MERCENARIES OF THE ANCIENT WORLD

MERCENARIES
OF THE
ANCIENT WORLD

―――――――

Serge Yalichev

Constable · London

First published in Great Britain 1997
by Constable and Company Ltd
3 The Lanchesters, 162 Fulham Palace Road
London W6 9ER
Copyright © Serge Yalichev 1997
The right of Serge Yalichev to be identified
as the author of this work has been asserted by him
in accordance with the Copyright, Designs and Patents Act 1988
ISBN 0 09 475750 X
Set in Linotron Ehrhardt 10.5 pt by
SetSystems Ltd, Saffron Walden, Essex
Printed in Great Britain by
St Edmundsbury Press Ltd
Bury St Edmunds, Suffolk

A CIP catalogue record for this book
is available from the British Library

For My Wife,
TAKIKO

Contents

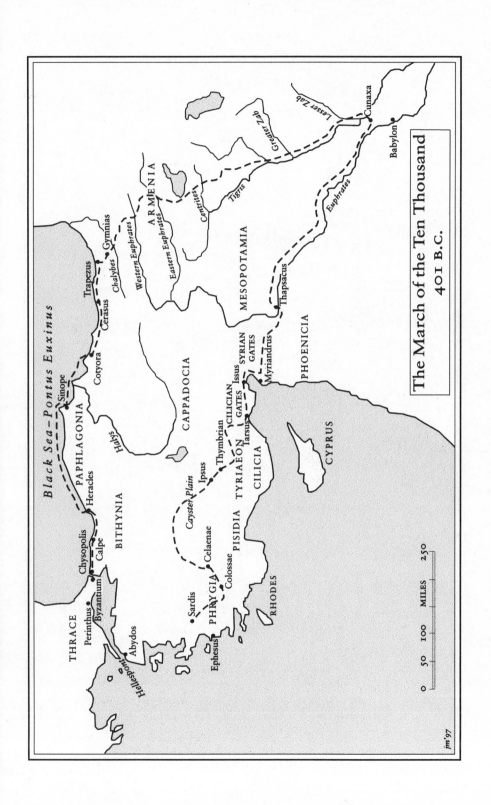

The March of the Ten Thousand
401 B.C.

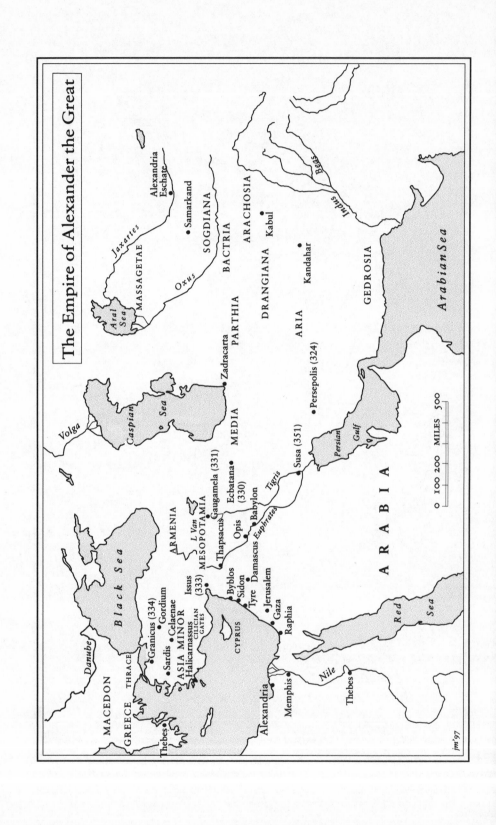

The Empire of Alexander the Great

MACEDON
GREECE
THRACE
Thebes
Danube
Black Sea
Granicus (334)
Gordium
Sardis ● Celaenae
ASIA MINOR
Halicarnassus
CILICIAN GATES
Issus (333)
ARMENIA
L Van
MESOPOTAMIA
Thapsacus
Byblos
Sidon
Tyre ● Damascus
Jerusalem
Gaza
Raphia
CYPRUS
Alexandria
Memphis
Nile
Thebes
Red Sea
ARABIA
Euphrates
Opis
Babylon
Gaugamela (331)
Ecbatana ● (330)
Tigris
MEDIA
Susa (351)
Persepolis (324)
Persian Gulf
Arabian Sea
GEDROSIA
ARIA
Kandahar
DRANGIANA
Kabul
ARACHOSIA
BACTRIA
Zadracarta
PARTHIA
Caspian Sea
Volga
Oxus
Jaxartes
Aral Sea
MASSAGETAE
SOGDIANA
Samarkand
Alexandria Eschate
Indus
Beas

0 100 200 MILES 500

jm '97

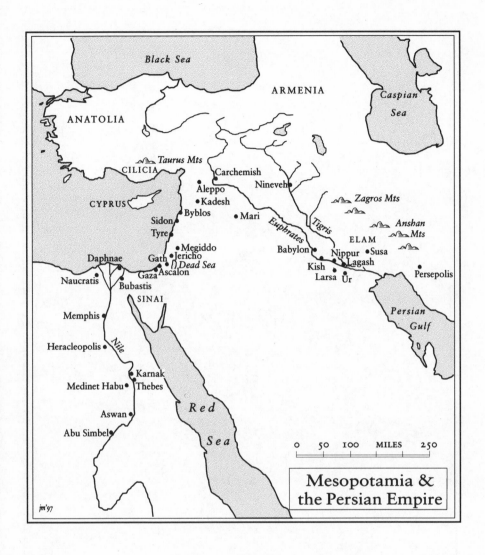

**Mesopotamia &
the Persian Empire**

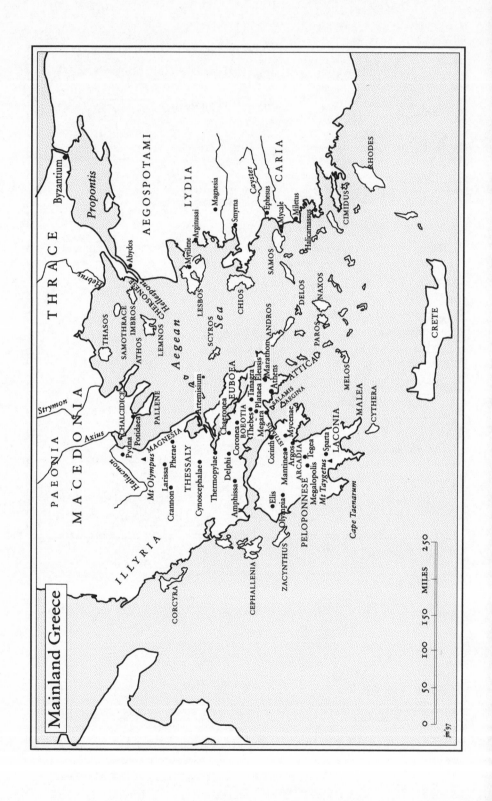

Mainland Greece

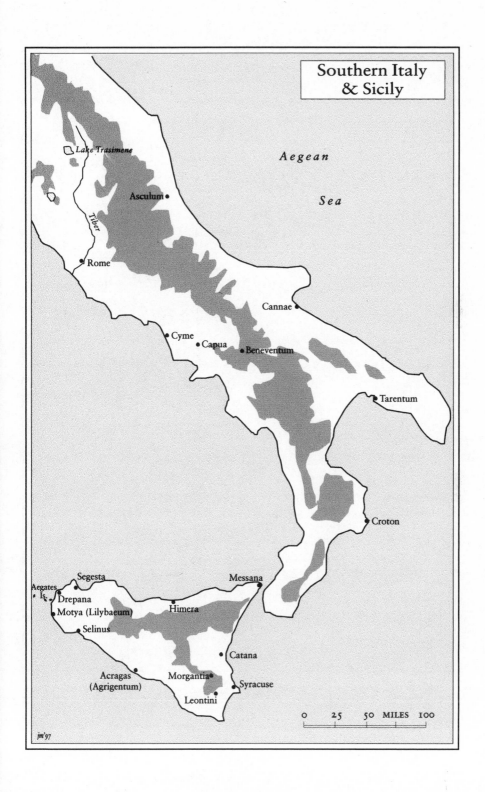

Southern Italy & Sicily

Aegean

Sea

Lake Trasimene

Asculum

Tiber

Rome

Cannae

Cyme
Capua
Beneventum

Tarentum

Croton

Segesta
Messana
Aegates
Is.
Drepana
Motya (Lilybaeum)
Himera
Selinus

Catana

Acragas
(Agrigentum)
Morgantia
Syracuse
Leontini

0   25   50 MILES 100

jm'97

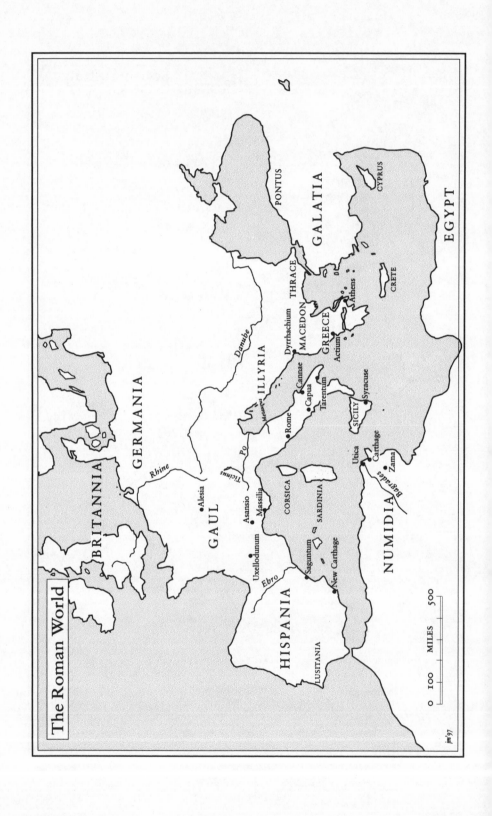

The Roman World

Acknowledgements

First and foremost I owe a debt of gratitude to my old friend Nevill Drury, without whose help, patience and encouragement the present volume would have remained just an idea. Madame Andrée Berland of Villeurbanne, France, spent an entire day at considerable personal inconvenience finding relevant materials in the bookshops of Lyons. *Merci de tout mon coeur.* Thank you also to Graeme Harrison, formerly of the Department of History at Sydney University and a born teacher such as one meets once in a lifetime. None of his students ever wanted to be the first to leave at the end of his seminars and he was never averse to continuing historical discussions for up to two hours after the official time, much to the discomfort of the nightwatchman, who was sometimes constrained to eject us from Graeme's room. Grateful thanks also to an old friend, Phil Hannon, who uncomplainingly endured hours of my reading the manuscript to him and made many valuable suggestions. Many thanks must also go to another old companion, David Knapp, for the very useful books he sent from England. Thanks to Hugh Myers for excellent material on the Assyrians and to my mother for information on the Roman Empire and Babylonia. I must express my gratitude to my wife, Takiko, who typed several chapters of the initial draft and to Judy Myers who did such a fine job on the final draft. Deep gratitude also to Marge Brewster for her invaluable help over a long period and to Jim Henderson for drawing my attention to David Harris' *Black Horse Odyssey*. Finally, I must acknowledge that my interest in mercenaries was kindled by a most unlikely source: the Irish traditional music group the Chieftains. Phil Hannon introduced me to their music during 1979 and I was immediately impressed by its happy-sad qualities. At about the same time I accidentally came across material on the

Irish 'Wild Geese'. Somehow the two events blended together. The nostalgic sounds of the Chieftains seemed appropriate to the story of self-exiled Irishmen fighting as mercenaries in foreign armies without a real hope of returning home. My MA thesis was largely related to the Irish but Graeme Harrison pointed out that mercenary soldiering was a very ancient profession and stimulated my interest in further research. Thus the present book is a product partly of Graeme's influence and Nevill's encouragement. It is my fondest hope that readers will find it interesting and perhaps engage in research of their own. Whatever errors are contained within its pages are purely mine and not attributable to anybody mentioned above.

Introduction

The very beginning of mercenary soldiering is lost in the remotest eras of the human past. The surviving evidence from the most ancient empires – fragments of old texts, clay tablets, relief carvings, wall paintings – is often obscure, imprecise, incomplete, tantalising and open to varying interpretations. Nevertheless, despite the relative paucity of material from the dawn of recorded history, it is abundantly clear that mercenary soldiering is – like prostitution – an extremely ancient pastime, perhaps almost as ancient as organised warfare itself.

The Sumerians, Egyptians, Hittites, Assyrians, Israelites, Persians, Greeks, Macedonians and, finally, the Romans all resorted for diverse reasons to the hiring of mercenaries at various stages of their histories. Nor did mercenary service disappear with the fall of the Roman Empire: fighting men still found plenty of work during the so-called Dark Ages, throughout the medieval period and in the Renaissance era. In the seventeenth century, the Thirty Years' War and the English Civil War, among other conflicts, provided a great many opportunities for mercenary soldiering. Irish, Scottish and German soldiers of fortune were also employed in Russia. At the same time, on the other side of Eurasia, Portuguese adventurers and expatriate Japanese *samurai* found work in the armies of South-East Asian rulers. During the eighteenth century, mercenaries still appeared in considerable numbers in many European armies right up to the outbreak of the French Revolution.

The rise of nationalism in Europe in the following century ended the large-scale employment of mercenaries and resulted in the pre-eminence of national armed forces raised by conscription or voluntary enlistment based on the concept of patriotic duty. Even so, the mercenary species did not die out. If Europe itself offered fewer prospects of employment, would-be mercenaries could still exercise their particular talents in colonial wars and wars of independence in exotic places like Latin America. Furthermore, the nineteenth century saw the creation of two of the most famous – if not legendary – mercenary formations: Britain's Gurkha regiments and the French Foreign Legion.

The major conflicts of the twentieth century were fought out by predominantly national armies but opportunities for mercenary soldiers were not totally lacking. Gurkhas and Legionnaires served with distinction both in the First and Second World Wars. During the Second World War, Germany's cause was tenaciously defended by the foreign volunteers who joined the Waffen SS. It is possible to argue forcibly that many – perhaps most – of these international volunteers enlisted for considerations other than personal gain, but whatever their reasons may have been, their service in a foreign army classified them as mercenaries at least in terms of status if not motive.

Since the Second World War, multinational bands of mercenaries have been involved in the independence struggles and post-colonial wars in Africa, Asia and Latin America, usually exacerbating already disastrous situations without having any decisive effect on their outcomes. During the 1960s mercenaries were employed in the Congo and the Nigerian Civil War and at least two mercenary commanders, Mike Hoare and Rolf Steiner, have left accounts of their activities. The long and controversial war in Indo-China also produced its crop of mercenaries, both South-East Asian and American. Among the Asians were Nung, Mu Ong and Montagnard tribesmen who – generously funded and trained by the US Central Intelligence Agency – collaborated with American forces, largely motivated by a traditional antipathy towards the Vietnamese in general and Vietnamese Communism in particular.

After the war in Vietnam a new generation of mercenaries emerged from among those American ex-servicemen whose belief in the righteousness of their country's frenetic anti-Communist crusade had remained essentially unshaken. Combining ideological zeal with a love of fighting and a disdain for peacetime military service, post-Vietnam mercenaries could find employment opportunities in the South African and Rhodesian armies or in the right-wing rebel forces ravaging Angola and Mozambique. At the end of 1979 came another opportunity, with the entry of the Soviet army into Afghanistan. There was also plenty of work to be found in the more traditional sphere of influence in Latin America where, in the same year, the Nicaraguan Sandinistas expelled an American-supported dictatorship.

Throughout the 1980s American mercenaries operated in El Salvador, Honduras and, most notably, in Nicaragua in support of Contra rebels whom they regarded as democratic freedom fighters, a perception much less obvious to the great mass of Nicaraguans, whose food-production centres, oil refineries, schools, hospitals, villages and children – rather than military targets – constituted the primary focus of Contra attacks.

In 1981, an older but still enthusiastic Mike Hoare recruited a group of mercenaries in an attempt to re-take the Seychelles Islands on behalf of their ousted first President, Jimmy Mancham. The operation proved to be an almost instant failure but it was not without its comical and even farcical moments and, though ultimately unrewarding, it did at least provide its leader with the subject matter for another book.

Mercenary activity has continued throughout the last two decades of the twentieth century, notably in the Bosnian conflict which followed the break up of Yugoslavia. European and American anti-Communist mercenaries operated alongside Bosnian and Croatian soldiers while Russian mercenary volunteers came in support of Serbia, a traditional ally with which Russia has a racial, religious and linguistic affinity.

In March 1997, the Government of Papua New Guinea sought to hire South African mercenaries recruited by the London-based firm Sandline International, in order to gain a definitive edge over secessionist rebels on the resource-rich island of Bougainville. However, the level of resentment among the troops of the regular PNG army was such that the mercenaries were promptly repatriated before they could be deployed for combat, while the PNG Prime Minister was forced to step down, pending a general election.

This recent incident, although one of the last involving twentieth-century mercenaries, is most unlikely to be the final chapter in the long history of the mercenary soldier. War breeds mercenaries and mercenaries thrive on war.

The present book is devoted to the Ancient World, that long period between the rise of Sumer around 3500 BC and the fall of Rome during the second half of the fifth century AD – a long period, indeed, given that nearly 4,000 of the 5,500 years of recorded human history fall into the category of Ancient History. The medieval period and the Renaissance era account for another 1,100 years, while the early modern (1600–1789) and the later modern (1789–2000) eras combined account for a mere 400 years. The approach of the book is broadly chronological, using the conventional time periods into which history has been divided largely for the convenience of historians, teachers and their students. Its chapters present a panorama of mercenary history, beginning with Sumer and ending with Rome, progressively examining the role and status of mercenaries in Akkad, Babylon, Israel, Assyria, Egypt, Persia, Greece and, of course, the Roman Empire.

To what extent were mercenaries employed throughout the Ancient World? Why were mercenaries used at all when governments could and did resort to conscription of native citizens on a regular basis? What use did employers make of their hired foreigners? What sort of relationships existed between the mercenaries and their employers? What were the advantages and disadvantages of using foreign troops? From what geographic and economic backgrounds have mercenaries originated? What factors led men to enter the mercenary life? Was it always just a matter of greed, poverty or adventure? It is with this range of questions that the present work is primarily concerned.

CHAPTER ONE

The Earliest Mercenaries

ANTHROPOLOGISTS and behavioural scientists argue passionately over the question of whether humanity has always been innately violent from the moment of its emergence as an identifiable species some 40–50,000 years ago, or whether external circumstances – the Fourth Ice Age, for example – rather than an unalterable genetic defect are responsible for human aggression. The potential for violence exhibited by human beings on an individual level or as part of a group is not in question and indeed cannot be denied. Hard evidence of warfare dates back to the most ancient civilisations and archaeological discoveries of the remains of walled cities, particularly Jericho, suggest that war was already a feature of life before the rise of the first empires. How far the practice of warfare reaches back into prehistory, however, cannot be precisely determined.

The British military historian John Keegan suggests that prehistoric people living in the post-glacial period from about 6000 BC to 3000 BC had no real reason to resort to violent action against fellow men, given the availability of sufficient resources for a still modest population. Land was plentifully available to those motivated enough to engage in sedentary subsistence farming in preference to the migratory life of the hunter and pastoralist. Furthermore, crop yields would initially have been far too small to attract the attention of raiders.[1]

Agriculture would have required then, as it does now, a cooperative effort from all the members of a farming community. Cooperation is the key concept emphasised by researchers optimistic about the human condition. In their view, cooperation rather than rivalry was the normal state of prehistoric societies and, if violence occurred, it was more in the nature of an aberration.

[5]

Perhaps. There may indeed have been tribal groups leading an essentially peaceful and cooperative mode of existence but *Homo sapiens* did not emerge at a time of relative abundance and favourable climate. The present species of humanity evolved during the Upper Pleistocene Period in a harsh and hostile environment dominated by the Fourth Ice Age, which began some 120,000 years ago and ended around 10000 BC. Did the relentless struggle for survival in such difficult and violent conditions intensify a cooperative spirit or merely sharpen the aggressive and possessive instincts of Upper Palaeo-lithic people?

Survival essentially meant a successful hunt. In an age when agriculture was impossible and, for that matter, unimaginable and unknown much before 7000 BC, hunting was the sole means of survival, yielding food, skins that provided a measure of protection against the elements, bones and horns that could be used for tools and weapons, or in shamanistic ritual ceremonies such as those depicted in prehistoric paintings in the Pyrenean Trois Frères caves (discovered in 1914). Hunting in groups, like farming, required cooperation and coordinated strategy. The earliest *Homo sapiens*, then, may have been cooperative rather than confrontational. With a population even smaller than that of the post-glacial agricultural era, hunting parties may have had little contact with outsiders and little opportunity to fight. What happened, however, when two separate hunting parties came across the same prey is a matter for speculation. Did such an event lead to cooperation, compromise or conflict? *Homo sapiens* must have learnt to kill in search of food or in self-defence almost from the first moment of its appearance on the planet. An ice age environment imposed an exclusively meat-based diet. Modern vegetarians may find the fact unpalatable but the earliest humans were carnivores not herbivores and a carnivorous diet necessitates killing, be it on the modest scale of a prehistoric hunt or on the grandiose scale of that Auschwitz for animals, the modern meat industry. How much of a leap of the imagination did it require for prehistoric man to realise that the weapons they used against animal prey could be used against their own species, during an argument over a woman, for example, or in a chance encounter with outsiders?

The surviving artefacts, cave paintings and skeletal remains from prehis-toric times are ambiguous and open to varying interpretations. Although some skeletal finds seem to suggest a violent denouement in the lives of the original owners of the skeletons, they do not in themselves throw conclusive light on the question of whether violence was an inherent or aberrant feature of life in the Pleistocene Period. It is not always possible to determine beyond doubt how the puncture marks, wounds and fractures found on skeletal remains came to be inflicted. Do they represent deliberate acts of violence or merely the results of accidents? It is, after all, nearly impossible to go through life without accidents that might leave scar tissue or broken bones and – *in extremis* – skull fractures. Some skeletons bear unmistakable signs of arrow and spear wounds or skull-shattering blows from clubs and axes that seem far from accidental. Even so, there is no consensus of opinion among prehistorians as to whether these are vestiges of primitive warfare.

The best that might be said about prehistoric life is that war was as yet unknown. If separate hunting parties did fight each other in a chance meeting – on balance, a reasonable presupposition – these confrontations consisted of individual duels fought out with stones, spears, clubs, axes, fists and fingernails and, much later, sometime after 10000 BC, bows and arrows.

If humanity has always been innately violent, right back to its very beginnings, unable to help itself owing to some genetic disposition towards aggression and acquisitiveness, then modern *Homo sapiens* seems to have little hope of reaching a more sophisticated and humanitarian approach to international relations and creating a more desirable world devoid of warfare. If, on the other hand, violence is external and not genetically programmed, the material and intellectual progress made by humanity over millennia of history and particularly in the last two centuries or so might conceivably be matched by a progressive reduction in the use of violence as a means of solving disputes. The question of human violence, however, remains essentially unresolved, except in the minds of sundry academics who dogmatically espouse either the optimistic view of human progress or the lugubrious perception that humanity may simply be beyond hope as far as aggressive behaviour is concerned.

Finally, there is the easy way out; the simple admission that human beings are more or less a mass of contradictions and that cooperation and conflict do coexist and need not be absolute opposites. Humanity, after all, is capable of cooperating to build and produce or to shatter and destroy. Whichever side of this slippery debate one might support, the record of human violence is clear and consistent. There can be no doubt about the frequency with which human beings have engaged in warfare, whether driven by natural inclination or external influences, ever since the dawn of history. A substantial portion of recorded history is military history.

Prehistoric fights, however frequently or infrequently they occurred, were very minor affairs – save to those directly involved. The emergence of

[7]

organised hierarchical urban societies brought the rather more serious business of organised warfare. Primitive cultures and sophisticated civilisations alike regularly embraced the practice of warfare with varying degrees of willingness as a means of achieving political, economic or religious ambitions. Among the most enthusiastic were the Assyrians who created the first permanent army known to history complete with cavalry, infantry, engineers, intelligence corps, paymasters and supply trains. By contrast, the Egyptians were far less addicted to expansionist warfare and viewed the soldier's life with a deep dislike which was already evident during the Old Kingdom and remained remarkably consistent throughout subsequent historical eras. Ordinary Egyptian citizens were far from enthusiastic about military service, nor were their Pharaohs, with the notable exceptions of Thutmosis I and Ramses II and III, particularly keen on building far-flung empires. Egypt's military activities were often confined to frontier defence and occasional punitive raids into neighbouring territories.

Popular or not, war was an inescapable part of life in the Ancient World. Intervals of peace were extremely rare and were regarded as temporary deviations from the normal course of events. Conflicts, conquests and martial exploits loom large in the surviving chronicles from the distant past. War was so frequent and pervasive that it was taken for granted and, perhaps for that very reason, its existence was rarely, if ever, questioned. Ancient historians like Herodotus, Thucydides or Polybius confined themselves to describing the motives and course of a particular war. The nature of war as a phenomenon, however, was never the topic of a philosophical dissertation.

The earliest wars were perhaps little more than summer skirmishes between neighbouring city-states using citizen militia forces raised by conscription and trained by a small core of professional soldiers who, along with priests and secular officials, formed a distinct class at the upper end of socially stratified societies. Militias were usually levied for brief periods and for objectives necessarily limited by the short terms of service, by the rudimentary military knowledge of the conscripts and by the need to keep commerce and agriculture as free from interruption as possible. Properly trained citizen militias were usually adequate for defensive actions or, at best, brief offensive operations such as punitive raids against nearby enemies. If an enemy city happened to fall, its attackers might be encouraged to range further afield and attempt other targets. Similarly, a city-state that survived an assault might launch a counterattack in revenge. Either way, the scope of military operations was effectively widened and relatively small wars gave way to protracted campaigns of conquest leading to the subjugation and sometimes to the genocide of the conquered people.

Prolonged operations aimed not just at the ravaging of enemy territory but at its conquest required something more effective than an army composed of militia units. They required men to whom soldiering was a speciality and, thus, ambitious rulers bent on the creation of empires began to employ professional fighting men drawn from two basic sources of recruitment. To some extent, their needs might be met by a city's hereditary warrior class or other native citizens tempted into permanent military service by the prospect of economic gain and social advancement. The second source was foreign mercenaries, operating for much the same set of reasons. As natural subjects of their particular ruler, the native citizens were not mercenary by status but they were certainly mercenary by inclination. Hired foreigners were mercenary both in terms of their status and their motivation.

Mercenary soldiers were usually well-trained fighters conversant with a wide range of weapons or specialists in the most effective use of one particular weapon. Unlike short-term citizen levies, they could be used to besiege enemy cities – time-consuming work which required patience and a rather more sophisticated knowledge of military technology than that available to ordinary militiamen. Provided that sufficient money was available to pay their wages, mercenaries could usually be retained for as long as they were needed.

Foreign soldiers were also employed as elite bodyguards. Dressed in a distinctive way, a corps of foreign guards often enhanced the prestige and power of the monarch. Hiring such a corps was an expensive proposition but the very fact that a ruler was able to afford the expense was in itself an indication of his financial and political power. As long as that ruler remained strong and respected and was able to provide adequate payment and rewards, he could normally rely on the fidelity of his foreign guards. During riots and rebellions, foreign mercenaries tended to remain loyal to their employer. They had no emotional links with the local population and no reason to sympathise with rebels. Native troops, on the other hand, might not always be reliable if they had sufficient cause for discontent. Mercenary bodyguards provided a ruler with a greater sense of personal security and, when the need arose, an effective police force.

Mercenaries were sometimes hired on a temporary basis but, quite often, they found permanent employment. Armies gradually ceased to be purely national and essentially amateur formations and became partially or totally mercenary in composition and character. The transition was not always a

[9]

simple linear process. Armies sometimes oscillated between the two extremes of being totally national or totally mercenary and the relative number of native and foreign troops varied widely according to time, place and circumstances. Nevertheless, it is clear that all the great empires of the Ancient World came to rely, partially or completely, on mercenary soldiers. Indeed, many of those empires owed their very existence to the use of professional troops both native and foreign.

THE PLAIN OF SHINAR – SUMER, AKKAD AND BABYLON

The oldest evidence of organised military activity comes in the shape of the Standard of Ur (British Museum) and the Stele of Vultures (Louvre), both produced in Sumer between 3000–2300 BC. These relics show uniformly attired footsoldiers armed with spears, socketed axes and large shields, and war-chariots each manned by a driver and a javelin thrower. Drawn by asses rather than horses, the chariots were lumbering contraptions lacking in manoeuvrability and may have been used purely to transport leading troops to the scene of yet another brotherly confrontation between the forces of rival Sumerian cities. Sumerian armies are depicted as well-disciplined, well-organised and well-equipped formations. The representation of precise formations is important for it implies that the Sumerians did not fight haphazardly but in units or regiments, each with its own standard, possibly organised, according to one expert, on a clan or territorial basis.[2]

Curiously enough, Sumerian troops were deficient in missile weapons such as bows and arrows (a major feature of Egyptian armament) and seem to have relied on the sheer momentum of charges and hand-to-hand combat. In the use of chariots, however, the Sumerians were 1,000 years ahead of the Egyptians who had never seen horses, let alone chariots of any sort, until their introduction around 1700 BC by the invading Hyksos.

The Sumerians settled in the southern part of the Plain of Shinar (later called Babylonia after 2000 BC), closer to the Euphrates than the Tigris, whose higher banks made the more easterly river less suitable for irrigation projects. There they established a cluster of about twenty city-states, including Uruk, Kish, Eshnunna, Umma, Khafaje, Lagash, Nippur and Ur. Initially a Stone Age people, the Sumerians progressively learnt metallurgy, working at first with tin and copper and then mixing these together in a proportion of approximately 80 per cent copper and 20 per cent tin to produce bronze, a much harder metal better suited to the production of edged tools and, inevitably, weapons of war.

The invention of writing separated history from prehistory and the development of writing was undoubtedly the most important achievement of the Sumerians. The cuneiform (wedge-shape) system enabled them to keep legal, business, trade and family records. It also enabled the Sumerians to make accumulative records of stellar and planetary motion and to produce a lunar calendar and a sexagesimal numeral system which divided the day into twenty-four hours of sixty minutes each with each minute being sixty seconds long – a system of time measurement still in use nearly 5,000 years later.

Along with a nascent science, the Sumerian writing system led to the creation of some of the world's earliest literature in the form of myths, legends, proverbs and quasi-historical works, the most famous being *The Epic of Gilgamesh*. The excavation of certain clay tablets from the city of Ur during the 1930s – tablets that had obviously been used for school exercises – clearly shows that the Sumerians established a system of education based on rote-learning with corporal punishment as an antidote for student misdemeanours. Literature formed part of the curriculum together with arithmetic, natural history and mineralogy.

The oldest written materials from Sumer, however, do not pertain to literature, science, education or religion, but to war, in this instance, war between Lagash and Umma. Writing enabled Sumerian monarchs to record military campaigns and victories. These narratives were invariably exaggerated and self-congratulatory and not always far removed from the mythical epics studied in Sumerian schools.

Sumerian society was essentially theocratic. Each city and its surrounding territory was an independent state headed by a *patesi*, who was at once a high-priest of the city's main temple and a secular prince. He was a judge, a chief engineer and a general and presided over the levying of recruits in time of war.

The earliest Sumerians seem to have been relatively classless, but the long civil wars between the city-states gradually altered the social structure to the extent that soldiers acquired greater prominence among the upper classes. Inter-city-state rivalry encouraged imperialism, that is, unification by conquest, rather than limited defensive actions. This, in turn, encouraged the rise of militarism and a professional military class.

[11]

The formation of a permanent soldier caste was perhaps inevitable, given the general unsuitability of part-time militia troops for prolonged campaigns.

The *patesi* and the secular princes almost certainly had a standing corps of guards to assure personal safety and enhance their prestige in the eyes of other Sumerians. The temples also maintained varying numbers of more or less professional soldiers – more or less, because some of them may well have been employed on agricultural and architectural projects during those infrequent times of peace.[3] Some would have been employed guarding temple treasures and in wartime they would be called upon to train and lead militia levies. The permanent soldiers of the Sumerian city-states served their respective employers in return for hereditary appanages which ultimately devolved upon their sons who were then required to continue military service in place of their fathers.[4]

The earliest armies of the city-states were primarily made up of short-term militia contingents. These were levied partly by the secular nobility who could call upon that most ancient source of army recruits, the agricultural labourers. Contingents were also supplied by the temples, selected from among urban clients and tenant peasantry working ecclesiastic estates. Alongside the temporary militias there must already have been a nucleus, at least, of permanent soldiers. Sumerian depictions of helmeted heavy infantry uniformly armed with spears and shields and operating with unity and precision strongly suggest the existence of trained professional troops. Acting together in formation with such unity and precision required long and regular training sessions involving men prepared to work practically full-time, rather than seasonal militiamen whose brief period of service produced little more than a basic level of training.

Owing to the vagueness and scarcity of reliable contemporary records, it is difficult to determine the average size of a fully assembled army of any particular city-state let alone the size of a larger army formed of individual contingents from cities and towns controlled by Ur, Kish, Lagash or Umma at the height of their power and territorial expansion, but given an initially modest population, the earliest Sumerian armies could not have been very large – perhaps 3–4,000 men. As cities grew in size and numbers of inhabitants, however, the available manpower grew concomitantly.

Throughout Sumer there was a gradual transition from citizen militias serving more or less from patriotic motives to permanent professional armies largely motivated by mercenary considerations. This mercenarisation began during the First Dynasty of Ur, continued during the Lagash Dynasty and the Akkadian period and reached its culmination during the Third Dynasty of Ur, which marked the resurgence of Sumer after a century of foreign occupation by the Guti and then its final downfall. The re-establishment of Sumerian independence by Ur Nammu around 2100 BC was largely attributable to his employment of Akkadian mercenaries who seem to have been more adept at fighting and more effective than the Sumerians.[5] The military forces of the Third Dynasty of Ur were entirely professional, partly mercenary in composition, completely mercenary in motivation and far removed from the predominantly militia armies of early Sumer. Moreover, they owed their allegiance to their pay-master, the king, not to the collective entity of the city-state.

The first solid references to mercenaries in Mesopotamia are to be found in documents from the Akkadian period pertaining to the royal guard of King Sargon (c. 2350–2300 BC). An impressive formation by the standards of that time – some 5,400 strong[6] – the royal guard must initially have been composed of native Akkadians but there can be no doubt that it later contained foreign mercenaries. There were several sources of mercenary recruits from the periphery of Sargon's empire, such as the Guti from the Zagros mountains and the Amorites living in Syria west of the Euphrates. There were certainly Amorites in Sargon's guard. The name of their commander, Nubanda Mardune, appears in Sargon's own correspondence together with the description 'captain of Amorites'.[7] The king's inscriptions show that he took excellent care of his guardsmen in terms of food, clothing, weapons and the land-grants he bestowed upon them to provide for their financial support. He also took care to show his appreciation of their martial prowess and military victories in the most glowing terms in inscriptions and pictorial representations that reflected their glory – and his.

What use did Sargon make of his army? After all, 5,400 professional warriors had to be kept occupied by more than drilling and guard duty. To some extent there was police work and the suppression of rebellions. Sargon treated the Sumerians with considerable sensitivity, paying particular respect to Sumerian religion, and, on the whole, his reign was characterised by internal stability. He did, however, face occasional revolts that erupted for reasons not always elucidated by surviving texts, particularly towards the end of his reign. His professional army proved its worth on these occasions, ruthlessly eliminating the malcontents. The foreign mercenaries in Sargon's guard would have been particularly savage towards an insurgent population with whom they had no blood-ties and for whom they could have no sympathy.

Sargon created an empire – the first empire worthy of the name – that stretched from the Persian Gulf across Mesopotamia to the eastern Mediterranean coastline. His army assured internal security, protected trade routes and guarded the frontiers of the empire but its main business was campaigning beyond Mesopotamia in what were purely and simply pillaging enterprises aimed at the forcible seizure of raw materials and merchandise from outlying territories.[8] Everything acquired in Sargon's campaigns was meticulously catalogued, from precious metals, fragrant timber, jewellery and *objets d'art* right down to mundane articles like vases. Needless to say, the main beneficiary of Sargon's looting expeditions was Sargon. The royal treasury was regularly replenished and – a not unimportant detail – his soldiers were regularly paid.

Sargon's army was a thoroughly mercenary organisation used by the king for thoroughly mercenary purposes. There can be little doubt that mercenaries played a significant role in the armies of the Akkadian period and continued to do so during the Third Dynasty of Ur and the Babylonian empire. Owing to the scarcity of surviving documents from earlier ages before the Akkadian conquest, it is not possible to determine precisely when foreign mercenaries first made their appearance in the various Sumerian armies alongside the citizen professionals and in what numbers. Some of the earliest mercenaries may have been Sumerian exiles. Expelled from their own cities, these desperate outcasts might offer their services to what were effectively foreign employers. The citizens of any one Sumerian city would naturally have regarded people from other cities as outsiders. Exiles have often been a source of mercenary recruits throughout history. That there were Sumerian exiles engaged in mercenary service seems to be a reasonable proposition but, without concrete evidence, one that must remain a matter for speculation.

Disgruntled individuals expelled from their native cities were not the only possible source of mercenaries. Nomadic tribesmen from the mountainous regions bordering the Fertile Crescent – the Taurus mountains in Anatolia and the Zagros mountains east of the Tigris – came to the Shinar Plain on an individual basis, attracted by its fertility and the wealth of its urban inhabitants. There they obtained work as manual labourers or mercenary soldiers or both, given that a clear distinction was not always made between civilian and military employment. Certainly such tribesmen – Amorites, Guti,

Hurrians among others – were taken into service sometimes in considerable numbers by the kings of Akkad and the Third Dynasty of Ur. There is no reason to suppose that the employment of such tribesmen was limited to the later periods of Sumerian history, but again there are only passing references in older Sumerian inscriptions to outsiders coming down from the mountains in search of work.

There was another source of foreign soldiers closer at hand, albeit an unlikely recruiting ground for reliable mercenary troops – Elam. Lying beyond the Tigris river to the south-east of Mesopotamia, the confederation of Elam was composed of urban centres of which the most important was Susa in the alluvial valley of Kerkha and highland territories in the Anshan mountains, a southerly continuation of the Zagros range. Each component territory was ruled by a prince owing allegiance to the Elamite king in Susa, so long as that king remained strong. The Elamites were a mixed group of people, partly semitic and partly west Asian, of indeterminate origin. Archaeological evidence suggests that the Elamites were already well-established by 3000 BC and thus they were not much less ancient than the Sumerians, with whom they enjoyed rather less than neighbourly relations. In effect, their relations with the inhabitants of the Shinar Plain, both Sumerians and Akkadians, were almost invariably hostile, with infrequent and abnormal periods marked by peaceful commercial and cultural contacts during which the Elamites – a literate people with their own writing script – absorbed a considerable amount of Sumerian culture.

The first thousand years of Elamite history is characterised by countless looting and pillaging raids motivated largely by greed and countless reciprocal campaigns to Elam conducted by the Sumerians and Akkadians. These were aimed not just at deterring enemy incursions and the collection of plunder but also at the acquisition of raw materials, in particular timber which was at a premium in treeless Mesopotamia.

The fortunes of war must have swung back and forth in favour of one side or the other but, although the Elamites could take advantage of the fact that the Sumerians were often at war with themselves, on the whole they came off second best in encounters with their neighbours across the Tigris. Held at bay by Sumer, conquered by Sargon of Akkad, ravaged by Rimush, Sargon's successor, and turned into a tributary state by King Shulgi of the Third Dynasty of Ur, Elam had to wait until 2006 BC to wreak revenge on the much-resented Mesopotamians. Weakened by internal political dissension and a relentless Amorite advance into Akkad, the city of Ur fell easily to a full-scale Elamite attack. With the collapse of Sumer, Elam began a golden age as a major power, a lengthy period which lasted until *c*.639 BC and the conquest of the Elamites by the Assyrian king, Ashurbanipal.

Throughout history there have always been people prepared to join foreign armies, even enemy armies, if sufficiently motivated or sufficiently desperate. During the Second World War there were Russian volunteers and prisoners of war who joined the Vlasov army out of a loathing for Stalinism or out of the more fundamental and compelling desire to avoid being worked or starved to death in a German prison camp. Understandable though their reasons might have been, the survivors of the Vlasov army were deported to the Soviet Union by their British captors to be tried and executed for treason and for having worked for Germany as a species of mercenary. In the Ancient World, however, service in an enemy army was not invariably seen as contradictory or reprehensible nor was there any apparent contradiction attached to the recruitment of foreign troops from among potential or actual enemies. Thus, Julius Caesar could conquer Gaul with less than a dozen Roman legions aided by a cavalry force made up almost entirely of Gauls. Subsequent Roman armies always had their complement of Gallic and Germanic horsemen. The Persians who had invaded Greece in the early fifth century BC could recruit large numbers of Greek mercenary hoplites in the latter half of the same century and continue this recruitment well into the following century.

King Shulgi of Ur (2095–2048 BC) also turned to a traditional enemy, now grudingly submissive but always prone to insurrection, and raised a type of foreign legion from among the Elamites. Some of the recruits appear to have been prisoners of war released on the condition of performing military service as auxiliaries, which was undoubtedly a better option than the forced labour usually imposed by the Sumerians on their captives. Most of the recruits, however, seem to have been volunteers and were therefore more in the nature of mercenaries than conscripts. Shulgi's Elamite recruits were placed under the control of a *Sukkal-makh* (Grand Regent), a high official in the service of the King of Ur. The *Sukkal-makh* was based at Lagash which lay closer to Elam – and hence closer to the recruiting grounds – than the capital city of Ur. The precise number of Elamite troops enrolled by the Grand Regent remains unknown but the *Sukkal-makh* progressively acquired considerable personal power and prestige – a circumstance made possible by direct control over a sufficiently large and impressive group of armed men acting both as police and border guards. The main function of the Elamite mercenaries was garrison duty and border patrol along Sumer's eastern frontiers. Their task was to deter raids by nomadic tribesmen from the Zagros mountains and incursions by their own nationals. They operated as part of larger Sumerian garrisons or on their own in small groups of five to twenty-five men and were maintained with a daily ration of barley bread and ale. It is unclear whether regular food and drink was the only inducement offered to prospective mercenaries but, unless the Sumerians were simply taking advantage of the desperation of hungry men, it can be assumed that service in the Elamite legion offered the opportunity of alleviating poverty as well as hunger. The Elamites seem to have performed their duties effectively enough and Sumer enjoyed a lengthy period of peace that lasted until the fall of the Third Dynasty of Ur. There is little information as to the role played by the legion at the time of the Elamite conquest of Ur but it is more than likely that they assisted the invading Elamite army as a kind of fifth column and highly unlikely that they died to the last man defending Ur against a concerted attack by their own people.

With the Elamite destruction of Ur, the control of Mesopotamia was left wide open to a number of rival city-states. The struggle lasted about a century and there were shifting alliances at various stages but, reduced to its essentials, the main contest involved Isin, Mari and Babylon on the one side and Larsa and the Elamites on the other. Initially, Isin gained the initiative, capturing the Elamite garrison at Ur. However, the apparent supremacy of Isin was shattered by Rim-Sin of Larsa whose troops captured and ravaged Isin around 1794 BC. But the fortunes of war did not favour Larsa for very long. The new Babylonian king, Hammurabi, attacked and conquered Larsa and expelled any remaining Elamite presence from Mesopotamia. For good measure, he then turned on his ally, Mari, which he also conquered, thus bringing the protracted war for control of lower Mesopotamia to a successful conclusion in favour of Babylon.

Hammurabi (c.1792–1750 BC), the second great imperialist after Sargon of Akkad, established a centralised administration that kept strict control over all provincial governers by means of regular correspondence, and equally strict control over all levels of Babylonian society by means of the 282 articles of a very precise code of laws, of which the most notorious clause was 'an eye for an eye, a tooth for a tooth'.[9]

Under Hammurabi's vigilant control, Babylonian agriculture, commerce and industry flourished; in particular, the textile industries, wool being the most widely used material for clothing in Mesopotamia and its neighbouring territories. Merchants acquired great financial power – as, indeed, did the temple priests. Babylonian temples were the centres of commercial life and, among other activities, they lent money at exorbitant rates, controlled substantial land holdings and presided over the buying and selling of merchandise. Needless to say, Babylonian religion supported the wealthy and was devoid of concepts like charity to the poor.

The Babylonian army before the reign of Hammurabi consisted of a small nucleus of professional soldiers who formed the royal guard and part-time militia troops levied from among the free citizens and the *mushkenu*, a lower and poorer class who were not slaves but were under obligation of service to the state, either in a military or civilian capacity. In Hammurabi's time, however, the borders of the Babylonian empire were protected by a strong standing army which numbered at least 10,000 men and seems to have reached 20,000 men at its maximum strength. The citizen militias were only mobilised on an irregular basis and then only in support of the professional army. Like the armies of Sumer and Akkad, the Babylonian army gradually underwent a transition from amateur to professional, from militia to mercenary. It was Hammurabi himself who completed the process of mercenarisation by establishing a kind of feudal system in which volunteers performed military service entailing long-distance campaigns or frontier garrison duty in return for land-grants. Thus, by motive or by status, the men of Hammurabi's army were effectively mercenary soldiers, whether they were native professionals or foreign recruits. The king's personal bodyguard contained many foreign mercenaries recruited both from within and without the borders of Babylonia and included contingents drawn from those perennial troublemakers, the Elamites.

Hammurabi's army also contained a proportion of slaves pressed into military service. How many there were remains unclear but, on the premise that a large number of armed slaves might prove dangerous to the state, their total number must have been relatively modest. If, on the contrary, it was substantial, the slave-soldiers must have been tightly controlled and closely supervised by other elements of the Babylonian army. The slaves may have been used in small groups as urban policemen or they may have performed garrison duty alongside the mercenary volunteers. On far-flung campaigns there was always the risk that slave-soldiers might desert. Desertion, however, might not necessarily bring freedom. Slaves were branded and their status was easily identifiable. Runaway slaves might be welcomed as potential recruits by an enemy and gain their liberty or they might merely have traded slavery to the Babylonians for slavery to someone else, perhaps in even harsher conditions.

After Hammurabi's death, the Babylonian army remained an essentially mercenary organisation while the citizen militias played a subsidiary role. The royal bodyguards were almost entirely recruited from outside the empire. Hammurabi's successors had inherited his impressive army but lacked the great king's skill, willpower and sense of purpose. Like the Sumero-Akkadians before them, the Babylonians were weakened by internal revolts and the loss of a sense of unity created by strong rulers like Sargon and Hammurabi. There was also the ever-increasing pressure exerted by new waves of intruders – Hittites, Hurrians and Kassites – from the north and east of the crumbling Babylonian empire. Babylon's mercenary troops were unable to prevent the Hittite army of King Mursilis I from sacking the city in 1595 BC. Fatally shaken by this large-scale expedition, Babylon fell to the Kassites, a highland people from the Zagros mountains. The Kassites ruled lower Mesopotamia for over four centuries until they in their turn were overthrown and Babylon was sacked yet again by the Elamites.

The Babylonian monarch, Nebuchadnezzar I, managed to expel the Elamites and ravage Elam with the help of a renegade Elamite lord, Ritti-Marduk, who fought as a mercenary in Nebuchadnezzar's army. Ritti-Marduk's intimate knowledge of Elamite military strength and dispositions must have been invaluable and he was subsequently well rewarded with material goods and privileges. But Babylon's partial recovery did not last long. Elam was defeated and ravaged but not destroyed and in the north there was the menace of Assyrian power. Babylon gradually fell first under Assyrian influence and then, in the reign of Tiglath-Pileser III, under actual Assyrian control and remained in a state of subjection until the decline of the Assyrian empire and the advent of the Chaldeans (Kaldu).

The Chaldean monarchs, Nabopolassar (626–605 BC) and his son, Nebuchadnezzar II (605–562 BC) rebuilt and restored Babylon, creating architectural marvels such as the Tower of Babel, the Hanging Gardens and the Ishtar Gate. They not only restored Babylonian civilisation but expanded the Babylonian empire, successfully contesting the possession of Syria–Palestine with Saite Egypt. The battles of Carchemish (605 BC) and Ascalon (604 BC), among others, must have been extremely fierce. At Carchemish, a major trade centre and strategic crossing point on the upper Euphrates, the Egyptian garrison with its substantial contingents of Ionian Greek and Nubian mercenaries was totally destroyed while other Egyptian troops in the vicinity beat a precipitate retreat, not without losing large numbers of panic-stricken men to the pursuing Babylonians. When Nebuchadnezzar and the Egyptian pharaoh, Necho II, fought again in southern Palestine, the Egyptians were again defeated but the additional Greek mercenaries recruited by the pharaoh to replace losses at Carchemish inflicted heavy casualties on the Babylonians. Nebuchadnezzar was forced to suspend his advance for a year in order to rebuild and re-equip his heavily depleted forces. He could do so, however, secure in the knowledge that he had broken Egyptian power in Syria and Palestine.

Although the great majority of Greeks involved in the war between Egypt and Babylon came from mercenary encampments established by the Egyptians, the Babylonians also had Greek mercenaries among their ranks, as evidenced by surviving inscriptions from Babylon pertaining to the presence there of Ionian Greeks. They are not all anonymous personalities for one of them at least is known by name. Antimenides, an expatriate from Mytilene, seems to have fallen foul of the newly-elected *tyrannos* of the island of Lesbos. Exiled along with his brother, Alcaeus, a poet and close friend of Sappho, Antimenides took service with Nebuchadnezzar. Alcaeus went to Egypt but whether this parting of the ways represented some difference of opinion between the two brothers remains unknown. Antimenides seems to have fought well on behalf of his employers and it is more than likely that he came up against other Greeks fighting for the pharaoh. If so, Antimenides survived these fratricidal encounters and finally returned to Lesbos where he apparently received a hero's welcome and could show off the sword with ivory pommel and gold trimmings that he had received from his recent employer.[10]

THE HABIRU

The long struggle for possession of Mesopotamia and Syria–Palestine began in the late fourth millennium BC and progressively intensified over subsequent millennia. It might be said that this struggle has continued in one form or another well into the twentieth century of the modern era and may not yet be over. The Sumerians, the first known inhabitants of the Shinar Plain, enjoyed more or less uncontested occupation over such a fertile area for about a thousand years and could indulge in the sheer luxury of being able to fight among themselves unimpeded by serious competition from outsiders. But their supremacy could not remain forever unchallenged. Waves of mainly Semitic invaders from the surrounding mountains advanced relentlessly westward into Mesopotamia and beyond to the Mediterranean. Non-semitic, Indo-European peoples such as the Hittites also exerted pressure from the north, ultimately coming into conflict with the Egyptians. Some of this intrusion resulted in a more or less peaceful blending of different ethnic groups, as in the case of the Akkadians and Sumerians, but more often it represented violent interaction, the conquest, subjugation and oppression of one group by another. From the Akkadians of the middle third millennium BC to the Hebrews who infiltrated from the Arabian Desert during the latter half of the second millennium, waves of immigrants entered the Fertile Crescent to be assimilated, repulsed or submitted to by previously established peoples. At some indeterminate point during these turbulent times, the earliest mercenaries were taken into service by foreign employers, driven by economic determinist motives or a predilection for fighting that came naturally to members of warrior societies. Historians have been able to trace their ethnic composition with varying degrees of certainty. Akkadians, Elamites, Amorites, Guti and Greeks; all of these have been readily identifiable in surviving records. One group, however, has defied permanent identification.

The *habiru* (also *hapiru*, *apiru*), whom the Sumerians referred to as *Sa-Gaz*, were already known in Mesopotamia during the third millennium, at least as far back as 2500 BC. The *habiru* and *Sa-Gaz* were in fact the same people. In Hittite texts found at Boghazkoi in Anatolia the two names are used interchangeably. The origins and ethnic composition of the people in question and the etymology of the terms *habiru* and *Sa-Gaz* remain obscure and have been the subject of controversy among scholars of Middle Eastern history and archaeology[11]. Researchers have sought to find the common link between the groups of people designated as *habiru* or *Sa-Gaz* in an attempt to fit them into a precise classification. They have been variously identified with the Kassite mountain people from Iran, the Aramaeans, the Amorites, the Hurrians, the Bedouins and most often with the Hebrews. The Hebrews may have been one group of *habiru* but there is no incontrovertible evidence which shows that the *habiru* were specifically Hebrews other than a possibly misleading resemblance between the words 'Hebrew' and '*habiru*'. Nor is there any compelling evidence for any direct connection between the mysterious *habiru* and the other ethnic groups mentioned above. The

[21]

Sumerian word *Sa-Gaz* was a pejorative one literally meaning 'head-smasher' and, by extension, 'aggressor', 'bandit', 'wrong-doer' and 'filibuster'. These nuances offer a clue to the true nature of the *habiru–Sa-Gaz*. They were not a homogenous group at all. The terms *Sa-Gaz* and *habiru* were not a designation of geographic or ethnic origin, but referred to the status and life-style of a group (or groups) of people composed of different ethnic origins and attracted to each other by their common condition, namely one of social isolation in whatever territory they happened to enter. Whoever they really were, the *habiru–Sa-Gaz* were omnipresent in the eastern Mediterranean area from Anatolia to Egypt.

Some *habiru* (both men and women) are known to have engaged in civilian occupations, working for city governments as interpreters or in private domestic service (as shown by contracts found in Nuzi). But the great mass of contemporary texts focus on their military skill and bellicose nature and clearly demonstrate that the usual activity of the *habiru* was mercenary soldiering, both as *condottieri* under contractual obligations to kings and princes, and on their own account in bands of raiders and pillagers. In this second capacity the *habiru* led a similar existence to the free companies in fourteenth-century France, performing startling feats of plundering and raping. Like the medieval free companies, the wandering *habiru* bands constituted an element of chronic instability in the eastern Mediterranean region. During the fourteenth century BC *habiru* bands seem to have been particularly active and powerful enough to threaten or actually capture cities in Phoenicia and Syria–Palestine, in much the same way that the larger free companies gained control of poorly-defended towns in France. The *habiru* played an important role in the decline of Egypt's Asiatic empire, both in independent rampaging bands and in the pay of vassal-kings seeking to throw off Egyptian rule. The insurrection of the vassal-kings led to civil war between the rebels and vassal-rulers who had remained loyal to the empire.

Large numbers of *habiru* were involved in the anti-Egyptian movement. Indeed, owing to their military prowess, they constituted the backbone of the rebel forces. The Amarna letters, some 300 small clay tablets, contain numerous references to the actions of the *habiru–Sa-Gaz*. Written by loyal vassals mainly to the Pharaoh Amenophis IV (also: Akhenaton 1377–1358 BC), the letters are among the oldest diplomatic correspondence in the world and amply illustrate the prominent role of the *habiru*, both as a focus for the rebellious elements and as an effective military force. The ruler of the Phoenician coastal city of Byblos, Rib-Addi, wrote a series of increasingly despondent reports and appeals to his god-king. Extracts from the sequence of letters leave little doubt as to the gravity of the situation.

'The *Sa–Gaz* soldiers are very hostile in my regard . . . all my mountain and seaside towns have gone over to the *Sa–Gaz* . . . the *Sa–Gaz* have become even more hostile . . .' Rib-Addi repeatedly appealed to the Pharaoh for a detachment of Sherden or Nubian merenaries who might reinforce his own Sherden garrisons and retrieve the situation, but Akhenaton, who had always shown a profound indifference to foreign affairs and was furthermore plagued by ill-health and advancing old-age, seems to have had other priorities. Rib-Addi's desperate correspondence remained unanswered. Nevertheless, he persisted in writing to his overlord.

'Why do you stand by and do nothing while the *Sa–Gaz* capture your towns, the dogs!'

'Byblos has gone over to the *Sa–Gaz* too . . . all my towns have joined the *Sa–Gaz* and everybody hates me . . .'[12]

Rib-Addi's pessimism seemed quite justified. He was attacked and wounded nine times by one of his own Sherden mercenaries who had apparently considered his current employer to be a lost cause. The vassal-ruler must have been possessed of considerable physical sturdiness, managing to despatch his assailant, despite his wounds and the element of surprise which had favoured the mercenary. This was not, however, the end of his troubles. His Sherden garrison was massacred by mistake by Bedouin mercenaries sent by an Egyptian official in Galilee to restore order in Byblos. The Egyptian had acted in the erroneous belief that Rib-Addi belonged to the rebel side. As for the Bedouins, they merely did their job with considerable enthusiasm without discriminating between friend and foe. The loss of his bodyguard and the defection of the citizens of Byblos forced Rib-Addi to flee, first to Beirut and then to Sidon where he was captured by rebel forces. His precise fate is unrecorded. However, given the turbulence of the era, the violence of the protagonists and the general cruelty of the Ancient World, there is little ground for optimism.

Other vassal rulers had their problems with the *habiru*. Zimriddi of Sidon wrote that, 'all the towns entrusted to my care by the Pharaoh have gone over to the *Sa–Gaz*.' A letter from the ruling house of Tubihi informed the Pharaoh that 'your towns, oh my lord, my deity, my sun, belong to the *Sa–Gaz*.' Abi-milki of Tyre advised Amenophis that the King of Hasor had defected to the *Sa–Gaz* and that his own subjects had also favoured the mercenary rebels. Maiarzana of Hazi sent a series of letters describing the fate of loyalist cities captured by the *habiru*. 'When the *Sa-Gaz* took Gilumi, one of your towns, oh king, they put it to the sack and burnt it so that perhaps one single house survived.' Maiarzana announced the destruction of several other cities in much the same style. He was pleased to report, however, that a *Sa-Gaz* attack on his own city of Hazi was repulsed, that the enemy were cut to pieces and that only forty of them escaped.[13]

Most of the Amarna letters refer to *habiru–Sa-Gaz* fighting against Egyptian domination in the Levant, but others clearly show that there were also *habiru–Sa-Gaz* in pro-Egyptian armies. Thus Biriawaza of Upe could inform Amenophis that he was prepared to strike wherever the Pharaoh thought best, 'with my bodyguard, my war-chariots, my allies, my *Sa-Gaz*, my Bedouins and Nubians.'[14] Despite their apparent identification with the struggle against Egyptian hegemony, the *habiru* were first and foremost mercenary adventurers prepared to fight for whichever employer offered the best remuneration and conditions of service. In this respect they were typical of most mercenaries throughout history. As it happened, the anti-Egyptian movement possessed sufficient financial resources to attract the great majority of the *habiru*, but it is not unreasonable to suppose that they would have served the pro-Egyptian cities in larger numbers had the pay and conditions matched or surpassed those offered by the rebel cities.

The *habiru* also found lucrative employment in the armies of the Hittites, a non-Semitic people from the Armenian mountains, who had invaded Anatolia shortly after 2000 BC. Under King Shubbiluliuma (r. 1380–1346 BC), the Hittite empire reached the height of its power, destroying the military state of Mitanni, a former ally of Egypt, around 1350 BC. The Hittites were determined opponents of Egypt's rule in the Levant and did all they could to encourage the anti-Egyptian revolution. With the cooperation of several disaffected vassal-kings, the Hittites invaded Syria, penetrating as far south as Kadesh.

Hittite armies underwent the gradual transition from citizen militia to mercenary professional common to most military establishments of the Ancient World. The earliest armies were composed of levies supplied to the king by the feudal nobility. By the reign of Shubbiluliuma, however, Hittite armies were standing forces made up almost entirely of mercenaries, including the king's Elamite bodyguard, Bedouins and *habiru*. Feudal levies were rarely mobilised. Hittite texts refer to 3,000 *habiru* in royal service being committed to garrison duties, a task best performed by regular rather than short-term militia troops.[15]

The *habiru–Sa-Gaz* operated as mercenaries in the eastern Mediterranean area for well over 1,000 years. As noted above, their origin and ethnic composition remain elusive. Contemporary texts do, however, offer some insight into their nature, motives and social status. They were déracinés, having no contact with their place of origin. They were foreigners wherever they went, with no local tribal loyalties. Records from such locations as Babylon, Alalah, Nuzi, Amarna, Ugarit and Anatolia show that the *habiru* generally led a nomadic life-style, although they often settled in urban areas after protracted wandering. They were landless and outside regular society, wanderers and outlaws in settled agrarian communities. Anatolian texts indicate that the *habiru* had their own pantheon of gods and were not assimilated into the religious and social life of the Hittites. The *habiru* were exiles, fugitives, adventurers or refugees. Archives from the Phoenician seaport of Ugarit emphasise the refugee status of many of the *habiru*.[16] Indeed, the terms *Sa-Gaz* and *habiru* seem to have been virtually synonymous with 'refugee'. Certainly, refugees seem to have been a major source of recruits for *habiru* bands. Newly-arrived refugees, despised by the native population, would naturally have gravitated to expatriate communities. The *habiru* appear to have possessed the right of residence in certain suburbs of cities under Ugaritic control even though they were regarded as a potentially dangerous element. Unlike the *habiru* bands described in the Amarna letters, they accepted local laws and paid taxes in kind (jars of wine) to the authorities for the privilege of living in the ghettos. Ugarit, a prosperous cosmopolitan trading centre, was a regular employer of mercenaries. Its infantry forces were largely composed of foreign soldiers. Given that the Ugaritic *habiru* were relatively docile, it is not unreasonable to suppose that their communities were among the sources of recruitment available to the city's rulers.

The *habiru* who fell into the refugee category were not always political exiles. Some recruits joined the mercenary bands for adventure and the chance of acquiring loot. Others migrated from their native land to escape inconvenient debts or onerous contracts. Sheer poverty would have been a powerful incentive for at least some of the refugees. Escaped slaves were another source of recruits for the *habiru*. Those escapees who joined bands of pillagers would have been particularly savage during the capture and sack of cities. Former slaves became the most vicious of masters.

In summary, it can be said that there were different types of *habiru*, ranging from uncontrollable marauding bands, through more or less disciplined *condottieri*-style companies serving local rulers under contract, to groups living a relatively settled civilian-military life subject to the authority and supervision of particular governments. The motives underlying the *habiru* choice of life-style must have varied according to circumstances and the mentality of the people involved. A single motive might have been sufficient in some cases – for example, poverty or greed or love of adventure. However, the actions of human beings are often governed by a subtle and complicated patchwork of inter-related motives. It is likely that many of those who joined the *habiru* did so for a variety of compelling reasons.

The *habiru* disappeared from written records around 1000 BC. Whether they were finally assimilated into local societies or were wiped out remains unknown. As wandering mercenaries the *habiru–Sa-Gaz* left very few tangible remains in archaeological sites.

It can be seen, in summary, that the military history of the earliest civilisations of Mesopotamia and its environs already reveals a recurrent pattern in the development of armies – one that was to become characteristic of the military forces of subsequent empires in the Ancient World. The intensification of warfare that went hand in hand with the rise of imperialism caused the armies of Sumer, Akkad, Babylon and those of the Anatolian Hittites to undergo a progressive transformation from part-time citizen militias serving more or less patriotically to permanent professional forces that were partly or wholly mercenary in composition and certainly mercenary in motivation and character. The creation of empires might be achieved with militia troops but the more difficult task of maintaining them required soldiers – native or foreign – prepared to serve full-time.

Although direct references to mercenaries are not extensive at this formative period in world history there can be no doubt that mercenary soldiers were active in the most ancient empires. The extant documentation provides some insight into their role and character. They are already found exercising several classic functions – classic in the sense that these same functions were repeatedly performed throughout subsequent ages. Picked mercenaries served as royal bodyguards: Sargon had his Amorite corps; Hammurabi and Shubbiluliuma had their Elamites and poor old Rib-Addi his Sherdens. Garrison duty was another recurrent function of mercenaries, as evidenced by King Shulgi's Elamite Legion and Hammurabi's system of land grants in return for service in remote areas. The Amarna letters show that mercenaries also functioned as policemen. Bedouins, *habiru* and Nubians were used by Syrian vassal-rulers loyal to Egypt to suppress anti-Egyptian rebels. The letters also reveal that *habiru* mercenaries operated in free companies, distant precursors of the free companies of medieval France and Italy. Mercenaries of the same ethnic origin could be found fighting on opposite sides, a situation which recurred continually right up to the twentieth century AD. Thus, there were *habiru* on both sides of the anti-Egyptian revolt and Greeks on both sides in the struggle between Egypt and Babylon. Rib-Addi's encounter with the regicidal Sherden bodyguard raises the question of the reliability of mercenaries. Soldiers for hire have often proved fickle throughout history. Thus, for example, the sixteenth-century Swiss hired by French kings were notoriously difficult and their loyalty was never certain. On the other hand, at the outbreak of the French Revolution in 1789, the Swiss Guard remained loyal to the monarchy and died as a result while the Gardes Françaises went over to the Revolution.

There is little precise information as to what extent Rib-Addi's experience was generally indicative of the reliability of mercenaries in ancient Mesopotamia, but it is not unreasonable to suppose that the attitude of mercenaries towards their employers ranged from absolute fidelity to complete unreliability. Certainly, examples of reliable and unreliable mercenaries may be found in any historical era.

Even at this early stage of history it is already possible to draw some conclusions as to the geographical origins of mercenary soldiers. The mercenaries thus far encountered – Amorites, Guti, Elamites, Hurrians, Nubians, Bedouins, Sherdens and Greeks – have largely come from arid or otherwise agriculturally unproductive regions: mountainous areas, deserts and, in the case of the Sherdens and the earliest Greek mercenaries, Mediterranean islands with rugged topography and limited resources. Driven by poverty, toughened by a difficult environment, montagnards and desert-dwellers alike were drawn to the fertile plains of Mesopotamia. They were also attracted by the opulence of Egypt and played an important role in the land of the Pharaohs.

CHAPTER TWO

Egypt from the Old Kingdom
to the New

IF THE EARLY HISTORY of Mesopotamia provides rather imprecise and often enigmatic glimpses of the use of mercenaries, ancient Egyptian history presents a much more substantial picture of the mercenary system.

Among the vestiges of the ancient past in the collection of the Egyptian Museum in Cairo are the earliest model soldiers yet discovered. Originally sealed in the tomb of Mesehti, a Theban prince of the Twelfth Dynasty (Middle Kingdom), the painted wooden figures have survived the ravages of time in remarkably good condition and represent spearmen and archers of the Egyptian army. The group of spearmen shows a detachment of native Egyptian heavy infantry on the march or on parade. The archers, however, are much darker in colour and are armed with bows of a different type from that commonly used by the Egyptians. In effect, the dark-skinned models depict Nubian archers and clearly attest to the important role played by foreigners in the armies of the Pharaohs. The Egyptians valued the skill of these specialist archers and repeatedly employed substantial numbers of Nubians, alongside other mercenary troops, from a comparatively early date in the history of Egypt. Nubians were already present in the armies of the Old Kingdom. Thus, for example, the military forces of Pepi I, second Pharaoh of the Sixth Dynasty, consisted of native conscripts and Nubian archers from various tribes. The energetic Pepi, who became Pharaoh around 2350 BC, used his militia-mercenary armies in five punitive expeditions against Bedouin raiders in Syria. The 'Sand-dwellers', as the Egyptians called their nomadic enemies, were soundly thrashed by the Pharaoh's troops under General Uni, who displayed considerable tactical skill. Avoiding the usual overland attack routes and a head-on confrontation, Uni embarked his army, sailed up the eastern Mediterranean coast to a point behind Bedouin strongholds and proceeded to surprise the enemy.[1] A victory song, written in honour of the general's safe homecoming, records the satisfying fact that the Egyptians ravaged the Bedouins' territory, destroyed their fortresses and, not the least aggravating detail from the Bedouin point of view, cut down the fig trees and grapevines, thereby restricting the wine supply. In subsequent ages of Middle-Eastern history, Bedouins were to be found in Egyptian service fighting against fellow-Bedouins employed by Hittite armies, *habiru* bands and other enemies of Egypt.

Egyptian armies began in the way common to most other armies of the Ancient World as citizen militias and, in a similar transition, ended up dominated by native professionals and mercenary troops. In the Old and New Kingdoms especially, the basic pattern is clearly discernible. The Middle Kingdom presents a somewhat different picture in that mercenaries, mainly Nubians, formed a limited part of the military forces right from the beginning of the Kingdom. Although their numbers gradually increased, they did not achieve the same preponderance as in the Old and New Kingdoms. The armies of the Middle Kingdom remained predominantly national, that is to say, they were composed mainly of militia levies, some native professionals and a minority of foreign mercenaries whose collective strength was dissipated by their dispersion into widely scattered garrisons. Nevertheless, despite the reduced use of mercenaries characteristic of the Middle Kingdom, it remains essentially correct to conclude that Egyptian armies evolved in much the same way as other ancient armies and that, for a long period of its history, Egypt was heavily reliant on mercenaries.

THE OLD KINGDOM

The earliest armies raised at the beginning of the Old Kingdom were composed of short-term militia levies recruited from each of the forty-two *nomes* that made up the Egyptian state. The *nome* was an administrative district, a miniature state with its own capital city and its own governor appointed by the Pharaoh. Each governor was responsible for financial, judicial and military affairs and architectural and engineering projects. The militia recruits spent much of their time in non-military activities in mines and quarries extracting the materials needed for extensive public works. They were often commanded by officials who did not necessarily possess any military expertise. In time of war, the militia contingents were assembled under the command of the Vizier, the Pharaoh's chief minister.

There were several weaknesses in the militia system. The recruitment of armies depended to a significant extent upon the loyalty of the local governors to the Pharaohs at Memphis. A forceful Pharaoh commanded respect but a weak ruler, such as the centenarian Pepi II, who could point to few outstanding achievements other than longevity, encouraged the governors to challenge royal authority and assert their independence. Another drawback inherent in the militia system was that the conscripts were directly loyal to the local governor rather than the Pharaoh. Like most militiamen in other places and in other times, they had a limited outlook. They saw themselves firstly as belonging to their particular *nome* and only secondly as citizens of the larger Egyptian state. The Egyptian militia levies also displayed a weakness common to most militia forces. That is to say, they were relatively inexperienced compared with mercenary or native professional troops. Working in quarries under civilian officials was no real substitute for regular military training. On the whole, Egyptian militias were indifferent fighting forces. This drawback was accentuated by another factor, namely the abiding disdain with which Egyptians regarded the military profession and their general reluctance to perform militia service. Literary men satirised the uncomfortable life of the soldier with its hunger, thirst, fatigue and brutal treatment at the hands of officers. When levies were called out, many men, perhaps up to half of the liable population, vanished from their villages with remarkable speed and went into hiding for the duration of hostilities.[2] In ordinary life, the Egyptians never carried weapons. Despite the imperial ambitions of some of their more vigorous Pharaohs, they were not a warrior-society like the bloodthirsty Assyrians. Indeed, they were probably the least warlike of any of the peoples of the Ancient World.

Militia service only involved a very small proportion of the available population, namely, one recruit out of every 100 men liable for duty. Even so, the number of men ultimately available was reduced by the temporary disappearance of able-bodied men from their villages, and further reduced by those legally exempt on grounds of physical or mental disability or illness. Sometimes the village heads managed to avoid the displeasure of their feudal lord by imprisoning all men who might contemplate a sudden absence. They had excellent personal reasons in carrying out this precaution. Unaccountable absences among the male villagers normally resulted in a beating at the hands of lord's representative. The men finally chosen for militia duty often had to be forcibly separated from their families by the Medjay police and marched away to the accompaniment of weeping and wailing from distressed women, who expressed their grief in traditional fashion by throwing dust upon their own hair and faces.[3] Such unwilling recruits were unlikely to make very effective soldiers.

Given all these circumstances, it is hardly surprising that the Pharaohs should turn to mercenaries to provide the expertise and effectiveness necessary to successful campaigns. Their military skill was not their only attraction for the Egyptian monarchy. Whereas the militias tended to give their loyalty to the provincial governors, mercenaries owed their loyalty solely to their pay-master, the Pharaoh, and could be employed both for external wars and for controlling domestic unrest. As foreigners, mercenary policemen would have no qualms about oppressing their employer's natural subjects. Thus, succeeding Pharaohs hired mercenaries in ever-increasing numbers so that, by the time the Old Kingdom came to an end, foreign soldiers made up the great majority, if not the totality of Egyptian effectives.

Among the earliest mercenaries to be recruited were the Nubians from Upper Egypt and northern Sudan. Divided into separate tribes, among whom were the Medjay, Iam, Warrat and Irtje, the Nubians lived in rather squalid and barbarous conditions in mud hut villages along the Nile or away from the river in sites around water wells. The extremely narrow strip of arable land watered by the river limited the Nubians to pastoralism and small-scale subsistence farming that contrasted sharply with the abundant agricultural production of the well-watered Delta to the north. Much of Nubia was a desert. As a result of these harsh conditions of life, the Nubians became a tough warrior people, always ready to engage in inter-tribal skirmishes or in raids on Egyptian territory. Their relations with Egypt varied according to the circumstances prevalent at any particular period. There were frequent raids, partly motivated by the prospect of loot and partly as a response to Egyptian attempts to colonise Nubia. If Nubia was of little use agriculturally to the Egyptians, it was a major source of gold and iron ore. It also offered vital trade routes to the sub-Saharan south from which raw materials could be obtained for the luxury goods demanded by the Egyptian nobility. Nubian raids brought retaliatory expeditions from Egypt, such as that of the Fourth Dynasty Pharaoh, Sneferu (c.2600 BC) which took 2,000 prisoners.[4] Owing to the disunity of the Nubian tribes, their raids were never a real threat to Egypt. At other periods, notably during the Sixth Dynasty (c.2423–c.2200

BC), many Nubian tribes accepted Egyptian suzerainty more or less with good grace, although some tribes remained recalcitrant.

Nubian warriors served the Egyptians both as auxiliaries and mercenaries. In the first case, they were levied by tribal chiefs who had sworn allegiance to the Pharaoh. In the second case, they were hired directly by Egyptian recruiters from tribes that were often independent of Egyptian control. The rulers of the Iamite tribe, for example, were not among the chiefs who had given allegiance to the Egyptian monarchy. Consequently, recruiting parties from Egypt had to offer gifts in return for permission to recruit individual subjects for the Egyptian army. The Iamite tribe features prominently in inscriptions found on a tomb in Aswan recording the trading–recruiting activities of Harkhuf, an Egyptian nobleman. Sent to the lord of Iam by Pharaoh Merenre (*c.*2300 BC), Harkhuf negotiated with the Iamite chief, not as a superior, but on equal terms, for trade-goods and mercenaries.[5] Among the Iamites brought back to Egypt by Harkhuf during his third expedition were leopard skins, ebony, oil, incense, elephant tusks and mercenaries. The records do not specify the size of the mercenary contingent but it was apparently large enough to have deterred attacks by other Nubian tribes desirous of relieving Harkhuf of his 300 donkey-loads of precious goods. On his fourth and final expedition the Egyptian lord brought back another impressive load of luxury goods, more mercenary recruits and one dancing dwarf, an item highly prized by the Egyptian nobility of the time as the last word in entertainment.

For the Nubians recruited by Harkhuf and other officials, the rigours of military service in Egypt were still preferable to life in the harsh environment of their homeland. Mercenary soldiering meant regular pay and the chance of acquiring valuable loot. It also meant the possibility of personal advancement for the more able and resourceful of the Nubian recruits. Among the avenues available to ambitious mercenaries were entry into the Pharaoh's guard, promotion to officer rank and employment in a wide variety of capacities, both in the military and civil service. Egypt offered wide opportunities for impoverished foreigners, many of whom grew extremely wealthy and were materially much better off than the Egyptian peasantry. The same possibilities existed even for Nubians captured in battle and working as slaves in noble households and government offices. Many mercenaries and slaves became indispensable middlemen between the nobility and the mass of the Egyptian people. Given the numerous attractions of Egyptian service, it is not difficult to understand the motives of Nubian mercenaries and their absolute willingness to fight against their fellow Nubians back home if required to do so by their employers in pursuit of foreign policy objectives.

The 150 years of fragmentation and chaos which followed the collapse of the Old Kingdom around 2200 BC, known as the First Intermediate Period, were characterised by foreign incursions (attacks by resurgent Bedouin tribes). There were peasant uprisings against the nobility at Memphis and economic dislocation and famine. The situation was worsened by a prolonged struggle between the feudal nobility of northern Egypt, whose base was Heracleopolis, and the southern lords centred on Thebes. The First Inter-mediate Period did not mark any reduction in the mercenary presence in Egypt. On the contrary, the breakdown of Egyptian unity and power offered the prospect of abundant booty. Mercenaries continued to be employed by all the competing factions and some rose to positions of power and influence as they had done during the Old Kingdom. Other mercenaries, notably Nubians and Libyans, formed independent bands whose effect on native Egyptian settlements was akin to the havoc brought about by the *habiru* in the Levant.

THE MIDDLE KINGDOM

Egypt was finally reunited when the Thebans achieved supremacy over Heracleopolis. Nubian mercenaries in Theban employ played no small part in the defeat of the northern forces. Although Nubians fought on both sides, the geographical proximity of Thebes to the Nubian recruiting grounds gave the southerners a distinct advantage. That they were able to recruit greater numbers of Nubians than the north seems probable in the light of archaeolog-ical discoveries made on the sites of ancient Nubian settlements. The mercenary inhabitants of these settlements often received part-payment for their services in the form of material goods and food. Most of the ceramics and other objects found on the Nubian sites have been of Theban rather than northern manufacture.[6]

Having firmly established its control over Egypt, Thebes turned its attention to Lower Nubia which had asserted its independence during the long civil war in the north. Military expeditions invaded Nubia to restore Egyptian hegemony, re-open trade routes and punish those Nubian tribes who had been tempted to raid their weakened neighbour. Nubian mercenaries participated wholeheartedly in the Egyptian expeditions. Their loyalties were

[33]

strictly local and they did not object to ravaging the territories of other Nubian tribes, so long as their own districts were left unmolested. Several fragmentary accounts of the Egyptian expeditions survive, including a set of graffiti engraved on a rock by Tjehemau, a Nubian mercenary officer, commemorating battles fought near Aswan.[7]

The reunification of Egypt by the Theban rulers, Mentuhotep I and Mentuhotep II and the subsequent reimposition of Egyptian control over Lower Nubia opened the second great era in the country's history, known as the Middle Kingdom. Under the energetic Pharaohs of the Twelfth Dynasty, Egypt enjoyed economic prosperity and increased trade links with Syria–Palestine, Sinai and Nubia. Middle Kingdom objects found in Crete and Aegean products unearthed in Egypt testify to a vigorous expansion in foreign trade. At the same time, there was a cultural renaissance which produced some of the most elegant examples of Egyptian art and several literary works that were considered classics in their own time. Notable among the latter was the *Tale of Sinuhe*, a romance dealing with the adventures of an Egyptian nobleman who chooses self-imposed exile to avoid the wrath of the Pharaoh Sesostris I. The plot of this story beings with a coup attempt and the murder of Sesostris' father. Sinuhe, although not connected with the rebels, fears that the Pharaoh might view matters differently. As a consequence, he leaves Egypt in somewhat of a panic and makes his way into the Levant. Sinuhe is welcomed by a Bedouin tribal chief, marries the man's eldest daughter and serves his host as a mercenary commander-in-chief for many years, winning great victories against Asiatic nomads. An amnesty finally permits him to return to Egypt and a touching reunion with Sesostris.[8]

Egypt's principal military activity during the Middle Kingdom centred on determined efforts to colonise Nubia, the motive again being the securing of trade routes and the control of gold mines in the Nubian desert. Other than this, the Pharaohs confined their wars to occasional punitive expeditions into Libyan and Bedouin territories, all of which seem to have succeeded in discouraging enemy raids into Egyptian lands. In the south, a series of massive fortresses was constructed to safeguard the frontier with Nubia and the trade routes. The fortresses were practically impregnable. Their carefully constructed defences, with double walls, bastions and ditches, enabled the garrison to direct enfilading fire against enemy attacks on all possible entry points. Because the fortresses presented such formidable obstacles to would-be attackers, they only required small garrisons. Judging by the extent of the living quarters, some of them seem to have been manned by little more than 300 soldiers. The garrisons were a mixture of national troops and Nubian mercenaries, the latter being in the minority.

It has already been noted that mercenaries were not predominant in the armies of the Middle Kingdom. The Pharaohs of that period continued to hire them, albeit in much smaller numbers. Having firmly established their control over Egypt and Lower Nubia and erected defensive forts requiring only modest garrisons, the Pharaohs no longer needed to employ substantial numbers of foreign troops. Furthermore, they had retained some of the more effective militia units in permanent employ, thereby creating the nucleus of a standing army. Although these units represented nothing more than a nucleus and were not numerous enough to constitute a credible permanent army, their existence did enable the Egyptian monarchs to reduce their employment of mercenaries. Finally, the Pharaohs were also mindful of the depredations perpetrated by mercenary bands during the previous civil wars and sought to exercise much tighter control over foreign soldiers. This accounts for the dispersal of mercenary contingents into the fortress garrisons protecting Egypt's frontiers and trade routes. Some of the mercenary units, in particular Nubians of the Medjay tribe, were employed as an internal police force, a classical function repeatedly performed by mercenaries throughout history. Having no emotional links with the Egyptian people, the Nubians were willing agents of repression and indeed 'Medjay' came to be synonymous with 'police'.

With the advent of the Thirteenth Dynasty, the cohesion of the Egyptian state gradually disappeared for reasons which are not entirely clear. The Pharaohs of the new Dynasty may have been of weaker character than their predecessors. An apparently successful attempt at usurping the throne incited the provincial lords to struggle against each other for ultimate power. Egypt was placed under external pressure from two directions. In the south, the Kushite kings from Upper Nubia sought to extend their influence into Upper Egypt, not so much out of territorial ambition but to maintain trade links with the Egyptians. In the north-east there was an infiltration of much greater consequence. Between 1730–1700 BC, Egypt was invaded from Asia by the Hyksos, a group of people of diverse but indeterminate ethnic origins. They seem to have originated in the Eurasian steppes near the Caspian Sea and the Caucasus but were joined on their westward advance by various Semitic peoples, among whom were Arab nomads.

Egypt was torn apart by internal rivalries and usurpations which resulted in a quick succession of Pharaohs. The Hyksos occupied Egypt except for Thebes, which was granted an uneasy independence in return for the payment of heavy tribute. They lived apart from their Egyptian subjects in fortified camps, some of which were capable of holding up to 10,000 men[9] and were not at first greatly influenced by the superior civilisation of the conquered. Their main activity was oppression and the extraction of tribute.

THE NEW KINGDOM

The Egyptians endured the harsh rule of the Hyksos for over a century until the Theban ruler, Kamose, began a war of liberation around 1600 BC. The odious presence of the Hyksos had gradually produced a rising tide of nationalist sentiment and a sense of indignation against the Asiatic oppressors – the first foreigners ever to shatter the pride and superiority of Egypt. By 1580 BC the Hyksos had been driven into Palestine by Kamose's young brother, Ahmosis. The Egyptians had beaten the Hyksos by learning to use the chariot, the very weapon that had made the erstwhile invaders so formidable. The triumphant Ahmosis founded the Eighteenth Dynasty and Egypt entered its third great period, known as the New Kingdom. It was an age marked by vigorous territorial expansion.

Egypt's burst of empire-building was a radical departure from its intro-spective and isolationist traditions. To some extent it was motivated by a desire to wreak revenge on the barbarians who had so humiliated Egypt. This sentiment was inextricably combined with other emotional factors, including an intense nationalism (and hence xenophobia) that affected all Egyptians regardless of social class. There was the euphoria of liberation and there was the need to re-establish the sense of security that had been taken for granted before the Hyksos invasion. Underlying the high emotion and patriotism was greed. Wars of conquest meant loot and the chance to acquire wealth. There were also commercial considerations in Egypt's change of attitude. The Pharaohs of the Old and Middle Kingdoms had fought wars which were essentially not much more than punitive actions aimed at keeping troublesome neighbours docile and trade routes open. Now the New Kingdom monarchs embarked on imperialist wars not merely to ensure the safety of trade routes but to achieve complete control over all foreign trade by a military occupation of the very sources supplying Egypt with precious metals and other commercial goods.

The initial military activity of the early New Kingdom was centred, not on the Levant, but on the south. Egypt's southern borders had to be made secure by the re-establishment of Egyptian control and influence in Nubia. To this end, the first four Pharaohs of the Eighteenth Dynasty, Ahmosis I (reigned 1580–1557 BC), Amenophis I (1557–1530 BC), Thutmosis I (1530–1520 BC) and Thutmosis II (1520–1501 BC), all fought a series of protracted campaigns to bring Nubia under control. Despite Nubian opposition, the Pharaohs managed to impose their control over the whole of Nubia and further south into Kush.

The next Pharaoh, Queen Hatsheput, was pacifist by nature, a circumstance which thoroughly enraged military leaders who longed for wars of conquest. Her successor, Thutmosis III (1484–1449 BC), more than gratified their wishes by immediately adopting a consistent policy of aggressive intervention in western Asia. The military leaders could campaign to their hearts' content for Thutmosis embarked on seventeen expeditions over a twenty-year period with armies made up of militia levies, native professional soldiers and foreign mercenaries.

At the beginnning of the New Kingdom there had been very few mercenaries, if any, in Egypt's armies. The traditional recruiting areas such as Nubia had become independent, openly hostile to Egypt and friendly to the Hyksos. Furthermore, the intense xenophobia felt by the Egyptians during the struggle against the Hyksos precluded any immediate recourse to mercenary hire. Thus, the earliest armies were national formations composed of a core of regular troops and militia contingents.

As Egypt committed itself to the creation of an empire, mercenaries were gradually re-employed, so that by the time of Ramses II (1298–1235 BC), Egyptian armies had undergone the usual transition and had become almost entirely mercenary in character and composition. The maintenance of empire over an indefinite period of time could not be left to seasonal soldiers. Permanent garrisons were required to watch over strategic areas. Short-term militia levies were not always immediately available in times of crisis. Once hired, mercenaries could be assigned to permanent garrison duty and be readily available for military operations at the first sign of a disturbance. Thus, the Pharaohs once again sanctioned the hiring of foreign mercenaries. The need to keep permanent garrisons in occupied territories was not the only reason for the reintroduction of mercenaries into Egyptian armies. The native professional military caste of Egypt had come into existence during the Middle Kingdom as an alternative to the over-hiring of mercenaries. The Egyptian monarchy had conceded important privileges to its permanent soldiers. There were hereditary land grants, tax-free stipends and the right to present lists of grievances directly to the Pharaoh, all in return for military service. The soldiers enjoyed a special status that set them apart from the rest of society. In addition to its domestic privileges, the military caste became increasingly rich (and hence, powerful) after each new success in Egypt's imperialist wars. Wealth, power, status, financial investments and personal concerns progressively reduced the caste's desire to engage in further military adventures, except on its own account. As a consequence the Pharaohs began to employ mercenaries who would be directly loyal to the monarchy as long as they were well-treated and well-paid.

Naturally enough, the Pharaohs first looked to traditional sources for mercenary recruits. The Nubian tribes once more provided the Egyptian army with courageous fighters, inured to hardship by the difficult living conditions in their native land. The Medjay re-appeared in substantial numbers in the domestic police force. Initially, the Nubians worked largely within Egypt itself, as policemen, bodyguards, and in border garrisons where they monitored the activities of other Nubians from different tribes. There were some Nubian contingents in the armies that Egypt sent across its borders to conquer Mesopotamia, but the majority of troops were native Egyptians. The desire for revenge and loot that had animated Egypt's imperial adventure had lasted through several reigns, so that, in the time of the aggressive Thutmosis III, there were still sufficient numbers of Egyptians, both in the military caste and the militia, willing to participate in the Pharaoh's frequent expeditions.

Egypt achieved its maximum territorial expansion during the reign of Thutmosis who was one of the most skilful generals of the Ancient World. At Megiddo his army, which included some Nubian detachments, won a spectacular victory over a Syrian–Palestinian coalition of 330 city-princes led by the Hyksos king of Kadesh (1479 BC). The battle was of vital importance to Egyptian imperial ambitions. Megiddo stood astride the most important commercial artery in Syria–Palestine, linking Egypt with all the main trade centres of Mesopotamia.[10]

In subsequent expeditions, Thutmosis III inflicted defeats on Egypt's chief rival, the Mitanni state, at Carchemish (1473 BC) and Aleppo (1471 BC). At the same time, a rebellious coalition of Syrian princes met defeat at the battles of Senjar and Kadesh. By the end of Thutmosis' reign, the Egyptians had achieved uncontested supremacy in western Asia. So awesome was Thutmosis' military reputation that small scattered garrisons of native Egyptian professionals and foreign mercenaries were sufficient to police the whole empire.

Egypt's position remained strong during the reign of the next Pharaoh, Amenophis II (1449–1425 BC). The city-princes of Syria–Palestine had entertained hopes of independence after the death of Thutmosis, but Amenophis crushed their rebellions with a brutality that contrasted with Thutmosis' usually magnanimous treatment of beaten enemies. Whereas Thutmosis often won over recalcitrant princes by leaving them in nominal charge, Amenophis tended to hang them for public display. After one successful campaign in Syria, Amenophis returned in triumph with large numbers of prisoners, including 550 Syrian nobles, 232 princes, 323 princesses, 640 Canaanite nobles and lastly 270 women selected from the harems of the conquered princes.[11] Having reaffirmed Egyptian domination, Amenophis devoted himself to a variety of pleasurable pastimes, some of which included the selected women.

His immediate successors, Thutmosis IV (1425–1413 BC) and Amenophis III (1413–1370 BC), maintained the Egyptian empire. Thutmosis entered into an alliance with the now docile Mitanni against a common enemy, the Hittites. Amenophis III, who was not partial to warfare, fought a campaign against rebellious tribes in Upper Nubia (c. 1400 BC). His army and, indeed, his elite personal bodyguard contained large numbers of mercenaries from Lower Nubia who had no reservations about fighting their Upper Nubian kinsmen. The rebels were defeated in battle at Ibhet (above the second cataract), losing 312 killed and 740 prisoners.[12]

The number of mercenaries in Egyptian armies had steadily increased from the time of Thutmosis III. As previously noted, this was partly as a result of the growing reluctance of the native professionals to take part in further punitive expeditions once the empire had been firmly established and once their fortunes had been made. The Egyptian desire for revenge born of the humiliating Hyksos occupation gradually waned after the death of Thutmosis III so that, while the military class became increasingly unwilling for reasons connected with newly-acquired wealth, the mass of Egyptians lost their patriotic ardour and returned to the traditional passivity and unwarlike nature of their ancestors. The Pharaohs were once again faced with the problem of large-scale avoidance of militia duty by citizens liable to conscription and increasingly resorted to the mercenary system. Militias were still levied but they were assigned to secondary roles. Their presence was required to make armies look formidable but their importance did not extend much beyond this essentially decorative function. Henceforth, the main fighting was done by foreign mercenaries.

CHAPTER THREE

Imperial Egypt:
The Sea Peoples and the Hittites

DURING THE REIGN of Amenophis III, there was a notable expansion in the number and variety of mercenaries employed by the Egyptians. Alongside the Nubians were Libyans, Bedouins and the redoubtable Sherdens (Shardana). The latter rapidly became the most important of the foreigners in Egyptian service. They were prominent in the garrisons of Egypt's Asiatic empire during the reign of Amenophis' successor, Akhenaton, whose indifference to foreign affairs encouraged insurrection in the Levant. The Sherden garrisons found themselves fully occupied against rebellious vassal–kings, Hittites and *habiru*. Rib-Addi's distinctly miserable plea for Sherden mercenary reinforcements to crush the rebels in Byblos and the lugubrious fate of his own Sherden garrison have already been described. Given the scale of the revolt and the prominence of the Sherden, the events in Byblos would have represented but one incident of Sherden mercenary involvement in the struggle to maintain the empire. With the eccentric Akhenaton too busy imposing monotheism on his unwilling subjects to care about events in the Levant, the Sherden were faced with a difficult task.

The Sherden were excellent warriors specialising in close combat with sword and shield. The Egyptians, by contrast, relied primarily on the power of the bow and volleys of arrows to discomfit enemies. Although their fighting qualities are beyond doubt, the origin of the Sherden remains problematical. They formed part of a diverse group of Indo-European tribes collectively known as the Sea Peoples. The exact origin of these tribes remains a matter of conjecture but their appearance in the eastern Mediterranean seems to have been part of a mass migration caused by famine rather than a planned invasion.

The term 'Sea Peoples' was first used in 1881 by the historian Gaston Maspero, who referred to the tribes as *'peuples de la mer'*, thereby creating the impression that the mysterious migrants had all reached Egypt by crossing the Mediterranean. While this seems to have been essentially correct for some tribes, more modern research suggests that other tribes came southward from Anatolia via the Levant, with the apparent desire to settle in some fertile area.[1]

The surviving evidence concerning the Sea Peoples is fragmentary, sometimes contradictory and far from conclusive. It is difficult to do much more than suggest possible ethnic and geographic origins for the various tribes. Consequently, any attempt to identify these origins has to contain less than satisfying qualifications, like 'possibly', 'seem' or 'appear'.

Many of the tribes, such as the Denyen, Teresh, Lukka and Peleset (Philistines), appear to have lived in various locations along the Anatolian coast and the Aegean islands. That the Peleset, for example, resided in Anatolia at some stage during the late second millennium is suggested by a comparison of the Peleset ox-carts depicted in Egyptian carvings with ox-carts still used in modern Turkey. The ancient and contemporary vehicles are essentially identical. This evidence is, however, no more than suggestive.

The Akawasha (Ekwesh) have most often been identified with Achaean Greeks displaced by a migratory wave of Dorians from Illyria. If they were from Greece, the Akawasha were atypical. A group of 2,201 prisoners captured by the Egyptians were found to have undergone circumcision, a Semitic practice running counter to traditional Indo-European ways.[2] Some of the Sea Peoples seem to have lived in the western Mediterranean area. The Shekelesh, who raided Egypt in the reign of Merneptah (*c.*1236–*c.*1220 BC) and later served Ramses III as garrison mercenaries, may have had some connection with southern Italy and the Sikel people of Sicily. Again the evidence is very meagre and mainly centres on the similarity of the names 'Sikel' and 'Shekelesh' and the discovery in Sicily of pottery reflecting Anatolian influence.

The Sherden have been linked with Sardinia and Corsica on somewhat more substantial evidence. Bronze statuettes found in Sardinia show warriors armed with round shields and distinctive horned helmets very similar to the Sherden type. Moreover, a Phoenician inscription also unearthed in Sardinia gives the name of the island as Shardan. In Corsica menhir-tombstones show warriors dressed in Sherden style. Although these artefacts strongly suggest a Sherden presence on the islands, it is unlikely that Corsica and Sardinia were originally inhabited by the Sherdens. The two islands provided ideal bases for piracy, an activity the Sherdens engaged in before selling their services as mercenaries. It is more likely that the Sherdens moved to Sardinia and Corsica from Anatolia. Horned helmets like those of the Sherdens were not yet worn by Aegean or European peoples, but were characteristic of Anatolia, Mesopotamia and the Levant. Thus, the Sherdens also seem to have come from eastern Anatolia but, for lack of more conclusive evidence, their origin must be recorded as unknown. As Indo-Europeans, the Sherdens and the other Sea Peoples must ultimately have come from some unidentifiable location deeper within the great Eurasian land-mass. Of all the Sea Peoples, the Sherdens had the most sustained contact with Ancient Egypt, both as elite mercenaries in Egyptian employ and as enemies of Egypt in alliance with other tribes of Sea Peoples and Libya.

The decay of Egypt's Asiatic empire occasioned by Akhenaton's lack of interest was arrested during the reign of Tutankhamen (*c*.1352–*c*.1344 BC), who remains more famous for his impressive gold coffin than his earthly deeds, and Horemheb (*c*.1342–*c*.1313 BC), the last Pharaoh of the Eighteenth Dynasty. Lost territories were regained in Palestine. The ambitious Seti I (1312–1298 BC), second Pharaoh of the Nineteenth Dynasty, re-established Egypt's policy of territorial aggrandisement and ushered in the period subsequently known to history as the Second Empire. In a series of bold campaigns, Seti recaptured twenty-three fortresses held by Bedouin rebels in Palestine and defeated an Amorite–Aramaean coalition in Canaan by catching the respective enemy armies on the march before they had managed to achieve their junction. At Kadesh (*c*.1299 BC) Seti defeated the Hittites and re-established Egyptian dominance in Syria. In all of these actions Sherden and Nubian mercenaries played an important role alongside the native Egyptian forces.

The influence and the importance of the Sherdens was even more apparent during the reign of Seti's successor, Ramses II (1298–1235 BC). The new Pharaoh proved to be a courageous but rash general, as evidenced by the close-run battle of Kadesh. He was a prolific builder of temples (Abu Simbel, Karnak, Thebes, Luxor and Abydos), the Ozymandias of Percy Shelley's poem. He was also a vigorous and experienced man of action (100 sons and over fifty daughters).

When Ramses succeeded his father, Egypt's position in the Levant was threatened by the expansion of the rival Hittite empire. A military confrontation being inevitable, Ramses and the Hittite monarch, Muwattalish, made their preparations. The Egyptian army was reorganised into four main divisions named after the gods, Amon, Re, Ptah and Sutekh. Each division contained about 5,000 men.[3] Although there were contingents of less-than-enthusiastic conscripts, the army was now largely composed of native professionals and foreign mercenaries, predominantly Nubians, with lesser proportions of Bedouins, Canaanites and Amorites who had been former prisoners of war. Alongside the four divisions was a *corps d'elite*, Ramses' personal guard made up of Sherdens recruited in Phoenicia. With their double-edged swords, unfamiliar to the native Egyptians, their horned helmets surmounted by a large ball, that may have been a regimental distinction, and round shields, the Sherdens not only represented a corps of skilled fighters but were also a visible symbol of the Pharaoh's financial power and social status. Like all elite formations of foreign bodyguards throughout history, the Sherdens heightened the monarch's prestige and impressed his subjects. The favours and privileges they enjoyed and the post of honour they occupied in battle aroused the jealousy of other branches of the army. Ramses capitalised on the mutual rivalry to encourage the fighting ardour of his troops.

While Ramses mobilised his forces to attack the Hittites, the enemy king, Muwattalish (1306–1282 BC), levied contingents of troops from vassal-kings and spent lavish sums of money hiring mercenaries and auxiliaries, among whom were Elamites, Bedouins, Cilicians, Mysians, Dardanians and Lycians. The total Hittite force amounted to some 18,000–20,000 men.[4]

Ramses set out on a month-long march to the Hittite stronghold of Kadesh which lay on the Orontes river (Asi river) north of Beirut and dominated the strategic pass into the Bekah valley and its network of military and trade routes. The Pharaoh, together with the Sherdens and the Amon division, led the advance with the Re, Ptah and Sutekh divisions following in the order mentioned. While the army was still *en route* to Kadesh, two Bedouin mercenaries, ostensibly deserting from the Hittite side, told Ramses that Muwattalish had retreated to Aleppo rather than face the Pharaoh at Kadesh. Encouraged by this apparent faint-heartedness, the Pharaoh rashly pressed on to Kadesh, leaving the Re division at least seven kilometres to the rear and the rest of the army much further behind. Ramses ordered the Sherden and the Amon division to set up camp outside Kadesh, confident that the seemingly undefended city would fall as soon as the rest of the Egyptian army rejoined his vanguard, not knowing that Muwattalish's entire army – the largest Hittite army every fielded – stood waiting near Kadesh.[5]

The following morning, when the division came within sight of Kadesh, the Hittites began their attack. They struck, not at Ramses, but at the Re division, a tempting target moving up in open order and unprepared for battle. Caught completely by surprise, the Re division was routed. Its surviving troops reached Ramses' camp as a disorganised rabble fleeing before the enemy, which did nothing for the morale of the Amon division. The Hittites now attacked the Pharaoh's isolated troops.

Normally, Egyptian Pharaohs did not personally engage in combat during battles, but on this occasion Ramses found himself at the centre of the action. At one point he claimed to have been surrounded by the enemy and left completely alone by his own troops. Ramses' account of the ensuing fight is an impressive scenario, one which he later recorded for posterity in the inscriptions and pictorial representations at the temple of Abu Simbel in Nubia.[6] Deserted by his panic-stricken men and surrounded by 7,500 men in 2,500 chariots – Ramses somehow found time to count them – the Pharaoh coolly and single-handedly defeated the enemy with a dazzling display of archery and, it seems, an unlimited supply of arrows. As a god-king, Ramses was entitled to claim all the credit, but his scenario represents little more than an obvious and blatant piece of self-adulation denuded of historical value, beyond being a superlative example of the propaganda that monarchs used to enhance their prestige.

The Hittite chariots were heavier than those of the Egyptians and were designed to crash through an enemy by sheer momentum. Thus by the time that the Hittites reached the Egyptian camp, their horses were largely blown and the mass of chariots lost its cohesion among the camp tents and equipment. The seemingly unstoppable Hittite wave broke up in confusion with groups of chariots inextricably jammed together. The initial wave of panic that had washed over the Egyptians receded as they gradually realised that the Hittite onslaught had slowed down. Egyptian, Nubian and Libyan archers began to pour a destructive fire into the Hittite chariot crews and a savage hand-to-hand struggle ensued as Egyptian troops armed with spears and bladed weapons attacked the Hittites at close quarters. The Hittites nevertheless broke through to the royal enclosure where they came up against Ramses' Sherden bodyguard drawn up in line to protect the Pharaoh. The Sherdens fully demonstrated the fighting value of loyal and reliable mercenary troops by holding up superior numbers of Hittites long enough to enable Ramses to organise a counter-attack with chariotry.

It was the Egyptian superiority in archery and the greater manoeuvrability

[45]

of their chariots which eventually decided the day in favour of the Pharaoh. Hittite chariot crews were mainly armed with javelins and could thus be destroyed at a distance by the Pharaoh's chariot-borne archers. Nevertheless, the Egyptians had to fight continuously for three hours until the arrival of a contingent of Amorite auxiliaries and the approach of the Ptah division forced the Hittites to withdraw into Kadesh. Muwattalish, for reasons unclear, failed to commit his reserve force of 8,000 spearmen, thus enabling the Egyptian divisions to escape what should have been certain destruction. The Hittites had lost heavily but the Egyptian breakout had been dearly won. Some 50 per cent of the Amon troops and the Sherdens had been killed, captured or dispersed.[7]

Kadesh was a drawn battle. But for the gallant resistance of Ramses' mercenaries it might have been a disaster. Ramses returned to Egypt immediately without capturing the town and began work on transforming a lucky escape into a major triumph. At best he had temporarily inhibited the southward advance of the Hittites. Muwattalish had little difficulty in fomenting anti-Egyptian rebellions in the Levant and Ramses was forced to undertake a series of campaigns in order to recapture lost cities such as Ascalon in Palestine.

Mercenary soldiers continued to play a vital role in all the battles between the Egyptians and the Hittites. There were Indo-European, Asiatic and African mercenaries on both sides and they constituted the elite forces of the opposing armies. Around 1278 BC hostilities ceased. There was a sudden *rapprochement* between the rival empires occasioned by a mutual disquiet over the gradual advance of Assyrian power. Ramses sealed the Egyptian–Hittite *entente cordiale* with a dynastic marriage to a Hittite princess, much to the amazement of his subjects. During the grandiose celebrations, mercenary troops from both the Egyptian and Hittite armies paraded together and fraternised openly. Not long before, they had been ready and willing to kill each other in the service of their respective employers.

The *entente* between Egypt and the Hittites brought peace to western Asia for more than fifty years. On the western border of Egypt, however, the Libyan tribes continued to be a chronic source of trouble. Few documents survive concerning Ramses' campaigns in Libya but it is known that, after one victory against Libyans, Ramses added to the ever-increasing number of mercenaries in the Egyptian army by incorporating Libyan captives from the Ribu and Meshwesh tribes.[8] By the end of his reign, there was only a very small minority of native Egyptians in the regular army. Foreigners of various backgrounds flooded into Egypt seeking lucrative employment and an easier way of life. In one contingent of 5,000 troops sent by Ramses to Wadi Hammamat for traditional peacetime employment in quarries there were no Egyptians at all. Over 4,000 of the soldiers were Sherden and Libyans and the rest were Nubians.[9] This contingent was not unusual.

For Egypt, the Libyan tribes constituted a source of mercenary recruits on the one hand and a chronic nuisance on the other. Libyan mercenaries were employed as far back as the Sixth Dynasty of the Old Kingdom for punitive expeditions in the Levant. In the New Kingdom they came to occupy an important position in Egyptian society, constituting a distinct warrior caste alongside other foreign mercenaries. Ultimately their power grew to such proportions that they were able to usurp the throne and found the so-called Libyan Dynasties (Twenty-Second and Twenty-Third Dynasties). The Libyans also represented a recurrent threat to Egypt right from earliest times. Successive Pharaohs of the Old, Middle and New Kingdoms were forced to undertake military expeditions in order to prevent large-scale Libyan incursions. The desert tribesmen always took advantage of weak Pharaohs to push eastward into the Nile Delta. Given their disunity, the Libyan tribes were normally defeated with relative ease. Egyptian campaigns in Libya were aimed at containing the eastward advance rather than at outright conquest. The Libyans, however, were never daunted by their set-backs and returned again and again to test the mettle of new Pharaohs who might prove unequal to the task of defending Egypt.

The Libyans were skilled warriors, well-armed with bows, spears and long straight swords. Their attacks on Egypt were largely motivated by economic and geographical considerations. Like many other mercenaries throughout history, they came from a relatively poor and unproductive territory incapable of supporting a large population. Libya was largely a desert country where agriculture and pastoralism were confined to two narrow coastal strips, Tripolitania and Cyrenaica. Not surprisingly, the Libyans were ceaselessly attracted by the fertility of the Nile valley, which contrasted so starkly with the harsh environment of their own land.

Around 1232 BC, during the reign of Ramses' successor, Merneptah, the Libyans, led by the Meshwesh, attacked Egypt in concert with the Sea Peoples, among whom were the Akawasha, Teresh, Lukka, Shekelesh and Sherden. The Sea Peoples, as previously noted, were in quest of a new homeland. On their way southward they had attacked Egypt's new ally, the Hittites, and seriously weakened their Anatolian empire. But Egypt with its rich soil, its wealth and abundant natural resources was their primary target. Libyans and Sea Peoples shared the same goal. The attack on Egypt by the Libyan tribes and the predominantly Greek and western Mediterranean Sea Peoples was not a mere raid. It was a deliberate attempt at migration. The soldiers came towards Egypt with their wives, children, cattle herds and all their worldly possessions.

The coalition army of about 20,000 men struck at Egypt's western border, advancing to Perire (northwest of Memphis), a location whose extensive vineyards and grainfields must have provided an agreeable sight after the deserts of Libya. It was at Perire that the invaders and the largely mercenary army of Merneptah came into contact. After a six-hour battle the invaders were soundly defeated by the superior archers of the Pharaoh's army. During the encounter, coalition Sherden fought their kinsmen in Egyptian service. Their Libyan allies also came up against fellow Libyans of the Kehek tribe working as mercenaries in the Pharaoh's pay.

Merneptah had thwarted the most serious attempt at invasion yet mounted by the Libyans. While the dead attackers suffered the indignity of selective mutilation, the prisoners finally did get to enter Egypt permanently, though not quite in the way they had intended. Despite their failure, Merneptah was impressed with the invaders' toughness and fighting qualities. As a result, the Pharaoh took the captives into his own army, settling them in special areas in the Nile Delta alongside previously established foreign mercenary encampments. Merneptah thus acquired a valuable addition to his military forces and, in offering regular employment and land grants to former enemies, gave them a motive for serving rather than harassing Egypt. The remainder of Merneptah's reign seems to have been peaceful save for a short punitive campaign in Palestine to suppress a rebellion.

When Ramses III succeeded to the throne, events beyond Egypt's border had taken a distinctly threatening turn. In 1200 BC the friendly Hittite empire had collapsed under the onslaught of the Sea Peoples, who were now moving southward into Syria. In the west, the Libyans had reorganised themselves after the defeat inflicted by Merneptah. Threatened on both sides, Egypt was caught in a gradually tightening noose. Her already substantial foreign population was further enlarged by Canaanites, Syrians and Bedouins who entered Egypt, with or without official permission, having been displaced by the advance of the Sea Peoples. Libyans also continued to arrive in significant numbers, looking for an easier mode of existence. Needless to say, many of the infiltrators found their way into the ranks of the Egyptian army.

[48]

Ramses (1195–1164 BC), the last great Pharaoh of the New Kingdom, was fully alert to the renewed threat of invasion. He built up a large fleet of boats, constructed new fortifications at the river mouths of the Nile Delta and issued weapons to the army, which had been relatively inactive since the time of Merneptah's victories. The distribution of arms and the subsequent struggle with the Libyans and Sea Peoples was recorded in considerable detail in inscriptions and pictorial representations at Ramses' mortuary temple in Medinet Habu.

'Bring forth the equipment. Send out the troops to destroy the rebellious (countries) which know not Egypt. [Give] . . . equipment to the infantry and chariotry, to the troops, the Sherden and the Nubians.[10]

The separate mention of the Sherdens and Nubians in this exhortation suggests that they were regarded as elite troops. Further along in the Medinet Habu inscriptions, reference is made to the positioning of the elite troops in vulnerable locations along Egypt's borders. As to the 'infantry and chariotry' arms, they too were largely made up of mercenaries and the relatively few native Egyptians who still cared for a military life. The difference between the 'infantry' and the 'troops' mentioned is unclear, but the latter may refer to militia levies which were still occasionally called out to build up numbers and provide labourers.

There were three possible points through which the enemy could attack Egypt: the Libyan border, the Levant and the Nile Delta. All three areas did in fact come under attack. The Libyan tribes, again led by the Meshwesh, gathered just beyond Egypt's western border with the intention of striking at Memphis. Ramses, however, anticipated the attack and moved first, catching the Libyans with their preparations incomplete. The Egyptians gained a clear victory and their scribes could record that over 1,000 captives were taken and that the heaps of hands and phalluses removed as trophies represented over 12,500 dead. The prisoners were later impressed into mercenary service as garrison troops.

The second attack, a confrontation on land and water with the Sea Peoples, came in 1186 BC. Among the invaders were the Peleset, Shekelesh, Tjekker, Denyen, Akawasha, Weshesh and Sherden. Few details are known about the land battle other than it was fought beyond Egypt's north-eastern border and resulted in another triumph for Ramses and his mercenary army. Once again Sherden encountered Sherden and the pictures at Medinet Habu show the

Pharaoh's Sherden scattering the enemy and looting ox-carts loaded with women, children and personal possessions.

Having repulsed the overland invasion, Ramses returned to the Nile Delta in time to meet the seaborne attack, having thoroughly prepared his defences by positioning his boats according to a carefully thought-out plan. Many of the boats were side by side so as to form floating ramparts across the various river mouths, thereby forcing the enemy boats to sail close to the shore. The naval forces were supported by masses of elite mercenary archers stationed along the river banks. After throwing the Sea Peoples into utter confusion with accurate archery, the Egyptians advanced, ramming and capsizing many of the enemy craft. Those of the attacking boats that did manage to get through or skirt the lines of defending craft found themselves trapped as the Egyptians closed up and cut off their escape routes.

Ramses' spectacular victory had saved Egypt and its Asiatic empire. Some of the Sea Peoples, namely the Peleset, settled in the southern part of the empire, accepted the Pharaohs' suzerainty and in time came to give their name to their new homeland, which was henceforth known as Philistia and, from the fifth century BC, as Palestine.

The numerous prisoners taken by the Egyptians met various fates. There were some who wound up as slaves in temples and others were taken to the Delta camps where they joined foreign mercenaries already in Egyptian service. Ramses required the new recruits to swear an oath of allegiance and provided clothing and provisions on a regular basis. The Sherden remained the most important of the Sea Peoples taken into the Pharaoh's service, but Weshesh, Denyen, Shekelesh and Philistines also served the monarch, both in the main army and in the garrisons of the empire.[11]

Ramses fought one final encounter with the persistent Libyans in the eleventh year of his reign. Led as before by the Meshwesh, the coalition of Libyan tribes crossed the Egyptian border and invested the fortress of Hatsho. Ramses acted with characteristic rapidity, attacking the enemy positions around the stronghold. Caught between the volleys of arrows fired by the fortress garrison and Ramses' forces, the Libyans were routed and relentlessly pursued by the Egyptians, who inflicted 2,175 casualties and took over 2,000 prisoners.[12] The Pharaoh treated the captives with a severity normally uncharacteristic of the Egyptians, executing all the Libyan tribal chiefs and sending all their followers – men, women and children – to fortresses and temples as slaves. Ramses' stern treatment may have been the product of Egyptian exasperation. The Libyans had attacked Egypt once too often and had to be taught a lesson.

Ramses' measures seem to have been effective. The disaster at Hatsho marked the last Libyan attempt to invade Egypt by force of arms. As it happened, they kept coming into the Delta region, but in small migratory groups tolerated by the Pharaoh, not as an army bent on conquest. They added to the sizeable foreign population permanently established within Egypt's borders. It was a cosmopolitan population of soldiers and civilians, which included Sea Peoples, Nubians, Libyans, Semites and Iranians. The preponderance of foreigners was not limited to the military forces. Ramses' entourage of palace officials, personal attendants and generals included many foreigners, among whom were Libyans, Syrians and Phoenicians.

The foreign mercenaries and civilians living in Egypt were susceptible to Egyptian influence and many adopted local gods and local customs and became thoroughly Egyptianised. But the presence of such a large cosmopolitan collection of people in Egypt also had a considerable impact on the native population. There was a linguistic influence as new words, many of Semitic origin, entered the Egyptian language and came into daily use. The Egyptians also took an interest in foreign gods such as the Syrian god, Baal, who gradually began to rival Amon in popularity. The most important influence was the complete disappearance among native Egyptians of any desire to perform military service. Distasteful activities like fighting could be left to foreigners.

The dislike of war felt by the Egyptians was a laudable sentiment from a moral point of view, but it was inappropriate, not to say fatal, given the gradually increasing power of neighbours like the Philistines and the particularly vicious Assyrians. The numerous foreign mercenaries who had taken over the task of conducting Egypt's wars might have been skilled at their profession, but the great mass of them had no heartfelt loyalty to the state. It was not so much a case of what they could do for the country but rather what they could do for their purses.

The spectacular victories won by Ramses III over the Libyans and the Sea Peoples delayed, but did not prevent, the collapse of the Egyptian empire and indeed of Egypt itself as an independent entity. The decay of Egypt's greatness did not begin at some decent interval after the Pharaoh's demise. It had already begun to manifest itself in the latter part of Ramses' reign. There was an attempt against his life which showed just how irrelevant the concept of the godlike nature and sanctity of the Pharaoh had become. An embittered

Ramses unintentionally contributed to the decline of the Pharaoh's power by making pious but foolishly generous donations, especially to the temple of Amon at Karnak. The priesthood of Amon received the lion's share of endowments from the royal treasury and of loot taken in military campaigns. As a result the priests became enormously wealthy and the monarchy correspondingly poor.

The overwhelming economic power of the Amon priesthood also gave it substantial political power. People then, as now, could be bought and sold by the wealthy. Ramses could only counter this priestly power with his army, made up of voluntarily or forcibly enlisted mercenaries and crown-owned slaves assigned to military service. As foreigners, the mercenaries had no special attachment to Amon, but on the other hand their loyalty to the Pharaoh would be placed in doubt if he proved unable to pay their wages.

Thus, Ramses' empire, which still looked outwardly splendid, was in fact in remarkable decay, with a greedy priesthood taking much of the country's wealth, greedy royal relatives wanting their share of the goods and a foreign entourage and army motivated by mercenary considerations. After Ramses' death, another nine Pharaohs bearing the same name, but not the same military ability, reigned rather than ruled over Egypt from 1164 BC to 1085 BC. During this woeful period, the Pharaohs came more or less completely under the domination of the Amon sect. The reduced status of the Pharaohs vis-à-vis the Amon High Priest was even pictorially represented on the walls of the Karnak temple. A relief of Ramses IX donating gifts to the High Priest shows both men in equal size and stature. In the days of the great Pharaohs this sacrilegious liberty would have been quite unthinkable.

Egypt's Asiatic empire collapsed along with its prestige. Nubia reasserted its independence. The degree to which respect for Egypt had faded is illustrated by the fate of a group of Egyptian diplomatic envoys sent to the Phoenician city of Byblos. The helpless envoys were detained by the local ruler – for up to seventeen years. Finally, they died in captivity, of natural causes.

The last Ramesside Pharaohs were little more than palace-prisoners and puppets of the Amon priesthood. Herihor, the High Priest of Amon, ultimately took the logical step and became Pharaoh after the last monarch of the Twentieth Dynasty passed unlamented into obscurity. But the arrival of the Twenty-First Dynasty did not bring about any dramatic reversal in the decline of Egypt as a great power. On the contrary, Egyptian unity effectively collapsed as the country was split into two territories, a theocracy ruled by the High Priests of Amon centred on Thebes and a separate principality in the Delta ruled by the merchant princes of Tanis. For over a century a divided and feeble Egypt saw a succession of weak and ineffectual Pharaohs who shared what little power they possessed with independent princes. Foreign policy was totally ignored since Egypt no longer had an empire to worry about but the Egyptian nobility clung to the pathetic fiction that Egypt still enjoyed a nominal suzerainty over Palestine. The real ownership of Palestine was in fact being contested by other peoples. To the Philistines and their rivals – the Israelites under Saul and David – Egyptian notions of sovereignty seemed somewhat irrelevant.

THE LIBYANS, THE NUBIANS AND THE MEN OF BRONZE

The fate of Palestine had already been decided in favour of the Israelites when the Twenty-first Dynasty was terminated by a Libyan mercenary chief in 950 BC. As previously described, the Libyans had finally renounced their traditional policy of attacking Egypt in favour of a gradual and peaceful migration sanctioned by the Pharaohs, who appreciated Libyan military skill. From the latter half of Ramses III's reign onwards, the Libyans arrived in such numbers that, by the beginning of the Twenty-first Dynasty, the Egyptian army was very largely composed of Libyans with lesser proportions of Nubians and Asiatics. The Sherden and other Sea Peoples rarely appear in documents after the time of Ramses III. Whether they continued to find employment in Egypt or whether they were totally displaced by the Libyans remains unclear. At any rate, the Libyans were predominant both in terms of numbers and growing political and military power. They were able to create veritable military colonies in the Delta, centred on the land grants given to them by successive Pharaohs as a form of payment. With Egypt retreating from empire, internally divided and largely at peace, the Libyans had little opportunity to display their valour in combat.

The most important of the Libyan mercenary commanders was Sheshonk (Shishak), Great Chief of the Meshwesh. As commander of the Libyan mercenary community at Heracleopolis, he enjoyed both prosperity and local authority and a considerable measure of influence over the powerless Egyptian monarchy. When the last Pharaoh of the Twenty-first Dynasty disappeared in obscure circumstances, Sheshonk moved his residence to Bubastis in the eastern Delta and proclaimed himself Pharaoh. Sheshonk I (950–929 BC), took care to 'legitimise' his usurpation by marrying his son and eventual successor, Osorkon, to the daughter of the recently defunct Pharaoh. The Amon priesthood at Thebes did not accept the Libyan Pharaoh without some resistance but Sheshonk was able to impose his authority, at least for the duration of his reign. Thebes, however, always retained its autonomy and its freedom from paying taxes to the royal treasury. It remained in a position to challenge the Libyan Dynasty when the strong and ambitious Sheshonk passed away.

Although Sheshonk could not count on Theban monetary contributions to his financial resources, he nevertheless managed to replenish the depleted Egyptian treasury. Around 935 BC he led his army into Palestine on a grand plundering expedition. It was the first time in nearly three centuries that an army from Egypt had penetrated into western Asia. The Libyan mercenaries looted and burnt down dozens of cities and, in particular, Jerusalem where they captured the great quantity of wealth amassed during the reigns of David and Solomon. Sheshonk had finally achieved what the Libyans had failed to do for centuries, that is to say, the conquest of northern Egypt. His successful campaign in Palestine partly restored Egypt's prestige in the eyes of its neighbours. The abundant loot enabled Sheshonk to undertake grand architectural projects that had been effectively neglected for over 200 years. Sheshonk was an early manifestation of a recurrent phenomenon in military history – a mercenary leader with territorial ambitions.

The death of Sheshonk I left a vacuum which his successors did not manage to fill effectively. Rivalry within the ruling Libyan royal house during the reign of Sheshonk III led to the formation of a breakaway Libyan dynasty (the overlapping Twenty-third Dynasty) centred on Thebes. Libyan mercenary chieftains who had regarded Sheshonk I and his successors as no more than *primus inter pares* asserted their independence from royal control and established personal authority over the military colonies they commanded. The brief resurgence of Egyptian power and prestige initiated by Sheshonk quickly faded as Egypt once more disintegrated into separate territories, an easy prey for potential foreign invaders. Towards 730 BC the threat of invasion became reality just as one of the Libyan lords, Tefnakht, ruler of Sais, was on the point of reunifying Egypt. The Nubian king, Piankhi, descended into Egypt, defeating the mercenary armies of the squabbling territories both on land and in battles on the Nile river. Thebes, Memphis and the Delta all surrendered to the invader. The Libyans had been overcome by the Nubians who treated their captives with chivalry and a remarkable degree of humanity. Curiously enough, Piankhi returned to Nubia shortly after his victory. Tefnakht took advantage of this withdrawal to re-establish, at least temporarily, the dominance of Sais in the Delta region. Tefnakht and his son, Bocchoris, ruled for some ten years before Shabaka, Piankhi's less humane brother, returned to Egypt in 715 BC, burnt Bocchoris alive and re-established Nubian supremacy.

The foreign policy of the Nubian rulers was largely determined by the relentless approach of the Assyrians. Thus, the Nubian monarchs encouraged the cities of Syria–Palestine to rebel against their Assyrian overlords in the hope of creating an independent buffer zone between Egypt and Assyria. When the Assyrian ruler, Sargon II, crushed the revolts, Shabaka practised a policy of appeasement which dissuaded the Assyrians from an immediate attack upon Egypt. But this was a mere respite. The consummate destroyers were bound to renew their advance sooner or later. The Nubian monarchs continued to foment rebellion in the reign of Sargon's successor, Sennacherib, and once again Egypt was temporarily spared from invasion. An Egyptian mercenary army, sent to the aid of Judah, was saved from total destruction by the timely spread of a pestilence among the Assyrian troops.

In 671 BC, however, Egypt's providential respite finally came to an end when the Assyrian king, Esarhaddon, exasperated by Egyptian subversion in the Levant, led his army towards the Nile. Crossing the Sinai Desert with the aid of Bedouins who supplied camels, food and water, Esarhaddon besieged Memphis and captured Lower Egypt. The various lords of the Delta who had been vassals of the Nubian monarchs now swore fidelity to Esarhaddon and were retained as local governors. Their actions were not among the most noble acts in the annals of the Egyptian nobility. However, given the Assyrian reputation for severity, the submission of the lords is readily understandable. Their newly-sworn fidelity disappeared as soon as Esarhaddon withdrew. Incited by the Nubians, who still held Upper Egypt, the lords rebelled and reaped their reward at the hands of Esarhaddon's son, Ashurbanipal, in 666 BC. A powerful army composed of native Assyrians and Syrian auxiliaries retook the Delta. In two subsequent expeditions, Ashurbanipal's army penetrated as far southward as the city of Thebes, which was thoroughly plundered (661 BC). The surviving members of the Nubian monarchy retreated deep into Nubia, never to return to Egypt, and founded a new capital and a purely Nubian state at Meroe. As for the rebellious lords of the Delta, they were taken to the conqueror's capital, Nineveh, where they suffered the grisly punishments characteristic of the Assyrians.

There was one survivor among the rebels. Ashurbanipal spared Necho of Sais, who had been popular among his own people and, as a willing collaborator, would be useful in controlling the subject population in the Delta. Necho's son, Psammeticus, was invested with the title of Pharaoh and given control of all Egypt, subject to Assyrian supervision, of course. Egypt seemed to be thoroughly under Assyrian domination, but as Ashurbanipal gradually became preoccupied with wars against the Elamites and rebellions in Babylonia (651 BC), Psammeticus had the opportunity to establish control over the country in his own right.

It was precisely at this moment that a new group of mercenaries appeared on the Egyptian scene and played a vital role in restoring Egyptian independence. In order to impose his rule in Egypt, Psammeticus' first task was to subdue eleven other Libyan mercenary lords in the Delta region. This he managed to do after first undergoing a short period of exile imposed by his rivals. The traditional story related by the Greek historian Herodotus (c.484–c.420 BC), was that Psammeticus was exiled to the Delta swamps where he planned revenge. Sending for advice to Egypt's most important oracle at Buto, he was informed that 'men of bronze' would come from the sea to help him achieve his ambition. Strange men wearing bronze armour, never before seen by the Egyptians, did in effect materialise. They were Greek raiders from Ionia and Caria. According to Herodotus, Psammeticus befriended them, persuaded them to enter his service and proceeded to defeat the other Libyan lords.[13]

The details of Herodotus' account were quite probably derived from fanciful folk-legends, but the essential fact remains that Greek mercenaries did aid Psammeticus, first against the local lords and then against the Assyrians who were expelled from Egyptian soil.

The mercenaries did not, however, appear accidentally or miraculously, as Herodotus' version seems to imply. Inscriptions left by Ashurbanipal show that they were deliberately sent to Psammeticus' aid by Gyges, King of Lydia. Having originally allied himself to Ashurbanipal against the threat of Cimmerian invasions, Gyges now sent hoplites to Psammeticus, whom he perceived to be the most effective source of opposition to the Assyrians. Shortly afterwards, Gyges himself was killed in battle against Ashurbanipal's forces but the troops he had sent were instrumental in the defeat of the Assyrians in Egypt.

Psammeticus and his successors in the Saite Dynasty clearly recognised the military effectiveness of the Greeks. Throughout the Saite Period (c.650–c.525 BC), the Greeks received favourable treatment from the Pharaohs, despite their unpopularity among the native population and the jealousy aroused among Egypt's Libyan mercenaries. The Greeks were permanently settled in large camps known as the Stratopeda in the Delta and in strategic border fortresses. Their numbers were regularly enlarged by the arrival of other Greeks who had been driven south by the pressure of overpopulation in Ionia. They were attracted by the employment opportunities offered by the Saite Pharaohs and, as members of a much younger culture, they were fascinated by the sheer antiquity of Egyptian civilisation, with its awe-inspiring monuments and time-honoured traditions and ceremonials.

There were two main Greek military settlements: Defenneh and Marea. Defenneh, which the Greeks soon altered to Daphnae, commanded Egypt's most vulnerable area, the eastern frontier. The settlement was a large one capable of holding over 20,000 men.[14] Its inhabitants guarded against Bedouin raiders or Assyrian attempts at reconquest. As it happened, the Assyrians under Ashurbanipal were on the defensive and were no longer capable or desirous of attacking Egypt. Whatever threat they still represented was completely eliminated in 612 BC when Nineveh was sacked by the Medes, Babylonians and Scythians. Although the Assyrians never came back, the Scythians attacked the eastern frontier around 625 BC. According to Herodotus, Egypt was saved from invasion when Psammeticus bought the Scythians off with lavish gifts.[15] But it seems more likely that the offer of payment was more attractive than the prospect of difficult sieges of fortresses manned by Greek mercenary hoplites. The Scythians were primarily nomadic mounted archers and did not possess the military engineering skills of the Assyrians.

The second Greek military camp at Marea protected Egypt's western border against the possibility of renewed Libyan incursions. Thus, the Greeks were responsible for the defence of all Lower Egypt. The Greek presence was not just a military affair. Traders and merchants followed the southward movement of mercenaries and established themselves in garrison towns on the coast. The main trading centre to which all the Greeks ultimately gravitated was Naucratis. Situated in the western Nile Delta, Naucratis rapidly became one of Egypt's most prosperous cities. It became the sole

[57]

destination of all the trading goods shipped from Greece and the city's Greek middlemen made considerable fortunes. At the same time the establishment of regular commercial links between Greece and Egypt proved beneficial to the Egyptians. The Pharaohs enriched themselves by encouraging trade and the native population at large benefited from the improvement in the Egyptian economy that resulted from the vigorous commercial activity.

The collapse of Assyrian power enabled the Saite Pharaohs to send military expeditions into Egypt's neighbouring territories. Psammeticus' immediate successor, Necho II (609–594 BC), partly re-established Egypt's Asiatic empire by defeating Josiah of Judah, capturing Jerusalem and retaking Syria as far north as Carchemish. In 605 BC, however, Necho's empire-building came to an abrupt end when Prince Nebuchadnezzar of Babylon attacked Egyptian forces at Carchemish and inflicted a decisive defeat. Relics found at the site in the ruins of a house – a Greek shield and sword, large quantities of arrow and javelin heads and human bones – attest to a bitter struggle. The artefacts also imply that Necho's Greeks came up against fellow Greeks in Babylonian employ.

With the Asiatic empire lost yet again, the next Pharaoh, Psammeticus II (594–586 BC), turned his attention to Nubia where the Kushite kings were preparing an attack on Egypt. His pre-emptive strike was successful and Egypt was spared another Nubian occupation. The victorious army contained Libyans, Phoenicians and Israelites but it was the Rhodian and Ionian Greeks and the Carians who made up its elite spearhead and it was they who left visible evidence of the expedition in the form of graffiti on the colossi of Ramses II at Abu Simbel. Some of the inscriptions refer to the generals who led the campaign, Potasimto and Amasis, and appeared to have been done by two of the Greek mercenaries, Archon and Pelekos. Others are of a simpler nature and merely record the presence of more humble participants, such as Pabis of Colothon, Elesibus of Theos, Telephus of Ialysus and Python – son of Amoibichos. Although these more trivial inscriptions have some historical value in identifying the provenance of some of the Greek mercenaries, they are in effect distant precursors of that species of modern graffiti which proclaims that 'Fred was here'. Whether or not the Greeks were guilty of soldierly irreverence for things Egyptian, they served the Saite Pharaohs continuously right up to the Persian conquest in 525 BC.

The army of Psammeticus II and his successor, Apries (588–568 BC), was composed of Greeks, Carians, Libyans, Syrians and Nubians. But it is abundantly clear that, notwithstanding their own Libyan origins, the Saite Pharaohs despised the old Libyan-dominated army and valued the Greeks above all other mercenaries. The Greeks displaced the Libyans from their pre-eminent position and became the elite troops of the army. Needless to say, the Libyan mercenaries did not accept the Greek usurpation with good grace. Already, in the time of Psammeticus I, Libyan garrisons in Upper Egypt had mutinied and fled to Nubia in protest over the partiality shown to the Greek mercenaries. Now, Apries' own partiality for the Greeks was to have an unfortunate result. Greek immigrants had founded an independent settlement at Cyrene during the reign of Psammeticus I and had gradually begun to encroach on Libyan territory. The Libyans called upon Apries to help them resist further expansion by the Cyrenians. Uneasy at the growth of a rival Greek colony beyond Egypt's control, Apries sent an army to assist the Libyan tribesmen. It did not contain any hoplites for the Pharaoh was wary of sending Greeks to fight other Greeks. They might, on the one hand, prove quite willing, like the Nubians, to destroy their kinsmen. On the other hand, they might well be tempted to desert and join fellow Greeks. As a consequence, Apries' army was made up of non-Greek mercenary troops. It advanced carelessly and confidently against the Cyrenian Greeks and was crushed. When the survivors returned to Egypt, the remaining non-Greek elements of the army rebelled against Apries, persuaded that he had deliberately sent their colleagues to their deaths while sparing the Greeks. The Pharaoh sent his palace chamberlain, Amasis, to parley with the rebels. Sensing an opportunity to become Pharaoh, Amasis did more than parley with the insurgents. He joined them. Apries was forced to lead his Greek contingents – 30,000 Carians and Ionians according to Herodotus – against Amasis but was defeated at Momemphis by vastly superior numbers. Taken prisoner, Apries was well-treated by his successor but when Amasis' supporters strongly objected to this lenient approach, the former Pharaoh was handed over to the malcontents and was duly strangled.[16]

At first, Amasis (568–526 BC) seemed to pursue an anti-Greek policy, but in reality the Greek residents retained their special status even when the Pharaoh restricted their right of free movement within Egypt and closed the camp at Daphnae in order to placate his irritated native subjects. Amasis still maintained good relations with the trading community and merely transferred the Greek mercenaries to his own city of Memphis where they acted as his personal bodyguard. The Pharaoh had close personal links with the Greeks in the shape of a Greek wife, but more important in his calculations was the fact that his personal safety and the prosperity of Egypt were dependent upon Greek mercenaries and merchants.

Greek mercenaries fought on both sides in the struggle between the last Saite Pharaoh, Psammeticus III (526–525 BC) and the Persian king, Cambyses (530–521 BC). The ultimate Persian victory was partly attributable to the defection from the Egyptian army of a disgruntled mercenary, Phanes of Halicarnassus, who, according to Herodotus, was dissatisfied with his conditions of service. The immediate causes of Phanes' dissatisfaction are not specified by the venerable Herodotus but the consequences of Phanes' desertion were all too clear to Psammeticus. As a high-ranking officer, Phanes had an intimate knowledge of conditions within the Pharaoh's army. He was able to elude his immediate pursuers but was caught in Lycia. Phanes escaped, however, by inducing his guards to drink themselves into a blind stupor, and made his way to the Persian court where he advised Cambyses to seek the help of the Bedouins in crossing the Arabian Desert. Cambyses took the advice and was able to lead the army to the Egyptian border. Herodotus described the terrible revenge inflicted on Phanes' sons in retaliation for their father's act of betrayal.[17] When the Persian and Egyptian armies had lined up for battle at Pelusium, the Pharaoh's Greek and Carian mercenaries brought out the hapless sons into the open ground between the two armies and cut their throats over a bowl. As Phanes looked on, his former comrades poured water and wine into the bloody bowl and each mercenary then drank some of the resultant brew. Shortly after this heart-rending display, the battle began. It was a ferocious encounter in which the Rhodian and Ionian Greeks in Egyptian employ fought against Ionian and Aeolean Greeks working for the Persians. The Egyptian forces were totally annihilated by the Persians but whether Phanes lived to see the destruction of those who had imbibed the grisly cocktail was a detail left unrecorded by Herodotus. Psammeticus III, at first generously treated by Cambyses, attempted to raise a rebellion and was forced to commit suicide to avoid the Persian king's wrath. The Saite Dynasty was effectively ended.

From 525 BC until 332 BC and the advent of Alexander the Great, Egypt remained under Persian domination, notwithstanding periods of temporary independence. During the reigns of Darius I (522–485 BC), Xerxes (485–464 BC) and Artaxerxes (464–424 BC) there were wars of liberation which were inspired by Persian defeats at Marathon and Salamis and, indeed, were encouraged by the Greeks themselves. Throughout all these insurrections,

Greek mercenaries fought both for Egyptian rebels and Persian conquerors alike. Their encounters on the battlefield were characterised by extreme ferocity and there was no question of fraternal feelings as fellow countrymen came face to face. The Greeks were to play an increasingly important role as mercenaries in Persian service. Ionian Greeks participated in Darius' invasion of Scythia and in the Persian attack on the Greek mainland, albeit in relatively modest numbers. The Peloponnesian War (430–404 BC) saw a marked increase in the use of mercenaries within Greece as Sparta and then Athens began to hire Arcadian hoplites on a large scale. When the war ended, thousands of mercenaries found themselves without work. Having known no other *modus vivendi*, they sought permanent employment elsewhere, primarily in the armies of the satraps who ruled the twenty provinces into which the Persian empire was divided. By the time Alexander the Great invaded Persia (334 BC), Greek mercenaries made up about half of the Persians' available infantry forces.

In Egypt, Greek mercenaries, this time in Macedonian employ, retained their significant position in the country's military structure. Having annexed Egypt and founded the city of Alexandria (332–331 BC), Alexander stationed some 4,000 Greeks under the command of the Aetolian, Lycidas, as garrison troops in strategic towns. After Alexander's death his leading generals – the *diadochi* – struggled for control of the Macedonian empire (323–281 BC). The end result of the wars of the *diadochi* was the fragmentation of Alexander's empire into three separate monarchies: Macedonia under the Antigonids, Asia Minor under the Seleucids and Egypt under the Ptolemies. The armies of the Ptolemies and, indeed, of the rival monarchies were overwhelmingly mercenary in composition and were primarily made up of Greek hoplites with smaller proportions of specialist mercenaries such as Cretan archers and Thracian broadswordsmen. The Greek preponderance in Egypt lasted until the coming of the Romans during the second half of the first century BC.

Given its enduring links with mercenary soldiers, Egypt provides an admirable case study. Other Middle Eastern states, however, such as Assyria and Israel, also resorted to the mercenary system at one time or another, although, unlike Egypt, they were never as thoroughly dominated by foreigners.

CHAPTER FOUR

Israel

THE EARLIEST ARMIES of the Israelites were composed of conscript militia contingents drawn from the Twelve Tribes and were entirely national. Although they were exclusively infantry forces, Israel's armies were characterised by a wide range of armament and by tribal specialisation in one or two traditional weapons or styles of fighting. The chief source of information in this regard is the Bible which provides in 1 Chronicles 12 some details, albeit incomplete, relative to the specific skills of the various tribes. Thus, the Benjaminites were ambidextrous archers and slingers. The Gadites and Reubenites were more adept at sword and shield techniques, while the Judeans and Naphtali specialised in spear and shield fighting. The Judeans in particular provided the heavy infantry and fought shoulder-to-shoulder in phalanx formation. Issachar tribesmen were noted not so much for their ability with weapons but for their scouting and intelligence gathering. Some tribes, however, such as the Zebulunites, are recorded as having been expert with all available weapons and fighting techniques.

The advance of the Israelite tribes into Palestine was a gradual process lasting over two centuries and had become a *fait accompli* by about 1200 BC. Moses, destined to become an enduring national hero, had led one group of tribes out of Egyptian captivity around 1250 BC to join other tribes who had already migrated from the Arabian Desert. Inevitably, the progressive invasion of Palestine by the Israelites brought them into contact – and conflict – with the Canaanites who had established themselves in the area 1,500 years before the infiltration of the Hebrews. The invasion also brought conflict with the Philistines, much more recent arrivals who had settled coastal Palestine around 1200 BC as part of the general migration of the Sea Peoples. Both the

Canaanites and the Philistines were city-based societies. The Philistines established a league of city-states which vigorously attempted to expand its domination inland from such centres as Ashdod, Ascalon, Ekron, Gaza and Gath, a process which was ultimately incompatible with the westward movement of the Hebrews. Canaanite civilisation was, with the benefit of a thousand years' head start, immeasurably more advanced than the rough culture of the Hebrews. The major Canaanite cities were centres of trade, industry and learning. Faced by a more sophisticated civilisation, the Hebrews who settled in northern Palestine abandoned their nomadic ways, adopted an urban lifestyle and a good deal of Canaanite culture. By contrast, in less fertile southern Palestine, the Hebrews who went there remained wanderers with a preference for tent-dwelling over solid houses up until the reign of King David.

In keeping with their more advanced civilisation, the military forces of the Canaanites and the Philistines were, initially at least, more sophisticated and more professional than those of the Hebrews. The Canaanites possessed effective chariot forces some 900 strong, manned by a noble elite of permanent soldiers. Inspired by this impressive array, the Philistines lost no time in building up their own chariot arm. The effectiveness of chariotry was clearly demonstrated at Mount Gilboa where the defeated Israelites were pursued by chariot-mounted archers who inflicted heavy casualties on Saul's unhappy host.

While Israelite armies remained national until the reigns of Saul and David, the armies of the Canaanites and Philistines had already undergone a considerable degree of mercenarisation and relegated militias to secondary status by the time that David began his conquest of Canaan and his struggle to contain the Philistines. In both cases, militia forces were still raised from among the peasantry but Canaanite and Philistine militias played no more than a supporting role behind elite formations of native-born professional soldiers and foreign mercenaries. Among the latter were Sutu Bedouin and *habiru* friendly to the Canaanites and the Philistines. In the course of their duties, the mercenaries were sent out by their employers to contain independent bands of Bedouins and *habiru* raiders who posed a recurrent threat, particularly to the more weakly-defended villages of Canaan and Philistia.

It was during the reign of Saul, the first King of Israel (1030–1010 BC), that mercenaries were added to the Israelite army.[1] Several reasons prompted Saul to recruit foreign troops. Despite a number of Hebrew successes against the Canaanites during the twelfth century BC, a cluster of Canaanite strongholds including Jerusalem still remained unconquered and effectively separated the Hebrews living in northern Palestine (Israel) from those in the south, that is, the Judean Hebrews. Furthermore, there were other rivals for the possession of Palestine. On its eastern borders were the Edomites, Moabites and Ammonites, while in the north were the Aramaean kingdoms, most notably Damascus, whose military forces were as advanced as those of the Philistines, if not more so. Aramaean armies contained infantry, chariotry and cavalry, the latter being one of the earliest historical instances of the use of horsemen. Finally, in the west was Philistia and the war against the Philistines was still going in the enemy's favour. The Israelites' lack of progress clearly demonstrated that a numerically smaller but permanent army of well-trained and experienced professionals could be more than a match for a larger army built up by short-term conscription. Therefore, Saul needed to establish a similar type of army to that of the Philistines.

The military situation was not Saul's only concern. There were sound economic reasons behind the creation of a mercenarised army. Compulsory militia service removed farmers from the vital task of food production. Preoccupied with the achievement of a (hopefully) bountiful harvest, the militia conscripts were not keen to serve beyond the end of the summer campaigning season. The longer they were kept away from their farms, the greater the risk of personal economic hardship and damage to the national economy. This presented Saul with a dilemma. From the military, if not the economic viewpoint, the normal campaigning season was too short. Further-more, the Philistines were not always so considerate as to confine their operations to the limits of the period during which Israelite militiamen could engage in military service without seriously compromising agricultural pro-duction. The hiring of mercenaries, although expensive, would enable Saul to release more Israelite conscripts for farm work and to establish a military force able to serve for longer periods of time and capable of effective resistance to the Philistine professionals.[2]

The effect of compulsory military service on economic production was a perennial problem which faced governments throughout the Ancient World. Indeed, it remained a problem in subsequent ages, and has, perhaps, not been completely resolved in the modern world. One solution, that of the Greeks, for example, was the creation of a standing army made up of national volunteers or foreign mercenaries or a mixture of both. Another solution was to hire mercenaries who could be retained for as long as they were needed beyond the normal campaigning season. Their professionalism, skill and experience enabled them to effectively replace nationals needed for productive labour and they could be dismissed when their services were no longer required. Dismissed *and* paid. Any employer who defaulted on payment was simply asking for trouble. Hiring mercenaries could be a costly business in more ways than one.

Saul was not, strictly speaking, the first Hebrew to recruit mercenaries. The Bible (Judges 9:4; 11:3) relates that, in earlier times, Abimelek and Jephthah had recruited mercenaries. However, this was for their own private purposes outside Israel and not for use as permanent troops alongside militia levies. It was Saul who created the nucleus of a professional army by taking into his service all the suitable volunteers he could find, whether Israelite or foreigner, so long as they were brave (I Samuel 14:52). Most of the volunteers were probably from his own tribe, the Benjamin, but there were other Israelites, notably David from Judah and a few foreigners like Doeg the Edomite (I Samuel 21:8; 22:18). Saul set up a corps of officers whom he rewarded with fiefs. He was, however, too poor to pay sufficient numbers of mercenaries and his professional army – the royal bodyguard – was limited to 3,000 men divided into three corps of a thousand men each. Such a modest nucleus was too small to prevent defeat at the hands of the Philistines. Wounded in the stomach by enemy archers during the battle of Mount Gilboa, Saul committed suicide. It was left to David to overcome the Philistine threat, to capture the remaining Canaanite cities, to defeat other external enemies and to establish an Israelite empire; all of which he did.

Famous for the slaying of the Philistine giant, Goliath, with a well-aimed stone to the cranium, David did not hesitate to follow a practical policy of recruiting Philistine and Canaanite mercenaries, and, it seems, he had little problem finding people prepared to fight for him against their fellow countrymen. Previous to his anointment as king, David himself had acquired first-hand experience of mercenary service working for the Philistines. Initially, he had been commander of Saul's bodyguard. Unjustly exiled from Israel after a disagreement with Saul, David recruited 400 and later 600 mercenaries, many of whom were fellow Judeans.[3] There were also several foreigners, including an Aramaean, an Ammonite and Uriah the Hittite, on whom David was destined to play a dirty trick (2 Samuel 11:3ff). With these followers, David entered the service of Achisk, king of the Philistine town of Gath. Goliath's countrymen rewarded him well, making him prince of Ziklag.[4] In return, David proved remarkably loyal to Achisk, rendering mercenary service when requested to do so. Among other missions, he was

[65]

sent by the king to border outposts to suppress Amalekite raiders. At other times, he worked on his own account carrying out ferocious raids against the Geshurites, Amalekites, Gittites and other tribes unfriendly to the Judeans and Philistines alike. During these excursions, David's mercenaries massacred all those who fell into their hands irrespective of age or sex. When the Philistines mobilised their forces to attack the Israelites, David willingly agreed to fight in Achisk's contingent. Had it not been for the implacable opposition of the other Philistine rulers who declared him to be *satan* (which in those days simply meant 'adversary'), he would have been present during Saul's defeat on Mount Gilboa, fighting against his own kind, without hesitation or remorse.

Upon becoming King of Israel, David proceeded to create a standing army around the core of loyal retainers and mercenaries who had followed him into exile and had returned with him. Still to outward appearances a vassal of the Philistines, David vigorously recruited Philistine, Carite and Canaanite mercenaries, relying on foreign troops rather than militia levies for the upcoming struggle with Philistia. Not that David ignored the tribal militias. On the contrary, he assigned permanent officers to each of the tribes to work alongside tribal chiefs in the training of young men liable for service. To reduce purely tribal loyalties and to encourage a sense of national unity, David organised the tribal levies into a national militia divided into twelve corps each containing some 24,000 men (I Chronicles 27:1). In peace time, each corps went on active service for one month while the conscripts of the other eleven corps were held in reserve and were permitted to pursue daily-life activities while waiting for their turn at militia duty. An individual corps was not composed exclusively of one tribal group but contained men drawn from all tribes. This led to a reduction in petty local loyalties while, at the same time, David was able to use tribal specialisation in weapons to the best advantage. His diversified corps possessed various types of weapons in differing proportions according to the task to be accomplished. Furthermore, David's new militia system meant that he always had at least one corps under direct control and ready for action at a moment's notice, while the presence of permanent officers among the other corps expedited a general mobilisation in time of war.[5]

The Israelite national militia was always numerically much larger than David's corps of mercenaries. Nevertheless, given the composition of enemy armies, it was his professional troops whom David placed in the forefront of battle and it was they who played the key role in his victories. David used

[66]

his mercenary corps to defeat the Philistines, the Aramaeans, the Ammonites and to capture the much-coveted Jerusalem. The wars against the Ammonites and Aramaeans clearly demonstrated the primary role played by the professionals. It was the corps of mercenaries who launched the first attacks, followed at a decisive moment by the militia contingents of Israel and Judah operating in support of the permanent troops (2 Samuel 2: 14–17; 12:26; 12:29; I Kings 20:15–20).

David's army was a clear example of the coexistence of national and mercenary troops in the same army. As was often the case in the Ancient World, the mercenaries were a part of the permanent establishment while the entire national militia was mobilised only in time of war. The permanent army – David's guard – was composed of two corps. The first was the *gibborim* (mighty men), largely made up of faithful Israelite retainers who had followed David in times of adversity and good fortune alike and shared common experience and a bond of personal loyalty to the monarch. Equally loyal to David was the second corps of foreign mercenaries commanded by Benaiah ben Jehoida, with the Philistine, Ittai of Gath, as second-in-command. Its nucleus was made up of Philistine mercenaries who had been with David from the earliest part of his career. David was able to recruit a further 600 volunteers from the town of Gath.[6] He had, after all, loyally served Gath as a mercenary commander and was well-known among the Gittites. His mercenary corps was mainly composed of Gittites along with Cherethites and Pelethites and possibly a contingent of Cretan archers. There was also a lesser proportion of Canaanite recruits. The mercenaries were highly efficient warriors, as evidenced by their battle record. Being more heavily armed than the Israelites, they provided the army's heavy infantry.

It is not difficult to understand the motives of David's foreign volunteers. They were rewarded with land-grants and ample remuneration which David, unlike Saul, was able to provide from the loot of conquered cities; reason enough for becoming a mercenary in Israelite service. They were also exempt from taxation and demeaning activities like forced labour. They were not, however, free agents able to work for the highest-bidding employer, being bound by an oath of absolute fidelity to the king, which they took seriously and, it seems, willingly.

The fidelity of the mercenary corps was severely tested during the rebellion led against David by his son, Absolom. The revolt was undoubtedly the greatest crisis of David's reign. He was forced to flee from his capital, Jerusalem, leaving behind the apparatus of government, his personal fortune and even his harem.[7] As a monarch – and an employer of mercenaries – he was looking distinctly threadbare. Yet, released by the fugitive king from their solemn oath, the mercenaries did not desert. On the contrary, they remained staunchly loyal and played a decisive role in restoring David's power by defeating the rebel militias and killing Prince Absolom who had become a fugitive in his turn. It might be said that the mercenaries remained loyal to David because his demise might well mean the end of their own privileges. A successful Absolom might have continued their employment without demur but, equally, being suspicious of men who had been so conspicuously loyal to David, he might have ordered the termination of their employment and, for that matter, their lives. The largesse of their paymaster was no doubt a motivating factor among the mercenaries, but it is clear that their attachment to his cause went well beyond pecuniary considerations. The nucleus of his foreign corps had known David and served with him when he himself was still a mercenary in the service of Achisk. Furthermore, he undoubtedly possessed in full measure that intangible but powerful and persuasive quality known as charisma, which has more than once throughout history been sufficient by itself to attract soldiers, whether native or foreign, to a particular commander.

The suppression of Absolom's revolt was an example of one of the four main functions required of mercenaries by their employers. The assurance or restoration of internal order and the protection of the monarch was a task well-suited to mercenary soldiers for the reason – worth reiterating – that they could have no sympathy with their employer's enemies. Their other functions were, of course, the defence of the employer's territory from external attack, the conquest of enemy territory and the training and leadership of conscript militia. The actions of David's men also showed that foreign mercenaries were capable of more than a temporary loyalty to their employers.

After David's death, much less reliance seems to have been placed by his successors on hired foreigners. The corps of mercenaries was certainly present as an escort to Solomon on the day he became king but henceforth it was rarely mentioned, if ever, in any document from his reign. Indeed, Solomon seems to have relegated the mercenaries to a subsidiary position and favoured instead the creation of a large force of chariots comprising 1,400 vehicles, each drawn by two horses.[8]

Solomon's mismanagement of state affairs – his reputation for wisdom was always overrated – resulted in the collapse of the United Monarchy, that is, the separation of Israel and Judah. Mercenaries are intermittently mentioned in the annals of subsequent reigns, both in Israel and Judah, but the references are not extensive. Cherethite and Pelethite mercenaries are known to have been employed in Judah, serving their traditional employer, the House of David. Rehoboam garrisoned newly-built forts with professional soldiers (2 Chronicles 2: 11–12) while Amasias recruited mercenaries in Israel (2 Chronicles 25:6ff). The tyrannical Queen Athaliah employed Carite mercenaries for internal oppression, practically eliminating the House of David in the process.

It is the annals of Sennacherib rather than Israelite sources that provide the last reference to mercenary troops in Judean service. During the siege of Jerusalem by the Assyrians in 701 BC, King Hezekiah's mercenaries made a realistic appraisal of the military situation and deserted, leaving the hapless king to sue for peace.[9]

The heyday of foreign mercenaries in Israelite service was during the United Monarchy ruled by David. Before his time, they were too few in numbers to have any decisive effect on the military campaigns of the Hebrews. After his time, their status and prominence seems to have been reduced. But during his time they played a fundamental role out of all proportion to their numbers. Indeed, David could not have created his empire without the loyal assistance of his mercenary troops.

CHAPTER FIVE

Assyria

IF THE EGYPTIANS demonstrated a deep dislike of warfare and military service, the Assyrians positively revelled in wars of conquest which they pursued with a relentless savagery and single-mindedness, paralleled in pre-twentieth-century military history only by the Mongols. Their treatment of conquered peoples was characterised by extreme cruelty, notable even in the context of a particularly cruel age. The Assyrians practised a deliberate policy of terror and psychological warfare and did not hesitate to massacre the entire population of a fallen city if it suited the particular strategy of a campaign. The prospect of a fixed payment per head encouraged the Assyrians to behead any enemies they could find, excepting persons of rank and those considered suitable for slavery. Needless to say, the entire army began the work of beheading as soon as the enemy were routed. Some soldiers left the ranks even before a battle was over in order to get a head start. Mass executions of prisoners was also a common occurrence. The victims were impaled or had their skulls crushed by executioners armed with heavy clubs. The Assyrians often mutilated prisoners reprieved from execution using techniques that included blinding with burning irons, cutting off the ears and nose, removing the tongue and passing a ring through the lips. Compared with the Assyrian repertoire of torture and execution methods, the Egyptian practice of removing hands and reproductive organs from the dead was quite unspectacular.

From the reign of Ashur-Dan II (934–912 BC) to that of Ashurbanipal (669–631 BC) – a period encompassing sixteen successive reigns – there were 157 recorded instances of the deportation of conquered peoples by their Assyrian overlords.[1] This sometimes involved no more than the forcible removal of the military and civilian ruling class of the subjugated state and in other cases it involved the resettlement of large numbers of a vanquished enemy, if not the entire population. The largest single deportation numbered 208,000 people deported from Babylonia to Assyria by Sennacherib but more typical groups ranged in size from 10,000–30,000 deportees.[2] From the reign of Tiglath-Pileser III onwards, the Assyrians practised the mass deportation of conquered peoples on a systematic basis. It was no coincidence that deportations increased dramatically during the time of Tiglath-Pileser III (745–727 BC). This monarch had clearly understood that Assyria would remain vulnerable to attack from all directions unless he conquered all the surrounding kingdoms or at least dissuaded their rulers from offensive action with a credible threat of retaliation. The dissuasion of potential enemies with the prospect of savage retribution was one of the factors underlying Assyrian treatment of vanquished peoples. Stern examples had to be made, in this case *pour décourager les autres*. Deportation was also used as a means of punishing rebellious populations or recalcitrant vassal rulers. The threat of deportation was a regular feature of treaties between Assyrian monarchs and their foreign vassals. It was no idle threat.

The policy of deportation was aimed at the emasculation of likely centres of resistance to Assyrian rule. Again, it was no coincidence that the largest deportations were from the southern and eastern regions of the empire, for Babylonia, Elam and Media represented the most likely sources of rebellion. Deportation also involved the movement of skilled and unskilled labourers wherever they were needed by the Assyrians for building projects and restoration work, boat-building or the reclamation of desolate land for agriculture. Thus, the Assyrians derived considerable economic advantages from the forcible resettlement of chosen groups of people.

The status of deportees seems to have varied considerably. Some were no better than slaves and were condemned to the misery of hard labour in quarries or other life-shortening work. Skilled captives were assigned to relatively easy tasks such as the ornamentation of palaces. Some deportees seem to have enjoyed the right to possess property – both human and material – and the right to engage in commerce or industry. Indeed, they had all the rights of free Assyrian citizens. Using a deliberate policy, the Assyrians did not separate male deportees from their families. This was designed to discourage any emotional temptation that might lead males to attempt desertion to their homeland; conversely, it encouraged an easier acceptance of resettlement in a new location.

[71]

Once they were settled, deportees received favourable treatment from the Assyrian monarch, that is to say they were better treated than the indigenous population among whom they had been resettled. Again, this was a subtle and intelligent policy designed to improve the security of the empire. Deportees were often settled among people known to be implacably hostile to Assyrian rule and prone to rebellion at the first viable opportunity. The native population naturally regarded the deportees as usurpers and potential or actual spies for the Assyrians. Faced with this universal resentment, the deportees had little choice but to side with the local Assyrian administration. This was purely and simply a matter of self-preservation. Any successful rebellion on the part of the autochthonous population would cost not just the lives of the hated Assyrians but of the hated deportees as well.

Deportation also had military advantages for the Assyrians. The native Assyrian population was relatively small. Consequently the native Assyrian army was never large enough to garrison all strategic points in the empire and still maintain a sufficiently large mobile reserve. Deportees, then, provided a ready source of auxiliary recruits. Many of them had been professional soldiers in the various armies defeated by the Assyrians. Others, fit and strong enough, received Assyrian military training. They were sent into foreign regions as far away as possible from their home territories. Isolated in a potentially hostile location with which they had no emotional ties, and supervised by native Assyrians, such auxiliary troops would be less tempted to desert. Those that did succumb and were recaptured could look forward to a painful death.[3]

The deliberate cruelty of the Assyrians was quite compatible with their religion and was, in fact, an integral part of Assyrian religious belief. The Assyrian king was regarded as the viceroy of the gods and held a sacred mission to uphold the dignity and power of the deity. Like the Sumerians before them, the warriors of Assyria believed that their particular deities fully sanctioned and encouraged their wars of aggression and their treatment of conquered peoples and they held a real conviction that they were doing God's work. There can be no doubt that the Assyrians were inordinately cruel but a number of qualifications need to be made. First, they were not unique in their cruelty. All the ancient civilisations were routinely cruel in varying degrees towards conquered peoples. The gladiatorial combats held in the Colisseum, where men from all over the Roman empire were forced to fight against other men and wild animals for the entertainment of the populace and its rulers, would scarcely qualify as the finest cultural achievement of Roman civilisation.

Second, the Assyrians were not unique in the use of mass deportation of subject populations; the Egyptians, the Hittites, the Babylonians and Chaldeans all resorted to the practice of deportation in fulfilment of specific strategic or economic objectives. What made the Assyrians stand out from other ancient civilisations was simply the fact that they deliberately advertised their cruelty as a means of dissuading potential rebels.

For all their barbaric treatment of defeated enemies, the Assyrians were not savages. They possessed in abundance all those manifestations which distinguish a civilisation from a mere culture. They were not nomads living from day to day, but a city-based people with a sense of permanence derived from living in fixed locations. The Assyrians possessed a writing system, so essential to the pursuit of learning and the recording of accumulated knowledge and experience. The ruling classes encouraged art, literature and music and commissioned monumental works of architecture as visual symbols of their wealth and power. Scholars translated Sumerian and Babylonian texts, studied astronomy and medicine and recorded their observations on clay tablets for the use of future generations. Ashurbanipal had the largest library in the Middle East, containing some 22,000 clay tablets. Admittedly, a great deal of Assyrian civilisation was based on the achievements of Sumer and Babylon. Nevertheless, it was a sophisticated civilisation in its own right.

The Assyrians were not originally a warrior people. Their initial inclination was towards agriculture and commerce. They appeared in north-eastern Mesopotamia between 3000 and 2500 BC and for more than 1,000 years they were obliged to defend their ill-defined frontiers, not always successfully, against the invasions of more powerful neighbours, among whom were the Hittites, Mitanni, Aramaeans, Syrians, Babylonians and Elamites. There was a brief period during the reign of Shamsi-Adad I (1749–1717 BC) when the Assyrians enjoyed political unity and independence and successfully repulsed the attacks of outsiders. But, on the whole, the early Assyrians tended to be overawed by more powerful neighbours. Shamsi-Adad's son, Isme-Dagan, was defeated by Rim-sin of Larsa and was later forced to become a vassal of the Babylonian king, Hammurabi. Worse was to come around 1450 BC when the Assyrians were subjected to a humiliating period of vassalage to the Mitanni kingdom, lasting about one century, until the Hittite king, Suppiluliumas, destroyed Mitannian power. It was the devastating experience of vassalage that turned an essentially agricultural people into an exceptionally tough and warlike people. On the premise that offence was the best defence, the Assyrians transformed their territory into the world's first military state.

During the reign of Tiglath-Pileser I (1116–1074 BC), Assyrian rule expanded into Anatolia and northern Syria. After his death, however, the Assyrians were pushed back to their home territory by Aramaean invaders and for about 200 years Assyria stagnated politically and economically. Her fortunes were restored by Adad-Nirari II (911–889 BC), Tukulti-Ninurta II (889–884 BC), Ashurnasirpal II (884–859 BC), Shalmaneser III (859–824 BC) and Tiglath-Pileser III. Syria was reconquered, Palestine and Babylonia fell under Assyrian rule and the Armenian kingdom of Urartu was defeated.

In any assessment of Assyrian military history, Tiglath-Pileser III must occupy a prominent position. His reorganisation of the army was indeed radical. From the earliest days of the Assyrian state, armies had been made up of militias recruited by provincial governors from among the farming population and artisan craftsmen. The only permanent troops were the royal guard, which would have supplied officers to command the militia contingents. Thus, the first Assyrian armies were essentially similar in composition to the earliest armies of the other states of the Ancient World. Tiglath-Pileser abandoned the militia system in favour of a permanent army. His reasons were similar to those that impelled other monarchs to transform their part-time armies into professional forces. As the Assyrian empire expanded, short-term militias proved inadequate for the task of policing distant territories. Provincial governors and vassal states allied to Assyria continued to provide contingents of troops, both professional and militia, when ordered to do so by the king but henceforth the permanent military establishment was the heart of the Assyrian army, a highly mobile force prepared to go anywhere at any time.

The creation of a permanent army gave the king much greater control over the military forces. Henceforth, the army owed its allegiance directly to the monarch. As was the case in Egypt, the militias had owed their primary allegiance to the provincial governors whose own loyalty was not always beyond question. In creating a permanent army Tiglath-Pileser achieved the transformation of Assyria into a military society. The army served the state and the state served the army. The *raison d'être* of the Assyrian state was continuous warfare and imperialism. As more and more farmers were taken permanently into the army, the plunder from captured cities replaced local agricultural production as the chief source of wealth. There was certainly no lack of plunder. The Assyrian standing army was the best-organised and most efficient military force in the world, capable of fighting over any type of terrain. It was an army made up primarily of heavy infantry (spearmen and archers) with a much smaller mobile strike force of chariotry and cavalry (mounted archers). The Assyrians were supplied with weapons and armour made of iron and thus enjoyed a decided advantage over enemies still armed with bronze weaponry. The infantry was supported by an effective siege train comprising movable towers, various types of battering rams with protective covers and missile-throwing engines.

Underlying the combat effectiveness of the Assyrian armies was a well-developed logistical organisation. A network of strategic roads was con-structed linking the large cities of the empire with outlying centres and border fortresses. Each road had a number of relay stations a day's ride apart where couriers and cavalry contingents could obtain remounts, often selected from horses given as tribute by conquered nomadic peoples. New roads were immediately built into recently acquired territories and the entire network was constantly kept in good repair. Thus, the operations of the Assyrian armies were made easier by an efficient transport and communications system.

The control of trade routes and the securing of frontiers was assured by a series of fortresses sited both on the borders and in the interior of the empire. The garrisons of these forts safeguarded the passage of merchandise from one part of the empire to another and backed up the collection of taxes from the local population by government officials. Assyrian fortresses also served as food-storage depots where armies headed for as yet unconquered territories could replenish their supplies. A notable feature of Assyrian military organisation was its surveillance and intelligence-gathering system. The fortresses were centres of espionage from which special detachments of scouts, known as *dajjali*, penetrated deeply into enemy territory to gather information related to the movements of enemy monarchs, generals and troops. The *dajjali* were ordered to bring back prisoners who could then be questioned with all the severity for which the Assyrians were noted. Among the *dajjali* were semi-nomadic Arab tribesmen whose wandering life-style suited them admirably for long-range missions.[4]

Having transformed the militias into an awesome instrument of conquest, Tiglath-Pileser III began the recreation of the Assyrian empire. His succes-sors, Shalmaneser V (727–722 BC), Sargon II (722–705 BC), Sennacherib (705–681 BC) and Esarhaddon (681–668 BC), undertook a series of almost yearly campaigns to spread Assyrian domination throughout the Middle East and to inspire continuing fear in territories already annexed to the empire. Given their efficiency and reputation, the Assyrian armies were spectacularly successful in conquering new territories. Syria, Palestine, Phoenicia, Judea, Babylon and Egypt all came under rigorous Assyrian control. In fact the Assyrian monarchy's insatiable desire for fresh conquests led to a gradual over-extension of the empire. There were not enough native Assyrian troops available for the task of keeping conquered territories in submission. As a consequence, the Assyrian kings initially resorted to the forcible recruitment of auxiliaries selected from the armies of conquered rulers, and, finally, to the hiring of foreign mercenaries from nomadic tribes such as the Scythians.

The auxiliary recruits were chosen on the basis of their physical strength and their proficiency with some particular type of weapon and served in separate contingents. While some units were issued with Assyrian military costume and weapons and hence were practically indistinguishable from ethnic Assyrian troops, others were permitted or required to retain their own weapons and national costume. Among the auxiliaries who feature most prominently in Assyrian records were the Aramaean tribes who served their overlords with varying degrees of enthusiasm and reliability. The Gerasimmu tribe, serving as auxiliaries in southern Mesopotamia, had a mixed record of loyal service and rebellion, while the Ituan tribe was of a very different order. It is the most frequently mentioned Aramaean tribe in Assyrian annals. Initially conquered and incorporated into the Assyrian military establishment by Tiglath-Pileser III, the Ituans seem to have submitted to Assyrian rule without any lingering resentment and displayed genuine loyalty. In return, they seem to have been accorded a privileged status among Assyria's auxiliary troops. They were organised into homogenous units and sometimes operated independently of other formations in the Assyrian army. The Ituans served in a number of capacities. There were, of course, the usual garrison duties and field service as part of the larger army common to all auxiliary units irrespective of their ethnic composition. But, more remarkably, the Ituans were used as a kind of Foreign Legion, somewhat reminiscent of King Shulgi's Elamite legion, and were sent to various locations both at the periphery and deep within the empire itself to carry out police actions and crush riots and rebellions. Correspondence from the time of the Sargonid monarchs – Sennacherib, Esarhaddon and Ashurbanipal – refers on several occasions to 'the King's Ituans' or 'the Palace Ituans', a circumstance which suggests that the Assyrian kings exercised direct control over the Ituans and may have included them in the palace guard. This was a privilege accorded only to troops whose loyalty and reliability were beyond question.[5]

Assyrian records left by the kings repeatedly refer to the forcible recruitment of subject peoples and indicate a consistent policy aimed at building up troop strengths. When Israel fell to Assyrian armies in 722 BC, Sargon II replaced his losses by recruiting fifty chariot crews from Samaria. From the Syrian city of Carchemish, which he took in 717 BC, Sargon conscripted fifty chariot crews, 200 cavalry and 3,000 infantry into his permanent army. His successor, Sennacherib, incorporated some 10,000 archers and 10,000 sword-and-shield men after a victorious campaign in Syria. In his annals, Esarhaddon referred to 'large numbers' (regrettably, unspecified) of sword-and-shield men which he added to his army in emulation of his predecessors. With the fall of Elam, Assyria's bitterest rival, in 639 BC, Ashurbanipal was able to recruit some 30,500 archers and the same number of swordsmen from among the Elamites and their allies and their Parsuan mercenaries.[6] Ashurbanipal, the last of Assyria's major rulers, continued the forcible incorporation of auxiliaries into the army. Alongside these he hired ever-increasing numbers of mercenaries, largely recruited from among the Scythians. These expert horsemen were not, however, the only source of mercenary manpower. There were also recruits of various ethnic backgrounds who might with justification be referred to as 'hungry mercenaries'. Assyria's struggle to maintain its empire against external enemies and internal rebellions had led to veritable economic and agricultural chaos among the Aramaeans, Chaldeans, Arabs and other tribes of the Middle East. The widespread famine and poverty created groups of extremely desperate people willing to fight in Assyrian armies purely for the opportunity of a regular meal. For their part, the Assyrians made the most of the situation by sending food to various tribes known to be suffering the pangs of hunger as an enticement to enter into military service. Indeed, the Assyrians deliberately exacerbated the effects of famine in regions bordering Elam by destroying whatever palm and date plantations they could find and massacring or removing cattle herds. With their means of survival destroyed, the semi-nomadic tribes, whose existence was precarious even at the best of times, had little recourse other than mercenary service.[7]

Despite their reliance on mercenaries and auxiliaries, the Assyrian monarchs found it increasingly difficult, and ultimately impossible, to recruit enough troops to maintain an over-extended empire. Expelled from Egypt by the Pharaoh Psammeticus, and faced with rebellions in Babylonia, Ashurbanipal no longer had the forces to restore order simultaneously in both territories. Egypt was permanently given up as lost. There was also external pressure on the Assyrian empire from the Medes under King Cyaxares, who had formed an alliance with the Babylonians. Assyria's imperial expansion had been rapid and seemingly unstoppable but it had taken its toll of the native Assyrian soldiers who had been the backbone of the army.

Mercenaries and auxiliaries now replaced native soldiers in ever-growing numbers. A large part of the infantry was henceforth drawn from subject peoples such as the Aramaeans and Chaldeans or were recruited from among the hill tribes living in the mountains bordering Mesopotamia. Aramaeans had been in the army ever since the beginning of Assyrian expansion but now, far from being a relative minority, their numbers increased to such proportions that the Assyrian army became 'Aramaeanised'. Mercenaries were offered land-grants known as 'bow-land' as payment for permanent service. Even so, the impressment of larger numbers of auxiliaries and the inducements offered to mercenaries failed to produce forces large enough or committed enough to stem the decline in Assyria's fortunes. Whatever their fighting quality may have been, the loyalty of resentful subject peoples like the Chaldeans was not to be relied upon. Unsurprisingly, the Scythian mercenary cavalry also proved unreliable. After the death of Ashurbanipal, the empire disintegrated rapidly and the Scythians abandoned the last Assyrian king, Sin-shar-ishkun and joined the Median–Babylonian forces, tempted by the prospect of looting Nineveh. After a two-month siege, Nineveh fell in 612 BC, never to rise again. A few surviving Assyrians now led by one of the king's officers, Ashur-uballit, escaped to the town of Harran where they were reinforced by a small group of Egyptians. But in 610 BC Harran also fell to the Babylonians and Scythians.[8] With the total collapse of the empire, Assyrian history effectively came to an end and the Assyrian nation ceased to exist as an independent entity. Needless to say, a heartfelt cry of joy and relief went up from all the oppressed peoples, not least from the Israelites, 27,000 of whom had been deported from Samaria by the Assyrians.

The armies of Assyria, then, began as militia forces and evolved into mercenary formations. But this transition occurred in a rather different way in comparison with the other civilisations thus far discussed. Unlike Egypt, where mercenaries were already present in the Old Kingdom, Assyria did not resort to the hiring of mercenaries until its empire was well and truly in decline. Whereas Egypt needed mercenaries to compensate for lack-lustre militia troops, the creation of a powerful army of citizen professionals by Tiglath-Pileser III obviated any immediate need to employ mercenaries. As the Assyrian empire expanded, Tiglath and his successors could conscript a wide variety of auxiliaries from conquered states. The irreplaceable losses suffered by native Assyrian soldiers resulted in a much greater reliance on auxiliaries. Despite the ever-increasing presence of auxiliary troops, however, the Assyrians were unable to recruit sufficient manpower to maintain their over-extended empire. They were forced to look beyond their borders for mercenaries, such as the Scythians to whom they offered land grants – an inducement already encountered in the military organisation of Sargon and Hammurabi. The mercenaries and auxiliaries exhibited varying degrees of reliability. That of the Ituans was particularly noteworthy. The Scythians, however, as mercenaries were so often prone to do, changed sides when it became obvious that Assyria would fall.

CHAPTER SIX

Greece and Persia

AROUND 1200 BC, the Bronze Age culture of Mycenaean Greece collapsed as successive waves of Dorians from Illyria invaded central Greece. The Dorians displaced the original inhabitants or sometimes merged with them, as was the case in the region of Boeotia. They were Greek-speaking tribesmen and, as such, were not completely alien invaders. Many of the dispossessed Mycenaean Greeks fled southwards to the Peloponnesus, principally to Arcadia whose rugged mountain terrain held little attraction for the incoming Dorians. Arcadia was to become a major recruiting ground for mercenary soldiers. Other fugitive Greeks went further afield. Athenians established themselves in western Anatolia and became known as the Ionian Greeks. Euboeans and Boeotians founded colonies in Aeolia. Some of the dispossessed from the northern Peloponnesus (Achaea) moved westward and settled in Sicily, southern Italy and ultimately southern Gaul. There was also a southward migration of Achaeans towards Egypt. As described in a previous chapter, there Greeks were known to the Egyptians as 'Akawasha' and were among the tribes of Sea Peoples who attacked Egypt in the reign of Ramses II.

Towards 1000 BC the period of invasion and resettlement came to an end. During the next four centuries the Dorians and the surviving pre-Dorians gradually coalesced into a relatively homogeneous people, with a common culture. But this cultural homogeneity was not matched by political unity. Greece was a peninsula with a deeply indented coastline. The southern part – the Peloponnesus – was almost cut off from the north by the Gulf of Corinth. In the east, Euboea was separated from the mainland by a narrow sea and was the largest of a cluster of offshore islands. Four-fifths of the

Greek landscape was made up of mountainous terrain with no navigable rivers. The arable land was extremely fertile, but given its relative scarcity, it could only produce a limited amount of food and never enough to adequately feed the entire Greek population. Hunger and economic hardship drove many Greeks overseas in search of civilian employment or mercenary service.

With political unification effectively impeded by physical geography, the Greeks were divided into a patchwork of small, independent territories each of which gradually evolved into a *polis* or city-state. By the end of the eighth century BC the city-states were firmly established and were to remain the characteristic unit of Greek political structure. Many of the cities grew up around an *acropolis* ('high city'), that is, a citadel which was both a political and religious centre. The boundaries of the city-states were ill-defined and not dependent on natural frontiers, and the various territories were more often than not in competition with each other for the possession of scarce agricultural and pastoral resources.

Some of the larger city-states gradually began to dominate or completely absorb smaller neighbours during the seventh and sixth centuries BC. Thus, for example, Athens gained control over the whole of Attica while, in the south, reactionary Sparta was the dominant city-state of the Peloponnesus, having conquered neighbours like Messenia and coerced or persuaded others into forming an alliance known as 'The Lacedaemonians and their allies', or the Peloponnesian League. By contrast, the small city-states of Boeotia remained more or less independent of each other. They were but loosely united in a federation which was led but not dominated by Thebes. Some of the members of the Boeotian League, Plataea in particular, were reluctant participants and kept aloof. During the Persian Wars, the Plataeans remained loyal allies of the Athenians despite their perilous position. The Thebans, jealous of Athenian prestige and power, openly took most of the Boeotian states over to the Persian side. Thus, the Greek city-states as a whole were incapable of offering a united resistance to the Persian threat. Sparta and Athens managed to overcome their mutual enmity, but the states of northern Greece attempted to remain neutral or supported the Persian invasion with varying degrees of enthusiasm. The Greek and Persian Wars were far from being a simple contest between the forces of democratic Greece (only Athens was in any sense democratic at the time) and autocratic Persia.

In keeping with common military experience in other parts of the Ancient World, the earliest armed forces of the Greek city-states were citizen armies. There were, however, marked differences between the Athenian militia

[81]

system which was representative of most of the Greek city-states and the Spartan military establishment which developed along different lines and was to all intents and purposes a standing army.

In Athens, able-bodied males between the ages of eighteen and sixty were eligible for military service. At the age of eighteen, Athenian youths were enrolled into one of ten regiments according to their tribal affiliation. Issued with a spear and shield, they took an oath swearing to defend the gods, their homes and the state. They also swore not to dishonour their sacred arms nor to abandon comrades during a battle. They then underwent a two-year training period. In the first year the aspiring hoplites (*neotatos*) were trained in weapons handling and toughened by gymnastics while in the second they were sent to fortresses in various parts of Attica where they were trained in field manoeuvres. Having completed their obligatory period of service, the trained men were registered in a 'catalogue' of available hoplites and then discharged. Between the ages of twenty and forty-nine they were liable for active service in times of crisis. After their forty-ninth year, with age gradually starting to slow their reflexes, the militiamen became known as veterans, or *presbytatos*, and were summoned for garrison duty rather than for the field army. Wealthy young noblemen tended to serve in the cavalry and were given an allowance for the purchase and maintenance of their horses. Men and animals were rigorously subjected to an annual fitness test. Membership of the cavalry was considered to be an honour but the equestrian arm was never very large. During the Persian Wars the Athenian cavalry amounted to no more than 300 men while at the start of the Peloponnesian War there were about 1,000 recruits.[1] Given that the Athenians could form an army of some 30,000 men during the fifth century BC, the cavalry arm was quite modest. The rugged Greek landscape was not suited to large-scale cavalry operations.

If Athens was more renowned for its arts and letters than for its military organisation, Sparta was, by contrast, essentially a city of barracks. Despite its militia system, Athenian society was not particularly militarised whereas Spartan society was utterly dominated by the military life. A Spartan was trained, toughened and indoctrinated from the earliest possible moment and remained a life-long soldier. Women and girls also underwent courses in gymnastics, wearing the flimsiest of garments, or quite often, nothing at all, much to the surprise and disapproval of non-Spartan Greeks. Shortly after birth, children were carefully examined. The weak and unpromising ones were promptly dropped over a suitable cliff or left to die of exposure on Mount Taygetus. Only potential soldiers and potentially energetic women were spared. From the age of eight, boys were removed from their homes, formed into companies under experienced instructors, and were brought up very strictly by the state. In the proto-fascist atmosphere of Sparta, emphasis was on physical activities, unbending discipline and obedience. That *bête-noire* – academic learning – was kept to a bare minimum.

At the age of twenty, Spartan youths became liable for service. Hardened, brutalised and inured to hunger, cold and physical suffering, they were enrolled in dining clubs, life-long associations aimed at fostering a sense of solidarity and comradeship. They continued to exist on a truly Spartan fare – a strictly limited ration of wine, barley bread and the culinary speciality of Sparta, namely a nasty haggis, unpalatable to any but a local citizen. After the age of thirty, Spartan men were permitted to live at home but were required to take their evening meals together with their comrades at communal tables. They had to be ready for active service at a moment's notice. Consequently, they were not permitted to leave the environs of Sparta. The daily routine centred exclusively on exercises, drills and weapons training. The Spartans were full-time citizen soldiers and did not engage in agriculture, commerce or any form of manual labour. Their income came from land-grants worked by helots, that is to say, conquered peoples reduced to the status of serfs. The helots paid half of their crop in rent to their Spartan landlords.

The constant training and ordeal which Spartan males were forced to undergo from early boyhood produced hoplites decidedly superior to those of other city-states, where training normally began in early manhood and military service was of relatively short duration. Spartan soldiers were particularly adept at fighting shoulder-to-shoulder in disciplined phalanxes that were the envy of other Greek states. Greek warfare in the Mycenaean age had involved individual contests on horseback, in chariots, or on foot. In Homer's *Iliad* the Trojans and Greeks attempt to bring each other down with spears or heavy stones thrown over varying distances. If the missile weapons failed to resolve the issue, the opponents resorted to their swords or beat a strategic retreat. Archers, such as Teucer, are also described as operating individually. Warfare in the *Iliad* is rarely characterised by disciplined manoeuvre or coordinated use of weapons. With the emergence of the heavily-armed hoplite around 700 BC, the throwing spear largely gave way to the thrusting spear. Warfare was henceforth characterised by precise team-

[83]

work rather than the individual skill required in man-to-man matches between gallant and not-so-gallant champions of the sort described by the venerable Homer.

Compared with Athens, the Spartan army was relatively small. The southern state never had sufficient population to raise an army of 30,000 hoplites. Indeed, Sparta's birth rate steadily declined in the fifth century BC. Around 500 BC the city could muster some 8,000–9,000 men but at the end of the century was down to about 4,000, including troops recruited from among the helots and *perioeci*, that is, citizens of subject cities.[2] Nevertheless, Sparta was able to compensate for her numerical inferiority *vis-à-vis* Athens. First, her hoplites were of premium quality, for reasons already indicated. Second, Sparta could rely upon contingents from the Peloponnesian League to build up numbers in time of war. Third, tough mercenary soldiers were available from nearby Arcadia. Thus, while Athens became the principal naval power in Greece, Sparta became the main land-based power and exerted an influence out of all proportion to her actual size. With the final repulse of the Persians at Plataea, Mycale (479 BC) and Eurymedon (466 BC), the grudging cooperation between Athens and Sparta gradually disappeared. Growing hostility between the two states and Athenian attacks on Spartan allies led to a series of conflicts collectively known as the Peloponnesian War (460–404 BC). Both sides employed mercenaries during their protracted struggle. Indeed, the second half of the fifth century BC saw a dramatic rise in mercenary activity. For the first time in history, native Greek mercenaries were used in significant numbers within the confines of the Greek peninsula by local employers.

Prior to the Peloponnesian War, mercenaries had played a very limited role in Greece. The tyrants of the seventh and sixth centuries BC employed mercenary soldiers primarily as bodyguards and in very small numbers. Some tyrants in the Aegean islands recruited permanent forces of over 1,000 men. Polycrates, who became tyrant of Samos around 535 BC, had a force of 1,000 Samian bowmen in addition to his mercenary bodyguard.[3] He used these troops to conquer islands adjacent to Samos and on lucrative piratical raids. The tyrants of the Greek mainland, however, disposed of smaller forces and normally used their bodyguards for personal protection rather than territorial expansion. The modest size of their mercenary formations was not the only factor that inhibited imperialist ventures into neighbouring states. Despite the popular support they often commanded, the *tyrannoi* did not always enjoy a secure domestic position. They were most commonly usurpers and their

[84]

assumption of power lacked the force of legitimacy. Thus, with their rule always open to challenge, the tyrants could not easily afford to be absent from their home territories.

The word 'tyrant', which seems to have come from the Lydian language, was originally a neutral term without the connotations associated with it in modern times. Tyrants were essentially revolutionary despots who governed with varying degrees of benevolence. As mentioned above, they often came to power on a wave of popular support, replacing ruling aristocracies whose lands they confiscated and redistributed among the peasants. Thus, tyrants were not necessarily tyrannical. Some, indeed, were cruel despots but others were more in the nature of constitutional monarchs whose power rested firmly on the goodwill of their peasant subjects. Theagenes of Megara, for example, who became tyrant around 640 BC, obtained permission to form a bodyguard.[4] Whether it was made up of mercenaries or citizen volunteers was not recorded at the time. Similarly, Peisistratus, who was tyrant of Athens between 546 BC and 528 BC, was offered a bodyguard by his supporters. Initially it was a modest force of fifty men armed with cudgels but it provided the nucleus for a larger corps of guards.[5]

The rule of such tyrants as Peisistratus and Periander of Corinth was extremely beneficial – economically, politically and culturally – to the peoples of their respective cities. Periander pursued a vigorous colonial and commercial policy and during his reign Corinth reached the height of its power. Nevertheless, the *tyrannis* system ultimately ran counter to prevalent Greek ideas of government, which favoured either Spartan-style oligarchies (Sparta never had tyrants) or Athenian-style democracies. The tyrants were arbitrary, unconstitutional rulers and their use of mercenaries to maintain their power symbolised the despotic nature – benevolent or otherwise – of their government. By the beginning of the fifth century BC, tyrannies were on the wane in mainland Greece and were largely replaced by bourgeois commercial oligarchies or incipient democracies. They did not, however, entirely vanish. They continued to appear intermittently during the fifth and fourth centuries BC alongside democracies and oligarchies. The tyrants of the Aegean islands actively cooperated with the Persian empire in order to preserve their power and contributed naval and army contingents to the Persian forces.

The almost total disappearance of tyrants during the early fifth century BC was accompanied by a corresponding decline in mercenary use, so that there are exceedingly few references to mercenaries in the records of the period. The modest role played by mercenaries in the preceding centuries became even more modest. There were hardly any mercenaries operating on the Greek mainland. And yet, Greece had already acquired a reputation overseas as a supplier of mercenaries. That is precisely where the overwhelming mass of Greek mercenaries were before the Peloponnesian War: overseas. In other words, there were more Greek mercenaries outside Greece than in it.

Along with the Ionian Greeks and the Carians, a majority of mainland Greeks found service in Egypt with the Saite Pharaohs. Some served various kings in Mesopotamian cities. Others worked for the Lydians and transferred their services to the Persians when Lydia fell to Cyrus the Great. Most of the peninsular Greeks in Persian service came from Arcadia, which, far from being the idyllic pastoral landscape depicted by Nicholas Poussin and Claude Lorrain, was a wild and mountainous terrain capable of supporting a large population. Limited opportunities for mercenary service within Greece led the Arcadians eastwards, where they found permanent employment as bodyguards of Persian satraps (provincial governors) and as garrison troops. The Asiatic rulers fully appreciated the superiority of the heavily-armed and armoured hoplites. Thus, when the Persians began their invasion of Greece, their forces contained Arcadian mercenary soldiers together with the Ionian and Aeolian Greeks who were direct subjects of the Persian monarchy.

The armies with which the Persian kings attempted the conquest of Greece were multi-national formations. Native Persians formed their nucleus. They were supported by foreign mercenaries and auxiliary contingents from the numerous nationalities brought under Persian domination. The transition from national to multi-national, from militia to permanent professional began almost as soon as the Persians overthrew the Median kingdom in 559 BC. It was a rapid change which enabled Persia to embark on wars of conquest. Imperialist wars were best fought with professional soldiers, native and foreign. Cyrus the Great (559–530 BC), the first king of an independent Persia, created the nucleus of a standing army in the form of a royal guard made up of both Persians and Medes. The latter were not really foreign mercenaries. They were now serving their legitimate sovereign. Furthermore, the Medes and Persians were closely related peoples of Aryan descent. As the Persian empire expanded, however, foreign troops, both mercenary and auxiliary, entered Persian service in ever-increasing numbers.

Having consolidated his power in Media, Cyrus met and defeated a Lydian invasion led by the proverbially rich Croesus. At Thymbra in 546 BC, Cyrus organised his greatly outnumbered army into a single square, a novel departure from the usual linear formation in which ancient armies confronted each other. Croesus' army awaited the Persians in the customary battle order. Its centre was made up of mercenaries sent from Egypt by the Pharaoh Amasis. According to Xenophon, these troops seem to have come from Egypt's non-Greek mercenary population. Whether they were Libyans, Nubians or native Egyptians tempted into mercenary service remains unknown.[6] The left and right flanks of Croesus' army were largely made up of native Lydians and contingents of Greek mercenaries. As the Persian square advanced, the Lydian flanks moved inwards to envelop it, creating gaps on both sides of the central formation. Cyrus immediately exploited these weaknesses. Persian archers poured concentrated showers of arrows onto the enemy, totally disorganising the Lydian flanking formations. The Persian cavalry then charged the gaps in the Lydian army, enveloping the Egyptian troops in the central column. Surprised by Cyrus' unusual tactics, the Lydians were utterly routed. The surviving Egyptian mercenaries, who had escaped death by crouching under their very large shields, were taken into Persian service. With Lydia now under Persian control, Cyrus could call upon Lydian troops for subsequent wars of expansion.

The sources of manpower increased even further as Cyrus conquered Parthia, Sogdiana, Bactria and Arachosia in Central Asia. Armenia, Assyria and Babylon also fell to Cyrus' troops and Persian domination was extended westwards to the Aegean as one by one the Ionian and Aeolian Greek cities of Asia Minor were absorbed into the empire (548–538 BC). Like the other subject peoples, the Asiatic Greeks were now required to perform military service as auxiliaries.

Cyrus was killed in battle before he could realise his ambition to conquer Egypt. As previously described, the task fell to his son, Cambyses, who invaded the Saite kingdom with an army composed of Persians and auxiliary troops, including the recently incorporated Ionian and Aeolian Greeks and contingents of Aramaean and Jewish mercenaries.

The Asiatic Greeks were once again summoned for military service in 511 BC by Cambyses' successor, Darius (523–486 BC) and took part in campaigns aimed at preparing the way for a Persian assault on Greece itself. In order to mount an effective invasion, Darius needed a base of operations adjacent to his intended target. He also needed to protect the northern flank of his empire against incursions by nomadic tribes. The annexation of Thrace would meet the first requirement. A campaign against the redoubtable Scythians would fulfil the second. Accordingly, the Persian army crossed the Bosphorus into Europe over a floating bridge constructed by the Greek contingent.

[87]

Darius took Thrace, overcoming the uncoordinated resistance of the local tribes without undue difficulty. He marched on to the Danube, which marked the south-western border of Scythian territory, and crossed over another floating bridge built by the Ionians. Sure of success, the Persian monarch ordered the Greeks to destroy the bridge and join the advance into Scythia (southern Russia). However, he rescinded the order on the advice of one of his Greek commanders from the isle of Lesbos, Coes of Mytilene. Coes pointed out that Scythia had no towns and no land under cultivation and that the Scythians had nothing for which they might stand and fight. He was not afraid of a direct confrontation but feared that the Persians might wear themselves out simply trying to catch an elusive enemy in Scythia's seemingly endless spaces. In the event, Coes' fears proved to be well-founded. Darius was drawn deeply into Scythia to the northern shore of the Sea of Azov, without catching up with the nomads. The Scythians avoided a pitched battle but continually harassed the Persian army by picking off straggling detachments in brief raids. They practised a scorched-earth policy, leaving nothing edible either for man or beast. Frustrated and exhausted, Darius' army began a two-month long retreat to the Danube. The Scythians parleyed with the commanders of the Greek contingents guarding the floating bridge and suggested that the Greeks destroy the structure, thereby ensuring Darius' entrapment and destruction. The failure of the Persian expedition to Scythia presented a distinct opportunity to deliver the Ionian Greeks from Persian domination but the mercenary self-interest of the Greek commanders triumphed over the possibility of independence and Darius was able to extricate himself from a potentially disastrous situation. Some of the Greek commanders had become despots in their own cities and their local power depended on Darius' patronage. If he fell, so might they. Accordingly, the Greeks gave the Scythians a false promise to demolish the bridge and removed a small portion of it to satisfy the Scythians who then withdrew without waiting to see the whole structure disappear. The only positive result of the Persian invasion, other than the annexation of Thrace and Macedonia, was that the Scythians, impressed by Darius' tenacity, did not raid his territories when the Persians finally began their prolonged assault on the Greek mainland (490–448 BC).

Darius' defeat in Scythia encouraged the Ionians to revolt against the local tyrants who had led the Greek auxiliary contingents during the Scythian expedition. The tyrants were overthrown in the cities of Ionia and expelled, with the exception of Darius' loyal friend, Coes of Mytilene, who was stoned

[88]

to death. Despite Athenian aid, however, the revolt was crushed by numerically powerful Persian forces, which included mercenaries and auxiliaries recruited from diverse parts of Darius' empire.

Darius, however, had learnt from the experience and wisely established democratic governments in the Ionian cities in place of untrustworthy tyrants. Thanks to Darius' forbearance, these cities became local centres of democracy in a wider and undemocratic Persian empire. The Persian king had handled the Ionian revolt with considerable restraint but Athenian intervention was an affront that invited response. Thus, Darius decided on a full-scale invasion of Greece. As a result, Ionian Greeks were once more required to serve the Persians against other Greeks alongside an impressive multi-national force that included Medes, Carians, Lydians, Egyptians, Cypriots, Phoenicians, Bactrians, Ethiopians and Indians from Gandara. There were also Greek mercenaries in Darius' army – the bodyguards of various Persian satraps – and they were less reluctant about fighting fellow Greeks than their Ionian brothers.

In September 490 BC, the Persians and their subject contingents landed in Greece and had already deployed on the Marathon plain by the time the Athenian army arrived to take up its position in foothills overlooking the flatland. Darius' army, some 20,000–25,000 men,[7] was drawn up with the native Persians in the centre and the auxiliary troops, including the reluctant Ionians, on the wings. The Greek army consisted of 10,000 Athenians (9,000 hoplites; 1,000 light troops), and 1,000 Plataeans. Its commander-in-chief, the War-archon, Callimachus, presided over a council of ten *strategoi*, or generals, who led the various contingents and acted as advisers. The most experienced and influential of the *strategoi* was the Athenian, Miltiades. A former tyrant of the Chersonesus, he had ruled over Greeks and Thracians with a private army of 500 mercenaries of unrecorded origin but presumably recruited from Greek and Thracian volunteers.[8] Miltiades had served Darius on the failed Scythian expedition and had first-hand experience of Persian battle tactics. Now the former tyrant was firmly committed to democratic Athens and justified his change of allegiance by reminding the Athenians that he had intended to destroy Darius' bridge over the Danube, but had been prevented from doing so by Histiaeus of Miletus and the other Ionian Greek commanders, all of whom owed their positions to the Persians. It was not that Miltiades had suddenly become enamoured of democracy. He had, in fact, been put on trial for his tyranny. But his knowledge of the Persian army, his support for the Ionian revolt and his anti-Persian sentiment ensured his acquittal. Down on the plain in the Persian camp was another Athenian, Hippias, son of Peisistratus, the last tyrant of Athens, and a bitter enemy of Miltiades. After his expulsion from Athens, Hippias had fled to the Persian court. Desirous of reimposing his tyranny, he had guided the Persians to Marathon.

When the Greeks learned that the redoubtable Persian cavalry had separated from the main army and had unaccountably gone away on its own they formed up and began to advance towards the enemy infantry. In contrast to the waiting Persian line, where the centre was much stronger than the flanks, the Greeks had concentrated their strength on the left and right wings in two large phalanxes linked by a thin line of troops in the centre. When they came within range of the Persian archers, the Greeks broke into a run in order to minimise losses. The two lines clashed and the elite troops of the Persian centre did not take long to repulse the under-strength Greek centre by sheer force of numbers. The Greek wings, however, easily routed the Persian wings, including the half-hearted Ionian contingents. They then turned inwards to attack the Persian centre which had confidently advanced in pursuit of the thin Greek centre line. Whether the enveloping movement happened by accident or design remains an unsolved problem of the battle of Marathon. At any rate, it proved decisive. The multi-national Persian army fled to its ships pursued by the triumphant Greeks. Most of the stampeding, panic-stricken invaders reached and boarded the waiting ships despite the best efforts of the Greeks to prevent their doing so. Nevertheless, the Persians had suffered disproportionately high losses; 6,400 men as compared with 192 Athenian casualties.[9]

Marathon was a significant psychological victory which boosted the morale of the Greeks opposed to the Persian invasion, but, despite the heavy casualties inflicted on the invaders, it was not a decisive military victory. The Athenians had won no more than a reprieve while, for the Persians, Marathon was no more than a temporary irritation. King Darius died before he was ready to resume the assault on Greece but his successor, Xerxes, was fully determined to achieve his father's ambition. In 480 BC, the Persians returned in much greater force. Xerxes' army was composed of all the nationalities under Persian rule from Ionia to India and also included mercenaries hired from beyond the borders of the empire. The king disposed of 100,000 troops at the very least and perhaps up to 180,000 men. Even though the actual size of the Persian army fell somewhat short of the five million men claimed by Herodotus, the invading force was formidable enough.

Having crossed this remarkable bridge – a feat of Ionian Greek engineering

– the Persian army marched westwards along the Thracian and Macedonian coasts, towards Thessaly. Once again the northern Greek states would be the first affected by Persian military operations. They could take the risk of opposing the invasion or they could collaborate in the hope of avoiding extensive pillaging of their territories. The Thebans and Euboeans, who had no love for southern Greeks, were prepared to 'medise', that is, cooperate with Xerxes.

To many Thessalians, Persian domination was not likely to be worse than the oppressive rule of the local aristocracy. Thus, the Thessalian appeal to Sparta and Athens came largely from the ruling class and was by no means a unanimous cry for help. Nevertheless, the anti-Persian confederacy despatched a mixed force of 10,000 hoplites to defend the mountain pass at Tempe in northern Thessaly. When the hoplites reached their destination, they found that there were at least three other usable passes by which the Persians could invade Thessaly. Northern Greece was clearly untenable. The Persian land forces marched into central Greece while, off the eastern coast of the Greek peninsula, the Persian fleet kept pace. Among its 1,200 vessels were 300 craft crewed by ever-reluctant Ionian Greeks. The majority of the ships, however, carried Phoenician, Egyptian and Cypriot crews along with Persian and Median marines. Xerxes intended that his fleet should carry supplies for his land forces, who could scarcely live off the land in a largely arid country like Greece. A second objective was to land troops behind the opposing Greeks who had taken up defensive positions at Thermopylae. The pass at Thermopylae was narrower and hence more easily defensible than the passes in northern Thessaly.

Awaiting the Persians was a mixed Greek force of 7,000 hoplites, including 4,000 Peloponnesians, 1,000 Phoenicians, 700 Thespians and 400 Thebans who had been persuaded to fight rather than collaborate.[10] The Greeks were led by King Leonidas of Sparta but the Spartan contingent itself was limited to 300 hoplites of the royal guard, which suggests that the Spartans were half-hearted about mounting any defence north of the Isthmus of Corinth. They were constrained to fight at Thermopylae by their alliance with Athens and their dependence on the Athenian fleet for the defence of the Laconian coastline. While Leonidas and his men waited for the Persian land forces, the Athenian fleet (about 330 vessels) stood off Artemisium at the northern end of Euboea. Its task was to prevent the Persian navy from landing troops in the rear of the Greek positions at Thermopylae.

When Xerxes reached the pass he waited for four days before attacking,

[91]

possibly convinced that the mere presence of his mighty army would induce the Greeks to run away. The hoplites, however, failed to be intimidated. On the fifth day the Persian army began its assault, only to meet with a bloody repulse. For two whole days wave after wave of Persians and their auxiliary and mercenary forces failed to make an impression on the Greeks. Even the 10,000 Immortals, Xerxes' elite corps, were beaten back by the defenders. The longer spears and heavier armour of the Greeks were more than a match for the lighter armament of the Immortals. Furthermore, the narrowness of the defile made it impossible for the entire 10,000 men to attack simultaneously. Towards the evening of the second day, however, Xerxes was made aware of a mountain path which could be used to turn the Greek position. His informant, Ephialtes, was a northern Greek who had little love for the southerners and was anxious to see the Persian army move southwards and out of his native Malis. Xerxes immediately ordered Ephialtes to guide his Immortals along the path.

During the two days of battle at Thermopylae, the Greek and Persian fleets came into contact off Artemisium. Xerxes' fleet had suffered severe losses as a result of violent storms but still out-numbered the Greeks. After three days of fighting, the Greek fleet was still maintaining its objective of preventing the Persians from landing behind Thermopylae. But the disastrous news that the Persians had taken the Thermopylae pass forced the Greek fleet to abandon its position at Artemisium and sail for Salamis.

Leonidas had sacrificed himself and his 300 Spartans in a heroic last stand aimed at covering the retreat of the other Greek contingents. The Theban troops surrendered to Xerxes saying that they had been forced to fight by Leonidas and had really been pro-Persian all along. Xerxes, unimpressed by this sudden protestation of loyalty, had them branded with the royal insignia. The Persian king's displeasure was perhaps understandable for the attack on Thermopylae had cost him some 20,000 casualties. The Greeks had lost 4,000 men, half of whom were not hoplites but light troops.[11]

The Greek defeat encouraged the states of central Greece to proclaim their submission to Persian rule. With the exception of Plataea, which remained staunchly pro-Athenian, the Boeotian states declared their support for Xerxes, and Thebes in particular provided the Persians with enthusiastic auxiliaries. Athens was Xerxes' next objective and the Thebans positively revelled at the prospect of attacking a hated rival, even if that meant playing a mercenary role alongside a foreign invader. Xerxes needed to conquer Attica and eliminate the Athenian fleet before launching a combined land and sea assault on the Peloponnesus. The Thebans had the immense satisfaction of seeing Athens fall to the Persian army. The city was largely deserted, having been abandoned by its citizens, but a small garrison had remained in the Acropolis to roll stones down upon the ascending Persian troops. After a two-week siege the Acropolis was taken and the surviving garrison massacred. Athens itself was pillaged and burnt.

There now remained the task of destroying the Greek fleet, which maintained its position in the bay of Salamis. The Greeks had about 300–380 ships of which 180–200 were Athenian and eighty-nine were Peloponnesian.[12] The Persian fleet still outnumbered that of the Greeks although its exact size remains unclear.

The burning of Athens and the sight of Persian columns heading towards the Isthmus of Corinth severely affected the morale of the individual Greek naval commanders. The Peloponnesians, especially, wanted to abandon the combined effort against the Persians so that each contingent could defend its respective home territory. That the famous battle of Salamis took place at all was due to the initiative and enterprise of the Athenian squadron commander, Themistocles, who according to Herodotus, sent a secret message to Xerxes informing him of the disunity and demoralisation among the Greeks.[13] If Xerxes attacked forthwith, Themistocles offered to join the Persians. Whether or not Themistocles really did contact Xerxes, it is probable that the Persian king was aware of the imminent fragmentation of the Greek fleet from his own intelligence sources. There were plenty of Greek exiles working as mercenaries in Persian service who could be used as espionage agents. At any rate, the Persians decided on an immediate attack to prevent the Greeks from escaping.

The main Persian fleet, largely made up of Phoenicians on the right wing and Ionians on the left, assembled at the mouth of the eastern strait while the 200 ships of the Egyptian squadron sailed round the south of Salamis island to blockade the western channel. At dawn on 23 September 480 BC, the invaders were lured into an unfavourable combat zone where superior numbers proved to be a distinct liability. The Greeks destroyed or captured 200 ships and lost forty of their own. Of all the auxiliary contingents in Xerxes' fleet, the Phoenicians suffered by far the highest casualties. Xerxes was more than a little upset at the failure of the Phoenicians and vented his rage on their captains by having them decapitated. As a consequence, the badly-mauled Phoenician contingent shrank even further, owing to a sudden and dramatic increase in its desertion rate. Large numbers of Central Asian

Saka mercenaries had also drowned. For obvious reasons, most of them had never learnt to swim. The Ionian auxiliaries, by contrast, escaped relatively unscathed from the debacle. Contrary to expectation, they had fought the mainland Greeks with unusual determination. Perhaps they had hoped to ingratiate themselves with their Persian overlord, or they feared capture by the mainland Greeks. At any rate, whatever the reasons, there were few Ionian desertions to the Greek side. The Egyptian squadron blockading the western channel also escaped disaster and Xerxes was left with at least 300 ships, but the defeat at Salamis had been decisive. He no longer had sufficient ships to supply and support his land army, which was still a powerful and unbeaten force.

Xerxes left Greece with 60,000 picked troops, not in mindless panic as depicted by the Greeks, but purposefully, in order to crush any revolts that might break out – and indeed did break out – in Ionia. The remainder of the Persian army returned to Thessaly under the command of Mardonius. There it still posed a threat to the states of the anti-Persian coalition. When he had restored order in Ionia, Xerxes sent his elite force back to northern Greece. The arrival of these reinforcements enabled Mardonius to pay off and dismiss various contingents of Central Asian mercenaries. He retained a smaller but more effective force made up primarily of Persian troops supported by detachments composed of the best of the auxiliary troops. Among the latter were Medes, Afghans, Bactrians, Thracians, Ethiopians, Libyans and Egyptians. There were also Phrygian mercenaries from the northern part of Anatolia and 20,000 northern Greek auxiliaries from Thessaly and Boeotia.

In the spring of 479 BC, Mardonius made an effort to win Athens (and its navy) over to the Persian side with offers of reparation and new territories. The Athenians, however, rejected the Persian overtures. Mardonius, piqued at the refusal, responded by reoccupying Athens and burning whatever building had survived the first Persian attack on the city. Sparta was sufficiently alarmed to despatch 5,000 Spartan hoplites, 5,000 *perioeci* and 35,000 helot light troops to assist the Athenians. It was not that Sparta had any sudden affection for Athens. It was the sober consideration that the Athenian fleet was still vital to the defence of the Peloponnesian coastline. Thus, the Spartans under King Pausanius marched northwards linking up with 5,000 Corinthians and contingents from smaller states such as Aegina and Megara. The Athenians contributed 8,000 hoplites and archers and the ever-faithful Plataeans provided 600 hoplites. The combined total of all the Greek contingents may have amounted to some 80,000 men about half of whom were hoplites.[14] There was scarcely any cavalry. Against this force Mardonius had 100,000–120,000 men but certainly not the 300,000 recorded by Herodotus in his ninth book.[15] As the Greeks advanced, Mardonius retreated into the Boeotian plain where his cavalry could be put to effective use on a battle ground of his own choosing. The 3,000-strong Megarian contingent was caught on open ground near Erythrae by Mardonius' horsemen and suffered grievously until rescued by a picked force of 300 Athenian hoplites and archers.

Mardonius had out-generalled Pausanius. Instead of risking an attack on the fortifications of the Isthmus, he had made the Greeks come to him. He had interrupted their communication and supply lines. Moreover, he had made the enemy very thirsty. With their water supply rendered unusable, the Greeks were forced to retreat to new positions near Plataea where potable water was available. The retreat was poorly coordinated. The various contingents failed to submerge their mutual animosities and the Athenians were particularly loath to follow the orders of a Spartan commander-in-chief.

To the Persian commanders, the dissension among the Greeks was plainly obvious. Mardonius observed the Spartans, the Athenians and the others strung out in three uncoordinated columns. He had intended to wear the Greeks down by attrition, but the opportunity which now presented itself was too good to miss. The Persian army advanced in pursuit of the Greeks. Pausánius' Spartans were the first to be attacked by cavalry and then by Persian infantry, including elite guardsmen. Thus, the finest hoplites in Greece came into contact with the best infantry in the Persian army and, indeed, it was the ·sheer tenacity of the Spartans that decided the battle of Plataea in favour of the Greek coalition. The Spartan hoplites waited patiently with perfect discipline for the order to charge, sheltering behind their shields as innumerable showers of arrows fired by Persian and auxiliary archers fell among them.

When the order came, the Spartans moved forward with savage determination, battered down a rampart of large wicker shields and, despite gallant resistance, gradually overcame their more lightly-armed opponents. Mardonius led his 1,000-strong guard to where the fighting was most intense in order to rally his men. With their commander-in-chief among them, the Persians and their auxiliaries fought with great bravery, grappling man-to-man with the Spartans and breaking their spearheads whenever they could. The Spartans were sufficiently hard-pressed to request assistance from the Athenians, who were on the left of the Greek line. The Athenians responded

[95]

positively and began to manoeuvre towards their Spartan allies but failed to get very far. As they attempted to close the gap, they were attacked by the right wing of the Persian army. A fierce struggle developed which prevented the Athenians from supporting the Spartans. But it was not a contest between Greeks and Asiatics. It was Greek against Greek as the Athenians faced Thessalian cavalry and Boeotian infantry. The Athenians managed to repulse the Boeotians with the help of other allied contingents but only with extreme difficulty. Their Boeotian enemies were the last to retreat from the field once Persian resistance had been broken. The Boeotian troops abandoned the rest of the shattered army and, protected by their cavalry, managed to retire to Thebes. Pursued by the Spartans, the survivors of the Persian army ran for the refuge of their fortified camp. But the Greeks rushed into the camp and a general slaughter began. Pausanius had ordered his men to take no prisoners and the Greeks struck down their enemies irrespective of whether they resisted, pleaded for quarter or merely waited, passive and motionless.

The decisive land victory at Plataea was complemented by an equally decisive naval triumph at Mycale on the coast of Asia Minor. The Greek expeditionary force landed at Mycale and stormed a Persian encampment. The outcome was decided when the Ionian Greek contingent in the Persian army changed sides at last and joined the attacking mainland Greeks. The destruction of the Persian army enabled the Greeks to burn some 200 enemy ships.

After Mycale the Greek coalition inflicted further defeats on the Persians, capturing the Hellespont and Cyprus. The Spartans and the other Peloponnesian allies then pulled out of the coalition, well satisfied that the Persians could never again threaten their territories. Athens continued the war against Persia, forming a new alliance known as the Delian League with the island and maritime states of Ionia and Aeolia (478–477 BC). During the course of hostilities, the Athenians won large battles near Eurymedon in Asia Minor (466 BC) and at Salamis in Cyprus (450 BC). In 448 BC the Peace of Callias brought to an end the great Greek and Persian wars.

In theory, the Persians should have triumphed over the Greeks. They enjoyed a significant superiority in numbers both on land and sea. The Persian army was a remarkably cohesive organisation despite the diverse ethnic backgrounds of its soldiers. The auxiliaries, who collectively outnumbered the native Persian troops, normally demonstrated a high degree of loyalty to their Persian overlords. The Phoenician and Cypriot sailors of the

Persian fleet were not inferior in terms of skill and experience to their Greek counterparts. Xerxes' soldiers were capable of fighting over most types of terrain and they were certainly no strangers to mountain warfare. The Persian army was a formidable fighting force with an awesome reputation. Furthermore, the Persians had a considerable number of sympathisers, not just in northern Greece but also in the south. The northern half of Greece collaborated more or less willingly, partly from fear and partly from a desire to see the south ruined and impotent. Xerxes found many willing mercenaries in the north.

If the Persian army was notable for its cohesion, the same could scarcely be said for its opponents in Greece. The anti-Persian coalition was composed of separate and rival states which had overcome their long-standing enmity only with considerable difficulty. Parochialism was the principal influence on the decisions and policies of the various component states. The Peloponnesians were especially notable for their local loyalties and a selfish, narrow-minded approach to the danger confronting Greece, but even the Athenians, who came close to a pan-Hellenic outlook, ultimately acted from self-interest. The Spartans did not exactly rush to the common defence of Greece when requested to do so by the Athenians. Nevertheless, when they did contribute troops, the Spartans played a fundamental role in repelling the Persians. They were, after all, the toughest hoplites in Greece. But Sparta was an exception. The armies of the other city-states were part-time citizen militias. Athens had a few contingents of professionals in the shape of Cretan and Scythian archers. These mercenary specialists had already been employed by the Athenians on a fairly regular basis during the sixth century BC both as soldiers and policemen. The Cretan archers hired by the Athenians during the Persian Wars were not auxiliaries officially sent by Crete. They were mercenaries working on their own account since Crete had refused to help mainland Greece in its time of peril. The Cretans were relatively few in number at this time and only rose to prominence as mercenary soldiers during the Hellenistic Period, that is to say the long era between the death of Alexander of Macedonia in 323 BC to the establishment of the Roman empire by Augustus in 30 BC. The Cretans had also been long involved in piracy, their island being ideally suited to such activities by virtue of its geographical position. During the fourth century BC, the increasing importance of Crete as 'a ready-made nursery for mercenaries' was matched by a corresponding increase in Cretan piracy. Indeed, piracy and mercenary service sometimes overlapped, particularly during the third and second centuries BC when

[97]

Cretan pirates were systematically employed by the main Greek states to carry out large-scale raids on the maritime cities of their rivals.

The Persian army also had its numerous militia contingents but there were many more professional fighting men among the Persian ranks than among the Greek. The 10,000 native professionals of the Persian Guard alone were equal or superior in number to the fully-mobilised militia of many a Greek city-state, excluding the largest, such as Athens. The city of Sparta was rarely able to mobilise 10,000 hoplites drawn exclusively from its own population. Little Plataea's average was 500 men. The Immortals were not the only professional troops in the Persian army. There were the Greek mercenary bodyguards of the satraps and Libyan–Egyptian and Jewish mercenaries also rendered good service to employers who had liberated them from the cruelties of Assyrian domination.

Why, then, was Persia defeated in Greece? Much of the answer must surely be attributable to the superiority of the hoplites over their more lightly-armed and scantily-protected opponents. The battles of Marathon and Plataea provide clear evidence of the superior fighting quality of the Greeks. The Greek victory at Plataea was not the result of brilliant leadership. Mardonius was arguably a better strategist than Pausanius. Plataea was won primarily by the Spartan hoplites whose tenacity, discipline and better armament enabled them to overcome Mardonius' men. The Persians themselves drew the relevant conclusions and began to hire Greek mercenary hoplites in ever-increasing numbers right up to the conquest of their territories by Alexander the Great.

But the Persians did not lose the war solely because they came up against a superior type of soldier. Historical events are rarely attributable to a single cause. The Persians were unable to make the most effective use of their elite heavy cavalry, which far outclassed the small cavalry arm of the Greek coalition, since the terrain on which the Greek chose (or were constrained) to meet the invaders generally prevented the large-scale use of horsemen. Thus, the Persian army was denied full use of its most potent arm. At sea, the Greek ships proved to be faster and more manoeuvrable than those of the enemy. The Greek shipbuilders had manifestly surpassed their Phoenician mentors. Salamis demonstrated not just the high quality of the hoplite–marines but also the general superiority of Greek naval strategy and tactics. If their land strategy was sometimes questionable, on the water the Greeks had a clear edge over their opponents and they continually turned the very size of the Persian fleet to their own advantage.

Greek technical superiority, unfavourable geography and mistaken tactics are basic to any explanation of why the Persian invasion failed. But added to these tangible considerations are psychological factors. To what extent did the sense of anger, fear and insult aroused by the invasion and the prospect of losing their cherished independence motivate the hoplites of the anti-Persian coalition? How did their fighting spirit, their will to win compare with that of the Persians? How enthusiastic were Persia's auxiliary troops about a prolonged campaign fought far from their native territories? Given that the auxiliaries formed an important part of overall Persian strength, their morale would need to be analysed to the extent permitted by surviving contemporary documents. In describing the battle of Plataea, Herodotus rates the native Persians as being the best of the enemy troops but also praises the regiments of Saka mercenary cavalry who were extensively employed by the Persians in every part of their empire.

Whatever judgement may be made about the relative importance of causal factors, the results of Persian failure remain abundantly clear. The Persian empire had been effectively prevented from spreading into Europe. The southern Greek states had successfully defended their freedom and independence and soundly beaten the invaders. But the Persians were by no means a spent force and a third invasion attempt remained a distinct possibility. It was to counteract such an attempt that Athens formed the Delian League and continued to fight after the Peloponnesians had gone home.

CHAPTER SEVEN

Sparta and Athens:
the Peloponnesian War

FOLLOWING THE EXPULSION of the Persians from Greek soil and the termination of the Spartan–Athenian alliance, Athens became the leading economic, cultural and naval centre in Greece under the leadership of Pericles. Needless to say, as Athenian power and influence expanded, Spartan jealousy and disquiet increased proportionately. Seen from a Spartan perspective, this concern was quite justified, for Athens had begun to follow a distinctly imperialist policy that would ultimately result in war between the erstwhile allies, one that would see the employment of mercenaries on a scale previously unknown in Greece.

The road to war was a gradual one and began with the reconstruction of Athens on the ruins left by the Persians. Pericles strengthened the city's trade connections with Thrace and southern Russia which was the main source of Athenian corn imports. To protect the overland section of the trade route, Pericles organised the construction of the Long Walls linking Athens with its seaport, Piraeus. The Spartans were alarmed to see a new, much stronger city rising phoenix-like from the ashes. Furthermore, the fortifications were not the only source of jealousy and apprehension. Athens continued along its provocative path by forming an alliance with Argos, Sparta's bitter enemy. To make matters worse, the Spartans were also afflicted by internal troubles. The Third Messenian War (a helot revolt) also made the Spartans that much more reluctant to commit their hoplites to long-distance expeditions and encouraged the increased use of mercenaries who would be prepared to undertake lengthier campaigns as long as they were paid.

While Sparta struggled with its domestic problems, Athens extended its influence into neighbouring territories by entering into alliances with Thessaly and, more significantly with Megara, which had previously been a member of the Peloponnesian League (460 BC). The Athenian expansion into Megara was the immediate cause of the First Peloponnesian War. Hostilities began in 459 BC with a clash between Athens on the one hand and Corinth and Aegina on the other. The two Peloponnesian states were heavily defeated. Aegina was besieged, captured and forced to join the Delian League. Corinthian troops invaded Megarian territory but were repulsed and utterly routed. One particular contingent of Corinthian hoplites was caught in a cul-de-sac enclosed by a deep ditch. Prevented from escaping by Athenian hoplites who barred the exit, the Corinthians were slaughtered to a man by stone-throwing *psiloi*, or light troops, who had surrounded the enclosure. Well-positioned, light troops could be used to devastating effect against heavy infantry.

The Athenian victories prompted Sparta to enter the war despite the exhaustion caused by the recent Messenian revolt. The first Spartan move was to conclude an alliance with Thebes with the object of restoring the Boeotian League as a credible counterweight to Athenian power. In 457 BC 1,500 Lacedaimonians and 10,000 allied troops confronted the 14,000-strong Athenian army in Boeotia. At Tanagra, near Thebes, the Athenians were defeated in a fierce battle during which the Thessalians deserted to the Spartan side. The Spartans, however, did not follow up their initial advantage. They did not have sufficient strength to risk an attack on a fortified Athens and consequently withdrew to the Peloponnesus, ravaging Megara along the way.

Some two months after Tanagra, the Athenians struck back, crushing the Boeotian forces at Oenophyta. They gained control of all Boeotia except Thebes itself. In the Peloponnesus, Achaea went over to the Athenians. Thus, by 456 BC Athens had, in the short space of five years, established its hegemony over central Greece. The Delian League was transformed from an association of autonomous states into an Athenian empire. It was apparent almost from the outset that Periclean Athens regarded the members of the League not as partners but as subservient client–states from which she extracted heavy monetary contributions. Ostensibly the headquarters of the Delian League was on Delos but there was no doubt as to where the real power lay.

Athenian imperial ambition seemed limitless. Confident of success, Athens had committed herself to a war on two fronts – against Sparta and against the Persian empire in Egypt. She had despatched an expeditionary force to assist Inaros, a Libyan prince, who had launched a rebellion against Persian domination at the head of a mercenary army. Athenian motives were largely commercial. Egypt was a rich granary almost as important as the grain-producing areas of southern Russia. In 454 BC, however, the Persians inflicted a devastating defeat on the Athenian auxiliaries, which left very few survivors. This was a serious blow to Athenian power and prestige and in Greece itself the tide of events gradually began to flow in Sparta's favour. Argos renounced her alliance with Athens and made peace with Sparta. In 448 BC, the Boeotian states successfully revolted, defeating a small Athenian army at Coronea. Oligarchies soon replaced the democracies set up by the Athenians. The Megarians also rebelled and slaughtered all the Athenian garrison troops they could capture.

In 446 BC, the Lacedaimonian army advanced through Megara, threatening to destroy the numerically inferior Athenian forces. But, surprisingly, the Spartans and their allies withdrew. Pericles may have persuaded the Spartans that Athens would respect the desire for independence demonstrated by neighbouring states or perhaps the fear of helot insurrections had led the Spartans to return home as quickly as they could. The facts are unclear, but, at any rate, the southerners had made their point. Athens had over-extended itself in undertaking a war against two separate enemies and had suffered heavy losses. Peace was clearly desirable and came in 445 BC with the so-called Thirty Years' peace, which, in fact, lasted fourteen years. Athens lost Megara and Boeotia but retained Aegina. She also retained her heavy-handed control of the Delian League. Thus, while Sparta was recognised as being the supreme landpower, Athens kept her status as the leading sea-power.

During the interval of peace between the first and second Peloponnesian Wars, Athens experienced a golden age of cultural activity that was ultimately of far more significance than her attempts at empire-building. The Parthenon was constructed under Pericles' guidance and decorated by a group of master-sculptors, including Phidias. Pericles undertook an extensive programme of public works, partly to provide work for hoplite militiamen left unemployed by the coming of peace. Together with the architectural and sculptural masterpieces and scientific speculation came the creation of classic literary works. Around 441 BC Sophocles (496–406 BC) was at work on his most popular play, *Antigone*. His friend, Herodotus (484–*c*.425 BC) began writing his *Historia*. The term originally meant 'research' and now came to mean 'history'. The years of peace also brought economic prosperity. Agriculture and industrial production flourished and Athens indulged in a good deal of colonisation, primarily on the shores of the Black Sea and in southern Italy.

The underlying causes of enmity between Sparta and Athens remained unchanged despite the Thirty Years' Peace. For the historian Thucydides, 'What made war inevitable was the growth of Athenian power and the fear which this caused Sparta.'[1] Whether or not war was actually inevitable, the continuation of Athenian imperialism certainly made it a distinct possibility, even though Sparta was reluctant, for the moment, to commit herself to further hostilities.

It was not Sparta, nor Athens, however, but Corinth which provided the catalyst for a renewed war. In 435 BC, the Adriatic colony of Corcyra (Corfu) went to war with its founding city, Corinth. After several defeats at the hands of the colonists, the Corinthians undertook a massive ship-building programme in order to gain a numerical advantaage over the Corcyraean fleet, which was the second largest in Greece at the outbreak of hostilities. As a result, Corcyra appealed to Athens for assistance. Last-minute intervention by Athens saved Corcyra (433 BC) but the Athenians were not yet in breach of the Thirty Years' Peace. The alliance between Corcyra and Athens was a defensive rather than offensive arrangement and as such was permitted under the provisions of the peace treaty.

Corinth now did all she could to persuade Sparta to take up arms against the Athenians. The Athenians in their turn did their best to exacerbate Corinthian indignation. Their next provocation came over Potidaea, a city founded by Corinth, but also a member of the Athenian empire. The Athenians demanded that Potidaea demolish her seaward walls and expel her Corinthian magistrates. When the people of Potidaea refused, Athens prepared to punish the city. The Corinthians immediately despatched 2,000 men (1,600 hoplites, 400 light troops) to Potidaea to assist in the defence of the city. According to Thucydides, this relief force was made up of Corinthian volunteers and mercenaries recruited in the Peloponnesus.[2] The precise origin of the latter is not specified in his account, but it seems likely that they came from Arcadia or perhaps Achaea, two regions with a well-established tradition of supplying mercenaries to overseas employers. At any rate, it is the first reference that Thucydides makes to the use of mercenaries within the confines of Greece itself. Up until the Peloponnesian Wars, the overwhelming mass of Greek mercenaries found work in Asia Minor, Egypt or Mesopotamia. Now there would be no lack of opportunity closer to home.

The Athenian siege of Potidaea lasted until the early months of 429 BC. By the time the Athenians had captured the city and released the volunteer–mercenary troops largely unharmed, the Spartans had committed themselves to military intervention and the second Peloponnesian War had begun in earnest. The siege of Potidaea, like the intervention in Corcyra, was a provocation that stirred up the Spartans, but it was not quite a flagrant breach of the provisions of the Thirty Years' Peace. Athens' next move, however, which barred Megara from every seaport under Athenian control, definitely contravened the spirit and the articles of the treaty. Athens justified her various acts of aggression in simple terms, informing the Spartans that she had earned the right through her past conduct. Her motives were the same as those of other states; a quest for security, the defence of her honour and self-interest. Thucydides would probably not have been surprised to learn that, two-and-a-half thousand years later, his succinct exposition of Athenian motives would still be applicable to the foreign policies of modern nation-states.

The Spartans were unimpressed by Athens' claims to special status, justified, in Athenian eyes, by the gallant victory at Marathon. They demanded that Athens lift the siege of Potidaea, grant independence to Aegina and permit Megara to use Athenian ports. Faced with a refusal, Sparta presented an ultimatum. A Theban attack on Plataea, which had, of course, remained loyal to Athens (March 431 BC) made war inevitable.

On every side, young Greek hoplites applauded the outbreak of hostilities. They were recruited from the upper echelons of Greek society and their arms and armour were highly visible symbols of their social status. There was some similarity with medieval Japanese *samurai*, who were distinguished from the rest of society, not so much by their apparel, which could range from a lord's expensive silk costume to the modest clothes of a low-ranking warrior, but by the exclusive right to carry two razor-sharp swords. It was considered disgraceful, both for hoplite and *samurai*, to lose or abandon his armament. For a *samurai*, it represented a total loss of honour, which could only be regained by ritual suicide. For the hoplite, the loss of a shield in battle was best kept quiet, if possible. One exception was Archilocus of Paros, a truculent, irreverent, bad-mannered character who flourished c.650 BC. He was primarily known as an iambic poet and, for reasons best known to themselves, was considered by the ancient Greeks to be on the same level of brilliance as Homer. He was also a wanderer, a gold-miner and a mercenary soldier. As a mercenary commander he led an expedition from Thasos into Thracian territory in search of gold. Defeated by the Thracians, Archilocus fled with his men, abandoning his shield.

> Some Thracian flaunts the shield I left behind;
> My trusty shield – I had to – in a wood
> Well, I have saved my life: so never mind
> That shield; I'll get another just as good.[3]

Needless to say, a *samurai* could never have expressed the sentiments contained in Archilocus' poem.

During the first year of the war, Spartan armies under King Archidamus invaded and ravaged Attica but failed to draw out the Athenian army from behind the Long Walls. Meanwhile, Athenian naval expeditions raided the Peloponnesian coastline. In the following year the Spartans invaded Attica for a second time and failed again to provoke a decisive encounter. Athens easily held out against the Peloponnesians and kept up her naval attacks on the enemy's home territories. When all seemed to be going well, disaster struck in the form of a plague that seems to have spread from Ethiopia, through Egypt into Asia Minor and finally to Piraeus and Athens itself. The pestilence destroyed one third of the total population of the city. Many a young hoplite who had looked forward to the glory of war with joyous anticipation succumbed to an insidious microscopic enemy against which spear and pretty shield could do nothing. The loss of 4,400 hoplites from the 13,000-strong garrison led to an increased use of mercenaries, as will presently be seen. Though a serious setback, the plague did not cripple Athenian power nor did it decrease the Athenian determination to emerge victorious. In 429 BC, Pericles passed away, a victim of the plague, and was replaced by Cleon, a vigorous proponent of continued war against the Peloponnesians.

Ironically, perhaps, the presence of the plague in Athens added to its impregnability. Anxious to avoid the contagion, the Spartans retreated and turned their attention to Plataea. At sea, Athens maintained her advantage. The Athenian admiral Phormio inflicted defeats on numerically superior Peloponnesian fleets. The Athenians also suppressed revolts on the allied, or rather, subject islands of Corcyra and Lesbos (427 BC). On the other hand, gallant Plataea was besieged by Spartan and Theban troops. The modest garrison of the city, some 400 Plataeans and eighty Athenians held out for two years against greatly superior forces.

Despite a remarkable local success on the island of Sphacteria, where Athenian troops captured 292 Peloponnesians, including 120 Spartans, the course of the war between 424–421 BC went largely against the Athenians. A further attack against Boeotia was defeated by the Theban general Pagondas. The Spartans decided on a new strategy which entailed attacks against Athenian colonies in Thrace. Their objective was the disruption of Athens' trade route to the Black Sea.

Accordingly, the Spartan general Brasidas invaded Thrace at the head of 1,700 men, of whom 700 were freed helots trained as hoplites and the rest mercenaries recruited in the Peloponnesus. The Spartans were not about to commit their main army to a distant campaign at a time when Athenian success at Sphacteria might encourage helot revolts. Spartan hoplites were also required for the defence of the Peloponnesian coastline. Thus, the Spartan authorities gave Brasidas the helots whom they were probably glad to get rid of and enough money for the hire of mercenaries. The latter would have no qualms about fighting far from home as long as they were paid.

In 423 BC, Athens requested a truce. Sparta, which was also on the point of exhaustion, readily agreed. Brasidas had his enemies in Sparta who were jealous of his progress. The diversion had been too successful and it had been achieved with mercenaries and ex-slaves rather than Spartan hoplites. The armies of Sparta and Athens ceased their operations in Greece but Brasidas ignored the truce and captured several more Athenian colonies. Cleon was finally forced to lead an expedition to Thrace to restore Athenian domination. His army consisted of 300 cavalry, 1,200 Athenian hoplites and a large but unspecified force of troops provided by allied states.[5] Both Cleon and Brasidas made use of Thracian mercenary peltasts, lightly armed troops carrying javelins and small shields. Despite the general disdain in which light troops were still held, the opposing generals seem to have appreciated that peltasts could play a useful role in harassing hoplite formations. Thucydides records that Cleon reached Eion and waited there for the arrival of Thracian mercenaries before marching on to confront Brasidas at Amphipolis. The Spartan general also reinforced his army with 1,500 Thracian peltasts, 1,000 Myrcinian and Chaldician peltasts plus an unspecified number of Edonian light troops.[6]

Arriving at Amphipolis, Cleon moved up close to the walls to reconnoitre the situation outside the city. Confident of victory, he had gone forward solely with his hoplites, leaving the mercenaries and auxiliaries still on the march towards the city. Brasidas' troops waited not on the walls but behind the gates, ready to make a vigorous charge against the Athenians. Cleon realised too late that, instead of having to besiege the city, he would have to face an immediate attack. He ordered his troops to withdraw as rapidly as possible, forming them into one long column which, as it happened, presented its unshielded side towards the city gates. Brasidas charged out of one gate with only 150 picked hoplites, hitting the centre of the retreating column, while the rest of his troops, including the mercenary peltasts, emerged from the second gate to strike at the end of the Athenian formation. Totally disconcerted, the Athenians broke and fled. Cleon was killed by a Thracian mercenary peltast from Myrkinos. Given his lack of affection for Cleon, Thucydides may have derived some pleasure in recording that Cleon had been struck down by a low-grade mercenary while running away.[6] It is possible that Cleon died in a more courageous fashion and that Thucydides in describing a cowardly and ignominious death had allowed his antipathy to colour an otherwise remarkably neutral account. The hoplites who were under Cleon's direct command are recorded by Thucydides as having temporarily stood their ground against Brasidas' men until their ranks were broken by showers of missile weapons thrown by mercenary peltasts. As the Athenians ran in total disarray, the mercenaries followed in relentless pursuit, striking down many a panicking hoplite. Brasidas seems to have chosen his mercenaries well. The Athenians lost 600 elite hoplites. His largely mercenary army had suffered just seven casualties. It was his last victory, for the Spartan general had been mortally wounded and lived just long enough to be told of the outcome of his daring plan.

The defeat at Amphipolis led Athens to negotiate for peace. Thus, in 421 BC, the Archidamian War (named after Archidamus of Sparta) came to an end. The Peace of Nicias restored the territories of Sparta and Athens much as they had been before the war. Neither side had achieved anything decisive and the causes of conflict – imperialism, jealousy, insecurity, commercial rivalry – had not been removed.

Despite a Spartan alliance with the Boeotian states and an Athenian alliance with Argos, Sparta and Athens remained in a state of uneasy peace. The *strategos* Alcibiades did his best to provoke war between Sparta and the Argive coalition. Argos and Sparta would weaken each other for the benefit of Athens. As part of his plan to embroil Sparta in a new war, Alcibiades encouraged the Argives to attack Epidaurus, a steadfast member of the Peloponnesian League. The imminent collapse of the Epidaurians stirred Sparta into action. She sent reinforcements to her hard-pressed allies and mobilised her entire army for a decisive confrontation with Argos. Among

[107]

the assembled contingents were the enfranchised helots and mercenaries from Brasidas' Thracian expedition. In all, King Agis of Sparta disposed of some 20,000 men.

In 418 BC, the Spartan army, divided into three separate corps, invaded Argos and Mantinea with the object of crushing the Argive forces and bringing the wayward states back into the Peloponnesian League. The battle that was eventually fought at Mantinea resulted in a complete victory for the Spartans. The opposing armies seem to have been equally matched in terms of numbers – about 10,000 men each – but Spartan training and discipline prevailed as Agis' hoplites routed the enemy troops almost immediately, to the accompaniment of groups of flute players whose music kept the Spartans in step. Among the fleeing troops who trampled each other in their eagerness to escape were the survivors of the Athenian contingent of some 1,300 men. Mantinea, the largest land battle of the Peloponnesian War, had been fought during a time of nominal peace. Needless to say, Sparta re-established her supremacy in the Peloponnesus. Argos signed a peace treaty and became a Spartan-style oligarchy. Mantinea and the other recalcitrant states rejoined the Peloponnesian League. Sparta chose not to declare war on Athens, despite the limited Athenian participation on the side of the Argives. Athens was now effectively excluded from Peloponnesian affairs and was forced to look further afield in her desire for imperial expansion.

In 416 BC, Athens was presented with an opportunity for expansion on a grand scale and again called upon a substantial body of mercenaries and auxiliaries. When Segesta, an allied city in Sicily, requested military assistance from Athens against Selinus, a Megarian colony and an ally of Syracuse, the Athenians saw a chance to conquer the whole island, although they wanted at the same time to make it look as though they were sending help to their own kinsmen and to their newly acquired allies there.[7] In effect, it was the prospect of territorial and commercial expansion, military glory and adventure, tribute and plunder that lured the Athenians into an enterprise that was to end in disaster. Originally founded by the Corinthians, Syracuse was the island's richest and most powerful city and a highly desirable prize but few Athenians had any real idea of the magnitude of the undertaking. It was scarcely appreciated that, in terms of surface area and population size, Sicily was comparable to the Peloponnesus. Nevertheless, once a firm decision had been taken, Athens mobilised her forces enthusiastically in anticipation of a straightforward campaign. She raised over 5,000 hoplites, 1,300 light troops and some 20,000 sailors. The Athenian cavalry, however, consisted of no more than thirty horsemen. Athens relied on its Sicilian allies to provide cavalry. The invasion force was placed under the command of three *strategoi*, Alcibiades, Nicias and Lamachus. It was a remarkable choice of generals; Alcibiades and Nicias disliked each other intensely. The ambitious, self-seeking and able Alcibiades fully supported the attack on Sicily in view of the personal glory he hoped to acquire. On the other hand, Nicias, a popular but inefficient general, questioned the wisdom of leaving Athens relatively unprotected when she was only nominally at peace with Sparta and had no more than renewable ten-day truces with the Boeotians. Furthermore, such an expedition would leave Athens less able to control her potentially rebellious subject-cities. Athens needed peace and reconstruction after the ravages of the plague and her losses in battle. The Syracusans were well-armed and well supplied and they were not reliant on food imports. Nicias emphasised the difficulties as much as he could, reminding the Athenians that they would have to carry all their supplies with them rather than depend on foreigners of dubious reliability. Syracuse was a first-rate military power. Consequently, Athens needed to raise a particularly large and versatile army made up not just of Athenian citizens and Delian League subjects but also of mercenary hoplites from the Peloponnesus and Cretan archers and slingers.

Far from being dissuaded, the Athenians immediately gave their generals *carte-blanche* to hire mercenaries and Alcibiades left Athens on a recruiting tour of Argos and Arcadia. As a result, 500 Argives, 250 Mantineans, 700 Rhodian slingers and 480 mercenary archers (including eighty Cretans), among other hired troops, joined the invasion force. There were about 120 exiles from Megara who served as light troops and a few exiles from Syracuse who hoped to return to their native city.[8] The Argives, who were Dorians, were motivated to serve Ionian Greeks against other Dorians by a deep hatred of Sparta and the prospect of making a quick profit. According to Thucydides, 'The Mantineans and other mercenaries from Arcadia were in the habit of marching against any enemy who was pointed out to them as such at the time, and the fact that they were serving for pay now made them regard the Arcadians in the Corinthian service (i.e. Syracusan service) as just as much their enemies as anyone else.'[9] The Cretans and Rhodians also joined up for the pay and loot and found themselves fighting fellow countrymen in Syracusan employ. Similarly, financial reward was the main motive that led Aetolian mercenaries to enlist in the Athenian forces. Some of the mercenaries, however, such as the Acarnanians, participated mainly out of goodwill towards Athens. There were also some Etruscan mercenaries who joined the Athenians in Sicily, primarily driven by an abiding hatred of Syracuse.

The Athenian invasion fleet – some 134 triremes and an equal number of supply boats – left Piraeus in June 415 BC, carrying its 27,000 soldiers and sailors. Shortly after it reached its destination, Alcibiades was accused of religious sacrilege and was recalled to Athens to stand trial. On the return journey he managed to escape to the Peloponnesus and sought asylum in a most unlikely place – Sparta. He revealed details of Athens' latest imperial ambitions. The Spartans were alarmed to learn that the Athenians first intended to conquer Sicily and then the Dorian colonies in Italy. Following this, they would attempt to conquer the Carthaginian empire and finally attack the Peloponnesians, aided by all the western Greek forces they could raise as well as a large number of Iberian mercenaries.[10]

The defection of Alcibiades now left the invasion force in the hands of Lamachus, who favoured an immediate attack on Syracuse before the enemy could prepare adequate defences, and the over-cautious Nicias, who preferred to sail for Segesta where he hoped to acquire extra funds with which to pay his hired troops. Nicias prevailed and the Syracusans were given precious time in which to strengthen their defences. In May 414 BC, the Athenians finally began the siege of Syracuse, having lost their initial advantage. The Syracusans came out of the city in an attempt to prevent its encirclement. In the battles which followed they were defeated and forced to retire behind the walls but Lamachus, who had foolishly exposed himself while leading the Argives, was cut down by Syracusan cavalry. The expedition was now under the sole command of Nicias, who had never believed in the appropriateness of the venture.

Having repulsed the Syracusans, the besieging army now began circumvallation works on the landward side of the city in order to sever its links with the interior of the island. Once the ramparts were completed it would be only a matter of time before the city fell. Syracusan morale began to deteriorate and was certainly not restored by the arrival of Sicel tribesmen and Etruscan mercenaries attracted by the prospect of looting Syracuse. The city's inhabitants were close to surrender.

Meanwhile, in Sparta, Alcibiades had persuaded his hosts to send an expeditionary force to rescue their Dorian kinsmen in Syracuse. The Spartans contributed 600 trained freed-men and helots while the Corinthians sent a mixed force of citizen hoplites and Arcadian mercenaries. Two hundred volunteers came from Boeotia while Sicyon raised another 200 hoplites.[11] Under the command of the Spartan general Gylippus, the relief force landed in Sicily unopposed. From the towns of Himera and Selinus, Gylippus received a small reinforcement of cavalry and light troops. A thousand pro-Syracusan Sicels also joined the expedition. In a bold move, Gylippus managed to reach Syracuse by crossing an unfinished and unguarded sector of the Athenian rampart. His arrival greatly improved the morale of the Syracusans. Nicias hesitated to attack Gylippus but the Spartan commander had no hesitation about taking on the Athenians. As a result, the besiegers lost control of the high ground around the city and were thrown back to their base-camp at the Great Harbour of Syracuse. The Syracusans then constructed a wall of their own, intersecting the Athenian rampart. This effectively prevented Nicias from closing his ring around the city. At the same time, the Syracusan fleet, reinforced by Corinthian ships, attacked the Athenian triremes in the confined space of the harbour, inflicting severe losses. Nicias informed Athens of the unfavourable turn of events. The Athenians, he stated, were no longer the besiegers but had, on land, at least, become the besieged. Sailors sent out on foraging duties were being killed by Syracusan cavalry. Slaves were deserting to the enemy.[12] The mercenary troops were also starting to disappear, now that their employers' fortunes had taken a turn for the worst. Being on the losing side holds no attractions, particularly for mercenaries.

> As for the foreigners in our service, those who were conscripted are going back to their cities as quickly as they can; those who were originally delighted with the idea of high pay and thought they were going to make money rather than do any fighting now find that, contrary to their expectations, the enemy is not only holding out against us but is actually opposing us on the sea, and are either slipping away as deserters or making off in one way or another – which is not difficult considering the size of Sicily.[13]

The beleaguered Nicias requested Athens to send more reinforcements, or alternatively, the order to withdraw. He fervently hoped to receive the latter but got 5,000 more troops and seventy-three ships, for the Athenians were not yet ready to give up. Like the initial invasion force, the second expedition, led by Demosthenes, was made up of 1,200 Athenian citizens, allied contingents and mercenary hoplites, archers and slingers. Upon his arrival in

July 413 BC, Demosthenes launched a night attack with the object of regaining the high ground around the city. After some initial success the Athenians were repulsed, first by the Boeotians and then by the Syracusans. Unable to tell friend from foe in the moonlight, Demosthenes' hoplites retreated down to the harbour in great disorder. They blundered into each other, mistook comrades for the enemy and fought each other hand-to-hand in blind panic. Some, uncertain of their direction, ran straight into Syracusan troops or fell over cliffs, meeting a terrible fate either way. In the morning, the Syracusans gathered up a large harvest of abandoned weapons and many of the decorated shields that were such objects of pride to the hoplites.

After this salutary lesson, Demosthenes favoured a complete withdrawal from Syracuse. Nicias, however, now added a further touch of irony to the course of events by refusing to retreat. He reasoned that the Syracusans must be short of money:

> Because of their payments to the mercenaries, their expenditure on fortresses in the open country, and then the maintenance, which had now lasted for a year, of a large fleet, they were already short of money and would soon not know where to turn. They had spent 2,000 talents already and had run up large debts in addition; and if, through failing to produce the pay, they were to lose even a small portion of their present force, they would at once be in a bad way, since they depended more on mercenaries than on men who, like the Athenians, were bound to serve.[14]

In Syracuse, Gylippus, aware of the dissension among the Athenian generals, was determined to keep the enemy on the defensive. Contrary to Nicias' expectations, the city's mercenaries, unlike many of his own hired troops, did not desert when their pay went into arrears. Perhaps they sensed imminent victory and the prospect of paying themselves with loot. Indeed, far from losing his mercenaries, Gylippus received reinforcements of Peloponnesian mercenaries among other hired troops sent out by cities allied to Syracuse. Thus, the Syracusans prepared to attack the Athenians on land and sea. With the Athenian expedition in such bad condition Nicias accepted the inevitable and agreed to a withdrawal. At this point, the moon, which had cast its cold, remote light with impartiality upon the horrors of the night battle, now went dark. Persuaded by his men, the highly superstitious Nicias changed his mind about withdrawing from Syracuse. The lunar eclipse was a bad omen. But adverse celestial phenomena were perhaps not the only factors which made

Nicias hesitate yet again. If he returned home in disgrace he had a very good chance of being put to death.

Nicias' hesitation sealed the fate of the entire expedition. Gylippus launched an immediate naval offensive. Although the Athenian fleet was still superior in numbers, its ships were in poor condition and its sailors weakened by disease. By contrast, the Syracusan fleet was manned by freshly-arrived contingents and its ships were more strongly built and in better repair. A Syracusan squadron of seventy-six ships defeated eighty-six Athenian ships, driving the survivors back into the Great Harbour. Gylippus' next move was to blockade the harbour mouth with old merchant vessels chained together. The Syracusan battle fleet was stationed in a semi-circle on the wings of the blockade so that it could attack the flanks of the Athenian fleet, which had no alternative but to attempt a breakout. Nicias loaded some 110 ships mainly with his surviving mercenary troops and ordered them to smash through the blockade. The result was a complete disaster. Although the head of the Athenian fleet managed to penetrate the blockade, the Syracusans, as planned, attacked the flanks and, in an action reminiscent of Salamis, forced the Athenian ships to crowd together. With scarcely any room to move, ships collided, rammed into each other, deliberately or unintentionally, and jammed together. Fierce fighting raged across the decks of the triremes, watched anxiously by Athenian and Syracusan hoplites stationed on shore. The Syracusan victory was clear and decisive. The Athenians broke and were chased back to land by the Syracusan troops.

Despite the bloody repulse they had suffered, Nicias and Demosthenes decided to make another attempt at breaking through the blockade on the following morning. Their sailors, however, had had enough and refused to man the ships. The Athenian generals now had no recourse but to escape overland. Thus, two days after the naval battle, the 40,000 surviving troops – soldiers and sailors – of the Athenian expeditionary force marched away from Syracuse towards Catania, an allied city, leaving their dead unburied and their sick and wounded comrades to the less-than-tender mercies of the Syracusans. The retreating hoplites were short of food and drinking water and were constantly harassed by Syracusan cavalry and infantry who prevented them from obtaining further supplies and forced them to change the direction of their march away from allied territory. The Athenians attempted to elude their tormentors by a night march but to no avail. When morning came, the rearguard under Demosthenes was surrounded by the Syracusans and forced to surrender. On the following day, Nicias' troops also found themselves encircled by the enemy but, driven by desperation and a raging thirst, they fought their way through to the Assinarus river. The sight of cool water destroyed whatever discipline remained. Many were trampled in the crush of bodies as they struggled to drink and to reach the imagined safety of the far bank and many were impaled by their own spears or those of their fellow soldiers.

The Syracusans closed in on this desperate and demoralised mass. Crossing the river, they occupied the steep opposite bank and began a sustained bombardment. Gylippus' Peloponnesian mercenaries descended to the river in order to slaughter more of the enemy at close quarters. Of the 40,000 troops who had begun the retreat from Syracuse, there were only 7,000 survivors.[15] Nicias surrendered to Gylippus, who was well-disposed towards the Athenian commander in view of the humane treatment which he had given Spartan prisoners in the past. But the Syracusans felt rather less sympathy. The hapless Nicias and his colleague, Demosthenes, were executed. Nor was much compassion shown to the survivors, who were placed in a narrow stone quarry where they suffered from exposure, malnutrition and thirst and ten weeks later the allied and mercenary prisoners were removed and sold as slaves. Mercenary soldiering was, and remains, a risky business fraught with unexpected consequences.

The failure of the attack on Syracuse and the total loss of her expeditionary forces came as a grievous blow to Athenian power and prestige. She had lost over 40,000 men together with their arms and equipment and an enormous amount of money which she had used to obtain material and to pay mercenary troops. Although Athens had employed foreign light troops, such as Cretan archers, for at least a century, the Syracusan expedition marked the first occasion on which she employed much more expensive mercenary hoplites. Owing to the hesitation and incompetence of Nicias, she did not get value for money. But the disaster of Syracuse was not the only crisis in Athenian affairs. While the siege was still in progress, Sparta had invaded Attica and established a permanent fortress at Decelea, a town which lay within sight of Athens. Thus, while Athenian troops were engaged in besieging an overseas city, Athens was itself in a state of permanent siege, with her agriculture effectively ruined by Spartan raids. Twenty thousand agricultural slaves deserted. Farm animals were slaughtered or removed and Athenian supply lines were disrupted. The destruction caused by the Spartan garrison of Decelea and the huge cost of the Syracusan expedition had such a deleterious effect on her finances that Athens sent away 1,300 Thracian mercenaries who had arrived too late to sail with Demosthenes' relief force. Even though the Thracians would have been useful against the Spartans at Decelea, Athens could no longer afford their fee of one drachma a day per man. In order not to disappoint the Thracians, however, the Athenians provided a general to lead them home and encouraged them to attack the Boeotian city of Mycalessus on the way. The peltasts could then pay themselves with plunder in lieu of the wages promised by Athens. When the mercenaries arrived, they found the citizens of Mycalessus unprepared for a surprise attack:

> The Thracians burst into Mycalessus, scaled the houses and temples, and butchered the inhabitants, sparing neither the young nor the old, but methodically killing everyone they met, women and children alike, and even the farm animals and every living thing they saw ... Among other things, they broke into a boys' school, the largest in the place, into which the children had just entered, and killed every one of them.[16]

The massacre at Mycalessus further increased the hatred felt towards Athens by her enemies. Nor were her allies particularly impressed. With the encouragement of the Peloponnesians, the Athenian empire began to break up as Chios, Miletus and Lesbos, among other members, revolted against Athenian rule. Furthermore, in 411 BC, Sparta began to receive money with which to finance her fleet from a former enemy. Persia had greatly enjoyed watching the struggle between the very states which had once combined to defeat her. Now that it was obvious which way the tide was running, Persia offered subsidies to the Peloponnesians in return for renewed control over the Ionian cities of Asia Minor.

But, despite her losses at Syracuse and the perpetual threat from Decelea, Athens continued to fight stubbornly until 404 BC. With stringent economy in government expenditure, she managed, almost miraculously, to replace a substantial part of her fleet. Also remarkable was the decision to recall the homesick Alcibiades, who fully justified his recall by defeating the main Peloponnesian fleet off Cyzicus in 410 BC and capturing Byzantium in 407 BC. In the meantime, Sparta rebuilt its fleet, received subsidies from Persia for the hire of mercenary seamen and appointed a new commander, the ambitious, unscrupulous Lysander, who ended Alcibiades' good fortune by inflicting a heavy defeat on the Athenians at Notium in Asia Minor. In one last remarkable effort, Athens replaced her naval losses and won a crushing victory over the Peloponnesian fleet near the Arginusae islands, but it was to be her last victory. In 405 BC, Lysander inflicted an irreversible defeat on the Athenian fleet at Aegospotami in the Hellespont after which he blockaded Piraeus while Spartan land forces under King Pausanius laid siege to Athens itself. After six months of misery and hunger, the Athenians surrendered in April 404 BC and the great Peloponnesian War came to an end.

Sparta, the self-declared champion of autonomy, now imposed military governors and garrisons in all areas under her control. She suppressed nearly all democratic governments and replaced them with oppressive oligarchies which, in retrospect, made Athenian dominance look somewhat benevolent. Athens was required to tear down the Long Walls and surrender her surviving battle fleet, save for twelve triremes for coastal surveillance. Henceforth, Athens was to be a member of the Peloponnesian League and was required to conform to the dictates of Sparta's foreign policy. Sparta was, for the moment, supreme throughout Greece but, being a military rather than commercial power, she derived little benefit from her ascendancy. Thebes did rather better. She enriched herself with loot taken during raids into Attica and made huge profits from the resale of captured Athenian goods which she had purchased at very cheap prices from her Spartan ally. The commerce of other states, especially Megara, was effectively ruined. In effect, the real beneficiary of the long and bloody war between the Greek states was Persia. She had recovered the Ionian possessions taken from her by the combined action of Sparta and Athens. The Spartan victory brought peace, at least temporarily, but it also ended any possibility of creating a united Greece. Athenian policy had tended towards political unification, whereas Sparta was interested neither in political unification nor autonomy. At length, Athens, Thebes, Corinth and Argos all rebelled against her harsh domination and the Spartans were finally defeated at Leuctra by the Thebans, much to the surprise of other Greek states, in 371 BC.

The Peloponnesian War had an irreversible effect on traditional Greek military organisation. In cities other than Sparta, the service demanded of eligible males had hitherto represented no more than a temporary interruption of an essentially civilian way of life. In other words, the conscripts were amateur soldiers and their *strategoi* were amateur generals drawn from the upper echelons of society. They were elected for the duration of an emergency on the basis of their social standing, popularity, courage, capacity for leadership and past military experience. But military expertise was not necessarily a prerequisite for election. The *strategoi* were more often than not elected for their ability to inspire and lead rather than for their generalship.

For that matter, the art of command was still a rudimentary affair. The concept of holding troops in reserve until the critical stage of a battle was largely unknown. Hoplite battles consisted of a direct clash on level ground between two armies of identically armed men. Specialist light troops were generally regarded with disdain and rarely used to maximum advantage. The *strategoi* deployed their men and immediately committed the entire force to a confrontation with the enemy. They promptly lost any overall direction of the ensuing battle by joining in the action, sometimes with dire personal consequences. Generals were rarely concerned with long-term strategy. Like conscripted soldiers throughout the Ancient World, Greek militiamen were keen to get back to civilian pursuits. Before the Peloponnesian War, Greek military operations were short, simple and amateurish. Twenty-seven years of almost continuous war, however, led to a transition from amateur to professional, from militia to mercenary.

The process of change was perhaps inevitable. The Peloponnesian War entailed not just an inordinately long period of time but also vaster distances and more complex campaigns than those to which the Greeks had been accustomed. Long-distance campaigns, such as the Syracusan expedition and Brasidas' foray into Thrace, required men prepared to travel extensively and fight well beyond the limits of the traditional campaigning season; in short, men willing to be professional soldiers. The Spartans took the first step towards the mercenarisation of wars fought within Greek territory. Unwilling to despatch their citizen army too far from home, they recruited paid citizen volunteers, freed helots and Arcadian mercenaries for long-distance attacks on Athenian possessions. Athens, which had already employed Thracian light troops well before the Persian War, followed suit by hiring mercenary hoplites from the Peloponnesus.

Another development which contributed to the mercenarisation of Greek warfare was the increasingly important role played by lightly armed troops who were very often professional fighting men. Although they were generally considered by the hoplites to be inferior soldiers, they became a significant factor in the conduct and the outcome of battles. There were several types of light troops, the most common being archers, slingers and peltast javelin men. For all the apparent simplicity of their weapons, light troops were specialist soldiers. Their way of fighting entailed a much higher degree of specialisation than the relatively straightforward spear-and-shield techniques of hoplites fighting in formation. Peltasts' tactics were based on speedier and more complex manoeuvres and, as a consequence, required more intensive and prolonged training. The accurate use of missile weapons was a skill acquired and maintained by regular if not constant practice. For this reason, light troops tended to be professionals. They were either foreign mercenaries mainly from Thrace, Crete and Rhodes or they were natives (*psiloi*) recruited from the impoverished lower classes of a particular city-state. They were enticed into military service solely by the prospect of pay and the consequent alleviation of their grinding poverty. Unlike the hoplites, these native troops were not militiamen motivated by a sense of obligation.

Athens was the first to transform some of its poorer citizens into light troops and her motives were economic. Foreign light troops were expensive and could not normally be hired in very large numbers. But natives could be recruited and trained to perform the same specialised functions provided by foreign light-armed mercenaries and, most importantly, they could be paid at a much lower rate of remuneration. Their professionalism was partly a product of their specialist skill and training but it was also encouraged by the very length of the Peloponnesian War. Once recruited the *psiloi* tended to stay recruited. After all, there was more money and food to be had as a low-ranking soldier than as a hopelessly poor civilian. Contrary to expectations, heavily armed footsoldiers did not always acquit themselves very well in encounters with light troops. Thus, for example, when the Athenian general Demosthenes invaded Aetolia in 426 BC with an army largely composed of hoplites, he expected an easy victory over an enemy army almost entirely made up of lightly armed troops. Instead, the invading army was routed by the Aetolians.

Greek hoplite militiamen did not generally welcome the growing presence of light troops in the armies of the city-states. It was not so much that a good peltast was a better soldier than a good hoplite. The amazing defeats inflicted on hoplite armies by lightly armed forces were, as noted, exceptional events. They were indications of the tactical skill of the winning general rather than symbolic of the superiority of the peltast over the hoplite. Such victories were won in geographical conditions favouring the light troops; that is, broken and hilly ground which prevented the hoplite phalanx from operating as a cohesive unit and enabled the attackers to pour down stones, arrows and javelins with little fear of being caught or killed by opponents in heavy armour. But there was no question as to the superiority of hoplites fighting together in unbroken ranks over level ground. Peltasts were certainly capable of closing in and cutting down dispirited and panic-stricken individuals or small groups of hoplites who had become separated from the main phalanx but no army of light troops could stand and fight shoulder-to-shoulder against an array of armoured hoplites with levelled spears. The damage inflicted by light troops was achieved by repeatedly attacking and then yielding quickly, much as the constant crashing and subsiding of ocean waves gradually wears down the hardest of rocks.

To some extent, the hoplites despised light troops because they were either foreigners or they were drawn from the lower, often poverty-stricken, classes of Greek society, while they themselves came from higher social strata. But the negative attitude of the hoplites *vis-à-vis* the peltasts was not just a function of the lower social status of the latter. They disapproved of what they considered to be the dishonourable fighting methods employed by the peltasts and they disdained weapons that killed indiscriminately at a distance. To meet the enemy eye to eye on level ground, to fight and die if need be for one's comrades was the supreme ideal for a hoplite, one that ultimately derived from Homeric times. There was no room for those afraid to meet an opponent man-to-man. But the reality was that peltast fighting techniques were effective, even though they might be below the dignity of the hoplites. Light troops were a fact of military life that could not be ignored and the more able generals learnt how to use them to best advantage. Thus, Demosthenes quickly drew conclusions from his defeat by the light-armed Aetolians and began to employ light troops on a much larger scale in coordination with heavy infantry. Using the very same ambush tactics that had routed his own force in Aetolia, he won several spectacular victories against the Spartans.

The very presence of specialist light troops was one factor that encouraged the rise of professional generalship, for the proper handling of such troops required something more than amateur leadership. The Peloponnesian War produced men who became generals by profession alongside thousands of rank and file hoplite militiamen who opted for the mercenary life. The militias had been more or less permanently mobilised during the seemingly interminable conflict. When peace finally came, the hoplites were disbanded and left to their own devices. There were those whose skills and financial position must have allowed them to resume civilian life if they so desired. But there were many hoplites who had known no other way of life than military service and who were literally good for nothing else. Some of them had acquired a taste for adventure and bloodshed and were psychologically incapable of re-entering a more peaceful mode of existence. Others were motivated by sheer poverty. These men had already been poor before the war or they had become poor through the loss of property and possessions during its long and bitter course. Either way, they had little or nothing to return to. There were also considerable numbers of displaced persons and exiles in various Greek cities, desperate people who had few options other than to seek work as professional soldiers. Wars, and especially long wars, breed mercenaries.

Population pressure also encouraged the growth of mercenary service. Despite the losses suffered during the war, Greece remained a heavily over-populated region. Over-population had already been a problem for several centuries given the scarcity of natural resources in the Greek peninsula. Farming lands had rarely, if ever, produced sufficient food for the total population at any particular period. The classical solution to the problem of population pressure had been the foundation of colonies, but, by the beginning of the fourth century BC, nearly all the available overseas territories had been occupied. Thus, many Greeks who might have found a relatively peaceful way of life in colonial settlements now saw mercenary soldiering as the only alternative to abject poverty and starvation.[17]

The exact number of people who turned to mercenary service during or after the Peloponnesian War cannot be determined with absolute precision but it is not unreasonable to suggest that, around 400 BC, at least 20,000 mercenaries were active in the eastern Mediterranean area.[18] In 401 BC, the Persian satrap, Cyrus, was able to recruit 13,000 volunteers for his ill-fated expedition against Artaxerxes II, but it is unlikely that he managed to recruit every single mercenary available at the time. There were many Greek mercenaries who were already gainfully employed by other Persian satraps or by local Greek paymasters. At any rate, whatever the total number of mercenaries may have been, it was certainly in excess of 13,000 men and was probably closer to the estimate of 25,000 suggested by the American historian, M. I. Finlay (an estimate he later increased to 50,000).[19]

There had been several precedents for Cyrus' employment of Greek mercenaries. Other satraps had also appreciated Hellenic military prowess and had recruited hoplites for self-protection and, indeed, for insurrection. What made the affair of 401 BC different from earlier incidents was its scale. Never before had such a large number of Greek mercenaries been brought together as a single unit. Most commonly known as the 'Ten Thousand', despite their actual number, Cyrus' Greek troops constituted a substantial army in their own right. After the death of Cyrus at Cunaxa and the dispersal of his Asiatic contingents, the Greeks were unexpectedly thrown on their own resources and were forced to act as an independent group in order to survive. The march of the Ten Thousand deep into the heart of the Persian empire and their perilous retreat was one of the most famous episodes of ancient Greek history and deserves a chapter in itself.

CHAPTER EIGHT

Greece and Persia:
The Ten Thousand

THREE GREEK eye-witnesses are known to have written detailed descriptions of Cyrus' expedition but only one – that of Xenophon – has survived in its entirety. The accounts of Ctesias of Cnidus, Artaxerxes' doctor, and Sophaenetus of Stymphalus, an Arcadian general of the Ten Thousand, have been lost save for a few brief and enigmatic fragments which sometimes confirm and sometimes contradict the story found in Xenophon's *Anabasis*. Also at variance with the *Anabasis* is the account written by Diodorus Siculus in the first century BC. His chief source was the *Universal History* of Ephorus, a work produced in the fourth century BC of which, unfortunately, not a single word has survived into the present era.

Written partly as an apologia by an ageing man looking back thirty years into the past, the *Anabasis* suffers from a number of serious shortcomings. In common with other Greek commentators, Xenophon greatly exaggerates the size of Persian forces with the usual aim of glorifying Greek capabilities and denigrating those of the enemy. His account contains occasional geographic inaccuracies and questionable details. It also contains an immoderate amount of self-adulation. Xenophon mentions Xenophon some 230 times from Book III onwards and quotes twenty of his speeches, all of which are considerably longer and more inspiring that those of his fellow-generals. The worthy Athenian did undoubtedly play a major role during the retreat of the Ten Thousand and the magnification of his own importance may well be an accurate depiction of events. However, Xenophon was but one of five new generals chosen to replace the initial Greek leadership which had been murdered by the Persian satrap Tissaphernes. At best, he might have been *primus inter pares* or perhaps he was merely 'one of the boys'. The available evidence, scanty though it might be, suggests the latter.[1] Diodorus, paraphrasing Ephorus, does not mention Xenophon at all.

Despite its imperfections, the *Anabasis* is probably the single most valuable document written by a mercenary about mercenaries. At its most superficial level it remains a highly readable adventure story, rich in detail. But it is also a study of human characters, motives and ambitions. The Greeks described by Xenophon are not an anonymous collection of mercenaries, but a lively and individualistic group, a self-contained society of soldiers who are responsible only to themselves. Xenophon did not, needless to say, record the names of every participant. A list of 13,000 names would have filled up a volume in itself, not to mention made rather dull reading, and Xenophon could not have been familiar with every soldier in the expedition. At the same time, he did not limit himself to naming a few high-ranking officers. The names of humble hoplites appear alongside those of generals and captains.

Cyrus raised his mercenary army in secret and in separate groups and locations. He had to conceal his actual intentions for as long as he could, both from Artaxerxes on the one hand and his Greek recruits on the other. Once he had raised sufficient forces, Cyrus proclaimed his apparent intention to attack the hill tribesmen of Pisidia who had often proved troublesome to the Persian satraps and also announced a private war against his fellow satrap and enemy, Tissaphernes. Wars between Persian governors were not unknown. Indeed, dynastic feuds had bedevilled the Persian empire ever since its foundation by Cyrus the Great. Thus, the younger Cyrus' stated intention seemed plausible enough and Artaxerxes seems to have accepted his military preparations at face value. Cunningly, Cyrus made a great show of fraternal loyalty by sending regular quantities of tribute from cities under his control to the king in Persepolis. Thus, Artaxerxes did not suspect that his younger brother was less than totally devoted to the promotion of family solidarity. The Greeks also had to be deceived, otherwise they might well refuse to participate in an insurrection against a legitimate monarch. As it happened, Tissaphernes readily suspected that Cyrus' preparations were much too large for a private squabble while the Greeks did indeed rebel when they discovered their true mission.

Cyrus' recruiters ranged far and wide throughout Greece, the Aegean Islands and Ionia. Peloponnesians made up over 50 per cent of the assembled hoplites (some 6,000 out of 10,000 men).[2] Cyrus was fully aware of the reputation established by Arcadian and Achaean mercenary hoplites. His own bodyguard included 300 Arcadians commanded by Xenias of Parrhasia and it was around this nucleus that he built up his mercenary forces. Recruits for the Ten Thousand also came from Sparta, Athens, Megara, Argos, Boeotia, Thessaly, Acarnania, Elis, Samos, Chios, Rhodes, Crete and Amphipolis, among other locations in the Greek world. Alongside the heavy infantry were some 2,400 light troops, which included 1,400 Greek peltasts, 800 Thracian peltasts and 200 Cretan archers.[3] Thus, some three years after the end of the Peloponnesian War, men who had recently been on opposite sides now came together to follow the mercenary profession in the service of a Persian prince.

With the exception of Cyrus' Arcadian guards and some other Peloponnesians, relatively few of the Greek hoplites appear to have been professional mercenaries of long-standing experience. The light troops were probably experienced mercenaries but the *Anabasis* identifies only one hoplite – the Laconian Perioec, Dexippus, who in 406 BC had led a band of mercenaries in the service of Syracuse. He had already established a reputation for unreliability before joining Cyrus' army and subsequently lived up to his reputation by deserting from the Ten Thousand during the retreat. Later, Dexippus met a suitable end, killed by the Spartan Nicander as a result of his involvement in intrigues at the court of the Thracian king. The fact that there is only one solid reference to an experienced mercenary hoplite in the *Anabasis* does not in itself prove the near absence of professional soldiers of fortune. There may well have been others not identified by Xenophon but it is nevertheless reasonable to conclude that the majority of the Ten Thousand, even the preponderant Arcadians, had been former militiamen rather than mercenaries.

Arcadia was certainly a long-established recruiting ground for mercenaries but during the Peloponnesian War there had been little need for young and adventurous Arcadians to enter into overseas mercenary service in emulation of their fathers, grandfathers or distant ancestors. Intervals of peace were extremely short and Arcadian hoplites found ample employment opportunities and excitement at home in the service of their own state. Furthermore in 401 BC the mercenarisation of warfare within Greece was not yet far advanced. During the Peloponnesian War, the rival states had found mercenaries increasingly useful but, on the whole, hired soldiers such as the Arcadians remained in the minority in most armies and the conflict was fought essentially with hoplite militiamen. The Spartans, of course, were full-time professionals but most were not mercenary soldiers. The process of mercenarisation did not really gather momentum until the early decades of the following century. When Cyrus recruited his troops, there was not yet a large, organised and permanent body of experienced mercenaries available for hire on a systematic basis. Even in Arcadia, recruiters seem to have gone from town to town or deep into the countryside looking for hoplites willing to work in remote locations. During the fourth century certain specific towns became famous, or perhaps, notorious, as open markets where unemployed mercenaries habitually congregated in large numbers while waiting for offers of work. Prospective employers could go to towns like Taenarum on the southern Peloponnesian coast and raise substantial forces of mercenaries on the spot. Taenarum was established in Spartan territory, not Arcadia, with the full approval and cooperation of the Spartan government. Alarmed by an ever-decreasing birthrate and a reduction in hoplite numbers, the authorities were forced to rely more and more on the recruitment of mercenaries to build up the Spartan army. Taenarum, a Spartan naval base, acquired a reputation as the best mercenary market in Greece. After the Macedonian invasion of Greece, Taenarum became the gathering point for anti-Macedonian mercenaries by virtue of its geographical location, which made it virtually impregnable to land attack.[4]

In Cyrus' time, however, such towns as Taenarum had scarcely come into existence or not at all. At least, there are no references to mercenary market places in fifth-century texts. It will be remembered that Cyrus' mercenaries came from nearly every part of the Greek world and not from a single town specialised in supplying mercenary hoplites for hire. Given these circumstances, it is not particularly surprising that many of the Ten Thousand were entering mercenary service for the very first time. Their commander-in-chief, Clearchus, had, however, done a great deal of fighting and, as Xenophon describes, he was extraordinarily devoted to war for its own sake.[5] Nevertheless, Clearchus, like many of his men, was a novice mercenary. His extensive experience of warfare had been in the service of his own city-state and it was not until his exile from Sparta and his fatal involvement with Cyrus that he became a mercenary soldier. Cyrus' Greeks may well have been newcomers to the mercenary trade, as implied in the *Anabasis*, but they were not inexperienced as soldiers. The Peloponnesian War had seen to that.

Like most civil conflicts, the Peloponnesian War had produced large numbers of exiles. Consequently, some of the Ten Thousand were men who had become *personae non gratae* in their home states and were forced to seek a livelihood elsewhere. Exactly how many recruits came to Cyrus motivated by the bitterness and desperation of exile remains unclear. Xenophon mentions very few such men by name and implies that exiles were not numerous in the Ten Thousand.[6] Apart from Clearchus, who had been exiled for ignoring orders from the Spartan government, there were Dracontius, also from Sparta, Archagoras from Argos and Gaulites from Samos.

A few professional mercenaries; a few exiles; a lot of former militiamen: such were the soldiers who made up the Ten Thousand. What were their motives? Naturally enough, Xenophon saw his colleagues as something more than a mere collection of impoverished men attracted by the prospect of making money. His comments, however, are somewhat ambiguous. On the one hand, he records that some participants brought servants with them, the implication being that they were already wealthy enough to afford servants and that such people also expended more money than was absolutely necessary on their arms and equipment.[7] Xenophon lavishes praise on Clearchus as a man devoted to the art of warfare rather than money:

> He could have lived in peace . . . but he chose to make war. He could have lived a life of ease, but he preferred a hard life with warfare. He could have had money and security, but he chose to make the money he had less, by engaging in war. Indeed he liked spending money on war just as one might spend it on love affairs or any other pleasure.[8]

Xenophon plainly rejects poverty as a motive for the Ten Thousand. And yet, almost in the same breath, he implies that money was indeed a primary influence:

> Most of the soldiers had joined up for this service because they had heard accounts of Cyrus' generosity and not because they had been hard up. [Some recruits] had left fathers and mothers or children behind at home with the idea of coming back again with the money to give them, since they had heard that the other Greeks with Cyrus were doing very well for themselves.[9]

Clearly Xenophon cannot have it both ways. There were undoubtedly recruits like Clearchus for whom money was a secondary motive – men who lived for war, any war, anywhere, any time and could never get enough blood and adventure. Clearchus was not the first to exhibit this particular mentality nor was he by any means the last. On balance, however, and with respect to the venerable Xenophon, deracination, the insecurity of life at home, disillusionment with the harsh oligarchies set up by a victorious Sparta and, not least important, the prospect of bringing money home to their families – Xenophon says it himself – must have been the main motives of the majority of Cyrus' Greeks. If the recruits were not hard up, as Xenophon claims, why would they bother to leave family and friends for the uncertainty and rigours of a long-distance foreign expedition? How many of them shared Clearchus' passionate pleasure in war for the sake of war? Once the expedition had begun, there were at least two occasions on which the Greek rank-and-file refused to march any further unless they were guaranteed an increase in pay. Hardly the behaviour of men uninterested in financial gain. Writing around 380 BC, when the mercenarisation of Greek warfare was much more advanced, the Athenian orator Isocrates regarded the Ten Thousand as scoundrels too base to earn a living in their own land.[10] Isocrates hated mercenaries in general and mercenaries who served the Persians in particular. He advocated a Greek crusade against the Persian empire. But Cyrus' Greeks were neither the mere rabble suggested by Isocrates nor the disinterested volunteers described by Xenophon. Some of them might well have been totally uneducated and incapable of any other activity but fighting. Others, however, and especially the Athenians, must have possessed some degree of education. Xenophon, although no intellectual, had studied under the guidance of the philosopher Socrates, and must have acquired a modicum of learning, despite the fact that Xenophon was later critical of his teacher. The Ten Thousand, then, were a diverse collection of men, more or less motivated by the chance of improving their financial status and their lot in life.

With his reputation for generosity, Cyrus was an attractive employer. Even though he had to operate discreetly, he experienced little trouble recruiting sufficient numbers of hoplites and light troops. Perhaps it was not money alone that attracted some of the Greeks. Cyrus was undoubtedly a charismatic leader and a good judge of character. Furthermore, he understood the psychology of the Greeks. He appreciated their fighting qualities, understood their sense of superiority over Asiatic troops and knew how to flatter them. He was a complex character – wily, perceptive, ambitious, cruel and vindictive towards his enemies; loyal and generous to his tried and trusted friends. He was a *bon vivant*, fond of good wine and food, which he often shared with those close to his heart. Such was their appreciation that practically all of his table companions died fighting for him at the battle of Cunaxa. Cyrus had a reputation for magnanimity that was occasionally justified but was more often apparent rather than real. He ruled his satrapy with an extreme severity somewhat reminiscent of Hammurabi and did not hesitate to order the blinding or mutilation of law breakers. Cyrus punished cowardice and lavishly rewarded those who displayed courage, talent and fidelity with governorships, gaudery and gold.

> Generals and captains who crossed the sea to take service under him as mercenaries knew that to do Cyrus good service paid better than any monthly wage. Indeed, whenever anyone carried out effectively a job which he had assigned, he never allowed his good work to go unrewarded. Consequently it was said that Cyrus got the best officers for any kind of job.[11]

To round off his admirable qualities, Cyrus was an enthusiastic amateur gardener who took time off from cultivating political ambitions to contemplate the growth of flowers.

Cyrus concentrated the bulk of his forces at Sardis in western Anatolia. He had in excess of 35,000 Oriental troops of which the infantry was under the command of the Persian general Ariaeus. There were 3,200 cavalry, including 600 horsemen of Cyrus' guard. Contingents of hoplites and light troops recruited by Greek mercenary captains arrived in Sardis one after another. Xenias the Arcadian brought the largest group, some 4,000 hoplites. Proxenus, a Theban mercenary commander, reached the city with 1,500 hoplites and 500 peltasts of unspecified origin. Then came Sophaenetus of Stymphalus, bringing 1,000 hoplites. Socrates the Achaean (not Xenophon's teacher) contributed some 500 hoplites. Pasion of Megara brought 300 hoplites and 300 peltasts. The origin of the latter is also unspecified by Xenophon but they were most likely Greek nationals given the preponderance of Greeks among the light troops recruited for the Ten Thousand.[12]

With these forces, Cyrus set out on a meandering march through Phrygia, to maintain as long as possible the illusion that his campaign was aimed at the Pisidians. His enemy, Tissaphernes, however, was not deceived. Cyrus' army was much too large for a mere punitive expedition against recalcitrant tribesmen and the satrap immediately travelled to Artaxerxes' capital at Susa (formerly the capital city of Elam) to inform the king of his well-founded suspicions. Turning south-east, Cyrus arrived at the Phrygian city of Colossae, where he was joined by another 1,000 hoplites and 500 peltasts led by the Thessalian mercenary captain Menon. Xenophon describes Menon, a bitter rival of Clearchus, in less-than-flattering terms as a cynical liar and cheat obsessed with acquiring wealth and honours. Owing to his intense dislike of Menon and his respect for Clearchus Xenophon undoubtedly exaggerated his description but it must, nevertheless, have contained some element of truth, just as the most insidious, effective and persuasive propaganda nearly always includes a modicum of truth, no matter how distorted. If Menon was as ambitious, greedy and perfidious as claimed by Xenophon, then he was even more of a mercenary than Clearchus, for whom material reward was supposedly subordinate to the sheer joy of fighting.

Cyrus moved on from Colossae in a north-easterly direction to the city of Celaenae where he spent nearly one month and received further reinforcements. Clearchus himself arrived with 1,000 hoplites, 800 Thracian peltasts and 200 Cretan archers, while Sosis the Syracusan also joined the army, bringing 300 hoplites.[13] Cyrus' army, now almost fully assembled, continued to march northwards away from Pisidia towards Agora and Keramon, cities that lay on the northern borders of Phrygia. His route must have puzzled both his hoplites and his enemies. Gradually, however, he turned eastwards and arrived at the city of Cayster Plain, where he encountered his first problem.

Cyrus had expended a considerable fortune in raising his mercenary forces and had liberally supplied his Greek recruiters with money. Clearchus, for example, received 10,000 darics, which Cyrus had obtained from the cities under his control. Now, however, his funds were running low and his mercenaries chose the moment to demand their pay, which was already three months in arrears. Cyrus was short of money but not of promises. The Greeks, however, wanted something more substantial and continued to demand their back pay, implying that their further participation in the expedition might be in doubt.

At this point, Epyaxa, the Queen of Cilicia, came to Cyrus' financial rescue, so that he was able to distribute four months' pay to his anxious mercenaries. The good queen had been sent by her husband, Syennesis IV, who was determined to be on the winning side of the struggle between Cyrus and Artaxerxes. He would make a great show of loyalty to the older brother by garrisoning mountain passes that lay along Cyrus' line of march while his wife showed the younger brother alternative routes by which he could outflank Syennesis' trooops. The Cilician queen's generosity did not end with her well-timed monetary donation. Her relationship with Cyrus rapidly went beyond the bounds of a purely platonic association.

His Greek mercenaries temporarily satisfied, Cyrus was able to continue his south-westerly march through Ipsus and Thymbrion. At the next city,

Tyriaeon, a somewhat comic incident confirmed Cyrus' faith in the martial abilities of the Greeks, if indeed any confirmation was needed. When Epyaxa expressed a desire to review Cyrus' army, he duly paraded his entire force and drove along its front in a chariot, while the queen followed in a covered carriage. The Greeks must have been an impressive sight in their bronze armour and uniformly attired in red tunics, their shields uncovered to reveal their various devices and decorations. They became even more impressive when, at a given signal from Cyrus, the Greeks began to advance in battle formation, heightening the effect with loud yells. Perhaps it was a manoeuvre designed to impress the assembled crowd of local citizens or a Persian idea of a practical joke, but the sight of thousands of shouting Greeks bearing down upon them with levelled spears and seemingly possessed by a lunatic frenzy proved too much for Cyrus' charming benefactor and her entourage. All the spectators fled in a considerable state of panic, not at all amused. Cyrus, however, was delighted. He could confidently expect a repeat performance with a much more important result when he confronted Artaxerxes.[14]

Inexorably, the confrontation drew closer, as Cyrus marched on from Phrygia to Lycaonia, a territory which the satrap's army thoroughly plundered. All the while, King Syennesis kept up the pretence of opposing Cyrus' advance while Greek troops led by Menon and guided by the queen marched by a shorter more southerly route to circumvent the Cilician troops.

The Greek mercenaries had suspected for some time that Cyrus was aiming at a much more substantial enemy than troublesome Pisidian hill tribes. This was not such a difficult conclusion to reach given that Pisidia now lay behind them and each day's march had taken them further away from their ostensible destination. They were now more or less convinced that the real purpose of the enterprise was the dethronement of a legitimate monarch whose capital lay at a distance of three months' march from the Aegean sea coast deep in the centre of Asia. Thus, the Greeks refused to advance any further and no amount of coercion by Clearchus could induce them to change their minds. Clearchus changed tactic, making an impassioned and lachrymose speech which Xenophon quotes, or rather, reconstructs, at some length in Book I of the *Anabasis*.[15] His stratagem was effective, for the assembled hoplites resolved to send a deputation to Cyrus to ascertain his real intentions. Cyrus again deceived the Greeks by claiming that he intended to attack his inveterate enemy, the satrap of Syria, Abrocomas, Artaxerxes' bastard brother. This sly declaration was plausible enough since Abrocomas had an army complete with his own Greek mercenaries stationed in northern

Syria. Cyrus' Greeks reluctantly agreed to continue the march, only half-convinced by his explanation, not without first having obtained a pay increase of three half-darics per soldier instead of the original one daric a month.

The crisis resolved, Cyrus continued to penetrate eastwards to the seaport of Issus, where he received a final reinforcement of 700 Lacedaemonian hoplites under Chirisophus. These troops had been transported from Ephesus by sea in twenty-five of Cyrus' triremes commanded by Tamos the Egyptian. At Issus, Cyrus received an unexpected bonus when the 400 hoplites employed by Abrocomas deserted in order to join his own forces.[16]

Leaving Cilicia behind, Cyrus' army passed unimpeded through the narrow mountain pass known as the Syrian Gates and entered Syria itself. Abrocomas, perhaps disconcerted by the desertion of his Greek mercenaries, failed to defend the pass and allowed Cyrus to penetrate into his own satrapy. Abrocomas retreated not directly towards Artaxerxes' forces but in an apparently circuitous and somewhat puzzling way which resulted in his rejoining Artaxerxes some five days after the climactic battle of Cunaxa, just in time to savour victory without having exposed himself to possible defeat.

When Cyrus reached the Phoenician seaport of Myriandrus, two of his Greek generals deserted. Xenias the Arcadian, who had originally recruited 4,000 hoplites, and Pasion of Megara boarded a trireme and promptly disappeared, taking their accumulated loot. In an act of magnanimity calculated to impress the other Greeks, Cyrus made a point of not punishing the women and children left behind by the two deserters, nor did he pursue them.[17]

From Myriandrus, Cyrus' army moved inland across northern Syria, reaching the famous Euphrates river at Thapsacus. With Abrocomas nowhere in sight, Cyrus could no longer dissimulate the real objective of his campaign. Again, the ordinary hoplites refused to march any further unless they received yet another increase in pay. Cyrus promised that each mercenary would receive five minae of silver, an amount equivalent to 500 Attic drachmas or about four months' pay. While the Greeks were still deciding whether or not to continue, Menon took the initiative by leading his contingent across the Euphrates. By a remarkable coincidence, the river level was unusually low and Menon's men were able to reach the eastern bank on foot without having to use the boats normally required for the crossing. Pleased with Menon's manoeuvre, Cyrus himself crossed the river and the rest of his army soon followed. A third crisis had been resolved but a fourth one arose shortly thereafter when Clearchus ordered the beating of one of Menon's soldiers as a result of a quarrel between the hoplites of Menon and those of Clearchus. Embittered by Clearchus' action one of Menon's hoplites threw an axe at him as he rode through Menon's camp later in the day. Although the missile missed its intended target, a shower of stones thrown by other hoplites convinced Clearchus that his presence among Menon's troops was unwelcome. Already unpopular owing to his harshness and his severe punishments, Clearchus was forced to seek shelter among his own troops. A fight appeared imminent as Clearchus led his Thracian peltasts and Thracian cavalry towards Menon's camp, but a sanguinary outcome was avoided by the timely arrival of the Theban general Proxenus, who positioned his hoplites between the two rival groups. Cyrus himself arrived and reminded the Greeks that dissension among them could only lead to disaster. Both sides saw the wisdom of Cyrus' words and withdrew. Both this incident and Menon's earlier crossing of the Euphrates on his own initiative clearly show that, up until the moment when they were thrown on their own resources after Cunaxa, the Greeks in Cyrus' army had a sense of belonging to distinct and separate contingents.[18] Their generals were rivals struggling for pre-eminence, both in the eyes of the entire Greek force and those of Cyrus.

In Babylonia, King Artaxerxes finally realised the magnitude of the threat posed by Cyrus' slow but inexorable advance along the course of the Euphrates. He had been tardy in mobilising his own forces and had expected Abrocomas to join him so that their combined armies could resist Cyrus at some suitable location, such as an irrigation trench or a defensive wall. He had not expected that his younger brother would penetrate so deeply into his empire and yet Cyrus had managed to overcome all the natural and artificial obstacles that lay in his path. Abrocomas had proved worse than useless and Artaxerxes could no longer wait for him to arrive. The king marched his army northwards to confront Cyrus. He hesitated at first to make contact with the invading forces, but finally the two brothers met at the village of Cunaxa to settle their differences on a permanent basis.

It is not easy to reconstruct the actual sequence of events at Cunaxa. The accounts of Xenophon, Sophaenetus and Diodorus (*pace* Ephorus) all differ in detail and contain claims that are improbable at best and, more likely, impossible. The behaviour of Cyrus and Artaxerxes is accorded quite different treatment from one version to another. Xenophon claims that Artaxerxes continued to lead his troops despite a wound inflicted by Cyrus himself, while Doctor Ctesias recounts that he treated the wound and that the king subsequently withdrew to a nearby hill to obtain some rest – a much more likely occurrence given the apparent severity of the injury.

Xenophon's description of Cunaxa is plainly unreliable on several counts, beginning with his utterly exaggerated claim for the size of Artaxerxes' army. The Persian king certainly did not have the 900,000 men claimed by Xenophon.[19] Contrary to the impressions created by the venerable Greek, ancient armies were rarely very large, their size being limited by the logistic problems posed by the maintenance of a large army. Artaxerxes could not have had more than 100,000 men and more likely had not much more than half this number.[20] The very fact that he chose to wait for Abrocomas, albeit in vain, and did not go out to confront Cyrus until the last possible moment suggests that the king's forces were not as large as he would have liked. Xenophon's fantastic figure was yet another instance of exaggeration aimed at making the Greek victory over the Persian left even more remarkable and reinforcing the idea – deeply rooted in the Greek mind – of the innate ability of hoplites to stand up to any number of lacklustre Asiatic troops.

In battle, Persian rulers normally stationed themselves in the centre of their battle lines so as to be able to exert an equal measure of control over the left and right wings of their armies in so far as was possible under battle conditions. Thus, following traditional practice, both Cyrus and Artaxerxes stationed themselves in the centre of their respective armies. On the insurgent side, Cyrus' centre was made up of his line and guard cavalry, with his Asiatic infantry under Ariaeus on the left and the Greeks under Clearchus on the right.

What did happen at Cunaxa as the two multi-national armies came into contact? Towards midday on an unspecified day in September, 401 BC, the king's army began to advance silently and purposefully towards the insurgent army. The battle opened auspiciously enough for Cyrus when the Greeks moved menacingly and noisily towards the enemy directly opposite them, provoking a nearly instantaneous atmosphere of panic among the king's men. It was a repeat performance of their memorable review in honour of the Queen of Cilicia and was achieved at the cost of one hoplite wounded by an enemy archer.[21] The battle-hardened veterans of the Peloponnesian Wars had proved their value and Cyrus was already receiving premature congratulations from his officers now that the throne of Persia seemed within reach. Artaxerxes, however, did not panic and, seeing that the rest of Cyrus' army had not advanced along with the Greeks, orderd the right wing of his army to wheel towards the left in order to envelop Cyrus' Asiatic troops. Noticing the enemy movements, Cyrus immediately led his 600 horse guards in an impetuous attack against the king, leaving behind in his haste and enthusiasm his 2,000 line cavalry. The sheer audacity of the charge unnerved the men of Artaxerxes' guard and Cyrus' men sowed confusion and disorder among a force ten times their numbers. Cyrus struck down Artagerses, the enemy guard commander, and, catching sight of his brother, rode towards him with definite fratricidal intentions. Animated by his hatred, Cyrus wounded Artaxerxes, although not fatally, with a blow that penetrated the king's breast plate. At this point, he himself was severely wounded through the eye by an enemy soldier identified by Ctesias as a Carian mercenary in Artaxerxes' service. Falling from his horse he was soon despatched along with eight of his favourite table companions who had rushed to his defence. Shortly thereafter, Tissaphernes' cavalry and Egyptian heavy infantry mercenaries routed Cyrus' Oriental troops and looted the insurgent army's camp, save for that section allotted to the Greeks and defended by hoplites who had been expressly detached from the main Greek force in order to guard their baggage.

With their employer literally gone to pieces, the Greeks were suddenly and unexpectedly left to their own devices and were called upon to surrender their arms by Phalinus, a Greek mercenary in Tissaphernes' service. Some of them proposed that the entire army should simply change sides and seek employment with Artaxerxes, to be used, perhaps, on an expedition to secure Persian domination over Egypt. Clearchus, mistrustful of Tissaphernes, dissuaded the Greeks from pursuing this line of thought and persuaded them to retain their weapons. Despite the unfavourable turn of events, very few soldiers deserted to Artaxerxes; but 300 Thracian peltasts and some forty Thracian cavalry, convinced that the Greeks were in a hopeless situation, disappeared from the Greek camp.[22]

Artaxerxes might, of course, try to destroy the entire force by overwhelming them with superior numbers but, given the way his men had failed to perform in the face of Greek combat superiority, this option would undoubtedly be very costly. Yet the king had to get the mercenaries out of Babylonia as rapidly as possible. The very fact that they had so very nearly penetrated to the capital itself had clearly shown up Artaxerxes' weakness, not least in the eyes of potentially rebellious satraps and the subject peoples of the Persian empire. Central authority had already been weakened by the Persian defeat in Greece and now the formidable Greeks had come largely unhindered to threaten the peace of his realm. Furthermore, had Cyrus not been killed at Cunaxa, Artaxerxes could be in little doubt that he would no longer be enjoying the title of Great King, nor for that matter, any of the other joys of life. The Greeks had to go before his prestige was irrevocably damaged.

The Greeks wanted to go. The question was by which route. The way they had come was impractical for they had already bought or looted all the supplies that had been available. For the inhabitants of the villages, towns and cities along the line of march, an army on the move had much the same effect as a plague of locusts on a farming community. Artaxerxes declared a truce applicable both to the Greeks and to Ariaeus' Oriental contingents whom the Greeks had managed to rejoin after the battle. With the king's approval, or rather, connivance, Tissaphernes offered to guide the Greeks along an alternative route where supplies were supposedly plentiful. Despite their mistrust of the satrap, the Greeks allowed Tissaphernes to lead them out of Babylonia northwards along the course of the Tigris river, always keeping a safe distance from Tissaphernes' own troops. Their mistrust was well-founded for Tissaphernes' intention was to lead the Greeks out of Persian territory and into the wild and dangerous region of Armenia where they would hopefully be destroyed by hostile mountain tribesmen. The Persians would thereby be spared the trouble of having to do the job themselves. The Greeks marched warily fearing that Tissaphernes might find some advantageous position from which to launch an attack against them. Ariaeus' men now marched and camped with those of Tissaphernes, a circumstance which did nothing to decrease Greek suspicions. The Greeks kept a constant watch on the movements of the Persians and the Persians reciprocated.

When both armies stopped and made camp near the confluence of the Zapatas river (the Great Zab) with the Tigris, Clearchus obtained an interview with Tissaphernes to ascertain the satrap's intentions and to lessen the mutual suspicion that animated both armies. He reassured Tissaphernes that the Greeks had no other goal but to go home. But Clearchus' straightforward soldierly approach was no match for Tissaphernes' subtlety and cunning. The Spartan gullibly persuaded his fellow generals and some twenty officers and 200 hoplites to accept Tissaphernes' friendly invitation to a banquet to be held in their honour on the following day, with the result that, when the generals were safely inside Tissaphernes' tent, they were

[135]

arrested while the officers and men waiting outside were massacred at a given signal. The generals were conveyed to Babylon, where they were put on public display and then executed.[23]

Tissaphernes was well satisfied with his *coup*. He could reasonably expect that the Greek army would lose its morale, cohesion and discipline and might simply surrender. Under similar circumstances, an Oriental army – especially one deep in hostile territory – suddenly deprived of its leadership, tended to lose the will to fight, if not to dissolve into panic, as was the case with Ariaeus' troops at Cunaxa. Indeed, the Greeks did become despondent when they learnt of Tissaphernes' treachery – many being unable to eat or sleep – but for one night only. It was at this point that the difference between the Greek and the Oriental mind became manifestly clear. The Greek hoplites were prepared to obey leaders whom they trusted and respected, and individuals were leaders only so long as they were accepted as such by their men. This was true both of military and civilian leaders in the democratic city-states of Greece. Very few of the Greek mercenaries had had any affection for the stern and somewhat brutal Clearchus but they had appreciated his toughness, his courage and his ability to inspire confidence. Unlike that of Oriental soldiers, their obedience was founded on trust and was liable to be withdrawn if the *strategos* proved incompetent. Their acceptance of orders was more in the nature of acquiescence as fellow participants in a democratic process not as subjects of a despot.

The Greeks had followed their former employer, Cyrus, 2,400 kilometres from Sardis to Cunaxa, but not without questioning his motives – they had expressed dissatisfaction and the threat of desertion when their pay had failed to materialise. Now their democratic traditions enabled them to react to their new adversity in a way unthinkable to the Oriental mind: the *election* of new leaders. For Xenophon, this was where the story really started, for it was he who reminded the Greeks that Athens had stood alone against superior numbers at Marathon and had triumphed. He exhorted the surviving officers to show leadership, stating that men determined to die with honour and dignity often survived while those desperate to preserve their lives at any cost often got killed. He suggested that the Greeks should march out of Persian territory using their prisoners as guides rather than relying on any of Artaxerxes' officers. As for Cyrus' native troops, they had proved cowardly and unreliable and Tissaphernes was welcome to them. Finally, Xenophon advocated the election of new *strategoi* from among the remaining officers and new officers from among the rank and file hoplites. Thus, five new generals were duly elected, including Xenophon himself and the Spartan, Chirisophus, who was *primus inter pares*. The Greeks burnt all unnecessary impedimenta, formed themselves into a hollow square to protect their baggage and camp followers (servants, prisoners and large numbers of women) and continued their march along the eastern bank of the Tigris, with Xenophon and his fellow *strategos* Timasion, commanding the rearguard.[24]

As they marched, the Greeks were confronted by Mithridates, a former Persian general in Cyrus' army, who had suddenly become an enthusiastic supporter of Tissaphernes' point of view. He had been sent by the satrap to ascertain Greek intentions and to impress upon them the supposed impossibility of escaping from the king's territory. Undaunted, Chirisophus responded that, so long as they were left unmolested, the Greeks would march out peacefully, refraining as much as possible from destroying the lives and property of the king's subjects, but that a vigorous resistance would be offered to anyone who tried to impede the retreating army. The Greek generals decided to have no further negotiations with Persian ambassadors for it soon became obvious that Mithridates had been sent to induce Greeks to desert from the Ten Thousand. His success, however, was limited to the Arcadian officer Nicarchus and some twenty hoplites who disappeared during the night after his visit.[25] Although these desertions showed that the solidarity of the Greeks was not quite perfect, twenty or thirty hoplites and the 340 Thracians who had deserted just after the battle of Cunaxa represented a remarkably low rate out of an army of 13,000 men. There were no mass defections among the Ten Thousand, who were held together by a common danger, a common desire to survive and a common urge to go home. There was also that special sense of camaraderie and solidarity characteristic of and specific to soldiers, particularly those who have seen action on a battlefield, a sentiment only partly expressible in words and not fully comprehensible to civilian outsiders whose lives have never been at risk.

After the Greeks crossed the Zapatas river, Mithridates reappeared not for further diplomacy but to launch an attack on the square with 200 cavalry and 400 archers and slingers. On this occasion, the Greeks were unable to retaliate effectively against this relatively modest force and the rearguard suffered badly, although Xenophon does not specify the number of casualties. The Greeks had no cavalry, the Thracian horsemen having already deserted. Their Cretan archers were outranged by the Persians and their range was even further reduced by their being in the centre of the square. When the hoplites charged out of the square, their heavier armour slowed their pace so that they were unable to catch the Persian light troops. Satisfied with his attack and contemptuous of the Greek response, Mithridates withdrew, having concluded that the retreating army would be easy to wear down.

Xenophon suggested that the Greeks fight fire with fire and create cavalry and light troops to counter those of the Persians. The removal of the best horses from the baggage train resulted in a cavalry force of some fifty men and at Xenophon's initiative a force of 200 slingers was selected from among the army's Rhodian hoplites. The sling had long been a characteristic weapon on the island of Rhodes and the Rhodians, who were in the habit of using leaden bullets instead of the usual stones, would be able to cast their missiles at nearly twice the range available to their opponents. In effect, when Mithridates returned with 1,000 cavalry and 4,000 archers he received a nasty surprise when the modest Greek force of desperate and determined men sallied out and routed his troops, capturing eighteen cavalrymen. Several days later, when Tissaphernes himself attempted to harass the Greeks with a much larger army, the Cretan archers, firing long Persian arrows which they had picked up in considerable quantities, and the Rhodian slingers did such damage to the satrap's men that he retreated out of range and merely followed the Greeks at a distance.[26]

But Tissaphernes had not given up the pursuit. He launched attacks whenever the Greeks were forced to abandon their square formation during the crossing of bridges or narrow mountain passes. With the Greeks crowded together in considerable disorder, Tissaphernes' attacks inflicted considerable casualties. The Greek generals tackled the problem by forming six special companies, each of 100 men, whose task it was to reinforce any weak point or gaps in the formation. This tactic worked well enough on level ground but when the Greeks reached hilly country they were vigorously attacked by Persian light troops. Encumbered by their armour, the hoplites made desperate attempts to charge uphill against the Persians but failed to catch any of their assailants. When they retreated towards the main army, they did so under a shower of missiles. The situation was retrieved by peltasts from the Greek right flank who climbed a range of hills higher than those occupied by the Persians. Under the threat of being caught between the hoplites below and the peltasts above, the Persians broke off their attack.

The Greeks occupied a village where they stopped for four days to treat their wounded and recuperate their strength. During this time a Persian attack was firmly repulsed. Taking advantage of the Persian dislike of fighting in the dark, the Greeks made a night march that gave them a temporary lead over their pursuers. The tenacious Tissaphernes, however, caught up and occupied a mountain top which overlooked the only pass by which the Greeks could once more reach level ground. In a repeat performance, Xenophon took his peltasts and 300 picked hoplites and climbed an even loftier mountain top, forcing the Persians to abandon their intended attack. Thus, the Greeks were able to proceed unhindered into the plain.

Their next major trial came when they entered the Carducian mountains, which marked the northern border of Media and lay outside the Persian empire. The Greeks attempted to parley with the Carducians but the Kurdish response was a series of attacks at every point suitable for an ambush. The Carducians were expert slingers and their archers fired arrows of impressive penetrative power that had little difficulty in making holes in the shields, breast plates and bodies of the sorely-harassed Greeks. Xenophon records that an Arcadian hoplite, Basias, was shot clean through the head by an enemy archer, while another comrade, the Spartan, Leonymus, died when an arrow penetrated his shield, his jerkin and then the man himself.[27] The Kurds rolled down large boulders from the hill tops, keeping up this pleasurable activity by day and by night. The Greek countermove of sending out detachments of light troops to occupy higher ground than that of the enemy was only partly effective for the Carducians retreated, not before having shot some of their attackers, only to renew their assault elsewhere on the Greek formation where there were no protective light troops. The Greeks took seven days to cross Carducia before reaching the River Centrites (Buhtan Su), which separated Kurdistan from Armenia. Those seven days had been more destructive to the Greeks than all their encounters with the Persians.

Carducia may have been fiercely independent of Persian rule but Armenia was a Persian satrapy and, as the Greeks prepared to cross the Centrites, they observed Persian cavalry and Armenian, Mardian and Chaldaean mercenary infantry on the other side of the river, for news of their coming had preceded the Ten Thousand. Behind them, the Kurds waited quite openly in the Carducian foothills with the all too clear intention of launching another attack if the Greeks remained on their side of the river. On their first attempt to cross the Centrites, the Greeks found the water too deep but the accidental discovery of a more shallow section enabled Chirisophus to lead the vanguard across the river. Xenophon, in the meantime, gave the impression that he intended to cross at the original point and the Persian cavalry waited close by on the opposite bank. The Persians retreated, however, upon observing that Chirisophus had successfully crossed the river and threatened to fall upon their rear. The mercenary infantry, seeing their cavalry move off without a fight, soon followed, abandoning the high ground they had occupied. Xenophon ordered his light troops to make a diversionary attack on the Kurds while the rest of the rearguard raced for the shallow ford. The manoeuvre was successful and the remaining Greeks managed to cross the river unmolested. Their enemies ran back into the hills, fearing a major Greek attack, but not without wounding a few peltasts who had ventured too far towards the Kurds.

The Greeks marched unchallenged for a week across plains and gently undulating hills. As the weather gradually turned colder, the first snows began to fall. When they reached the Teleboas river (Murad Su), the local satrap, Tiribazus, suddenly appeared and informed the Greeks that he would not attack them as long as they did not burn the villages along their route. When the Greeks discovered that this was a deception, their response was swift. An immediate attack led by light troops on the Persian camp took the satrap by surprise and his men fled without offering resistance. The Greeks marched on through the pass where Tiribazus had intended to ambush them before the satrap had time to concentrate his scattered forces.

The Greeks marched across central Armenia, relatively unbothered by the enemy, save for marauding bands who picked off any stragglers and captured baggage animals too tired and too weak to continue carrying their loads. They crossed the eastern branch of the Euphrates near its source without undue difficulty. But, if human enemies did not present a serious impediment at this stage, Nature took a vicious toll. The intense cold and deep snow killed many of the animals, the slaves, the camp followers and, notwithstanding their toughness, claimed some of the hoplites as well. At one stage, those that survived the weather found shelter in curious underground houses, where the inhabitants gave the Greeks a wide variety of food and a potent barley wine.

Leaving their genial hosts, the Ten Thousand moved on through the Armenian mountains and crossed the Phasis river, which flowed towards the Caspian Sea and lay near the northern border of Armenia and the land of the Chalybes. One last mountain pass and the Greeks would descend into the plain beyond. The pass, however, was blocked by Chalybian tribesmen and the Greeks had to resort once again to the tactic of occupying higher ground in order to dislodge their enemy. The army was able to reach the plain and marched across Chalybes, not without fending off constant attacks from the local inhabitants who fought the Greeks at close quarters with spears, stones and daggers and decapitated any prisoners they took, waving the heads at the Greek army to the accompaniment of singing and dancing.

Crossing the River Harpasus (Çoruh), the Greeks reached friendlier territory and another week's march brought them to the large and prosperous city of Gymnias, where they received the welcome news that only five more days of march lay between them and Trapezus, a Greek city in Colchian territory on the Black Sea. Indeed, a few days later the vanguard reached Mount Thekes and caught sight of the sea. The joyous cry of *Thalassa! Thalassa!* (the sea! the sea!) was progressively taken up along the entire Greek column.

For the citizens of Trapezus the sudden and unexpected descent from the Armenian mountains of the Ten Thousand was a far from welcome development. Although they had lost about 4,000 men on the march from Cunaxa to Trapezus, the surviving 9,000 still represented a substantial group of warriors, extremely toughened and hardened after their fight for survival against ferocious mountain tribesmen and their endurance of lethal weather conditions. The city had been on good terms with the Colchians and their friendly relations were being compromised by the depradations of an army of mercenaries. There was, however, no question of imposing control over this travelling democratic community which was a law unto itself, for the local hoplite militia would be no match for these men.

Much to the relief of the people of Trapezus, the mercenaries moved on westwards along the shore of the Black Sea (Pontus Euxinus) under the leadership of Xenophon. Trapezus had been able to provide only a few ships which were used to carry the wounded, the older hoplites, the soldiers' women and the children who inevitably increased the population of camp followers. The march from Cerasus to Sinope via Cotyara took the Greeks through the territory of the savage Mossynoeci tribes who, fortunately for the Greeks, perhaps, were engaged in a civil war over the possession of their capital city and were consequently incapable of offering any united resistance to the passage of the Greeks across their lands.

At the city of Cotyora, the reputation of the Ten Thousand had preceded their actual arrival and they found the gates barred against them. Cotyora was a colony of Sinope, the main Greek settlement on the Black Sea, and shortly after the arrival of the mercenaries, Sinopian ambassadors reached the city and threatened to make an alliance with Corylas, Governor of Paphlagonia, against the Ten Thousand if they attempted to plunder Cotyora. After being assuaged by Xenophon, the ambassadors moderated their stance and Xenophon's army was able to travel to Sinope in a fleet of ships provided by the city. The Sinopians, in turn, provided ships for the onward journey to Heraclea, glad to get rid of their unwelcome guests.

Now that the Greeks were so much closer to Greece itself they became increasingly conscious of the fact that they were coming home from their adventure with relatively little to show for their enterprise. The death of Cyrus had, of course, deprived them of a paymaster who had promised so much and they had also had to abandon considerable quantities of the loot they had taken on the march, for it had been impossible to fight for survival and carry plunder at the same time. Thus, against the advice of Chirisophus and Xenophon, the majority of the army voted to express their gratitude to the Heracleans for their hospitality by demanding a substantial monetary contribution.[28]

This incident clearly shows, if more evidence is needed, that whatever Xenophon may have written about the motives of the Ten Thousand, they were primarily driven by economic determinism. It is also a further indication that, unlike Asiatic military commanders, Chirisophus and Xenophon were indeed only *primus inter pares* – elected leaders and not autocrats. They led by persuasion and argument not by virtue of superior social status or god-like prestige. Their proposals were subject to a democratic vote and were acceptable only so long as they accorded with the general will of the army. Chirisophus' opposition to the greedy demand for 10,000 Cyzicene staters (a Cyzicene stater was worth twenty-eight Attic drachmae, or one daric, i.e. the average daily pay of a mercenary hoplite) effectively meant the end of his leadership of the army.

The Heracleans responded to their visitors' blackmail by quickly bringing their trade goods into the city and manning the ramparts. Foiled in its extortion attempt, the mercenary army fell apart. The 4,000 Arcadians and Achaeans suddenly discovered that their local loyalties no longer permitted them to serve under a Spartan and an Athenian and separated from the army. The remainder split up into two groups – 1,400 hoplites and 700 Thracian peltasts stayed with Chirisophus while 1,700 hoplites and 300 peltasts chose to follow Xenophon.[29] The Arcadians and Archaeans sailed away first on ships obligingly provided by the Heracleans, bound for the Greek port of Calpe, where they disembarked with the object of attacking Thracian villages in Bithynia. In the meantime Chirisophus and Xenophon also headed for Thracian territory, albeit by different routes. The Arcadian–Achaean contingent organised itself into smaller detachments, each given the task of attacking a separate village. With the element of surprise, the Greeks were able to capture several villages, which they thoroughly looted. But one raiding party was caught at a river crossing by a Thracian attack and was wiped out to a man. Other groups returned to a previously determined rendezvous point, only to be surrounded by large numbers of Thracian horsemen and peltasts. With few, if any, light troops of their own, the Greeks were unable to escape a constant barrage of arrows, javelins and stones and were forced to ask for a humiliating truce. They were rescued from certain destruction by the arrival of Xenophon's contingent.[30]

After this salutary lesson, the Arcadians and Achaeans returned to Calpe where they agreed to reunite with Xenophon's troops and those of Chiriso-phus. At this time Chirisophus died suddenly as a result of illness and was replaced by Neon of Asine by a democratic vote. The need to obtain fresh supplies caused Neon to send some 2,000 men back into Bithynian territory. After an initial loss of 500 men caught plundering, the Greeks set out again into the interior of Bithynia and encountered Persian–Bithynian forces drawn up in battle formation. A series of spirited charges decided the issue in favour of the Greeks. The Bithynians fled at the sight of a determined phalanx of hoplites advancing noisily, behind a solid row of shields, spears levelled and ready. Pharnabazus' cavalry observed the rout of their allies from a nearby hill. In what was, perhaps, the most remarkable aspect of the whole affair, tired Greek footsoldiers, having seen off the Bithynians, then charged uphill and dislodged a large force of cavalry, which fled without striking a blow.[31] The sole purpose of the Greek expeditions had been the acquisition of plunder and they were now able to loot the countryside untroubled by the enemy. They travelled on to Chrysopolis (modern Scutari), plundering at every opportunity.

During the months that the Ten Thousand had been fighting their way back home, Sparta and Persia had maintained a precarious peace and the immiment arrival at Chrysopolis of an army of mercenaries pleased no one, for it introduced a further element of instability into an already sensitive diplomatic relationship. To Pharnabazus, the mercenaries represented a threat to his satrapy, while the Spartans had neither the inclination to employ such an independently-minded body of men, especially one led by an Athenian, nor the desire to enter into hostilities with Persia at that particular moment. To accommodate Pharnabazus, Admiral Anaxibius agreed to ferry the entire mercenary army across the Bosphorus straits to Byzantium and gave Xeno-phon's men a promise of pay as an incentive. The army duly crossed over to

Byzantium where it ran into further trouble. The city of Byzantium was a vital strategic and commercial centre which handled the importation of grain from southern Russia, and Anaxibius had no intention of paying the mercenaries or of allowing them into the city in any substantial numbers. He permitted the sick and wounded to be quartered within the city walls and announced that pay would be distributed only outside the city, whereupon he shut the gates, leaving the hoplites without food or money. Impelled by a sense of betrayal, the mercenaries managed to force open the gates and would have looted the city had not Xenophon ordered the entire army to assume parade formation in a large city square. He reminded the incensed hoplites that, though Byzantium was under Spartan control, it was not a Spartan city. It was wrong, he said, to punish its inhabitants on account of Spartan duplicity. Furthermore, such an act would mean war with Sparta, which at present controlled the whole of Greece owing to its victory in the Peloponnesian War. Sparta could call upon contingents from every part of Greece, even Athens, if she decided to destroy the remnants of the Ten Thousand and, with a hostile Tissaphernes and a vengeful Persian king waiting in Anatolia, there could be no retreat from Greek territory. These sober considerations calmed the army, which left Byzantium and marched into Thrace, leaving behind some 400 sick and wounded men who were promptly sold into slavery by the newly-appointed Spartan governor, Aristarchus.[32]

Faced with the prospect of spending a miserable midwinter in Thrace with few resources at their disposal, some of the hoplites deserted, no longer attracted by the mercenary life, and made their way individually or in small groups back to their ancestral homes or to the nearest cities in the hope of finding employment of some kind. Other hoplites suggested a return to Asia, Tissaphernes notwithstanding, but Xenophon was fully aware that the Spartans would sink any ships carrying the Ten Thousand in order to maintain peace with the Persians. There was only one recourse open to the Greeks who remained with the army: further mercenary service not on behalf of a Greek employer but on behalf of Seuthes, a minor Thracian king who lived largely by brigandage and was involved in what was essentially a civil war between native tribes for predominance over Thrace. Seuthes negotiated with Xenophon and promised to pay each rank and file hoplite a stater of Cyzicus per month, double pay for the captains and four times the standard rate for the generals. The money would be obtained from the sale of booty captured in plundering expeditions against rival Thracian villages.

To seal the bargain, Seuthes invited the Greek officers to a rather remarkable feast which Xenophon describes in considerable detail. The Thracian king drank copious amounts of wine without any apparent inebriation and exhibited somewhat idiosyncratic table manners by throwing pieces of bread and meat to or at the guests. Still, the hoplites were hungry and the banquet with entertainment provided by professional buffoons seems to have literally been a roaring success.[33] The Greeks spent the bitterly cold winter looting and burning villages belonging to the Thynians, Seuthes' main rivals. Many of the prisoners taken were sold into slavery or merely speared to death on the spot. With an unbeatable combination of heavy-infantry hoplites, light troops and cavalry at his disposal, Seuthes was able to overcome the resistance of enemy forces solely composed of light troops. The Greeks, however, were in for an unpleasant surprise, for Seuthes' Greek agent, Heraclides, had only managed to obtain twenty-eight days' pay for the hoplites after the sale of booty in the Greek city of Perinthus and it became apparent that Seuthes had no real intention of making up the balance. He was, after all, first and foremost a bandit chief. Not paying one's mercenaries is never a wise move but the providential arrival of two Spartan envoys seeking the services of Xenophon and his men circumvented any serious confrontation between Seuthes and the Greeks.

The radical change in the Spartan attitude to the Ten Thousand was a result of the outbreak of war against Persia in the spring of 399 BC. The war itself had been provoked by Tissaphernes who had decided to incorporate the late Cyrus' territories, including the Ionian coast, into his own possessions. The Greek cities of Ionia appealed to Sparta for assistance against Tissaphernes. In response, Sparta decided in favour of intervention, her confidence increased by the daring and ostensibly successful march of the Ten Thousand into the heart of the Persian empire and back again. It made sense to increase the size of her forces by hiring the very men who had accomplished this feat and they were duly hired at the standard rate of one daric a month per hoplite, two darics per officer and four darics per general.[34] How long Xenophon stayed with the army remains uncertain. He seems to have returned to his native Athens where his pro-Spartan sympathies earned him a poor welcome, ultimately followed by exile. At any rate, he was again involved in mercenary service in 396 BC, fighting in Asia Minor for King Agesilaus of Sparta, and was present, two years later, at the battle of Coronea, when he fought once more for Sparta against Thebes, an ally of Athens.

King Seuthes was glad to see the Ten Thousand go, now that they had served their purpose and given him control of Thrace. That the Greeks had been employed by another foreigner in order to resolve domestic conflict was not remarkable in itself but the fact that their employer had been a Thracian was unusual if not unique. Ever since the first recorded hiring of Thracian mercenaries around 540 BC by the Athenian *tyrannos* Peisistratus, Greek city-states had employed Thracian peltasts and cavalry on a fairly regular basis. Seuthes, however, was the first Thracian to hire Greeks and on a substantial scale at that. The Ten Thousand were the first large Greek army to have served two separate foreign employers and now they were the first large army of mercenaries to be taken into Spartan employ. They marched out of Thrace, sailed to Lampsacus and then made their way to Pergamon where they were incorporated into the Spartan army commanded by Thibron, thereby losing their identity as an independent unit.

To many of their contemporaries, the march of the Ten Thousand was proof of the weakness of Persia. Men like Isocrates reasoned that if an army composed of what he regarded as the scum of Greece could march deep into the Persian empire unopposed until the very last moment, then Persia must indeed be ready to fall to a Greek invasion. King Agesilaus of Sparta was similarly enthusiastic at the prospect of spreading Spartan domination beyond the confines of Greece at the expense of Persia. To writers in later periods of history beginning with Arrian (2nd century AD), the Ten Thousand were the precursors of Alexander the Great. Their exploits were a prologue to Alexander's conquest of Persia – a sort of dress rehearsal that had shown how easily the Persian empire might be taken. Arrian vigorously promoted his view in his work *Anabasis Alexandri* and his choice of the word *anabasis* was a conscious emulation of Xenophon's account.[35] The idea that there were direct parallels between the Ten Thousand and Alexander's invasion was perpetuated by subsequent historians right up to modern times. At best, however, it is only a half-truth.

The ease with which Cyrus' army penetrated into the Persian empire may be attributed to a number of factors but the superior combat prowess of the Greeks was not among them, for the mercenaries did little, if any, serious fighting before Cunaxa. From Sardis to Cunaxa the insurgent army passed through territory whose people were openly friendly to Cyrus or, at least, cooperative in the hope of being on the winning side. Cyrus' troops also passed through stretches of land that were sparsely inhabited, if at all. The Persian empire was a huge agglomeration of productive areas linked by arterial roads and often separated from each other by mountainous or desert regions that were simply not worth garrisoning. Seen in this context, the

Cyrean army's smooth passage through Anatolia and beyond was, in fact, not as remarkable a feat as it seemed to be to Xenophon's contemporaries in the Greek world.

At Cunaxa, Artaxerxes' army was not much larger than that of Cyrus and was quite unrepresentative of the military resoures available to the king. He had substantial forces garrisoning various parts of the empire but only a limited number available for immediate use around Babylon. For that matter, the result of Cunaxa may be viewed from differing perspectives. It is true that the Greeks swept the field in front of them and, had Cyrus lived, he may well have become the new king. But Cyrus' Asiatic troops had failed to perform adequately and their leader's death rendered the Greek victory meaningless. Artaxerxes, even if by default, was the real victor. The Greeks had won their part of the battle but the war was lost. Alexander the Great fought his battles to much greater effect.

After Cunaxa, the Greeks did not attempt to conquer Babylon although they had come so close to the capital city. They retreated. Indeed, they were forced to retreat by the threat of the overwhelming numbers that Artaxerxes could gradually bring against them. A retreat is very rarely the logical consequence of an incontestable victory. In addition, the Greeks were *allowed* to retreat relatively unmolested by the Persians. Tissaphernes had been speaking no more than the truth when he had said that the Persians could have destroyed the mercenaries had they really wanted to do so.[36] Even without a concerted Persian attack, the entire campaign had been a failure. The Ten Thousand had lost nearly half of its men. The peltasts, who arguably saved the Ten Thousand from total destruction at the hands of the hill tribes, suffered particularly heavy casualties, given that they were always engaged in protecting the hoplites from enemy peltasts.

The march of the Ten Thousand did not represent a deliberate invasion of Persian territory by a foreign power, unlike Alexander's campaigns which aimed at nothing less than the conquest of Persia. The Ten Thousand had simply been hired on a temporary basis for the resolution of a family feud. A Cyrean victory would merely have resulted in a change of king but the integrity and strength of the Persian empire would have remained intact. Cyrus, ambitious as he was, might even have organised another full-scale attack on the Greek mainland. The Ten Thousand had no serious thoughts of conquest and no intention other than to help Cyrus win a throne – a goal they grudgingly accepted – and to go home to Greece richer if not wiser. They were first and foremost mercenaries disinterested in the rights and wrongs of the cause for which they had been hired. They had no other *raison d'être* beyond their role in the resolution of a domestic struggle. Had Artaxerxes offered to hire them *en masse* after Cunaxa it is quite probable that many would have accepted and it was only mistrust of Persian intentions that prevented a change of allegiance. It was also a weakness of the whole affair of 401 BC that the entire Greek participation depended on the private ambitions and the survival of one dominant personality.

In some senses the Greeks were the precursors of Alexander but the differences between his expedition to Persia and that of the Ten Thousand seem greater than any apparent parallels. Conversant with Xenophon's *Anabasis*, Alexander clearly understood that any serious attempt to conquer Persia could only be effected by an army with a substantial component of cavalry. Cyrus' army had been relatively deficient in horsemen. An invasion force made up purely of infantry, no matter how proficient, could not hope to prevail against the large cavalry arm that constituted Persia's main strength and at the beginning of the fourth century, despite the embarrassing episode of the Ten Thousand, despite a gradual decline in royal authority and despite the rivalry between satraps in outlying provinces, the Persian empire was not yet ready to collapse.

The military operations of the Spartan general Thibron were partly successful to the extent that some Aeolian towns were freed from Tissaphernes' control but his efforts were compromised when his troops and chiefly the former Cyrean mercenaries looted the property of the very people they had come to assist. Thibron was replaced by Dercyllidas and was later killed when his forces were surprised by Persian cavalry (392 BC). His successor did rather better, freeing more Greek cities but avoiding the depredations perpetrated by the mercenaries by quartering his army well away from liberated areas. Dercyllidas avoided attacking Tissaphernes and instead marched into Phrygia, the satrapy of Pharnabazus, with whom he concluded a truce after having acquired enough loot to maintain his 8,000 men for a whole year. Dercyllidas next attacked Tissaphernes but without any decisive result.

In the winter of 397 BC, Agesilaus himself arrived in Asia Minor, took over the Spartan army, which still included the remnants of the Ten Thousand, and enthusiastically began operations against Tissaphernes. The Spartan expedition into Asia Minor achieved its goal of restoring the independence of the Greek cities and proved once again the superiority of the hoplites. But Agesilaus' success really represented not much more than a plundering expedition. He had neither the cavalry nor the siege equipment for a serious strike deep into the heart of the Persian empire. He was no more a precursor of Alexander than the Ten Thousand had been. Although the Persian satraps had been beaten by the Greeks, Persia was still capable of a powerful riposte: the naval battle of Cnidus (394 BC). Outfought on land, the Persians decided on a major naval offensive against Sparta. The ensuing Persian victory was as complete as the Spartan victory had been at Aegospotami. Perhaps there was an added piquancy to this particular victory for the admiral of the Persian fleet. He was none other than the former Athenian admiral Conon, who had been trounced by Lysander at Aegospotami and was now doing good mercenary service for the Persians. There was also an ironic touch in the fact that the Persian fleet had been largely manned by Greek crews. One naval battle effectively terminated Spartan supremacy in the Aegean Sea and Spartan attempts to establish an empire in Asia Minor. The Greek cities invited their Spartan garrisons to leave as promptly as possible and once more acknowledged Persian suzerainty.

Sparta was also facing difficulties closer to home for Persia had also engaged in a diplomatic offensive against her. She had not endeared herself to Artaxerxes by supporting Cyrus in his attempt to usurp the Persian throne and encouraging every would-be mercenary in her territory to join his expedition, even if only to get rid of potentially troublesome unemployed soldiers.

Thus, the Persians did everything to exacerbate the discontent felt by Greek states resentful of Spartan supremacy. They were encouraged by an anti-Spartan insurrection that had already broken out on the island of Rhodes. Their ambassador, Timocrates, was himself a Rhodian and he approached Athens with an ample and tempting supply of gold which added solidity to the Persian diplomatic overture. Promoting a war against Sparta was not very difficult under existing circumstances. Athens, Corinth, Argos and Thebes came together to form a coalition against her, supported financially and militarily by the gleeful Persians. Civil war once more ravaged Greece and provided more work for mercenary soldiers.

CHAPTER NINE

Greece: Civil War

THE FORMATION of the anti-Spartan coalition and the outbreak of the Corinthian War forced the Spartan government to recall Agesilaus from Asia Minor. He, in turn, was forced to abandon his grandiose designs against the Persian empire. Hostilities began in Boeotia before Agesilaus could arrive. The Spartans suffered defeat at the Boeotian town of Haliartus where Lysander was killed. Sparta promptly lost control of Greece north of the Isthmus of Corinth and her discomfiture at Haliartus cemented the alliance between Athens, Thebes, Corinth and Argos and encouraged the Locrians, Euboeans, Acarnanians, Thessalians and Chalcidians (Thracian Greeks) to join the Coalition.

Agesilaus was still on the march from Asia Minor when the next major clash took place between the forces of Sparta and the Coalition at the battle of Corinth (July 394 BC). The Lacedaimonian hoplites numbered some 6,000 and their allies – Elis, Sicyon, Epidaurus, Tegea and Pellene – collectively provided 10,000 men. There were about 24,000 hoplites and a large but unspecified number of light troops in the Coalition army.[1] At this early stage of the war most of the participants seem to have been natives of their respective city-states. Athens' hoplites were all citizen militia but her light troops contained both impoverished Athenians and foreign mercenaries, most probably of Thracian origin. Both armies, composed as they were of contingents from numerous city-states, were unusually large, by most previous standards, for Greek armies fighting on Greek soil.

The battle of Corinth was in some ways similar to Cunaxa in that the right wing of each army defeated the enemy directly opposite. Thus, the Spartans who were posted on the right of the Peloponnesian army broke through the

Athenian contingent but the Corinthians, Argives and Boeotians on the right of the Coalition army routed Sparta's allies. Sparta won the encounter, inflicting heavy losses on the enemy, but she had really gained nothing because the strategic Isthmus of Corinth with its system of fortifications remained in Coalition hands.

At Amphipolis, Agesilaus received the news of the Spartan victory at Corinth without enthusiasm for he understood that the battle had changed nothing. When he reached Chaeronea, there was another of those dreadful solar eclipses which never failed to excite and disconcert the superstitious peoples of the Ancient World. In this case, the darkening of the sun did indeed seem to portend evil events. Shortly thereafter, Agesilaus received news of the Spartan naval defeat at Cnidus – news he carefully concealed from his army for he was intent on fighting a battle as soon as possible and had to keep the morale of his men unimpaired by disastrous tidings. He had already been working on their morale by offering prizes of money and weapons to the mercenary commanders of the best turned-out companies of hoplites, peltasts and archers.[2] He was able to recruit new mercenaries along the way, all of whom were attracted by the prospect of prizes.

When Agesilaus arrived in central Greece, the Coalition forces took up position near Coronea and brought the Spartan king to battle. Agesilaus positioned his Spartans on the extreme right of his line, along with his substantial contingent of mercenary troops. There were, of course, the remnants of the Ten Thousand (Xenophon among them) who had seen a good deal of campaigning over the six years that had elapsed since their adventure with Cyrus. There were also Lacedaimonian mercenary hoplites sent as reinforcements by Sparta and mercenaries from the Greek cities of Asia Minor, both hoplites and peltasts.

Remarkably the battle of Coronea took a rather similar course to that of Corinth, with the right wing of each army routing their immediate opponents. The Thebans charged first, chasing the Orchomenians off the field while Herippidas, commander of Agesilaus' mercenary troops, led the mercenary contingents, including the Cyreans, against the Argives. Faced with a concerted attack by both light-armed troops and hoplites operating together, with the Spartan contingent advancing in support, the Argives broke and fled without coming into contact with their assailants. Agesilaus then turned his forces towards the left, hoping to catch the Thebans by a flank attack. But the Thebans, initially disconcerted, rallied immediately and, according to Xenophon who must have done considerable fighting that day, a vicious fight ensued during which Agesilaus was almost killed. The Thebans repulsed Spartan attempts to cut them off from their allies and left the field to Agesilaus, but not as a dispirited or vanquished force.[3] From the point of view of mercenary involvement, Coronea was significant given that it was the first major battle in Greece itself where mercenaries played a significant if not decisive role in securing victory for their employer.

As with the engagement of Corinth, Coronea changed nothing. The Isthmus of Corinth still lay firmly under Coalition control and Spartan domination ws confined to the Peloponnesus. The war dragged on in a dreary, indecisive way – a war of attrition. The Corinthians built long walls between Corinth and its western seaport of Lechaeum to prevent any Spartan passage north of the Isthmus. Agesilaus laid siege to the fortifications over a two-year period. The defenders of Corinth were reinforced by a large force of mercenary peltasts recruited by the Athenian admiral Conon in the Hellespontine region and Thrace and placed under the command of the Athenian mercenary general Iphicrates.[4] In pitched battles in the confined spaces of the Long Walls, the peltasts were not in their element and were driven back by Corinthian exiles fighting as mercenaries in the Spartan army.[5] But on raiding expeditions the peltasts were extremely effective against hoplites and Iphicrates scored his greatest triumph in the destruction of 600 Spartan hoplites near Lechaeum.

Iphicrates' mercenary peltasts were highly trained and, unusually for light troops, operated in precise formation even though they fought in open order.[6] They seem to have been well paid by their Athenian employers for, unlike other mercenaries, they maintained a high standard of discipline and, indeed, their general seems to have been a stern disciplinarian who on one occasion personally killed a sentry found asleep at his post.[7] The destruction of the Spartans earned Iphicrates undying fame (or opprobrium) as a mercenary commander of peltasts and, needless to say, enhanced the reputation of light-armed troops who, as previously described, had always been regarded as inferior fighting men by the hoplites.

At one point in the siege of Corinth, the Spartans broke through enemy defences and made a gap in the Long Walls. They were prevented from exploiting their success by the onset of winter and the arrival of Athenian militia–levy hoplites and masons who sealed the gap. The following spring, Agesilaus renewed the attack on the Long Walls and captured the seaports of Lechaeum and Piraeon (the latter connected Corinth with Boeotia) and seemed on the verge of isolating Corinth and gaining control of the Isthmus.

But right at this moment of sweet success Iphicrates destroyed the 600 Spartans who were *en route* from Lechaeum to Sicyon. This disaster did serious damage to Spartan morale and Agesilaus withdrew from Corinth. Iphicrates continued to use his mercenaries to good effect, recapturing all the towns taken by the Spartans except for Lechaeum. The retention of Lechaeum meant that Sparta had gained access to the north but her reputation had suffered badly at the hands of Iphicrates and his light troops and the war itself had more or less reached a stalemate. Sparta turned her attention eastwards, aiming to re-establish her influence in Asia Minor and regain Persia as an ally.

Corinth had not been the only state to erect defensive Long Walls. Taking advantage of the decline of Spartan power north of the Isthmus, Athens rebuilt its own Long Walls which it had been forced to demolish at the end of the Peloponnesian War. The reconstruction had been a gradual process owing to a shortage of funds but was completed thanks to money donated by Pharnabazus, who bore an abiding resentment against Agesilaus for having ravaged his satrapy. Protected by her new walls, Athens was once more free to contemplate maritime expansion and made alliances with, or resumed control of, several Aegean islands, including Lemnos, Imbros, Scyros, Chios and Delos. This did not represent a major reconstitution of the Athenian empire but it was suggestive of renewed imperial ambition.

The Athenians also scored a success against the Spartans in Asia Minor in 388 BC. The Hellespontine city of Abydos had been the only centre to remain in Spartan hands after the battle of Cnidus and its location made it an excellent base from which a Spartan fleet could harass Athenian shipping and interrupt the all-important supply of grain from southern Russia. Sparta provided its admiral, Anaxibius, with enough money to raise 1,000 mercenaries from the cities of Aeolia.[8] These constituted his main force, along with a small contingent of Lacedaimonians and 250 hoplites from Abydos. Alarmed at any possible tampering with her food supply, Athens sent the redoubtable Iphicrates with 1,200 mercenaries to confront Anaxibius.[9] Iphicrates did not disappoint his native city. Setting up an ambush along a narrow mountain defile, he waited for Anaxibius, who was returning to Abydos from its allied city of Antandrus. Iphicrates caught Anaxibius' men in the worst possible position, strung out on the march with the hoplites from Abydos in the vanguard, followed by the mercenaries and the rearguard of Lacedaimonians. Waiting until the enemy columns had begun to descend towards the plain of Abydos, Iphicrates' mercenaries charged down after them. Taken completely by surprise, Anaxibius' mercenaries lost some 200 men while the Abydene hoplites lost about fifty.[10] Casualties among the Lacedaimonians remain unknown but as they were the first to be attacked they must have suffered considerably. Anaxibius himself did not survive the encounter and his men were pursued all the way to Abydos by Iphicrates' triumphant warriors.

Iphicrates' attack effectively confined the Spartans to Abydos and gave Athens control of the Hellespont. Artaxerxes, still cool towards Sparta, was not overly alarmed at Athens' successes in the Aegean and Asia Minor and was content to remain allied to the Athenians, despite diplomatic missions from Sparta seeking to persuade Persia to change sides. But in 390 BC Athens was suddenly placed in an embarrassing position when, in Cyprus, King Evagoras of Salamis, who was a tributary of the Persian king, attacked other cities on the island, both Greek and Phoenician. Evagoras, who was a great friend of Athens, wanted full control over, and independence for, the entire island. Much to the surprise of observers like Xenophon, the Athenian government, its alliance with Persia notwithstanding, was persuaded to send a modest force of ten triremes carrying mercenary peltasts to Cyprus.[11]

The peltasts seem to have been chosen from among those who had defended Corinth against Agesilaus. Up until the lifting of the siege of Corinth, the peltasts had been paid with money provided by the Persians. Now their pay came from Athenian sources, not the government but private individuals who had been exiled by the oligarchy (The Thirty) established by Sparta immediately after its victory in the Peloponnesian War and who had been welcomed by Evagoras. Among the contributors were Lysias, an orator and speech writer for litigants, and comic poet and playwright Aristophanes.[12] In the event, the money was wasted for the Athenian force was intercepted and destroyed by the Spartan admiral Teleutias before it could be used by Evagoras against the Persians. Artaxerxes, however, noted the Athenian gesture with a degree of displeasure and suspected that Athens did indeed have renewed imperial designs. When in the following year the Athenians sent a further ten triremes with 800 peltasts, Artaxerxes' suspicions became certainties.

The peltasts also came from the garrison at Corinth and had been placed under the command of the Athenian general Chabrias when Iphicrates was reassigned to make war on the Spartans at Abydos. Chabrias' force, battle-hardened at Corinth, proved extremely effective and Evagoras was able to conquer most of Cyprus, albeit for a brief period. Evagoras was slain by a eunuch, and under the terms of the King's Peace of 387 BC, Cyprus was to lose its independent status and was no longer to be supported by Athens.

Sparta and Persia were able to impose the King's Peace after a sudden reversal of fortune in Sparta's favour. With Persian subsidies no longer available, Athens now ran very low on funds with which to continue the war. Even worse, her grain supply was cut off when the Spartan commander Antalcidas led a fleet of eighty ships to blockade the Dardanelles. The fleet was composed of Spartan, Persian and Syracusan ships. Syracuse, of course, had no love for Athens after the siege of 414 BC. Athens had no real choice but to acquiesce in a general peace mediated by Artaxerxes – hence the name 'King's Peace'. To many pan-hellenists, like the Athenian Isocrates, the peace treaty was a national humiliation. After all, Persia had proved itself weak against the Ten Thousand and Agesilaus had also routed the Persians in Asia Minor. The Persians might still have a powerful cavalry but they were becoming more and more dependent on Greek mercenary infantry and on Greek sailors for their fleets. Isocrates blamed Sparta and to a considerable degree he was correct. Sparta was prepared to betray the Greek cities in Asia Minor yet again in order to secure Persian assistance but Athens had been equally guilty of soliciting a Persian alliance.

Under the terms of the treaty Sparta remained predominant in Greece although Athens was allowed to keep the northern Aegean islands she had regained and other Greek states were, in theory at least, guaranteed autonomy. The Greek cities in Asia Minor were duly sold out while Persia imposed its domination over Cyprus by force of arms. With the re-establishment of peace one of the first acts of both Athens and Sparta was to dismiss their hired troops. An outbreak of peace represents the worse calamity for a mercenary but work was available elsewhere. Artaxerxes' expeditionary force against Cyprus contained a sizeable contingent of Greek mercenaries, the largest thus far hired by a Persian king. They had been recruited not from Asia Minor but from the Greek mainland and now that Evagoras had been abandoned by Athens as a result of the peace treaty, they had no problem in serving Persia against a fellow Greek.[13] Chabrias had also abandoned Evagoras, partly because Athens could no longer allow him to stay and partly because his falling into Persian hands if and when an invasion came would be construed as an Athenian breach of the King's Peace. Chabrias had been sent to Cyprus not in an independent capacity but as an allied general, even if his peltasts were themselves freelance mercenaries. Thus, when the Persians attacked, their Greek mercenaries did not encounter Chabrias' peltasts, although Evagoras did have other Greek mercenaries in his employ, 6,000 of his own Cypriots and contingents of Syrian and Egyptian auxiliaries sent by the Pharaoh, Achoris, who was also fighting for independence from Persia. In 386 BC, Chabrias went to Egypt at the invitation of Achoris and was given a high command in the Egyptian army. Just as an earlier generation of mercenaries had left graffiti at Abu Simbel, some of Chabrias' warriors left their own inscriptions near the Great Pyramid of Gizeh and, like the earlier variety, these were largely a matter of names and cities of origin. The fourth-century inscriptions, however, show a much higher proportion of mercenaries from the Greek mainland – half the inscriptions were done by Athenians – whereas their earlier counterparts came largely from Asia Minor or the Aegean islands.[14] This was perhaps a small indication of the progressive mercenarisation of Greek warfare that began towards the end of the Peloponnesian War and gradually gathered momentum during the fourth century. Chabrias did excellent service on behalf of the Pharaoh but was peremptorily recalled to Athens when Persian ambassadors went to his native city to put forward the proposition that Chabrias' presence in the rebellious Egyptian army was incompatible with the provisions of the King's Peace. Chabrias was not strong enough to operate as an independent *condottiere*. He went home and was placed in charge of the Athenian fleet, which was not the ideal position for a general so skilled in land warfare. However, Chabrias undoubtedly adapted his skill to naval warfare for in 376 BC he won a momentous victory over the Spartan fleet between the islands of Paros and Naxos.

Iphicrates, like Chabrias, was not minded to lay down his arms after the peace of 387 BC. Like Xenophon before him, he went to Thrace straight from his successful operations in the Hellespont, attracted by the employment opportunities opened up by civil war between rival Thracian families. Iphicrates remained in Thrace for some fifteen years, serving as a commander of peltasts, but from 374 BC to 372 BC he was in Persian service as commander of the king's mercenaries. Pharnabazus, who was in command of the Persian expedition against Egypt, had first noticed Iphicrates at the battle of Cnidus. The latter was then no more than eighteen years old, not yet famous, and was serving as a mercenary in the Persian fleet. Pharnabazus made an official request to Athens for Iphicrates' services and Iphicrates, always ready for a good fight, agreed to serve the Persians. The satrap had recruited a substantial Greek mercenary army numbering somewhere between 12,000–20,000 men (the estimates vary according to the source), of which 8,000 were hoplites.[15]

But the offensive against the recalcitrant Egyptians did not go well. Pharnabazus, ageing and increasingly lacking in initiative, opposed all of Iphicrates'
suggestions, including a daring plan for a raid on the Egyptian capital at
Memphis. Disgruntled, Iphicrates finally abandoned the Persian army,
including his own mercenaries, and, under cover of darkness, left Egypt by
boat and returned to Athens.

While Iphicrates had been spending his time gainfully employed in Thrace,
war broke out again in Greece itself. Indeed, the King's Peace could not last
for Sparta had learnt nothing and forgotten nothing and continued her
extremely heavy-handed policy of suppressing democracies with her Peloponnesian dependencies while at the same time she vigorously combated the
formation or growth of any new confederation of cities, rather hypocritically,
in the name of protecting the autonomy of individual states. Sparta aimed to
keep Greece as disunited as possible and was thus playing Persia's game.
Needless to say, Sparta was keen to promote the autonomy (read: disunity) of
cities north of the Isthmus of Corinth while in the Peloponnesus she punished
cities deemed to be less than loyal or enthusiastic about her domination.

Sparta's enemies, of course, had their ambitions. Thebes wanted to
maintain and expand the league of Boeotian states, which Sparta did its best
to dismember, while Athens, encouraged by the re-establishment of its links
with the north Aegean islands, was working towards the creation of a new
naval league to counter Spartan domination. But war did not break out
between Thebes or Athens on the one hand and Sparta on the other. It was
the substantial growth of a confederacy of cities at the north-eastern extremity
of Greece that caused Sparta to resume war on a serious scale. Originally
founded by the city of Olynthus, the Chalcidian League had steadily grown
into a union based on equality between the cities and common legal and
commercial rights.[16] But the very existence of a thriving confederation was
reason enough for Spartan aggression. The pretext came when two Chalcidian
cities – Apollonia and Acanthus – refused to join the League and appealed to
Sparta for help. Sparta responded by providing a modest force of hoplites,
partly because of the perennial threat of helot risings in Lacedaimon and
partly because the population of fully-trained Spartiates had been in steady
decline as a century of prolonged warfare gradually took its toll. Her
Peloponnesian allies were loath to send their own nationals to the northern
borders of Greece, particularly when the campaign would entail lengthy
sieges and there was harvesting to be done back home. Thus, in a distant
precursor of the scutage system of the medieval era, Sparta allowed her allies

to provide money in lieu of men, so that the expeditionary force was substantially composed of mercenaries and of peltasts in particular.

Against the Peloponnesian force of 10,000 men[17] the Olynthians had 800 hoplites, about 2,000 peltasts and 500 cavalry.[18] But, at first, the campaign went badly for the Spartans and the mercenaries hired by their allies. The Spartan general Teleutias proved unequal to the task and his use of mercenary peltasts was incompetent. In open battle before Olynthus, the peltasts were foolishly ordered to attack enemy cavalry independently of hoplite support and were badly mauled. Teleutias was killed in an Olynthian counter attack and his successor, King Agesipolis, fared little better, dying of fever while Olynthus held out under siege. The city finally capitulated in 379 BC, starved into surrender, and the Chalcidian League was dissolved, only to rise again at a later date.

Sparta gained an unexpected benefit from her northern campaign. She was able to control Thebes for a period of three years, owing to the treachery of Theban factions who favoured oligarchy over democracy. The Spartan garrison and the oligarchs were expelled in a popular uprising led by Theban exiles who secretly returned to the city. Needless to say, Sparta and Athens were once again at war. After an abortive march on Piraeus by a Spartan commander, Sphodrias, Athens entered into an alliance with Thebes, albeit unwillingly. Her resolve was strengthened by Agesilaus, who invaded Boeotia with an army of 20,000 men intent on permanently destroying the Boeotian League.

Agesilaus fought two campaigns in Boeotia, neither of which achieved his objective of crushing Thebes. He captured mountain passes, notably those in the Cithaeron mountains, which gave access to the Theban plain. There were numerous skirmishes between mercenary peltasts, which sometimes ended in the nearly total destruction of one particular contingent of peltasts by those on the opposite side.[19] Such an event occurred in the Cithaeron mountains when peltasts led by the Spartan general Cleombrotus surprised a force of 150 peltasts in Athenian service. But in 376 BC when Cleombrotus attempted to occupy the Cithaeron passes for a second time, the Athenian and Theban mercenary peltasts were waiting in ambush and the Spartan peltasts were routed with a loss of forty men.[20] Against Boeotian cavalry the peltasts hired by Sparta performed poorly when they were unsupported by Lacedaimonian hoplites.[21]

The Boeotian campaign was indicative of the extent to which Greek military forces had become mercenarised. Agesilaus – and his enemies – were able to hire mercenaries by the contingent from all over the Greek mainland, even from small urban centres which maintained groups of mercenaries alongside their own native levies for border wars and garrison duties. The small Arcadian city of Clitor, for example, provided Agesilaus with its entire contingent of peltasts whose services he retained with a month's pay in advance.[22] Agesilaus was also able to recruit mercenaries in the north and the fact that even modestly-sized cities could afford to maintain mercenary troops suggests that mercenaries had become readily available and were relatively cheap, given that supply had created the demand for them. The only constraint on the number of mercenaries that could be hired was the state of a city's treasury at any particular time. Some cities could only afford a small contingent while others could build up sizeable armies.

Sparta was losing the war. By 374 BC, Thebes had recaptured, by force or by persuasion, all but three Boeotian cities. Theban prestige was greatly enhanced by the victory of its general, Pelopidas, in a chance encounter with a Spartan force twice the size of its own near Tegyra. The Spartans were routed by the newly-formed Sacred Band, made up of 150 pairs of passionate homosexual lovers who had sworn to live or die for each other. Whether or not undying love was the cement that held the gay young blades together, their performance is beyond question. Thebes had successfully fought fire with fire and created a match for the Lacedaimonian hoplite.

In an ancient precursor of gunboat diplomacy, the Athenians indulged in some trireme diplomacy aimed at scaring the Spartans and demonstrating their command of the seas. A fleet under Timotheus, son of Conon, sailed right around the Peloponnesus, within view of land, to the western island of Corcyra (Corfu), a newly-acquired Athenian ally. Alarmed, Sparta launched an attack on Corcyra, sending a force of Lacedaimonian hoplites and 1,500 mercenary hoplites and peltasts under the command of Mnasippus. At first the campaign was successful and Corcyra, with its abundance of agricultural produce and wine, proved to be a mercenary looter's paradise. The Corcyreans retreated into their city and, as the siege progressed, faced the spectre of famine. They appealed to Athens and received a reinforcement of 600 mercenary peltasts but further Athenian aid was slow in arriving.

Mnasippus, confident of an imminent victory, began to discharge some of his mercenaries prematurely, physically mistreated others and relaxed his guard *vis-à-vis* the city. Furthermore, although he had sufficient funds available, he allowed the wages owed to the mercenaries to fall two months in arrears, with the apparent intent of enriching himself at their expense. His unpopularity and deceit lowered the morale of his mercenary troops who no longer evinced a desire to fight or obey Spartan orders, let alone die uselessly for an avaricious commander. Taking advantage of a moment when the Spartan army was clearly off-guard, the Corcyreans counter attacked and achieved a complete rout of their besiegers. Mnasippus paid for his misuse and mistreatment of his mercenaries with his life. An Athenian relief force led by the formidable Iphicrates and Chabrias arrived too late to assist in the Corcyrean victory but just in time to intercept and capture a Syracusan fleet of ten triremes carrying Sicilian mercenaries despatched to Sparta's aid by her ally Dionysius of Syracuse.

During the Corcyrean episode, Iphicrates, although an official ambassador of Athens, behaved somewhat like an independent *condottiere*, hiring his troops out without Athenian permission to the Acarnanians, who were engaged in a border war with their Thyrian neighbours, and made a tidy profit for himself. He maintained his army by exacting contributions from allied states on the mainland and in Ionia using the threat of military force as blackmail. Iphicrates' behaviour was symptomatic of the changing nature of military leaders during the fourth century. Gone were the amateur *strategoi* – politicians and prominent citizens appointed as temporary generals – of the fifth century. Generalship, like all other levels of soldiering, was progressively becoming a professional affair and the new breed of generals were no longer statesmen but specialist soldiers hired by statesmen and entrusted with the recruitment and payment of an army. To some extent, Iphicrates was transitional. He was, on the one hand, a general doing the bidding of his native city. He went wherever he was directed to go by the Athenian government and returned to Athens when recalled. He remained an Athenian citizen and was primarily loyal to Athens. He remained so even when his Thracian father-in-law became an enemy of Athens after 365 BC. He agreed to serve Cotys in a defensive capacity but refused to lead his mercenaries in any attack on Athenian territory. Iphicrates never quite forgot his primary allegiance, even when towards the end of his career he fell out of favour in his native city. On the other hand, Iphicrates certainly used his men for his own private purposes in border wars that had nothing directly to do with Athenian policy. Mercenary service on the side, as it were, was very lucrative. But, even though many of his troops were out-and-out mercenaries with little passionate attachment to any particular cause and Iphicrates himself had seen considerable mercenary service in Thrace and in Egypt, he was not a completely independent mercenary commander and he took care to ensure that his private campaigns did not conflict with Athenian interests. Thus, Iphicrates alternated between or combined two positions: he was sometimes a leader of mercenaries in the service of his own city and sometimes a mercenary leader working on his own account.

In either capacity, Iphicrates was a remarkable commander fully aware of the capabilities and limitations of mercenary light troops and thus able to use them appropriately to maximum effect. He was also credited with a number of modifications to the equipment of his light troops, namely the replacement of large shields with *peltae*, so as to lighten the soldier's load and gain greater mobility and speed. He introduced the so-called Iphicratean boots, which were easier to tie and untie and appear to have been a modification of Thracian boots. Iphicrates also lengthened the peltast's sword and spear. This third innovation, which effectively turned light troops into a species of pikemen, may have come as a result of Iphicrates' experience in fighting Egyptian heavy infantrymen whilst in Persian service. A lengthened spear would have been of no advantage in his earlier battles with the Spartans.

Iphicrates' reforms may well have had a major effect on the fighting style of Greek light troops and they are believed by some scholars to have influenced Philip of Macedon in his creation of the Macedonian phalanx. There is, however, no contemporary evidence as to the extent to which Iphicrates' reforms were adopted or any recorded instances of their use (and hence their effectiveness) in combat. References to Iphicrates' reforms are all second- or third-hand from Diodorus Siculus, who describes them in a parenthetical comment, and from Cornelius Nepos, who more or less reiterates the former. At any rate, the reforms which Diodorus Siculus attributes to the year 374 BC, when Iphicrates was in Persian service, were a feature of the latter stages of his career. Iphicrates' most spectacular victories – the destruction of a Spartan *mora* in 390 BC and of Anaxibius' mercenaries in 389 BC – pre-date his reforms and were a result of superior generalship not improved technology.

Unlike Iphicrates, Timotheus, the commander of the fleet that had sailed around the Peloponnesus to Corcyra, was a general of the old school who would have been more at home among the *strategoi* of the fifth century than among the mercenary generals of the fourth. He served as a commander of mercenaries, as a servant of Athens, always with a sense of duty and patriotism. But Timotheus was a very wealthy citizen, having inherited a fortune from his father, Conon. He could afford to be perpetually patriotic, but men like Iphicrates and Chabrias – men of initially modest means – could only become rich by mercenary service. Timotheus was a man out of his time. Iphicrates was half loyal citizen, half mercenary. Other generals of the fourth century became much more independent of their native cities and did not hesitate to sell their services to rival city-states or to foreign employers when they found themselves unemployed or *personae non gratae* at home. Nor did they hesitate to fight against their own city-states, if by doing so they could acquire wealth or, even better, become tyrants in their own right. Among the more prominent of these mercenary adventurers was Dion, an exile from Syracuse, who in 357 BC returned to Sicily with an army entirely composed of Peloponnesian mercenaries to overthrow his brother-in-law, Dionysius II, whose own army was entirely made up of Greek, Sicel and Campanian mercenaries. Dion enjoyed a short-lived triumph before being murdered by some of his own mercenaries. Other mercenary adventurers went north to Thrace or eastwards into Asia Minor to seek fame and fortune. In the same year that Dion invaded Sicily, the Athenian, Chares, led a mercenary army to assist the satrap, Artabazus, who had revolted against King Artaxerxes Ochus. There was also Charidemus, a Euboean mercenary general and the first non-Athenian to command mercenary armies in Athenian service. Like Iphicrates, Charidemus saw mercenary service in Thrace and married another of King Cotys' daughters. Unlike Iphicrates, he was not averse to using his mercenaries against Athens when Cotys decided to oppose Athenian expansion into the Chersonese. And, like many a mercenary general, Charidemus dreamed of becoming a tyrant over his own kingdom, an ambition he achieved, albeit temporarily, by capturing a few cities in Artabazus' satrapy. Towards the end of his career he re-entered Athenian service, for Athens, desperate for mercenaries in her struggle against Philip of Macedon, overlooked his past record of unreliability. Dion, Chares, Charidemus and Iphicrates were notable mercenary commanders but perhaps the most illustrious of all was King Agesilaus himself. As a young man he had seen Sparta's triumph in the Peloponnesian War. Now as an old man he had lived to see the unthinkable: the decline of Spartan hegemony and the invasion of the Peloponnesus by Thebes.

Sparta was indeed in dire straits. The fiasco at Corcyra had severely lowered Spartan morale. A series of devastating earthquakes did nothing to restore it. There was one positive development when, early in 371 BC, Sparta and Athens made a peace, whereby they agreed to dismember their respective Leagues, but Thebes, also invited to make peace, refused to disband the Boeotian League and consequently remained at war with Sparta while Athens once again withdrew into a state of armed neutrality. Agesilaus, whose hatred of Thebes was particularly intense, called for an immediate attack on Boeotia with the object of destroying Thebes itself. Accordingly, his fellow monarch (Sparta was a duel monarchy), Cleombrotus, led the Spartan army of 11,000 men into Boeotia and was crushed by the 6,000 men of the Theban general Epaminondas in a battle that amazed, delighted or disconcerted all of Greece. At Leuctra the traditional Spartan formation – a long line twelve ranks deep – was defeated by new Theban tactics employing a dense column fifty ranks deep with the Sacred Band at the forefront. Estimates of casualties nearly always vary, but the Lacedaimonian army lost at least 1,000 men and probably closer to 2,000.[23] Some 400 native Spartans, including Cleombrotus, were killed out of 700 present in the field – an irreplaceable loss.

The Spartans absorbed the shock of Leuctra with studied calm and indifference. The Athenians, more and more jealous of Thebes, received the news without joy. Arcadia, however, was thrown into turmoil as all but three of its cities (Tegea, Orchomenus, Heraea) asserted their independence from Sparta by forming an Arcadian league – a move actively supported by Epaminondas. Mantinea was rebuilt, complete with walls, and, in order to avoid inter-city jealousy, a new city named Megalopolis was established to serve as the capital of the pan-Arcadian federation.

To make up for its losses in manpower, Sparta raised another mercenary force in Corinth whose task was to defend the Isthmus against Theban attack. But the Arcadian League launched an attack on the cities that had remained loyal to Sparta, and the mercenaries were recalled, leaving the gateway to the Peloponnesus wide open to Epaminondas who invaded the Peloponnesus in mid-winter and inflicted a heavy defeat on Sparta's mercenary forces outside Orchomenus. The mercenaries were mainly peltasts who had advanced too far without hoplite or cavalry support. They demonstrated a rare loyalty to Sparta for the survivors made their way through hostile territory to rejoin the main Spartan army under Agesilaus and they remained loyal even during Sparta's darkest moments. But the Spartan treasury was practically empty and the Corinthian mercenaries seem to have disappeared after the expiry of their contract.

In 369 BC, an increasingly alarmed Athens made an alliance with Sparta and sent mercenary reinforcements, while Dionysius of Syracuse came to Sparta's aid, sending twenty triremes with 2,000 Iberian and Celtic mercenaries whose wages for five months' service he had paid in advance.[24] Thus, Sparta effectively received a free gift from Dionysius. A second free gift of mercenaries sent by the Syracusan tyrant, commanded by Cissidas, helped the Spartan general Archidamus to win the Tearless Battle (so called because there were no Spartan casualties) over the Arcadians and Messenians. Sparta also received 2,000 mercenaries on loan from the Persian satrap of Phrygia, Ariobarzanes. Their wages were also fully paid up. Sparta, increasingly reliant on mercenaries to make up for the loss of native Spartiates, but unable to afford more than a few of her own, had been assisted by foreign powers.

If humble montagnards found it lucrative to become mercenaries why not a king? Sparta's pecuniary difficulties were such that Agesilaus, at the ripe old age of eighty-four, twice went into mercenary service, first for Ariobarzanes in 364 BC and then for rebellious Egyptian princes in 361 BC. The second occasion was after the battle of Mantinea, a Theban victory won at great cost. Agesilaus went east in the guise of an ambassador but in his motives he was a mercenary pure and simple. He earned 230 silver talents, so that Sparta with its rapidly decreasing population of native hoplites would not have to rely on humiliating free gifts of mercenaries lent on a temporary basis. It was Agesilaus' last service to his beloved city for he died on the way home, never to see the sad spectacle of his hard-earned money being used for mercenary hire by a once all-powerful state.

Sparta in decline; Thebes in the ascendancy; Athens remaining aloof or behaving like a weathervane; Arcadia asserting its independence with military forces made up largely of mercenaries returned from service in Persian armies. Such were the main players in the struggle for supremacy. For a short time there was another serious contender, one with a real chance of imposing its authority over central Greece: Thessaly. Jason, tyrant of the Thessalian city of Pherae, occupies a brief but notable place in the history of mercenary soldiers simply because during his reign he maintained the largest mercenary army of any city-state. He had a private army of 6,000 mercenaries largely paid for from his personal fortune.[25] The very presence of such a relatively large body of men was of itself sufficient to persuade other Thessalian cities to accept Jason's rule. Pharsalus, the only city to resist, also yielded when its appeal to Sparta was refused. With all the cities under his control, Jason was able to build up an army of 8,000 cavalry and 20,000 hoplites – both citizen levy and mercenary – in addition to his existing 6,000 men.[26] Their pay was provided by contributions demanded of all the Thessalian cities. Jason, then, had achieved supremacy solely by the employment of a large army of mercenary soldiers and was in a position to expand beyond Thessaly thanks to that army.

Jason was an enigmatic personality. He was ostensibly an ally of Thebes and led his troops southwards to assist the Thebans, although he arrived too late to fight at Leuctra. On the other hand, he dissuaded the victorious Thebans from an all out attack on the remaining Spartan forces in Boeotia, urging negotiation over battle as a means of removing the Spartans. The total destruction of Sparta's army would leave Thebes in too strong a position. Did Jason mediate a Thessalian takeover of Greece? Isocrates maintained that Jason wanted to organise a pan-Hellenic crusade against Persia, but he himself was a staunch advocate of such a crusade and might have been attributing his own desires to Jason. Whether Jason wanted to control other parts of Greece or whether he really wanted to create a sort of Hellenic United States will never be known. He was murdered in 370 BC by seven conspirators for reasons which are also obscure, but had he lived, Jason would have had a real chance of achieving either ambition, given the size of his mercenary army.

The death of Jason showed up the fragility of a state whose cohesion and stability depended on the will and well-being of one dominant personality. The enforced unity of the Thessalians quickly vanished as their cities took sides either in support of Jason's successors at Pherae or against them. Macedonian aid was called in by several cities opposed to Pherae but the Macedonians merely annexed the very cities (Larissa and Crannon) they were supposed to save. Caught between the Macedonians and the very savage and bloody regime established at Pherae, the Thessalian cities, which were still struggling to assert their autonomy, appealed to Thebes. In a series of campaigns (369–364 BC), the Theban general Pelopidas repulsed the Macedonians and, at the battle of Cynoscephalae, decisively defeated the murderous Alexander of Pherae. Thessaly became a protectorate of Thebes but the Thebans stopped short of outright annexation, Boeotia being more important. Thus, the Thessalians retained a degree of independence, although they were, of course, no longer major contenders in the great game being played for control of Greece. In the Peloponnesus, the Arcadian League began to disintegrate as the northern Peloponnesus followed Mantinea and returned to the Spartan fold while the south sided with Tegea and, hence, Thebes. The *rapprochement* between a large part of Arcadia and Sparta strengthened the latter and, needless to say, weakened Theban influence. Epaminondas was forced to invade the Peloponnesus for a fourth time with an army made up of the Sacred Band, militia levies from all the Boeotian states, pro-Theban Peloponnesians and a modest force of mercenary peltasts. At Mantinea, his forces came up against another composite army of Spartans, Athenians and anti-Theban Peloponnesians. Epaminondas defeated his enemies in much the same way as at Leuctra but at the moment of victory he received a fatal spear thrust from a desperate Spartan.

The death of Epaminondas broke the spirit of the Thebans and effectively ended their period of hegemony. The belligerents, exhausted and short of funds, made peace. The Spartans were a shadow of their former selves and were kept in check by Megalopolis and Messenia. Athens had done rather better, owing to her naval power (about 250 ships in 360 BC), securing her hold over the Hellespont. With Thebes and Sparta more or less impotent, Athens could once again consider imperial expansion into Thrace and the Chersonese. She recaptured Euboea in 357 BC and, after the death of King Cotys, took coastal Thrace. But not everything was in Athens' favour. Although she remained moderately prosperous, her desire for renewed expansion placed an immense burden on her finances. Her large fleet was extremely expensive to maintain and her possessions outside the mainland required large numbers of mercenaries prepared to do long periods of garrison duty – mercenaries who demanded regular payment. To some extent, Athens could rely on contributions from allied cities, but some of these (Corcyra, Chios, Rhodes, Byzantium and Cos), suspicious of Athenian imperialism, abandoned the Athenian League and, of course, the payment of subsidies. No amount of taxation at home or piracy in the Aegean (to which Athens resorted) could prevent the ultimate bankruptcy of the League. Needless to say, the mercenary troops hired by Athens were not regularly paid and compensated themselves by raids on allied cities, thereby increasing Athenian unpopularity.

Athens attacked her recalcitrant allies (War of the Allies 357–355 BC) with a fleet under the command of Chabrias, carrying a large force of mercenaries led by Chares. But Chabrias was killed at Chios, Chares was forced to retreat and Iphicrates, in command of reinforcements, performed well below his usual standard. Although acquitted in a subsequent trial, Iphicrates was never given another command and died a few years later. After two years of largely unsuccessful efforts, Athens made peace and recognised the independence of the secessionists. Other allies, such as Mytilene and Perinthus, also seceded and Athens was left exhausted and a thousand talents poorer. Her mercenaries, underpaid and discontented, left Athenian service in large numbers to resume service for the Persians or to seek any location where a war was in progress.

While Athens was struggling with her erstwhile allies, another city-state

[166]

asserted its independence from the Boeotian League. Phocis had fought alongside Sparta at Leuctra and had been forced to join the League by the triumphant Thebans, very much against her will. An independent Phocis, particularly if in alliance with Athens or Sparta, presented a threat to Thebes' lingering control over Boeotia. Thebes needed a pretext to take action against Phocis and found one in the Greek religious establishment. The shrine at Delphi was Greece's most sacred religious centre, dedicated to the worship of Apollo, and was open to pilgrims from all over the Greek world. Like other shrines it was maintained and protected by leagues (Amphictyons) formed by several city-states in combination.

When the Delphi Amphictyons imposed a fine on the Phocians for cultivating land near the temple the Phocians refused to pay and elected a tyrant, the prominent and wealthy citizen Philomelus, to organise their resistance.

Philomelus appealed to the Spartans, who avoided direct involvement but provided money with which the tyrant raised a modest force of mercenaries and recruited 1,000 Phocian peltasts. In 356 BC, Philomelus captured Delphi. He killed the bitterly anti-Phocian Thracidae clan and confiscated their wealth. He was able to recruit more mercenaries and now had 5,000 in his employ. The Locrians, allies of Thebes, attacked the Phocians in an attempt to drive them out of Delphi but suffered a catastrophic defeat in a battle that was literally and metaphorically a cliff-hanger. The engagement was fought at the edge of the Phaedriad cliffs overlooking Delphi and the Locrians were either captured in substantial numbers or jumped over the cliffs to avoid possible torture and slavery.

Thebes was forced to act in order to redress the situation and declared war on the Phocians. Philomelus realised that he would need to hire a much larger army of mercenaries, in view of the fact that he had Spartan and Athenian sympathy but not their military support. The mercenaries were available but how to pay them? Extortion, no matter how thorough, did not provide sufficient sums of money. If farming sacred land had constituted a species of sacrilege, Philomelus now committed sacrilege *par excellence* by raiding the accumulated gold and silver treasures of the temple of Delphi, promising to repay what he claimed was only a loan at the end of hostilities. Although a great number of Greeks were scandalised by this action, the 10,000 mercenaries he was able to raise made absolutely no objection to this bold method of payment.

Thebes entered the war which raged on indecisively until, in 354 BC,

Philomelus was defeated at the battle of Neon and was forced, in a fitting end perhaps, to jump off a cliff to avoid capture. But Phocian fortunes revived under the leadership of Onomarchus, who invaded Locris, inflicting several defeats on its armies. The Thebans, however, began to have financial difficulties and in emulation of Agesilaus, sent General Pammenes to Asia Minor to earn money in the service of the Persian satrap Artabazus. For some reason, Artabazus became suspicious of Pammenes and imprisoned him, thereby denying Thebes her hoped-for finances. Her Thessalian allies appealed to Philip of Macedon for assistance. Philip responded by entering Thessaly and chasing out the Phocian mercenary army but was then defeated and forced to withdraw to Macedonia by Onomarchus and his entire army of 20,000 men. Phocis was at the height of its power – a power made possible solely by the recruitment of a large mercenary army and the requisitioning of sufficient means to support it. In effect, Philomelus and Onomarchus were not unusual. Nearly all tyrants in Greece and in Syracuse had based their power in mercenary troops, whether a relatively modest bodyguard or a sizeable army.

Onomarchus' final triumph was the capture of Coronea, which was held by a mixed force of citizen militia and mercenary soldiers. The events at Coronea were remarked upon by the philosopher Aristotle as a contrast between the calculated courage of mercenaries and the irrational courage of citizen soldiers. When the mercenary commander was killed, the mercenary troops retreated in the face of overwhelming Phocian numbers, bent on living to fight another day, while the citizens remained and died fighting.[27]

Philip of Macedonia returned to Thessaly in 354 BC and crushed the Phocians in a battle that destroyed at least 6,000 of the mercenary troops. Another 3,000 were captured. Onomarchus was killed while the prisoners were subsequently all drowned upon Philip's orders for their role in the sacrilege against Delphi.[28] The Phocian mercenary army had been wiped out but Phocis was saved from occupation by the prompt action of Athens, which sent troops to hold the pass at Thermopylae in order to prevent the Macedonians from penetrating further south. Temporarily thwarted, Philip consoled himself by conquering Thrace and expelling Athenian mercenary garrisons stationed there. Remarkably, Phocis managed to revive a second time, forming a new mercenary army which was reinforced by a further 2,000 mercenaries from Pherae, 1,000 troops from Sparta and 2,000 Achaeans.

In the meantime war broke out again in the Peloponnesus. With Thebes kept occupied by Phocis, Sparta attempted to destroy Megalopolis. The

Phocians had recovered strongly enough to repay Spartan help by sending 3,000 mercenary infantry to assist Sparta.[29] But the war proved indecisive. The Arcadians, Argives and Messenians fought effectively and prevented Sparta from realising her ambition. In 350 BC, the Theban financial position was substantially strengthened by King Artaxerxes who donated 300 talents in return for a temporary loan of Theban hoplites. The Thebans were then able to expand the size of their army by hiring more mercenaries. The war between Phocis and Thebes dragged on until 346 BC while in the north Philip of Macedon expanded his domains. Chalcidice made an alliance with Macedon against Athens and then changed sides. Philip, unimpressed, marched into Chalcidian territory. Most of the cities submitted without a fight but Olynthus, the chief city of the reconstituted Chalcidian Confederation, resisted and was destroyed, despite the presence of 6,000 mercenaries sent by Athens. The Athenians suffered another blow when Philip successfully encouraged Euboea to revolt. An expeditionary force sent by Athens failed to recapture the rebellious cities and the Athenians were forced to recognise Euboean independence and withdraw. In 346 BC, Athens made peace, at least temporarily, with Macedon and left Phocis in the lurch. The Phocians were forced by Philip to break up all their cities but one into villages and to repay the Delphic shrine in instalments of sixty talents a year.[30] But the Macedonian king did not exact any bloody retribution against the Phocians. Macedon, which had been traditionally regarded as barbarous by the Greeks, was accepted into the Amphictyon of Delphi in place of Phocis.

Philip's successes in Thrace, Thessaly, Chalcidice and Phocis evoked two diametrically opposed points of view in Athens. Isocrates advocated that Greece should unite under the leadership of Philip and conquer Persia. Besides the satisfaction of confirming Greek superiority over the Asiatics, there was a practical purpose behind Isocrates' view. Greece was plagued by a large number of wandering mercenaries whose very presence was a threat to society. Colonisation was the obvious answer to the problem of getting rid of these itinerant troublemakers. But all available territory in the west was already colonised by the Greeks or was solidly in the hands of rivals like the Carthaginians. The Persian empire was perceived as the weakest and most obvious target. Opposed to Isocrates was the orator and politician, Demosthenes (384–322 BC), an Athenian patriot, who mendaciously claimed that Philip wanted to destroy Athens, and gradually persuaded his fellow citizens that Philip had to be stopped by force of arms. Under his influence, the Athenians provoked the otherwise pro-Athenian Philip and delivered a fatal insult in the form of an anti-Macedonian alliance with Thebes. Distasteful as such a liaison might be to both sides, given their mutual hatred, Athens and Thebes realised that if either one fell to Philip's forces, the other would have to stand alone with every probability of being beaten.

In a supreme effort, Athens raised a mercenary army of 10,000 men under the command of Chares while her citizen levies joined the main coalition army alongside the Thebans and smaller allied contingents – both mercenary and militia – from Corinth, Megara, Achaea and Boeotia. To cut off Philip's two possible approach routes, the mercenary army was stationed near Amphissa while the main army waited in northern Boeotia.

Philip, in effect, attacked in both directions. He first shattered the mercenary forces in a rapidly executed assault. The survivors retreated eastwards to rejoin the main army. The Macedonians followed and caught up with their enemies at Chaeronea. Both armies had about 35,000 men. Demosthenes, who had done more than anyone else to provoke a confrontation, was among the Athenians, serving as an ordinary hoplite. He carried a splendid shield inscribed with the words *Agathe Tyche* (with good fortune) in gold letters. But fortune did not favour the anti-Macedonian forces. On 1 September 338 BC, Philip won a spectacular victory that gave him virtual control of Greece. The Theban Sacred Band died fighting to the last man, true to its oath, while Demosthenes fled with his compatriots, with or without his shield.

CHAPTER TEN

Macedonia, Persia and India

THE ARMY with which Philip defeated his enemies was for all practical purposes a permanent and professional force, largely national in its composition, although mercenaries were certainly present among its ranks. Philip is credited with having created a new type of phalanx in which his men were armed with lighter shields and longer spears in emulation of the so-called reforms of the Athenian mercenary general, Iphicrates. Philip, in fact, created two types of hoplites, distinguished from each other mainly by the length of their spears. The *pezetaeri* carried the longer *sarissa* (about 5.5 metres) while the *hypaspists* were armed with a somewhat shorter version (about 4.6 metres)[1] The *hypaspists*, by virtue of their lighter armament, could move more rapidly than the *pezetaeri* and operated as a link between the cavalry and the heavier infantry. They were, however, a sort of light hoplite rather than a species of peltast. Philip reintroduced the wearing of breast plates, which were of a lighter and thinner construction than had traditionally been the case. Thus, the Macedonian phalanx was deeper and more heavily armed than its Greek counterpart and yet, despite its heavier armament, it remained every bit as mobile, if not more so, than the Greek phalanx and was able to perform a great variety of tactical manoeuvres, all in perfect formation.

Philip's creation of a citizen army imbued with national spirit and a deep personal loyalty to the king was indeed a radical event in Macedonian military history and there can be no doubt that Greek mercenaries helped Philip to effect this transformation.[2] Mercenaries had already been employed by previous Macedonian monarchs on a modest scale and Philip certainly had a corps of mercenary troops serving alongside his national forces. He made use of his mercenaries in three ways, all of which were classical functions of the mercenary soldier: as garrison troops in newly conquered territories; as instructors for his native recruits and as expeditionary troops sent to assist pro-Macedonian friends wishing to establish tyrannies in their native cities by force of arms. Among other examples of the last mentioned were mercenary expeditions despatched to Euboea to install tyrants in Porthmus, Oreus, Chalcis and Eretria. The precise number of troops in Philip's mercenary corps remains unknown, but given that Alexander the Great initially had 5,000 Greek mercenaries (not allies) in the army with which he invaded the Persian empire, it is not unreasonable to suggest a similar figure for Philip's mercenary troops. At Chaeronea, he seems to have included about 6,000 mercenaries – most probably peltasts – in his army.[3] The mercenary corps was not commanded by Greek mercenary generals – although a few of these were among Philip's entourage – but by native Macedonian commanders of whom two are known by name: Parmenio and Adaeus the Cock.

With his professional army, Philip was able to defeat the Illyrians (inflicting 7,000 casualties in one battle on a total force of 10,000 men), take control of Thessaly, Thrace and the Hellespontine corn route from southern Russia and finally impose Macedonian domination over the Greek mainland south of Thermopylae. Philip treated Athens leniently out of respect for her culture and her still considerable naval power. He dealt with Thebes rather more harshly for having changed sides. He ravaged Spartan territory so that, when he convened a congress of all the Greek states at Corinth, Sparta was conspicuous by her absence. Philip, however, did not force Sparta to comply.

At Corinth, Philip announced his intention to lead a combined force raised from all over Greece against Persia, which was ostensibly weaker than ever. Around the time of Chaeronea, the strong King Artaxerxes Ochus had been murdered and replaced by the ineffectual King Arses. Isocrates, the passionate champion of pan-Hellenism, lived long enough to see Philip's victory but, while Philip was able to impose his will on the Greeks, he failed to create an atmosphere of unity. The Greek states grudgingly provided contingents of troops because they had no choice but were ready to rebel at the slightest favourable opportunity. Nevertheless, Philip initiated his grand design to invade Persian territory by sending Parmenio and a largely mercenary force of 10,000 men to Bithynia as an advance guard (336 BC). In the Hellespontine region Parmenio's troops came up against 5,000 mercenaries led by the Greek general, Memnon of Rhodes, a member of the Persian ruling class by virtue of his marriage to the sister of Artabazus. Despite their distinct numerical superiority, Parmenio's mercenaries were held in check by those of Memnon, who displayed considerable tactical skill. This was as far as Philip got in his campaign for he was murdered during the summer of 336 BC for reasons that have occasioned much speculation but have remained obscure owing to the swift demise of the assassin immediately after his capture.

Philip's murder was the signal for a general revolt throughout Thrace, Illyria, Thessaly and the territories south of the Thermopylae pass. In Athens, Demosthenes was exultant but Philip's son and heir, Alexander, did not panic. He rapidly marched into Greece as far as Corinth in a highly visible show of Macedonian military power. The Greek confederacy organised by Philip recognised him as its leader. It had, of course, little choice other than another risky confrontation on the battlefield. Alexander then turned northwards to deal with Thrace and Illyria.

While Alexander was restoring order in the north, Thebes revolted against Macedonian rule on the strength of an unconfirmed report that the new king had been killed in Illyria. The rumour proved to be greatly exaggerated for Alexander soon returned, defeated the Theban army and captured the city, slaughtering some 6,000 of its inhabitants (335 BC). All of Greece was impressed by the fate that befell Thebes and the urge to revolt against Macedonian hegemony rapidly subsided. There was, however, little sympathy for Thebes, which had, after all, sided with the Persian invaders during the previous century and had been as domineering as Sparta at the height of its power. Like Philip before him, Alexander treated Athens leniently, despite the activities of Demosthenes and the anti-Macedonian faction. He had need of the Athenian fleet. With his domination over Greece firmly re-established, he could focus all his boundless energy on the conquest of the Persian empire, which was now ruled by Darius III Codomannus, Arses having been poisoned in 336 BC.

In the spring of 334 BC, Alexander began his adventure at the head of some 32,000 infantry and 5,000 cavalry, taking care to leave 12,000 Macedonian infantry and 1,500 cavalry under the command of Antipater to assure domestic order in Macedonia and Greece. He was able to cross the Hellespont unopposed by the Persians, owing to the continued presence of Parmenio and his advance guard of Macedonians and Greek mercenaries. Parmenio, although contained to the eastern shore of the Hellespont, had not been dislodged by Memnon of Rhodes. Needless to say, estimates of the size of the Macedonian army, let alone narrative and interpretative details, vary in the accounts of Alexander's campaigns left to us by Arrian, Diodorus Siculus, Plutarch and Curtius. But it is reasonably certain that Alexander's initial

[173]

force was made up of 12,000 Macedonian hoplites, 7,000 Greek troops provided by the Corinthian League, 7,000 Thracians and Illyrians, 5,000 Greek mercenaries and 1,000 light troops. The cavalry contained 1,800 Macedonians, 1,800 Thessalians, 900 Thracians and Paeonians and 600 Corinthian League Greeks. The addition of Parmenio's troops who, despite losses inflicted by Memnon, still represented a significant force, increased the size of Alexander's army to over 40,000 men.[4]

The 5,000 Greek mercenaries are the only Greek troops recorded as being mercenaries, having been directly recruited by Alexander. But it is likely that the contingents provided by the Corinthian League also contained sizeable numbers of mercenaries hired to replace unenthusiastic citizen militia hoplites. Scutage was by that time a well established practice. The precise number of mercenaries cannot be known, given that they operated as part of contingents officially supplied in the name of particular city-states, not as independent units.

The light troops were mercenary contingents made up in roughly equal proportions of Agrianians from a small Balkan kingdom just north of Macedon and Cretan archers. The latter had a long-established reputation as the best archers in the Greek world but they also had a well-established reputation for unreliability that may explain their relatively modest numbers in Alexander's army. The Agrianians, by contrast, enjoyed a solid reputation as tough and reliable fighters. They served continuously throughout Alexander's campaigns with great distinction and were regularly reinforced with new recruits. Alexander valued them highly and they certainly impressed Arrian, who mentions them nearly fifty times in his account. The precise status of the Agrianians has been debated by scholars.[5] Their king, Longarus, was a long-standing friend and a *de facto* subject of the Macedonian king and consequently they might be regarded as auxiliaries or allies rather than straight-forward mercenaries, but when Alexander discharged them along with his Greek mercenaries at a later stage of his campaign, they re-enrolled as mercenaries.

At the beginning of his campaign, Alexander's army was not preponderantly a mercenary army, simply because the Macedonian king could not afford to hire them on a large scale. His financial problems were to some extent alleviated by contributions from the Corinthian League and the Greek cities of Asia Minor but it was not until after the battle of Issus that Alexander's pecuniary situation was improved by the acquisition of loot from the Persians. Alexander's own Macedonian phalanxes were as effective as any mercenary troops and always formed the spearhead of his army, along with the cavalry. He did not need mercenaries as shock troops. But although he was not reliant on mercenaries he nevertheless needed them for a number of purposes and, according to H. W. Parke, he employed over 42,700 Greek infantry and 5,180 cavalry between 334–329 BC.[6] He recruited Greek mercenaries on a regular basis to make up for losses but only 10,000–12,000 seem to have been included in Alexander's field army at any one time. Field operations were not the main purpose for which Alexander hired Greek mercenaries. Other than those he retained for service as support troops in the field army, Alexander used his mercenaries for four basic functions: garrison duty, the protection of supply lines, detached expeditions to attack targets by-passed by the main army and the creation of colonies in distant parts of his empire. As Alexander's empire grew larger, he had perforce to recruit more and more mercenaries to garrison every newly-acquired city, fortress or other strategic location. His creation of colonies after the battle of Gaugamela was partly a method of settling soldiers who had passed their optimum value as fighting troops and also represented a conscious effort to promote the permanent establishment of Hellenic civilisation in the furthest reaches of the Macedonian domains. To this end he supported the intermingling of his Greek and Asiatic subjects and encouraged Eurasian marriages.

The deeper Alexander penetrated into Asia, the more his army became mercenarised, but at the beginning of his campaign it was the Persian army that contained by far the largest number of Greek mercenaries. At Granicus, he faced some 20,000 Persian cavalry and about the same number of mercenaries. At the end of the battle he captured 2,000 of the latter and sent them in chains to a dreadful existence doing hard labour in Macedonia as a punishment for having fought against fellow Greeks.[7] Until this incident there had been little opprobrium attached to the performance of mercenary service in Persian armies. Individual hoplite militiamen had been able to go to Asia as mercenaries without losing their citizenship or any other rights they possessed as natives of a particular city-state. In fact, the governments of Greek city-states had even replaced the hiring of mercenaries on a private and individual basis by offering whole contingents of citizen hoplites and peltasts to Persian satraps as a money-making venture and as a way of temporarily removing potentially unruly elements. As described in a previous chapter, even kings resorted to mercenary service. Alexander's action in enslaving his Greek captives might have been approved of by Isocrates and the pan-Hellenists but as word spread among other Greek mercenaries in

Persian service it merely intensified their resistance and no troops are harder to overcome than those who feel they have nothing to lose by fighting to the bitter end. Alexander, however, realised his mistake and in subsequent encounters he spared the surviving Greeks on condition that they took service in the Macedonian army. And he encountered them in nearly every city and strategic point. At the siege of Miletus, Alexander was deeply impressed by the courage and loyalty of some 300 mercenaries who had obviously decided to fight to the death and refrained from attacking them when they agreed to serve in his own army. At Halicarnassus in Caria, Alexander's forces were fiercely resisted by a garrison composed of Persians and 2,000 Greek mercenaries, the latter commanded by Ephialtes, an Athenian exile. Memnon, who was in overall command of the city, ordered a night sortie by the Greek mercenaries aimed at burning Alexander's siege engines. The attack came close to achieving its objective and was barely repulsed by veteran Macedonian troops. Memnon withdrew from Halicarnassus, not before setting fire to the city, so that Alexander was left in possession of burnt-out ruins. The Macedonian king left some 3,000 Greek mercenaries and 200 cavalry to reduce two nearby strongholds (Salmakis and the Arconnese) still held by the enemy and to establish control over the rest of Caria while he marched on to Phrygia.[8] This was an instance, among many others, of Alexander's use of mercenaries on detached expeditions while the main army operated elsewhere.

On the way to Phrygia, Alexander captured the fortified town of Hyparna. Its mercenary garrison, much less obdurate than that of Halicarnassus, surrendered without a fight. The fate of the mercenaries is unrecorded, but it seems likely that Alexander would have taken them into service. Alexander next established his control over Lycia. He took the city of Telmissus not with a phalanx of hoplites but with a troupe of dancing girls. These charming entertainers and their slave attendants were sent into the city by one of Alexander's generals, Nearchus the Cretan, as a gift to the Persian commander. With daggers hidden in their flutes and small shields secreted in their baskets, the girls waited until their delighted hosts had imbibed sufficient quantities of wine and then used their daggers. Deprived of leadership, the citizens of Telmissus submitted to Alexander without further ado.[9] With Lycia under control, Alexander attacked Pisidia. He used light troops against light troops – Agrianians against Pisidians – and supported them with Macedonian heavy infantry. Alexander captured western Pisidia but did not bother with the rest. Like the Persian satraps before him, he

[176]

perhaps felt that a handful of tough and barbaric tribesmen were not worth the effort. He entered Phrygia and at the town of Celaenae came across a garrison of 1,000 Carians and 100 Greek mercenaries who agreed to surrender if Persian reinforcements did not arrive by a certain specified date. Celaenae surrendered when relief forces failed to materialise.[10] Again, the fate of the mercenaries remains unknown, but Alexander had probably learnt his lesson regarding captured mercenaries. Alexander continued on to Gordium, leaving Antigonus of Elimiotis with 1,500 men to guard Celaenae, which lay at the junction of several strategic main roads.

Alexander continued his march via Cappadocia and reached the Cilician Gates, the very same narrow pass in the Taurus mountains through which Cyrus and the Ten Thousand had travelled. The pass was an ideal spot for Persian resistance against the invaders but, at the approach of Alexander's *hypaspists* and Thracian mercenary light troops, the Persians fled without having offered any resistance. Darius, increasingly disconcerted by Alexander's uncontested approach, recalled all the Greek mercenary troops, including those sent to garrison the Aegean cities captured by Memnon.

Alexander moved on through Issus and crossed the Syrian gates. At this point, he was forced to retreat by Darius' attempt to cut him off via the northern passes of the Amanus mountains. Darius' thrust from the north was a sound piece of strategy for he had effectively cut Alexander's lines of communication and supply. According to Arrian, however, Alexander positively revelled in what was actually a stroke of good fortune. In a rousing speech to his somewhat perturbed officers, he pointed out that the Macedonian army was fighting for the cause of Greece while Darius' Greek mercenaries were only fighting for money, the implication being that men inspired by a noble cause must perforce fight better than men motivated purely by financial gain.

At best, Darius might have had 100,000 men but it is much more likely that his army was only marginally larger than that of the Macedonians. The 30,000 Greek mercenaries claimed by Arrian was an exaggeration. Allowing that the mercenaries had been in the forefront of fighting at the River Granicus and had lost some 3,000–4,000 casualties and 2,000 prisoners, J. B. Bury's figure of 15,000 seems reasonable.[11] Darius might have deployed up to 20,000 Greek mercenaries if he received reinforcements from among the Greek troops recalled from Asia Minor but this speculative figure represents the upper limit. He certainly had more than 10,000 Greeks.[12] Ten thousand mercenaries survived the battle of Issus, despite their presence at the most bitterly contested part of the field, and a loss rate of some 5,000 men seems a credible figure.

At the start of the battle, Alexander's army was drawn up with the Agrianian light troops, placed on the extreme right to protect Alexander's forces there from a detachment of Persian light troops which had outflanked the Macedonian army. Then came Alexander himself and the Companion cavalry; six Macedonian phalanxes and the *hypaspists*; Cretan archers and Thracian peltasts and, finally, Thessalian and Greek allied cavalry on the extreme left of the line. Alexander's Greek mercenaries, unlike those of Darius, never the spearhead of Macedonian armies, lay in reserve behind the phalanxes.

The Persian army opposite was arrayed in two lines, with Darius and his bodyguards in the centre of the first line and the all-important Greek mercenaries on either side. Both extremities of the line were held by Persian *kardakes* who were a species of peltasts. The second line was made up of Asiatic levies, who were no real match for hoplites. Darius' army might have been larger but in reality the Persian king had fewer good-quality soldiers – Greek mercenaries and Persian bodyguards – than his Macedonian opponent.

Alexander opened the battle of Issus by using the Agrianian light troops to drive away the Persian light troops threatening his right flank. Satisfied that his flank was now secure, he now led the Companion cavalry in an attack that shattered the *kardakes* and archers of the Persian left. But his impetuous if successful charge opened up a gap between his cavalry and the phalanxes, whose progress had been slowed by their crossing of the Pinarus river, which flowed between the two armies, and the steep and uneven ground covered with brambles which lay on the other side. It was this gap that Darius' Greek mercenaries exploited, attacking the disordered phalanxes with savage determination. Thus, the main struggle at Issus took place in the centre of the field and its intensity may be gauged by the fact that the Macedonians lost 120 officers and their general, Ptolemy, son of Seleucas.[13]

In his speech before the battle, Alexander had spoken lightly of the mercenaries, and his attitude to his own Greek mercenaries often bordered on mistrust, hence their employment as reserves rather than frontline troops. But in ascribing purely pecuniary motives to Darius' Greeks, Alexander had under-estimated both their motives and their determination. Darius' mercenaries were largely made up of professionals toughened by long years of service in Persian armies. Some were self-exiled and embittered opponents of

Macedonian control over Greek affairs. At any rate, as Arrian recorded, the fight was animated 'by the old racial rivalry of Greek and Macedonian'.[14] For some time, the battle hung in the balance until Alexander wheeled leftwards with his cavalry and *hypaspists* and attacked Darius' mercenaries on the flank. On the left of his line, the Persian cavalry attacked the Thessalian and allied horsemen and there, too, a desperate fight ensued which was only broken off when the Greek mercenaries in the centre began to retreat in the face of Alexander's cavalry onslaught and it became apparent that Darius himself was fleeing the field in undignified haste, leaving behind his mother, wife and children (whom Alexander treated with respect).

After Issus, Alexander did not pursue Darius deeply into the interior of the Persian empire, but chose instead to complete the conquest of Syria and Phoenicia and then march on to Egypt. Above all, he aimed to capture Phoenician seaports, for the Phoenician fleets were by far the most important element in the Persian navy. Possession of the Phoenician coastline would effectively give Alexander control of the eastern Mediterranean.

The cities of Phoenicia had enjoyed complete freedom from Persian interference as long as their ships were placed at the disposition of the Persians when required. To some extent Alexander's task was facilitated by the fact that the coastal cities were in a state of commercial rivalry rather than federal union. Byblos, Sidon and Aradus yielded without any resistance but the inhabitants of Tyre felt that submission to Alexander might be premature, given that the Persians were not yet decisively defeated. The siege of Tyre, however, proved to be the toughest objective that Alexander had to face and it took him seven months (January–August 332 BC) before he was able to capture the city. Macedonia now replaced Persia as the supreme naval power in the eastern Mediterranean.

The fall of Tyre now enabled Alexander to gain control over Syria–Palestine and continue into Egypt. The town of Gaza, however, decided to resist, laid in plentiful supplies and hired an army of mercenary Arab troops. There is no indication in the Ancient sources as to the motives of the Arab soldiers. Whether their service was purely a matter of money or whether it was informed by some other sentiment, the Arabs fought with great spirit and it took four major assaults over a two-month period before the city was taken by storm. Arrian relates that the Arabs and the native levies died fighting to the last man.

With Gaza conquered, Alexander moved on to Egypt where he received a warm welcome, particularly from the Egyptian priesthood. The Persian satrap of Egypt, Mazaces, had the good sense to submit to Alexander rather than sacrifice himself for a lost cause like Darius and was duly rewarded with an administrative position in the new government established by Alexander. The Macedonian king, like most citizens of the Hellenic world, had a kind of mystical reverence for Egyptian civilisation and treated the Egyptian religious establishment with genuine sensitivity, unlike the hated Persians. At Memphis in November 332 BC he was crowned Pharaoh and henceforth combined the functions of a god and a king.

While he was in Memphis, Alexander received a valuable reinforcement of 400 Greek mercenary cavalry commanded by Menidas and 500 Thracian cavalry. Unlike Darius, who relied largely on Greek mercenaries for effective infantry, Alexander placed a secondary value on mercenary hoplites, preferring to employ his native Macedonian phalanxes. The disposition of the Greek mercenary infantry at the rear or on the flanks of his army in his three main battles against the Persians clearly illustrates his attitude, but mercenary cavalry was another matter. Right up to and including the battle of Gaugamela, Alexander was deficient in light cavalry while his opponent had an ample supply. At Gaugamela, which was primarily a cavalry battle, Alexander's light-horsemen, posted on the right of his battle line, were extremely hard-pressed by the more heavily armoured Scythian and Bactrian cavalry sent by Darius against the Macedonian right flank. The mercenary cavalry and infantry faced up to ten times their number and barely managed to hold out while Alexander launched a frontal attack that crushed Darius' household guard and his Greek mercenaries and transformed a potentially dangerous situation into a spectacular victory.

The battle of Gaugamela was Darius' last chance to stop Alexander. Darius' army certainly outnumbered Alexander's forces. Arrian offers a figure of 40,000 infantry and 7,000 cavalry, which, for once, seems a reasonable claim. The Persian king had 30,000–40,000 cavalry but his infantry forces had been substantially weakened by the desertion of 8,000 Greek mercenaries after the *débâcle* at Issus. He now had a mere 2,000 left, which were nevertheless placed in the centre of his line along with 2,000 troops of his household guard. The 8,000 deserters led by Amyntas marched away to Tripolis, sailed to Egypt, where Amyntas lost his life in an abortive attempt at conquering the country, and finally wound up in the service of the Spartan king Agis. While Alexander was busy reducing the Persian empire, Agis had decided to attack Megalopolis but met defeat at the hands of the Macedonian general Antipater. The survivors of the 8,000 deserters from Issus were sent back by Antipater to Alexander who settled them in colonies in Bactria. After Alexander's death, the Issus mercenaries – always anti-Macedonian – played a role in a general revolt of Greek mercenaries against their more-or-less forced settlement in the colonies that the Macedonian king had established in an attempt to fuse the Hellenic and Asiatic subjects of his empire into one universal monarchy.

The attack by the Bactrian and Scythian cavalry against Alexander's mercenary cavalry and infantry (which included both the 'old mercenaries' who had been with Alexander from the start of his campaign and the newly-recruited mercenaries under Menidas) was, as previously mentioned, a precarious moment during the battle of Gaugamela. The Persian cavalry was far superior in numbers and armament and the Scythians especially were no mean warriors. But the very act of sending such a large body of cavalry to attack Alexander's right opened up a gap between the attacking cavalry and Darius' left centre. Observing this, Alexander immediately charged with the Companion cavalry and the closest Macedonian phalanxes. In a few minutes the tide of battle turned in Alexander's favour. Darius' guard and the 2,000 Greek mercenaries gave way before Alexander's onslaught while the Scythian and Bactrian cavalry still engaged against the Greek mercenaries suddenly found its own right flank exposed to attack and, although undefeated, was forced to withdraw. The Persian king saw his centre wavering, took the hint and barely managed to flee, abandoning along the way his chariot, his bow, 4,000 talents and the last vestiges of his authority and prestige. As the realisation that Darius had once again deserted spread through the Persian horsemen, they broke off their attack and fled. Alexander was free once again to resume his pursuit of Darius and chased the unfortunate monarch with unrelenting vigour throughout the night. Darius, however, had gained a substantial head start and escaped to Media. Nevertheless, Alexander could derive great satisfaction from the events of 1 October 331 BC. Gaugamela was one of history's most decisive battles for it marked the end of the Achaemenid dynasty and the Persian empire.

Alexander ceased to pursue Darius and marched to Babylon where he declared himself the legitimate successor to the Achaemenid dynasty. He took a conciliatory approach, thereby winning the cooperation of the Persian nobility, which had always provided the empire with its administrators. For the Persians, supporting Alexander was much better than being demoted into oblivion and meant a retention of their prestige and a measure of power.

Leaving Babylon, Alexander marched on to Susa, which had already been secured by an advance party of light troops under Philoxenus. On the way, Alexander received a substantial reinforcement of 1,500 cavalry and 13,500 infantry recruited in Greece and Macedonia by Amyntas.[15] About one third of these troops were native Macedonians and the remainder were mercenary volunteers. When he reached Susa, Alexander found, much to his delight, some 50,000 talents in gold and silver bullion and an extra 9,000 talents of minted gold coins, which would come in useful as Alexander gradually had to encourage his soldiers to march further east by liberally increasing their pay.

In January 330 BC, Alexander left Susa bound for Persepolis. In order to reach Persia by the closest possible route, Alexander had to cross the Zagros–Anshan mountain ranges and here he encountered two obstacles. The first consisted of the Uxian tribes, who were eventually attacked and practically annihilated by Craterus, one of Alexander's generals. The second obstacle was the satrap Ariobarzanes, who had built defences across a pass known as the Persian gates and awaited Alexander with an army of some 40,000 infantry and 700 horsemen, some of them survivors of Gaugamela. A frontal assault against Ariobarzanes' men was bloodily repulsed but the Macedonian king was able to lead troops behind the enemy lines and crush the Persians in coordination with another frontal attack launched by Craterus.

Just outside Persepolis, Alexander was welcomed not by city officials but by a strange and unsettling deputation of mutilated men. These pitiable figures were aged Greeks who had been mercenaries in the service of the Egyptian Pharaoh, Nectanebo, or other equally rebellious Persian satraps and had been punished by Artaxerxes III Ochus in the usual oriental fashion. They all bore brand-marks on their foreheads and lacked hands or feet. Alexander's first impulse was to repatriate these unfortunate ex-mercenaries but, on being told that there was nothing for them back in Greece and that they wished to form a farming community in Persia, Alexander provided them with cash, seeds and animals. Persepolis itself was burnt to the ground in revenge, Alexander claimed, for Xerxes' destruction of Athens. It was a foolish and wanton act, criticised at the time by Parmenio, and later regretted by Alexander.

Alexander left the ruins of Persepolis and marched towards Media. He had heard that Darius was at Ecbatana, attempting to raise another army. Alexander's progress was so rapid that the Persian king was unable to raise any substantial forces. He still had the majority of the 2,000 Greek mercenaries who had fought for him at Gaugamela and had remained remarkably loyal. There were also some satrapal contingents which included

Bactrians and Arachosians, but Scythian and Cadusian reinforcements upon which Darius had counted failed to arrive. With his preparations incomplete and his army too weak (3,000 cavalry and 6,000 infantry), Darius fled towards Bactria and Alexander entered Ecbatana unopposed.

Up until his entry into Ecbatana, the proportion of mercenaries and allies in Alexander's full army had remained more or less constant. He had progressively enrolled Greek mercenaries who had formerly been in Persian service into his own forces and had received reinforcements from Greece, but most of these were left as garrison troops in the towns and fortresses taken during his advance into Asia. Many of the mercenaries who entered his field army were merely replacements for losses incurred along the way. Alexander's army had remained primarily a citizen army and its mercenary component still stood at 5,000–6,000 men in a force that averaged about 40,000 men. Now, however, Alexander effected a change during his sojourn in Ecbatana that effectively mercenarised a much greater part of his army. With the Persian empire all but conquered, the purpose of the Corinthian League had been achieved. Consequently, Alexander discharged all the allied troops, including the Thessalian cavalry, paying each cavalryman a bonus of one talent (6,000 drachmas) and each infantryman 1,000 drachmas in addition to their normal pay. For the horsemen the bonus amounted to eight years' accumulated pay while to the footsoldier it represented three years' pay.[16] Alexander was nothing if not generous and possessed a rather nonchalant attitude towards financial matters. His munificence did not end there for he offered an inducement of three talents (18,000 drachmas) to those who re-enlisted on the spot as mercenaries in his army.[17] This was, of course, additional to their normal pay. Despite his princely offer, some of the League troops preferred demobilisation and were provided with a cavalry escort back to the Aegean coast and were safely transported by ship as far as Euboea. Alexander seems to have calculated that these returning veterans would act as recruiting agents by recounting tales of his benevolence and generosity. Although there are no precise figures for those who chose to re-enlist, all the ancient sources devoted to Alexander's career are unanimous in recording that the Macedonian monarch found no lack of applicants. With the expenditure of some 12,000–13,000 talents Alexander had bought himself a ready-made mercenary army.[18] The former League troops now owed their allegiance directly to their paymaster and not to their native cities. His own Macedonian troops, although not mercenary by status, had become mercenary by nature, seduced by Alexander's liberal rates of pay – they too received

[183]

bonuses – and the large quantity of loot that had resulted from their king's successful campaigns.

While Alexander was mercenarising his army at Ecbatana, Darius' fortunes continued to decline. His immediate retinue of Persian nobles, notably Bessus, the satrap of Bactria, now considered the king to be a completely lost cause. Only foreigners – the Greek mercenaries led by Patron of Phocis and Glaucus of Aetolia – remained loyal, partly out of a genuine sense of attachment and partly in apprehension of what Alexander might to do them if they were caught. Bessus seized Darius, deposed him as king of Persia and finally killed him. Darius' Greek mercenaries, wanting no connection with Bessus whom they regarded as a traitor, broke away and headed north towards the Caspian Sea. Not all mercenaries were prepared to simply change sides when their employer's luck ran out.

Bessus then escaped to Bactria, where he began to raise another army, while Alexander advanced to the town of Zadracarta and took the unconditional surrender of Darius' surviving Greek mercenaries. At first he threatened them with dire consequences for having fought against the Greek cause by serving Darius but, in a more conciliatory mood, incorporated them into his army as a unit henceforth to serve at the standard rate of pay.

After a quick campaign to subdue Mardia, Alexander resumed his march towards Bactria. However, he was forced to break off his pursuit of Bessus when he received news that the satrap of Aria, Satibarzanes, who had ostensibly submitted to Macedonian rule, was now in open revolt. Alexander could not afford to have enemies behind him as he advanced further east. A rapid descent into Aria caught Satibarzanes completely by surprise. The Persian fled to Bactria, where Bessus gave him 2,000 Bactrian cavalry so that he could again foment rebellion in Aria. On this second occasion, Alexander made characteristic use of his Greek mercenaries. He did not deal personally with Satibarzanes but sent Artabazus, who was not averse to fighting a fellow Persian and rival satrap, with a Greek mercenary force of 6,000 footsoldiers and 600 cavalry. The latter, under the command of Erigyius of Mytilene, was composed of mercenary horsemen long in Alexander's service and former Corinthian League troops now become mercenaries after their official discharge and re-enrolment at Ecbatana. The infantry included Darius' former mercenaries (about 1,500 men) under Andronicus who had initially accepted their surrender and had been appointed their commander by King Alexander. In the event, Satibarzanes' second revolt was short-lived. In a short and sharp encounter between the Greek mercenaries and the rebels,

Erigyius hit Satibarzanes in the face with a spear, thereby effectively terminating the rebellion.

With Aria now secure, Alexander incorporated Drangiana, Arachosia and Gedrosia into his empire. This was a huge territory, not easily won, which stretched from eastern Iran through Afghanistan and Baluchistan to modern Pakistan west of the Indus river. The welcome arrival of 6,000 mercenaries – Illyrians and Lydians in almost equal proportions – sent by Antipater enabled Alexander to found Herat in north-western Afghanistan, the settlement then being known as Alexandria of the Arians.[19] Alexander progressively established several cities that bore the name Alexandria, followed by some geographical qualification, such as Alexandria of the Caucasus (near Kabul), of Margiana (western Bactria), of Tarmita on the Oxus (northern Bactria) and Alexandria Eschate, the easternmost settlement (northern Tajzikistan). All of Alexander's settlements were primarily established as garrison cities, although some of them also became commercial centres. Their garrisons were largely made up of Greek mercenaries, more or less settled under compulsion, who were beyond their peak as fighting men or whose loyalty was not above suspicion. This latter criterion certainly applied to more than just a few of the Greeks. On receipt of a false report that Alexander had died during his campaign in India, 3,000 Greek settlers in Bactria revolted and made their way back to Greece.[20]

From Arachosia, Alexander marched north across the Hindu Kush into Bactria in extremely adverse weather, there to settle accounts with Bessus who retreated north into Sogdiana (modern Uzbekistan and Tajzikistan).

When he reached the River Oxus (Amu Darya), Alexander was faced with a mutiny. His Thessalian mercenary cavalry, who were already upset by Alexander's murder of his popular general Parmenio (in Drangiana), on suspicion that he *might* turn traitor, refused to continue in the atrocious conditions in which the king chose to operate. Alexander could not prevent the Thessalians from leaving and he released them, not without paying them their bonuses and severance money.[21] He made up for his sudden deficiency in cavalry by recruiting local Bactrian horsemen. This was not the first time he had recruited Asian troops, for he had already incorporated a modest number of Iranian light cavalry into his army, but from this time onwards he began to employ non-Hellenic soldiers on a more substantial scale, not always with the approval of his fellow Macedonians.

In retreating from Bactria without a fight, Bessus lost the confidence and support of the Sogdian feudal lords led by Spitamenes. He was arrested and a message was sent to Alexander to the effect that Bessus would be available for collection by a Macedonian officer of Alexander's choice. Ptolemy was despatched to Sogdiana and returned with Bessus, who was subsequently flogged, mutilated, given a show trial and then executed. Regicide was the one crime that stimulated a common sentiment among all monarchs, even when the victim happened to be the enemy. In sentencing Bessus, Alexander undoubtedly remembered his own father's death at the hands of an assassin.

The betrayal of Bessus by the Sogdians gave Alexander the false impression that Sogdiana was prepared to submit to his authority and the Sogdians, for their part, thought Alexander had merely wanted to capture Bessus. He moved on northwards to Samarkand and the Jaxartes river (Syr-Darya), which he wisely determined would be the limit of his empire, for beyond the river lay the limitless steppe. It was on the Jaxartes that he laid the foundations of Alexandria Eschate (Alexandria the ultimate).

Alexander summoned the Sogdian feudal lords to a conference but was faced with a revolt instead. The Sogdians captured seven fortresses which Alexander had established on his way to the Jaxartes and massacred their Greek mercenary garrisons. Spitamenes' forces, which included Kirghizian nomads and Scythian allies, laid siege to Samarkand. Alexander despatched sixty Companion cavalry, 800 mercenary cavalry and 1,500 mercenary infantry to the assistance of Samarkand, forcing Spitamenes to lift the siege.

Despite a costly campaign in which Spitamenes' guerrilla tactics took a heavy toll of Alexander's mercenary garrisons, Spitamenes' movements were gradually made more difficult by the increasing number of forts that Alexander established throughout Sogdiana and Bactria, all garrisoned by mercenaries under Macedonian officers. Nevertheless, he induced the Massagetae to contribute 3,000 horsemen to a raid he proposed to make on a Sogdian border stronghold. The Scythians – natural fighters and natural mercenaries, living in relative poverty with no towns or cities of their own – were always ready for a good *razzia*. But the raiders were soundly defeated by Coenus, the Macedonian commander of the area. Spitamenes' Bactrian and Sogdian followers deserted him, and the Massagetae, wishing to placate Alexander, removed Spitamenes' head and sent it to the Macedonian king with a message to the effect that the hostilities had all been a needless misunderstanding.

Alexander was now ready to embark on his ultimate adventure, the invasion of India. He was motivated partly by the desire for world domination which had gradually come to possess him as the sheer momentum of his military success progressively increased the size of his empire and led him further east. Alexander's more immediate justification was the fact that Cyrus the Great had once ruled parts of the Punjab and that, as heir to the Achaemenid empire, he was now entitled to reclaim these lost territories which were reputed to be fabulously wealthy. India, largely unknown and legendary, beckoned him on like the sirens in Homer's *Odyssey*.

The size of Alexander's invasion force is unknown and has variously been estimated as low as 20,000 and as high as 120,000.[22] Some 50,000–60,000 would not be improbable, given the military resources at Alexander's disposal, and a similar number of camp followers is well within acceptable limits because the character of the army had utterly changed from that of earlier Macedonian forces. Whereas Philip of Macedon had strictly limited the non-military component of his armies, Alexander's military establishment had become a veritable ambulant city – even more so than Xenophon's Ten Thousand – a city that contained not just soldiers and their personal servants but engineers, doctors, scientists, geographers and teachers, clerks and secretaries, tradesmen, traders and money-changers, poets, musicians and literary men, athletes, jesters, jugglers, cooks, seers and other assorted charlatans and, of course, a large number of women and children, which increased exponentially. Alexander's army had also ceased to be a predominantly Hellenic one. He had begun to recruit 30,000 Asiatic youths who were to be taught Greek and to be trained as hoplites in Macedonian fighting tactics.

Other than the mercenary cavalry and a few thousand footsoldiers, Alexander did not take many Greek mercenaries with him into India for he had left most of them to perform garrison duty in his newly-acquired provinces. There were nearly 10,000 of them in Bactria alone. The mercenary component of his army was largely Asiatic. He had at least 1,000 Scythians (Saka and Massagetae) who, despite their recent confrontation with Alexander, now happily participated in the expedition as mercenary horse archers and proved their worth against the forces of King Porus. Alexander's cavalry also contained Arachosians, Bactrians, Sogdians and Dahae. Among the infantry were the reliable Agrianians.

North-western India was a patchwork of small states. Some of them were republics ruled by oligarchies made up of tribal representatives or heads of families drawn from the *Kshatriya* caste – the warrior caste of Indian society. Assemblies of the oligarchs were presided over by a *rajah* – a non-hereditary position whose occupant was a chief rather than a king.[23] The republics of the Punjab tended to be more tolerant and receptive of unorthodox ideas, such as Buddhism and Jainism, more ready to assimilate foreigners and foreign influences. Other north-western states were monarchies ruled by hereditary kings, who were considered divine and were also mainly from the *Kshatriya* caste. But whether they were republics or monarchies, the Punjabi states were considered by other Indian states as being somewhat suspect because they had been contaminated, as it were, by foreign ideas and philosophies during their occupation by the Persians.

The armies of the Punjab and, indeed, of India as a whole, were largely professional. India, after all, had a hereditary warrior class which was, theoretically at least, ranked second after the Brahmin caste. Thus, the Indian states possessed sizeable standing armies made up of *Kshatriya* and mercenaries. The latter were not foreigners from beyond India's northern borders but native Indians often formed into free companies, somewhat akin to the mercenary companies of medieval Europe, who hired their services to various rulers throughout the sub-continent. Indian monarchs could also call upon the part-time soldiers of the guild-levies – tradesmen and craftsmen who received military training on a regular basis and were mobilised in time of war. But these were normally the only militia troops. The peasantry was largely left alone to till the fields in order to feed their social superiors in the warrior and Brahmin castes. The armies of India, then, were extremely tough and professional. During the Persian invasion of Greece, the Punjab had provided Persia with some of its finest troops.

Fortunately for Alexander, the states of north-western India were utterly disunited and gripped by the same sort of neighbourly rivalry and hatred that characterised almost every other region of the world, not least the Hellenic world. There was certainly no question of a united resistance to Alexander. Thus, when the Macedonian king invaded the Punjab in 327 BC, he was able to form an alliance with Omphis (Taxiles to the Greeks), the *rajah* of Takshashila (Taxila), against King Porus of the Pauravas, whose kingdom lay between the River Hydaspes and the River Acesines.

Alexander opened his campaign by crossing the Hindu Kush, overcoming fierce resistance from the local hill tribes of the region, and marching towards the Kabul river. He was met on the way by Taxiles, who provided about 5,000 men and gave Alexander twenty-five elephants (which Alexander used for transport rather than combat). The Macedonian monarch then divided his army into two. He sent Hephaestion, Perdiccas and Taxiles through the Khyber Pass to the Indus where they were to build a bridge of boats. They took with them about half the Companion cavalry, all of the Greek mercenary cavalry, three phalanx battalions and all of the baggage and made an untroubled march to Ohind on the Indus, bridging the river in accordance with Alexander's instructions.

Alexander, meanwhile, marched up the Kumar river to attack the hill tribes of Bajaur and Swat in order to secure the left flank of Hephaestion's forces. This proved to be an extremely demanding task, for the hardy and warlike natives offered furious resistance. Nevertheless, he gradually captured a series of hill-forts, often massacring all of the inhabitants. At Massaga, the capital of Swat (site unidentified), Alexander encountered some 7,000 mercenary troops who had been recruited from the interior of India. These men fought so valiantly that Alexander's assaults against the city were repulsed with heavy losses for the besiegers, even though the Macedonians had succeeded in making a breach in the walls. It was only when their leader was killed that the Indians surrendered. Alexander, highly impressed with the Indian mercenaries, decided to include them in his own army and allowed them to march out of the city in full possession of their weapons. However, during the night after their surrender, Alexander ordered his troops to surround the Indian mercenary encampment and slaughtered the entire force along with the women and children. His justification was that a report had reached him that the Indians had no desire to fight against other Indians and were planning to desert.[24] This official explanation *might* be admitted if the Indians had already taken an oath of loyalty to Alexander. If they had not then Alexander's action was nothing less than treacherous and impulsive and represented an indelible stain on his career.

Alexander continued to reduce the remaining strongholds in Swat. In some centres, like Bazira, Indian resistance was only intensified by the news of Alexander's massacre of the mercenaries. Other towns, like Ora, quickly surrendered to Alexander after a preliminary assault, probably wishing to avoid a general massacre at the hands of the besieging forces.

With Bajaur and Swat now under his control, Alexander could afford to rest his battle-weary troops before marching to the River Hydaspes (Jhelum) for an unavoidable confrontation with Porus, who was the Macedonian's most redoubtable opponent. Detailed descriptions of the battle of the Hydaspes may be found in Arrian and Plutarch and in the critical analyses of modern historians. The battle has long been regarded as Alexander's tactical master-piece, one in which he faced not just cavalry, infantry and chariotry but a force of elephants variously estimated by the ancient writers to have contained between eighty-five and 200 of the formidable beasts. Fortunately for Alexander, the lumbering animals did not always discriminate between friend and foe and at one vital stage of the battle began to crush Indian cavalrymen returning from a failed counter attack on Alexander's line. The Macedonian footsoldiers soon learnt to dodge the elephants and to slash at the trunks or attack from the side. Alexander made good use of his Scythian mercenary horse archers who destroyed nearly all of Porus' 180 chariots in a single charge. The Indian king's army found itself surrounded by the enemy cavalry and suffered terrible losses as Alexander's men closed in. Porus, although wounded, fought with supreme gallantry until, exhausted and weakened through loss of blood, he surrendered to Alexander, who treated him with dignity and honour. Porus had fought with such courage and tenacity that Alexander reinstated him as king and restored his lands. Genuine admiration underlay Alexander's decision, and genuine calculation, for the permanent removal of Porus might have enabled Taxiles to grow too powerful. Alexander chose the tried and trusted method of divide and rule. Porus, for his part, demonstrated an absolute loyalty to Alexander.

The battle on the Hydaspes had been a major victory but it had taken its toll on the morale of Alexander's men. The Macedonian king was able to move on to the River Hyphasis (Beas) and there his progress ended. His men respectfully but resolutely refused to continue and no amount of rousing speeches, sulking or emotional blackmail (would they really abandon their king in a hostile land?) could persuade them to reconsider. In the past, Alexander had been able to manipulate his men by playing on their greed and ambition but even promises of increased monetary rewards failed to move them. Now, forced to give up his dreams of world conquest, Alexander followed the course of the Hydaspes and then the Indus down to the ocean. Part of the army travelled down river by boat while the rest proceeded in two columns along either bank. At the Indus Delta, Alexander divided his army into three corps, sending one under the command of the Cretan Nearchus back to the Persian Gulf by sea while a second corps under Craterus was sent to Arachosia to put down a revolt. He himself began a march overland across the harsh and inhospitable land of Gedrosia, losing large numbers of soldiers and camp followers through hunger, thirst and heat exhaustion. At last, in the spring of 324 BC, he was back in Susa, only to find that during his absence his empire had fallen into confusion and was in danger of falling apart.

Many of Alexander's satraps – Persian and Macedonian alike – had not expected the king to return from his foray into India. Consequently, they had indulged in luxurious and riotous living, embezzled funds from money supplied by Alexander, hired private armies of mercenaries, oppressed the local population, plundered temples and tombs and behaved as independent rulers. The satraps had little difficulty in recruiting Greek mercenaries, for many of these had deep anti-Macedonian sympathies and a personal hatred of Alexander, whom they more or less served under duress. The mercenaries did not appreciate being forcibly settled in Alexander's new garrison towns nor did they have much time for his idea of a universal monarchy uniting Greeks and Asiatics.

This state of affairs was potentially disastrous and Alexander ruled with alacrity and extreme severity, deposing and executing any satrap who had abused his trust. In Media he also executed some 600 mercenary soldiers who had desecrated religious centres. But Alexander's main solution to restoring order was to deprive his satraps of the resources with which they might rebel by ordering them to disband their mercenary troops and by instructing the Greek cities to take back all those disaffected souls whom they had exiled and who had subsequently gone to Asia to engage in mercenary service. This was a significant decree for there were some 20,000 exiles from all parts of Greece. Such was Alexander's severity that his order regarding the disbanding of satrapal armies was promptly obeyed by those wishing to retain their positions, not to mention their lives.

One official who chose flight over submission was Harpalus, Alexander's finance minister. Convinced that he had seen the last of the king, he too spent Alexander's money with sustained profligacy until he received the dreadful news that his monarch was alive and well and on his way back. Harpalus left Babylon together with 6,000 mercenaries, whom he had hired at Alexander's expense, and 5,000 gold talents, which he had stolen from the treasury. He sailed first to Tarsus in Cilicia and then to Athens, where he had previously bought honorary citizenship. The Athenians were not so foolish as to provoke Alexander by admitting Harpalus and his mercenaries, even though they longed to throw off Macedonian rule and Harpalus' campaign-hardened veterans would be useful in any insurrection. Harpalus sailed for Cape Taenarum which had become a centre for disgruntled anti-Macedonian mercenaries, its existing military population being swelled by returned exiles and disbanded troops. After a brief visit to Athens, Harpalus and his men found employment in Crete but the renegade treasurer fell victim to a Macedonian assassin acting in collusion with Harpalus' second-in-command and with the full knowledge and approval of Alexander.

Having restored order throughout the empire, Alexander pressed ahead with his grand design of Hellenising Asia and Asianising Europe. He held mass weddings and up to 10,000 Greeks and Macedonians took Asian wives and were liberally rewarded with cash. His Asianisation of the Macedonian army proceeded apace. The 30,000 Asiatic youths whom Alexander had recruited were now trained and brimming with enthusiasm. When this new army arrived at Susa, its presence generated intense discontent among the Macedonian veterans. Alexander paraded the Macedonians at Opis on the Tigris river and there discharged some 10,000 aged, unfit or wounded veterans. Dismayed, the troops shouted abuse while Alexander, now accustomed to oriental servility, arrested and executed thirteen of the closest and most vocal recalcitrants.[25] Still enraged, Alexander discharged the entire Macedonian force and sent the troops home under the command of Craterus. Antipater, who had been left to assure peace in Macedonia and Greece, was directed to bring freshly recruited troops to replace the veterans. Alexander returned to Babylon where he found 20,000 Persian troops who had been recruited by the Macedonian general, Peucestas. In addition, he received new contingents of Lydian and Carian mercenaries led by Menander and Philoxenus. With these forces at his disposal and his 30,000 'Successors' (as he called his young Asian troops) he was ready to embark on his next campaign, the conquest of Arabia, without which his empire in the East seemed incomplete.

In the event, Alexander never set out on his expedition to add the final Arabian piece to his Asian empire. He fell ill after a bout of immoderate drinking, contracted a fever and died on 13 June 323 BC. Alexander's empire did not survive his death for its unity and continuity depended far too much on the sheer determination and force of personality of its creator rather than on an enduring set of institutions that could survive, irrespective of changes in leadership.

CHAPTER ELEVEN

The Hellenistic World

THE DEMISE OF Alexander rekindled Greek hopes of independence and led to the so-called Lamian War. Athens and Aetolia formed an alliance but Sparta, unsurprisingly perhaps, held back. In order to confront the Macedonians, the Athenians would need to hire mercenaries. They found the ideal recruiting agent in Leosthenes, who had been a commander of mercenaries in Alexander's army and was conversant with Macedonian battle techniques. He recruited 8,000 men at Cape Taenarum, using Harpalus' money, and marched north to Aetolia where he was joined by 7,000 Aetolians, 5,500 Athenian citizen hoplites and an extra 2,000 mercenaries.[1] These developments posed a real threat to Antipater whom Alexander had left in Macedon with only 13,000 infantry and 600 cavalry available for immediate use. At first, the war went in favour of the Greeks and Antipater was besieged in Lamia, which gave its name to this particular war. But the tide turned when Leosthenes was killed in battle and the Macedonian fleet inflicted a devastating defeat on the Athenian fleet at Abydos – one that finished Athens as a naval power. Craterus arrived to support Antipater with the 10,000 veterans discharged by Alexander during his fit of pique. Meanwhile, Athens and its allies missed out on reinforcements of their own, for the rebellious Greek mercenaries whom Alexander had settled in Bactria were intercepted in their march towards the west by the Macedonian general Peithon, disarmed and forced to return to their settlements. On the way, they were surrounded and massacred by Macedonian troops. Shortly thereafter, Athens lost the battle of Crannon to Antipater's forces and, with her defeat, any remaining pretensions to being a land power. Aetolia held out, the only territory outside of Sparta where Macedonian rule had not been restored. In retrospect, the northern Greek rebellion had been premature, for Macedonia had remained powerful despite Alexander's death but the Athenians and their allies could not have known at the time that they had mistimed their coup and that Alexander's successors would soon be involved in a prolonged struggle that would last for over forty years and result in the fragmentation of all that Alexander had created.

Perdiccas, who had been appointed regent by Alexander, claimed authority and was immediately opposed by Antipater, Seleucus, Eumenes, Ptolemy, Craterus, Antigonus, Cassander and Demetrius as well as other contestants. The struggles between these ambitious men were complex and the *minutiae* of shifting alliances, intrigues, bribery, assassinations and military confrontations have been well described elsewhere,[2] but it can be said that the war of Diadochi engulfed most of those responsible for its outbreak, one way or another.

The confusion and ferment occasioned by the generals' war was exacerbated in 282 BC by the sudden invasion of Macedonia by an army of marauding Gauls. The precise provenance of these invaders, be it Gaul itself, Italy or some location further east, remains conjectural but they had been wandering through the Balkans for several years before descending on Macedonia. Ptolemy Ceraunus, who had in his turn become King of Macedonia, attempted to stop the Gallic invasion but was captured and decapitated. In 278 BC a second wave of invaders was repulsed by the Aetolians in battles around Delphi and Thermopylae and withdrew to Thrace. Antigonus Gonatas, son of Demetrius, also fought a pitched battle with the Gauls at Lysimacheia in Thrace. He won a decisive victory over the 18,000-strong Gallic army and then took the survivors into mercenary service. With the help of Phocian pirates, he was able to capture Cassandreia, a city which had for some years been independent of the kingdom of Macedonia and presented the only remaining obstacle to the establishment of his rule over the entire region. During the fighting, Antigonus' newly-enlisted Gauls encountered other Gauls hired by the city's tyrant, Apollodorus, but it is unlikely that brotherly affection played any role in their meeting. Antigonus Gonatas was now King of Macedonia, an outcome he owed entirely to his army of mercenaries. A fourth group of Gauls crossed over into Asia Minor at the invitation of Nicodemes I, King of Bithynia, who used them successfully to resolve a civil war in his favour. The Gauls settled in the Phrygian plain, supporting themselves by mercenary service, and, after the end of the Wars of the Diadochi, were to be found in all the armies of the Hellenistic kingdoms. Nicodemes' introduction of Gallic tribesmen into Asia Minor had serious consequences both for himself and for the region as a whole. Shortly before his death, Nicodemes was forced to fight to maintain his throne against his exiled son, Ziaelas, who had hired the very Gauls introduced into the region by the king. Once settled, the Gauls were able to gain control of central Anatolia, which became known as Galatia.

Although all the warring generals retained a nucleus of Macedonian troops, their battles were fought with armies that were predominantly mercenary, both in motive and composition. The cavalry was almost entirely made up of Asiatic troops and gone were the days when the Greek mercenary infantry were relegated to a secondary role. They now fought alongside Asiatic infantry drawn from every province conquered by Alexander and every adjoining territory. Even pirates were employed, both in naval operations and on land.[3] There were plenty of mercenaries available and plenty of money with which to pay them, for Alexander's far-flung conquests had turned the generals into very wealthy men and they could afford to spend lavishly.

The mercenaries proved fickle, easily changing from one employer to another, from loser to winner, from one generous paymaster to an even more generous one. This was common and accepted practice and was not regarded as particularly reprehensible either by the victors or the vanquished. The Macedonians also behaved like the mercenaries, swapping sides, albeit for different reasons. The war was not popular among the ordinary Macedonian soldiers nor did any one particular general enjoy an outstanding popularity over the other contenders. By joining whoever happened to be victorious at a given moment, the soldiers might help to end the war and effect a decisive resolution of the struggle for succession. But there was no one capable of replacing Alexander, no one capable of maintaining the unity of the empire against those who sought to dismember it.

Out of nearly half a century of chaos emerged three great Hellenistic kingdoms, three great dynasties. There was the Antigonid kingdom of Macedonia founded in 297 BC by Antigonus Gonatas. Of the three kingdoms, it was the weakest, owing to a relative lack of resources and the relentless hostility of the Greeks. In 273 BC, Antigonus temporarily lost control of Macedonia, when Pyrrhus of Epirus, the mercenary king and adventurer, gave up his costly war with Rome and invaded the Antigonid kingdom, which he held for just over a year. Pyrrhus defeated Antigonus in battle with an army containing large numbers of mercenary Gauls paid for by money provided by the Queen of Egypt, who desired the Macedonian throne for her son. Antigonus' troops, both native Macedonian and mercenary, deserted to Pyrrhus, except for his own Gallic mercenaries who fought practically to the last man.[4] Antigonus, however, recovered from his defeat and attacked the Epirote king in a battle fought in the streets of Argos. The issue was settled whey Pyrrhus was killed by a tile thrown from a roof. The Epirote army surrendered and Antigonus, following the usual pattern, most likely incorporated Pyrrhus' mercenaries into his own army.[5] But the benefits of Antigonus' victory did not last. Ptolemaic Egypt continued to foment Greek rebellions. Liberally supplied with Egyptian subsidies, Sparta and Athens began the so-called Chremonidean War in 266 BC. Antigonus managed to defeat the Greeks and reimpose Macedonian control but only after five years of hard-fought campaigns. During the reign of Antigonus Doson, Sparta, led by King Cleomenes and again financed by Egypt, attempted to throw off Macedonian rule. Doson, with an army of 28,000 infantry and 1,600 cavalry (13,000 Macedonians, 9,000 Greek allies, 5,000 mercenaries, including 1,000 Agrianians and 1,000 Gauls),[6] met and defeated Cleomenes at Sellasia (222 BC) and occupied Sparta. His successor, Philip V, was forced to defend Macedonia against an Aetolian attack (217 BC), launched with the full support of Rome. The suspicion of the latter had been aroused by Philip's aid of Demetrius of Pharos who was engaged in piratical activities in the Adriatic against Greek cities friendly to Rome. Philip forced the Aetolians to make peace and continued his adventurism, provoking a full-scale response from Rome. A series of three Roman–Macedonian wars finally ended in the battle of Pydna (168 BC) where the Romans and their Numidian allies (some 37,000 men) utterly destroyed the 44,000-strong Macedonian army, which included 10,000 mercenary troops (Greek, Cretan, Thracian and Gallic among others). The Antigonid dynasty came to an end and Macedonia was partitioned into four independent states. In 146 BC Macedonia became a Roman province.

The second great dynasty, that of the Seleucids, lasted rather longer, until its termination by Pompey in 64 BC. In terms of size it was the largest of the three kingdoms but its integrity was always under challenge from external threats and internal secessionist movements. Ostensibly, Seleucid rule stretched from Asia Minor to the Punjab but the area actually under Seleucid control soon contracted owing to a loss of territory at both the eastern and western extremities of the empire. In the east, the Punjab was lost to Chandragupta Maurya, who had reputedly known Alexander and was sufficiently inspired to attempt the creation of his own empire. He defeated Seleucus in a military campaign (303 BC) but shortly thereafter gave the

Macedonian his elephants and established diplomatic relations on a permanent and friendly basis, entailing a regular exchange of ambassadors.

The surrender of some marginal territories to Chandragupta was not fatal to the stability of the Seleucid empire. But in other areas the fortunes of the Seleucids were not as favourable. In 275 BC, Antiochus I Soter, Seleucus' successor, managed to stop the Gauls from penetrating further east beyond Phrygia, but he was unable to expel them from Asia Minor. The Persian satrap Mithridates, declared independence and, supported by a mercenary army of Gauls and Asiatics, established the kingdom of Pontus on the southern shores of the Black Sea. Antiochus II (261–246 BC) and Seleucus II (246–226 BC) were unsuccessful in several attempts to recapture the eastern Mediterranean coastline. Threatened on three sides, the Seleucid empire seemed close to total collapse.

Antiochus III (223–187 BC), considered to be the greatest of the Seleucid kings, brought about a remarkable recovery of Seleucid power, despite an unpromising start. He attacked and overran Palestine with an army of 62,000 infantry and 6,000 cavalry. At Raphia in 217 BC, the elephant corps and Greek mercenaries of Antiochus' right wing easily defeated the left wing of Ptolemy IV's army, while the Greek mercenaries of Ptolemy's right wing overcame Antiochus' left wing, which consisted largely of Arab and Median troops. Having restored Seleucid rule in Armenia and influence in Parthia, Antiochus gained revenge over Egypt by defeating the forces of Ptolemy V at Panium (c.200 BC) and acquiring all of Syria–Palestine. The Seleucid king's' successes encouraged him to extend his influence westwards. He invaded Greece, ostensibly to recover lost territories in Thrace, and in doing so alarmed the Roman senate, which despatched an army under Marcus Acilius Glabrio. The Roman army included Pergamene, Achaean and Latin allies, Cretan mercenary archers and Thracian and Macedonian mercenaries. The Seleucid army was even more multi-national, containing Gauls, Medes, Dahae, Cretans, Thysians, Cappadocians, Syrians, Phrygians, Lydians, Arabs, Carians, Cilicians, Lycians and Pisidians. The two armies came into contact at Magnesia and in a single encounter decided the fate of Asia Minor. As at Raphia, the right wings of both armies routed their immediate opponents but a determined charge by the Roman centre decided the outcome in favour of the anti-Seleucid coalition (189 BC). Antiochus lost control of Anatolia west of the Taurus mountains and did not survive his defeat.

His immediate successors, Seleucus IV (187–175 BC) and Antiochus IV (175–164 BC), managed to hold the remaining empire together. Antiochus even launched two attacks on Egypt that would have terminated the Ptolemies had not the threat of Roman intervention forced his withdrawal on the point of victory. After the death of Antiochus, the Seleucid empire was further weakened by a long Jewish revolt led by the Maccabees (Judas, Jonathon and Simon Maccabaeus) who, as orthodox Jews, resented any Hellenisation of Jerusalem (165–141 BC).

The course of the revolt itself alternately favoured the Seleucids and then the Maccabees. The Jews, particularly in the south, were a hardy pastoral and agricultural people well-versed in the use of weapons, their fighting spirit animated by a fierce nationalism and religious zeal. They had been used as mercenary garrison troops by Egyptian Pharaohs for several centuries and some were serving the Ptolemies as soldier–settlers in return for land-grants.[7] The Maccabean forces contained no mercenaries for theirs was an intensely nationalist struggle. In the war of the Maccabees all the mercenaries – including Greeks, Cretans, Anatolians, Arabs, Persians and (non-orthodox) Jews – were in the Seleucid armies. The conflict dragged on for nearly a quarter of a century. In 141 BC the Maccabean rebels gained substantial concessions from the Seleucid king, Demetrius II (145–138 BC), to the extent that Judea effectively became an independent kingdom, despite sporadic attempts by subsequent Seleucid monarchs to reassert their control.

In defeating Antiochus III at Magnesia, the Romans had gained a great victory over the Seleucids and substantially weakened their empire but in doing so they unintentionally made possible the resurgence of the Parthians, whose expansion Antiochus had temporarily halted. Parthian expansion had suffered a setback when Demetrius' brother, Antiochus VII, had defeated the new Parthian king, Phraates II (138–124 BC), and regained Mesopotamia. However, the unrestrained looting of Antiochus' mercenary troops upset the people of Ecbatana, who rose in revolt – and the Parthians launched a surprise attack during which Antiochus was killed. In customary fashion, the Parthians incorporated some of Antiochus' mercenaries into their own army but these troops did not accept their impressment willingly and promptly deserted when they were required to fight against invading Scythians. Antiochus VII was the last Seleucid king to recapture any territory, no matter how briefly. The *coup de grâce* to the Seleucid dynasty was administered in 64 BC by the Roman general Pompey, who, fresh from his victories over Mithridates of Pontus, now marched into Syria. He annexed Palestine for good measure and returned to Rome to a tumultuous welcome.

Of the Hellenistic kingdoms, that of the Ptolemies in Egypt survived the longest and was undoubtedly the most prosperous and strongly-centralised of the three. The Ptolemy kings regarded Egypt's wealth as their own personal property and organised a large bureaucracy to control its systematic exploitation. Thus, the Ptolemies nearly always disposed of sufficient cash with which to subsidise any disaffected elements among their rivals and were chiefly responsible for many of the conflicts which weakened and ultimately destroyed the Hellenistic kingdoms. But if the Ptolemies played a somewhat negative political role, their patronage of science and literature made Alexandria the cultural capital of the Hellenistic World.

The Ptolemaic empire remained stable during the reign of the first two monarchs, Ptolemy I Soter (304–285 BC) and Ptolemy II Philadelphus (285–246 BC). But from about 250 BC onwards, the native Egyptian population gradually began to react against Graeco-Macedonian domination. The Ptolemies faced the growing discontent in a conciliatory and realistic fashion and the fact that Ptolemaic rule lasted as long as it did owed partly to the acceptance – grudging or otherwise – of Egyptian aspirations and influences by what was after all a foreign dynasty. Egyptians were introduced into the bureaucracy and the military forces where they were incorporated both into the royal guard and the regular army. The number of Egyptians gradually increased so that at the battle of Raphia some 20,000 fought alongside the 25,000 Graeco–Macedonian troops present on the field.[8]

The earliest armies of the Hellenistic kingdoms were those inherited from the Wars of the Diadochi, that is they were made up of a core of Macedonian phalanx troops who fought alongside large numbers of mercenaries – Greek, Gallic and Asiatic. As described above, Antigonus Gonatas owed his throne – and the restoration of his throne after the death of Pyrrhus – to his use of mercenaries, while Ptolemy Soter and Seleucus Nicator were also, initially at least, reliant on mercenary troops, native Macedonians being very much in the minority. Mercenaries were always present in every Hellenistic army right up to the Roman conquest of Macedonia and its rival kingdoms. The reasons for which mercenaries were hired had remained essentially unchanged and were just as valid in the Hellenistic period as they had been in previous eras. There was the continuing need for garrisons to assure the security of borders and strategic centres, a task best done by full-time professionals. The performance of tedious garrison duty by mercenaries reduced the disruption to agriculture, commerce and industry caused by too much reliance on the conscription of native citizens. Moreover, mercenaries were still in demand as specialists in a particular weapon not routinely used by their employers.

Thus, Cretan archers were regularly employed in practically all the armies of the Mediterranean world, with the exception of the Carthaginian army which placed greater reliance on Balearic slingers rather than archers for its missile troops. The Cretans and Neo-Cretans (newly enfranchised citizens drawn from the lower classes) were particularly active during the late third and throughout the second century BC both as mercenaries and pirates. They became the most prominent of Hellenic mercenaries and were employed in relatively large numbers. At Raphia, Antiochus III had about 3,000 Cretans and Neo-Cretans[9] while at Magnesia 2,500 Cretans were present in the Seleucid army.[10] The Cretans worked overseas as auxiliaries sent by various Cretan governments or as individually hired mercenaries. Some acquired fame, fortune and rank as generals, admirals, diplomats and administrators by virtue of their native ability, but most drew their wages as ordinary footsoldiers. Even so, this was preferable to life at home, which to most recruits meant unrelenting impoverishment. There were certainly a number of exiles driven from their homeland by domestic political events, but poverty, exacerbated by an economic crisis which swept the Mediterranean world during the second century BC, not ideology, was the ever-present motive that drove men with a proverbial attachment to their native soil into foreign mercenary service.[11]

Mercenaries, then, continued to play an important role in the Hellenistic world but the rulers of Macedonia, and of the Seleucid and Ptolemaic kingdoms sought to reduce their reliance on straight mercenary hirelings, whose loyalty was not always above suspicion, and to solve the perennial problem of payment – the single most difficult aspect of relations between mercenaries and their employers. In order to achieve their goal, the three kingdoms reorganised their military establishments, albeit in different ways. Once his authority had been imposed, thanks to his mercenary troops, Antigonus Gonatas reconstituted the Macedonian national levy, which he called out only in times of emergency. His permanent army consisted of his own bodyguard – the *Agema* – made up of Macedonians and of mercenary troops retained for garrison duty. Whether he had any other standing army is unclear, but it seems that Antigonus and his successors relied primarily on the phalanxes of the reinvigorated national levy to defend the Macedonian kingdom and supported them with mercenary troops as the occasion demanded. The phalanxes constituted anywhere between 30 and 65 per cent of Antigonid armies and in most cases more than 50 per cent. At Sellasia, the phalanx represented only 34 per cent of total army strength, owing to the large number of Greek allies who had come out in support of Antigonus Doson against Sparta, but this was rather an exceptional case.[12] There was a trend, already evident during Gonatas' reign, towards the recruitment of barbarian mercenaries – Gauls, Illyrians, Thracians – rather than Greeks, although Cretans, of course, were always in demand. Antigonus Gonatas had sometimes employed whole tribes of Gallic mercenaries and his successors continued this practice, although not on the same scale. Doson had 1,000 Gauls at Sellasia and Perseus, the last of the Antigonid monarchs, had 2,000 in his employ. There were two main reasons for the rise in the number of barbarian mercenaries. The first was that there were simply not enough Greek mercenaries in Greece itself to meet the demands of all the local employers. Greek mercenaries had been in constant demand overseas well before the accession of Alexander the Great and the supply of mercenaries was not inexhaustible. The second reason for the increased use of barbarian mercenaries was that they were relatively cheap. They came under the category of light troops, who were always paid at a lower rate than heavy infantry hoplites.

There is very limited evidence that Antigonid mercenaries were paid in anything but cash. Macedonia does not appear to have adopted any system of granting land in return for military service, at least not on any significant scale. The Roman historian Titus Livy makes passing reference to 'a large settlement of Gauls and Illyrians, who were energetic farmers.'[13] There is, however, no indication as to the actual size of this particular settlement or whether or not it was unique. Whether the barbarians were granted land conditional to the performance of military service when required or whether they received the land as a reward for past services remains unresolved.

In summary, Antigonid Macedonia was able to place less reliance on mercenaries by recreating and revitalising the tough, disciplined phalanxes for which the Macedonians had been renowned ever since the days of King Philip. The Antigonid monarchs could also count on substantial numbers of Greek allied troops provided at the expense of the allied governments and were, thus, spared the expense of hiring large numbers of extra mercenaries in time of war. Mercenaries were not unimportant and they were continually present during every reign from that of Antigonus Gonatas to that of Perseus – garrison duty was an important if boring and inglorious function – but they were no longer preponderant, as they had been during the Wars of the Diadochi.

Like the Antigonids in Macedonia, the Ptolemaic and Seleucid dynasties also owed the creation of their kingdoms to their use of mercenaries but once their control was established they then sought to diminish their dependence on purely mercenary forces who might display absolute fidelity or who might desert to the enemy. Both circumstances had been known during the Wars of the Diadochi, but the latter situation was by far the more prevalent. The Antigonids had been able to create what was essentially a citizen army supported by Greek and barbarian mercenaries. The Seleucid kingdom, however, was a multi-national organisation, while Ptolemaic rule represented in effect the occupation of Egypt by a foreign monarchy. Recruiting and arming large numbers of Egyptians might have adverse consequences.

For both monarchies the solution to the problem of ensuring loyalty from the military forces and to the problem of payment lay in the *kleroi* system, whereby recruits undertook to provide military service in return for land grants. The possession of land gave the soldiers a permanent income and a personal motive for supporting the monarchy. It was, of course, among the Macedonians and Greeks that the Ptolemies and Seleucids first recruited their *kleruchs* (soldier-settlers). Many, perhaps most, of the Greeks would have been mercenaries. Very few of the Macedonians, however, came directly from Macedon. There was no question of direct recruitment in what was, after all, enemy territory and, in any case, the Antigonids had banned Macedonian citizens, who were required for service in the national levy, from performing military service overseas without permission. There were in fact very few native-born Macedonian soldier–farmers.

Although the Seleucids and the Ptolemies shared the same aim of creating a reliable standing army in place of their mercenary formations, they established very different systems of land-grants. Seleucus Nicator continued Alexander's practice of founding cities as military settlements. He and his successor, Antiochus I, built some forty new military settlements, while Antiochus IV was responsible for fifteen. In the Seleucid system, land was assigned to a military community, that is, the soldiers received the land as a group not as individuals and the grant was communally worked. The military settlements were self-defending and self-supporting strategic points in the Seleucid empire. By contrast, the Ptolemaic system entailed the granting of individual plots of land whose size varied according to the rank of the recipient. The members of a particular regiment were not required to live in close proximity in a commune. Each individual was responsible for the cultivation of his own land and was under individual obligation to perform military service. The Ptolemies saw no need to create large military cities whose very presence might cause resentment among the Egyptian people. A decentralised population of farmer–soldiers was less intrusive and co-existed more easily with an essentially rural society.

The Ptolemaic *klerouchoi* were directly responsible to the king. Under the first two Ptolemies, the soldier–settlers had the use of the land but not its ownership. The *klerouchoi* could sub-let the land but had no right to sell it. They were taxed like any other land owner but, on the other hand, they were regularly paid. There was a gradual transition in subsequent reigns towards hereditary ownership so that, by the early second century BC, the *klerouchoi* had become hereditary soldiers with full rights over their property. They could transfer their land to others, although the new owners were still required to perform military service as a condition of ownership. In effect, the lessening of royal control over the land-grants was not inimical to the interests of the monarch. The *klerouchoi* could be trusted to make the best possible use of their land out of self-interest.

Although the Hellenistic kingdoms had reduced their reliance on mercenaries, they could not dispense with them altogether. They had gone about the creation of new military establishments in different ways but there was one common feature. The Macedonian levies and the soldier–settlers were equally part-time warriors. They were not required to serve all year – farms had to be maintained – and in times of peace their training and efficiency was bound to suffer. Mercenaries were still required for garrisons and in emergencies they were immediately ready for action, while the mobilisation of citizen levies and soldier–farmers perforce took considerable time.

CHAPTER TWELVE

Carthage, Syracuse and Rome

TOWARDS 800 BC, Phoenician (Canaanite) settlers from Tyre founded the city of Carthage at a strategic point on the north African coast which lay relatively close to Corsica and Sicily and dominated the trade routes along the southern Mediterranean. The Carthaginians went on to dominate most of the north African coastline and extended their influence further afield by founding colonies in southern Spain (Iberia), Corsica and western Sicily, although the Greeks remained firmly established in the eastern half. The Carthaginians, however, gained control of Corsica, Sardinia, the Balearic Islands and south-eastern Iberia.

The struggle for domination in the western Mediterranean was given further impetus around 500 BC by the rise of Syracuse as a significant maritime, military and commercial power. Under the tyrant Gelo (also known as Gelon), Syracuse became the most important of the Greek cities in Sicily and a serious rival against Carthage. At Himera, in 480 BC, Gelo inflicted a decisive defeat on the Carthaginians at the head of an army composed of Sicilian Greek allies and mercenaries in his own employ.

On the Italian mainland another potential aspirant to Mediterranean domination had gradually come into being – Rome. Modern scholarship suggests that Rome as a city, rather than a cluster of villages, began its existence some time after 700 BC, perhaps more than a century after the founding of Carthage and contemporary with the reigns of the Assyrian kings Sennacherib and Essarhadon.[1] After the expulsion of the last Tarquin king, Tarquinius Superbus, and the establishment of an oligarchic republic by Rome's patrician class, the Romans gradually began to expand their control and influence over central Italy by making alliances with neighbouring

Latin tribes and by destroying Etruscan power after the nine-year siege of Veii.

The spread of Roman power southwards was welcomed and encouraged by some of the Greek cities on the southern Italian coastline (Thurii, Locri, Rhegium) as a deterrent to the barbarian Oscan hill tribes whose plundering expeditions had been a chronic nuisance to the Greek commercial centres. The city of Tarentum, however, reacted differently, alarmed at the elimination of Samnite power as a counterweight to Roman expansion. Tarentum was the wealthiest of the coastal cities and had a 15,000-strong citizen army trained and led by mercenary officers, which Greece had produced in such large numbers during the fourth century BC. When other Greek cities requested Roman garrisons, the Tarentines sank a Roman flotilla and sought the assistance of King Pyrrhus of Epirus, the greatest mercenary commander of his age. Pyrrhus gladly complied, bringing an army of 25,000 veteran Greek mercenaries to Italian shores in order to protect Greek settlements against the citizen militia army of Rome and its allies.

Pyrrhus fought two battles with the Romans at Heraclea (280 BC) and Asculum (279 BC) and achieved the narrowest of victories each time, thanks largely to his elephant corps which disconcerted the horses of the Roman cavalry. Pyrrhus' mercenary phalanxes, experienced as they were, did not intimidate the citizen legionaries, who gallantly stood their ground until the charging elephants created gaps in the Roman line. After these indecisive victories, which had cost more than they were worth, Pyrrhus, never persistent if events did not immediately favour his cause, turned his attention to Sicily, where he gained yet another indecisive victory against the Carthaginians, who at that time maintained friendly relations with Rome. He returned to southern Italy in 275 BC and brought the Romans to battle at Beneventum where, after a desperate struggle, Pyrrhus' mercenaries were routed by an enemy superior in numbers. The Romans had learnt to deal with Pyrrhus' elephants in much the same way as Alexander's men had learnt how to counter those of the Indian king, Porus. They also unleashed an additional secret weapon in the form of squealing pigs, which ran among the disgruntled elephants, causing them to panic and lumber back into the Greek lines crushing many a hoplite in the process.[2] Pyrrhus withdrew to Tarentum and shortly thereafter left Italy and returned to Greece, ultimately to keep his appointment with the rooftile thrown by an irate Argive woman. Tarentum made peace and accepted Roman supremacy. The victory over Pyrrhus and his mercenaries left Rome in effective control of the entire Italian peninsula and had brought her into closer contact with the wider Mediterranean world. The perception grew among the Romans that their power could be extended beyond the confines of Italy. Rome now became a participant in the struggle for supremacy in the Mediterranean and her entry into the game brought her perforce into conflict with Carthage, with whom she had previously enjoyed nearly two centuries of peaceful diplomatic contract.

The Roman armies of the monarchical and early republican periods were citizen militias (*legio*) levied from among the nobility and richer peasantry, classes which had a vested interest in the maintenance of the security of the Roman city-state and the expansion of its power. Around 450 BC the militia system was expanded to take in more recruits from among the plebeians. All land-owning citizens except for the poorest were liable for military service. The wealthiest citizens who could afford to buy horses, normally the patricians and their retainers, were recruited into the cavalry. The Roman militias were levied only when emergencies arose and service in them was usually of short duration. Although all land-owning citizens other than the very poor were liable for militia service, in practice conscription was always selective and militiamen were bound to serve for no more than one year. The annual rotation of manpower and the provision of troop levies by allied city-states, matching the Romans in numbers of infantry and often out-numbering them in cavalry, are among the factors that explain why Rome never mobilised her full manpower at any one time, even during dire emergencies.

As Rome gradually subdued its neighbours in the Italian peninsula, campaigns became more protracted and short-term levies became increasingly impractical. Long sieges required a permanent ring of troops to maintain the pressure on an enemy city but such troops had to be maintained and compensated for any loss of income occasioned by their absence from their farms. Thus, at the end of the fifth century BC, Roman citizen militiamen, who had hitherto provided their own equipment at their own expense and had served without pay, now began to be paid on a regular basis. By the time of the Punic Wars the state had begun to supply standardised armour and weapons to the recruits. These two developments and the frequent wars in which Rome was involved were effectively, if perhaps unintentionally, the first steps in the creation of a standing army supported by troops from allied city-states.

The Roman army's effectiveness was based on a number of factors, including a willingness to learn from adversity. Although the Greek-style phalanxes which the Romans had adopted during the reign of the penultimate king, Servius Tullius, in the sixth century BC, were completely adequate against frontal attacks by similarly armed hoplite forces, this was not the case against a more mobile (and taller) enemy like the Gauls, who smashed a Roman army at Allia in 390 BC by operating in open order and delivering savage attacks on the vulnerable flanks of the formation. The phalanx was also defective in hilly country, as was amply demonstrated during Rome's wars with the Samnites. It was probably the Samnite Wars, even more than the Gallic invasions, that caused the Romans, at some point during the fourth century BC, to abandon the hoplite phalanx in favour of the legion. In theory, each legion contained 6,000 men, but 4000–4,500 was closer to the usual strength. Each legion was made up of thirty smaller formations known as maniples. There are many excellent accounts relating to the precise composition of the Roman legion[3] and it is sufficient here to make a few remarks on why the legion was generally superior to other fighting formations. It was, first of all, a formation that possessed much greater flexibility, versatility and mobility. It could defend itself against attacks on its flanks and on its rear. Its component maniples could fight as independent units, meeting attacks from any direction, or in close coordination with the other maniples comprising the legion. The legion could operate efficiently over level or hilly ground and was an altogether more effective formation than the Greek phalanx, as was shown by Rome's victory over the mercenary forces of Philip V of Macedon at the battle of Cynoscephalae (197 BC). If the legion had a defect, it was, perhaps, its inability to operate cohesively in wooded territory, an inherent defect in any formation reliant upon shoulder-to-shoulder fighting for its effectiveness, as evinced by the destruction of three legions in AD 9 by the German chieftain Arminius in the Teutoberg Forest, although on this occasion the Romans had additional *impedimenta* in the form of their families and a long baggage train. The gradual abandonment of the long thrusting pike in favour of two throwing javelins (*pila*) increased the mobility and striking-power of Roman legions while the adoption of an oval shield in place of the round hoplite shield afforded much greater protection against slashing sword cuts. The Romans retained their shorter swords, which they had learnt to use in the most effective way, with rapid thrusting motions that exposed relatively little of the legionary's arm but inflicted deeper wounds than slashing swords. The Romans first disordered their opponents with a shower of javelins and then followed up with an immediate charge.

The effectiveness of the legion, however, was not just a matter of speed, versatility and fighting technique, fundamental though these were. Unlike the lack-lustre militiamen of Ancient Egypt, the Roman citizen soldier was particularly tough, aggressive and imbued with a deep national feeling and fighting spirit. The Romans took war seriously, not as a game to be casually indulged in by the belligerents. Permanent conquests, not looting expeditions, became the ultimate aim of Roman warfare.

The armies of early republican Rome were exclusively composed of Roman citizen levies and allied contingents of native militia. These two sources of conscription provided more than adequate manpower for Rome's war within Italy. Rome had fought against foreign mercenaries called in by Tarentum but at this stage she felt no need to employ mercenaries of her own. The mercenaries were in the Hellenistic kingdoms founded by the Diadochi. They were in Syracuse and, most prominently, in Carthage.

The city of Syracuse was founded in 734 BC, according to tradition, by Dorian Greek colonists from Corinth and was thus somewhat younger than Carthage but probably reached the status of a city before Rome. Syracuse gradually rose to prominence as the greatest of the Sicilian Greek cities. In matters of government the Syracusans alternated between democracy and tyranny and reached the height of their power and influence under the thirty-eight-year rule of the tyrant Dionysius. In military matters, Syracuse came to depend on mercenary soldiers for its defence rather than on its citizen levies, who were neither very experienced nor very keen on the performance of military service. In general, the democratic governments tended to favour Greek mercenaries rather than Sicilian mercenaries like the Sicels while the tyrants hired non-Greeks – Sicels and Campanians from southern Italy – for the perennial reason that foreign mercenaries, having no sympathy or blood link with the local populace, would side with their employer during any rebellion. Many of the Syracusan tyrants, especially Dionysius, owed the acquisition or maintenance of their power to their employment of mercenary troops.

Hostilities between Syracuse and Carthage began in 480 BC. A Carthaginian army under Hamilcar invaded Sicily and attacked the town of Himera. However, a Syracusan relief force inflicted a total defeat on the invaders and Hamilcar was killed. In 474 BC Syracuse achieved another victory, defeating the Etruscans who had attacked the Greek city of Cyme, situated on Italy's Campanian coastline. The main concern of Syracuse was to stop the Carthaginians and Etruscans from forming an alliance against Syracuse aimed at dividing up Sicily between them.

The next ordeal for Syracuse came not from the direction of Carthage or

Etruria but from Athens, which sent a large citizen militia and mercenary force to capture the city. The course of the siege has already been described in connection with the Peloponnesian War and it suffices to say that Syracuse emerged triumphant but exhausted, a tempting target for a renewed assault from north Africa. In 409 BC the Carthaginians returned and destroyed Selinus. They besieged Himera, which fell to an attack by Iberian mercenaries and was razed to the ground.

At this point, a Syracusan exile, Hermocrates, returned to Sicily after a period of mercenary service for the Persian satrap Pharnabazus, built five triremes and raised a small army, which consisted of 1,000 mercenaries and 1,000 survivors from Himera, all of whom were ill-disposed towards the Carthaginians. Hermocrates launched raids into territory held by the Carthaginians and as his successes grew so did his army, which increased to 6,000 men, both mercenaries and citizens. Hermocrates hoped to be recalled to Syracuse as a reward for his efforts but he had been a supporter of tyrannical rule and the democratic government then in power at Syracuse refused him admission. Hermocrates decided to gain entry and recognition by force but when he secretly went into the city with only a few followers his presence was discovered and the local populace quickly massacred the entire band, including its leader.

Although Syracuse disowned Hermocrates, this response failed to placate the Carthaginians who had in any case decided on another invasion. They arrived in 406 BC in even greater strength, bent on conquering all Sicily, and began by besieging the city of Acragas, a wealthy settlement which had hitherto remained aloof from the struggle between Syracuse and Carthage. Acragas had prepared for the Carthaginian attack, appealing to its rival, Syracuse, for help against their common enemy and by hiring a group of Campanian mercenaries. The defence was led by the city's own generals and a Laconian mercenary commander, Dexippus. Acragas held out gallantly and the Carthaginians were soon affected by a plague which claimed their leader, Hannibal. But just when it seemed that Acragas would successfully withstand the siege, the Carthaginians intercepted a Syracusan food-supply fleet and the city ran short of food. The rashness of Acragas' over-reliance on mercenaries was made all too clear when the Campanians, deprived of regular rations, deserted and were taken into Carthaginian service. The Carthaginians entered the city and used it as a base for further military operations.

To meet the renewed threat, the Syracusans elected a new set of generals, including a public-office clerk, Dionysius, who had fought bravely at Acragas.

Dionysius, who had been a supporter of Hermocrates, faked an attack on his life and was granted a bodyguard of 600 foreign mercenaries, which he later increased to a thousand men. This was a development which the democratic government came to regret as Dionysius, backed by his mercenaries, gradually established a military dictatorship and enjoyed practically unlimited power. He replaced the officers of the Syracusan citizen militias with his own mercenary officers and, for good reason, sent Dexippus back to Greece, thereby ridding himself of a rival mercenary leader. Dexippus went on to join Cyrus' Ten Thousand four years later and, as described earlier, came to a bad end in Thrace.

On the whole, Dionysius ruled carefully and moderately in the sense that he did not indulge in murder and oppression for motives of personal revenge but rather for reasons of state. His more reprehensible actions were always politically motivated and were not inspired by petty private hatreds. He was capable of great severity but equally he was capable of calculated acts of mercy that were remarkable not just by the standards of tyrants but by the standards of the Ancient World in general.[4] But Dionysius' rule was unconstitutional and illegitimate and could not fail to provoke rebellions among the partisans of democratic government. In 403 BC, Dionysius faced his first revolt and was besieged in a fortress he had built in Syracuse harbour by local citizens philosophically opposed to tyranny. For some time, his situation seemed hopeless and some of his foreign mercenaries, seduced by promises of citizenship, deserted to the rebels. Dionysius did not lose his nerve. He secretly contacted the Campanian mercenaries who had previously deserted Acragas and requested assistance. The besiegers, already convinced that their victory was as good as accomplished, had begun to disband when a contingent of 1,200 Campanians arrived and re-established Dionysius' rule without undue bloodshed. Dionysius enhanced his reputation by not inflicting any punishment on surrendering rebels and treating them with unexpected kindness. He did, however, confiscate the weapons held by Syracusan citizens while the latter were outside the city gathering in the harvest and progressively increased the size of his mercenary army. He had access to diverse sources of recruitment. There were, of course, Greek and Sicel mercenaries native to the island and there were western Mediterranean recruits from Iberia, Liguria and Campania. Many of his Greek mercenaries came from territories in Greece directly or indirectly controlled by Sparta. At the time of Syracusan revolt against Dionysius, the Peloponnesian War had just ended and Sparta, with whom Dionysius had an alliance, reigned supreme. There were plenty of mercenaries available and Dionysius was able to recruit with the full permission of Sparta throughout the Peloponnesus and, indeed, in any other area under Spartan control.[5] His mercenaries performed the classic functions so often required of soldiers-for-hire, that is they acted as bodyguards, police, garrison troops and combat troops.

With his army of 83,000 men – foreign mercenaries and trusted citizens – he began a campaign of aggrandisement. He captured the rival city of Aetna and then turned his attention to the Ionian Greek cities of Catane and Naxos, both of which he took, owing to the cooperation of traitors who opened the city gates in return for a substantial reward in gold. Dionysius, a Dorian Greek, behaved with unusual severity towards the Ionian Greeks of the captured cities, selling the entire population into slavery. Catane he gave to Campanian mercenaries as payment and as a residence. He went on to recapture Leontini, which had formerly been a Syracusan possession but had achieved independence – an independence guaranteed by Carthage.

Confrontation with Carthage could not be far away. Dionysius positively welcomed a decisive encounter and did not wait for a Carthaginian attack. In 398 BC, while Rome was still engaged in the siege of Veii, the Syracusan tyrant attacked the Carthaginian town of Motya in western Sicily, which he took after a protracted struggle and not without considerable loss. His mercenaries entered the town, slaughtering most of the population without restraint in revenge for the Carthaginian depredations at Himera. Dionysius finally stopped the carnage, not from an excess of humanitarian concern, but from a desire to make a little profit by selling the survivors into slavery. Some Green mercenaries found in Carthaginian service were crucified as traitors to the Greek cause.[6] Dionysius returned to Syracuse, leaving Motya in the hands of a Sicel garrison.

In 396 BC, Dionysius besieged Segesta but was forced to break off his operations when a Carthaginian army under Himilco invaded Sicily, recaptured Motya and all the other centres captured by Syracuse and began a siege of Syracuse itself. Dionysius had failed to stop the Carthaginians – at least that was the perception among the Syracusans, whose democratic sympathies suddenly intensified now that the tyrant was no longer enhancing Syracusan prestige by conquering neighbouring cities. The pro-democracy elements appealed to the Peloponnesian mercenaries who, however, refused to become involved in a rebellion against their employer. They had come to help Dionysius against Carthage not democrats against Dionysius.[7]

In the meantime, plague once more severely afflicted the Carthaginian camp and Dionysius took advantage to launch a concerted attack. On this occasion he demonstrated a ruthless streak by deliberately sacrificing some 1,000 mercenaries, whom he seems not to have trusted, in a feint against one part of the Carthaginian camp while he attacked another with the bulk of his forces. The decoy mercenaries were overwhelmed as Dionysius had intended. At the same time, he defeated the Carthaginian land and naval forces – defeated but not destroyed, for a continued if reduced Carthaginian presence (hence threat) was essential to the maintenance of his power, his justification for a continued tyranny. He was the protector of Syracuse. Thus, he allowed Himilco and the Carthaginian nationals to escape after secret negotiations. Carthage's mercenary contingents, however, were left behind to be killed or enslaved, except for a particularly gallant band of Iberians who entered into Dionysius' service. The greater part of Sicily was now in Greek hands.

The Carthaginians remained undaunted and a second war broke out in 392 BC. Dionysius again defeated the Carthaginians, confining them to the western tip of Sicily. In the space of eight years, Dionysius had taken control of all the Greek cities of the southern Italian peninsula. He paid for his wars and his mercenaries by imposing special taxes above those normally levied and by looting temples wherever he could. In 383 BC, Carthage struck again. Dionysius won the first battle at Cabala, during which the Carthaginian commander, Mago, was killed but, in a devastating riposte, Carthaginian troops routed those of Dionysius at Cranion (379 BC). Dionysius was forced to make peace. He attempted to restore Greek rule over the territory he had lost as a result of his defeat at Cranion by launching a fourth war in 367 BC, but achieved no decisive result. Dionysius died while the war was still in progress, not in battle but after a session of immoderate drinking.

Dionysius was succeeded in 366 BC by his son, who had his father's name but not his acumen. The amiable but ineffectual Dionysius II made peace with Carthage and attempted to save money by reducing the wages of the older mercenaries among the troops he had inherited from his father. When the mercenaries – mainly Campanians and Iberians – seriously threatened to revolt, Dionysius was forced to back down. The commander of the mercenaries, Heracleides, was held responsible for stirring up the soldiers and had the good sense to disappear from Syracuse, despite Dionysius' best efforts to apprehend him, and to reappear in Carthaginian territory.[8]

In 357 BC Heracleides met Dion, the most famous of Syracusan exiles, in Corinth and together they planned the overthrow of Dionysius II with the aid of mercenary troops. Dion sailed to Sicily ahead of Heracleides and was at first spectacularly successful in his enterprise. He had no more than 1,000 mercenaries but was able to recruit volunteers during his march out of Carthaginian territory (where he had landed) towards Syracuse. Dionysius happened to be in Italy at that moment and Dion was able to enter Syracuse without a fight, warmly welcomed by the inhabitants, who were not at first disconcerted by Dion's mercenary bodyguard. Dionysius returned in haste and besieged Syracuse with a mercenary army. But Dion's mercenaries and the Syracusans held out against all attempts to capture the city. Both sides encouraged their mercenaries with monetary rewards and golden crowns.[9] Dionysius, confined to the island fortress in Syracuse harbour, abandoned his attack shortly after the arrival of Heracleides and 1,500 mercenary reinforcements.

Heracleides proved even more popular than Dion and was elected admiral, an appointment initially resisted by Dion who resented the favours shown to a rival. Heracleides further enhanced his prestige by defeating a naval squadron under Philistus, an old admiral and historian who had remained loyal to Dionysius. Whereat, Dionysius escaped to Italy, leaving his son Apollocrates and a garrison of mercenaries to hold the island fortress. Dion, on the other hand, lost his popularity among the Syracusans, who had come to realise the true nature of his ambition. There were complaints about the behaviour of some of his mercenaries and the Syracusans refused to provide wages for Dion's Peloponnesians, even though they had delivered the city from the tyranny of Dionysius. Dion might have attempted to impose his will by force – his unpaid Peloponnesians would have supported him against the Syracusans – but he chose to retire to Leontini together with his 3,000 loyal mercenaries.[10]

Syracuse was now more or less devoid of mercenary soldiers. With Dionysius gone and Apollocrates' men close to surrender owing to lack of food, there seemed to be no further need of Dion and his mercenaries. But Syracusan complacency was shattered by the arrival of Italian mercenary reinforcements under Nypsius of Neapolis. Heracleides inflicted another naval defeat on the new arrivals and the Syracusans spent the night drinking themselves into a drunken stupor. Before dawn, Nypsius' Italian mercenaries had scaled the city walls, killed the sleeping guards and captured part of Syracuse. The mercenaries pillaged and raped at will while the Syracusans were forced to swallow their pride and recall Dion. Magnanimously, Dion obliged, returning with all possible speed. In a decisive battle, which saw Peloponnesians fighting Italians and Italians fighting Italians, his mercenaries encountered those of Nypsius and routed them. Nypsius disappeared and Apollocrates surrendered. Dion at first agreed to share power with Heracleides – the two rivals having undergone an ostensible reconciliation – but he later acquiesced, not without some reluctance, to the murder of Heracleides, who had sided with the democratic forces in Syracuse. Dion established himself as a tyrant, although he continued to pose as the liberator of Syracuse. In 354 BC, he was assassinated at the instigation of his trusted friend Callippus by a group of mercenaries from Zacynthus. Callippus, briefly popular, became a tyrant in his turn and, fittingly perhaps, suffered the same fate as Dion when he was murdered, during an unsuccessful campaign against Dionysius in Italy, by mercenaries dissatisfied by Callippus' poor leadership and their equally poor rate of pay.

The death of Dion encouraged Dionysius to return to Syracuse at the head of a mercenary army. He recaptured the island citadel in Syracuse harbour while the Syracusans appealed for help to the tyrant of Leontini, Hicetas, whom the Syracusans elected as their general.

Fortunately, Syracuse had also appealed to its mother-city, Corinth. The Corinthians responded sympathetically, recruited 700 mercenaries and placed them under the command of Timoleon, a man passionately devoted to democratic government. Timoleon had hitherto lived in seclusion for having been involved in the murder of his brother. He had once saved his brother's life in battle but later agreed to fratricide when the latter schemed to become tyrant of Corinth. Now, in 344 BC, he was being sent to Syracuse with a force largely made up of Phocian mercenaries recruited from the survivors of the Phocian army that had desecrated the temple of Delphi. On the way to Syracuse, Timoleon received another 300 mercenaries from Canegra and Leucas.

In Sicily, Hicetas had inflicted a defeat on Dionysius, destroying 3,000 of his mercenaries. The Syracusan tyrant was once more confined to the citadel in Syracuse harbour. Meanwhile, Timoleon landed in Sicily, having eluded a Carthaginian fleet sent to prevent his return to the island. In the Sicel town of Hadranum the citizens were divided between those who favoured Hicetas and those who would summon Timoleon. Hicetas arrived first with 5,000 men and was still in the act of settling in his troops when Timoleon attacked with 1,200 men (he had recruited an extra 200 men in Sicily itself). Despite his numerical inferiority he completely overcame Hicetas' forces and occupied Hadranum, but Hicetas escaped to Syracuse. Dionysius offered to surrender on condition of being granted a safe passage to Corinth and the retention of his personal possessions. Timoleon readily agreed. Dionysius preserved both his life and his property and headed for a tranquil exile in Corinth while Timoleon gained the citadel with its arsenal of 70,000 weapons and the welcome addition to his forces of 2,000 mercenaries who changed from one employer to another with a minimum of fuss.[11] Remarkably, Timoleon had not taken possession in person. He had remained at Hadranum, which was now his headquarters, and had sent a small force of some 400 men to enter and garrison the fortress and to ensure that Dionysius was conveyed safely away from Syracuse .

Now that Timoleon had proved his worth, Corinth recruited another 2,000 infantry and 200 cavalry and sent them to Hadranum. The arrival of mercenary reinforcements from Corinth and Timoleon's growing prestige caused Hicetas to request additional help from Carthage. One hundred and fifty Carthaginian vessels duly arrived in Syracuse harbour laden with troops but Timoleon's garrison, although under pressure, remained in possession of the citadel. Timoleon marched towards Syracuse with all his forces. Fortune favoured him yet again when the Carthaginians suddenly withdrew. It was not just Timoleon's approach that prompted the Carthaginian decision. There had been considerable fraternisation between Hicetas' Greek mercenaries and those of Timoleon's garrison each time both groups had gone fishing in the harbour, even though they were quite prepared to kill each other if they met in battle. Mago, the Carthaginian commander, suspected that the Greeks might combine against his forces and sailed home to Carthage where he committed suicide in atonement for his precipitate retreat.[12] With the Carthaginians gone, Timoleon easily expelled Hicetas from Syracuse and restored freedom to the city. He behaved at all times like a liberator, never seeking to impose his will on the Syracusans. New migrants arrived from Corinth to help repopulate the city as did thousands of native Syracusans who had been exiled by the tyrants. Timoleon went on to restore democratic institutions in other Sicilian cities. Their tyrants, including Hicetas of Leontini, submitted one by one to the Corinthian general and to democratic government. Timoleon was one of the very few mercenary commanders throughout history who used mercenaries to bring freedom rather than suppress it.

Tyranny had been successfully extirpated from the Greek cities of Sicily but Timoleon now had to deal with the perennial problem which faced many a mercenary commander – the provision of adequate payment. Syracuse and Corinth defrayed expenses to some extent but Timoleon's mercenaries could scarcely be allowed to make up for unsatisfactory wages by looting other Greek cities – the very cities they had liberated from tyranny. Timoleon's solution was to conduct a raid on Carthaginian territory in western Sicily. The enterprise was successful and Timoleon was able to provide his mercenaries with both back pay and an advance.

Carthage, needless to say, was outraged and in 399 BC, a large Carthaginian army once more landed in Sicily intent on punishing Syracuse. Timoleon was certainly outnumbered several times by the superior Carthaginian forces but he was not intimidated. He did not wait for the invaders to penetrate into Greek territory, choosing instead to confront the Carthaginians inside their own domain. On the way to western Sicily he was deserted by 1,000 mercenaries whose pay had again fallen into arrears and who were, in any case, unenthusiastic about facing a much larger enemy force. To prevent them from joining the Carthaginians, Timoleon did not stop them leaving, promising instead that they would be paid if they marched back to Syracuse. He persuaded the remaining force (6,000 mercenaries, 5,000 Syracusan and allied citizens)[13] to continue and met the advancing Carthaginians at the River Crimisus. He attacked the elite troops of the Carthaginian army (also known as the Sacred Band) and destroyed the entire formation after some hard fighting.

Timoleon's victory was complete, as complete as any victory could be, but he took no advantage of it, even though he was in an excellent position to inhibit any further Carthaginian expansion and indeed terminate the Carthaginian presence in Sicily altogether. He was forced to act against the former tyrant of Catane, Mamercus, and against Hicetas, both of whom had re-established tyrannies in their respective cities with the aid of Carthaginian mercenaries. Timoleon overcame both tyrants, not without losing two contingents of mercenaries who were destroyed by superior enemy forces. Hicetas was betrayed by his own mercenary troops and handed over to Timoleon. Mamercus surrendered and both tyrants were executed by the Syracusans. Carthage made peace and Timoleon retired to an estate presented to him by the grateful people of Syracuse. He died blind in 337 BC, much lamented by all of Hellenic Sicily, perhaps the most unusual mercenary commander of his age, or of any age.

The history of Sicily in the period after the death of Timoleon and the First Punic War is rather obscure owing to the scarcity of relevant documents and artefacts but it seems that the island enjoyed some two decades of relative peace after which the work of Timoleon was undone by the re-establishment of tyrannies effected, needless to say, by the use of mercenaries. Most prominent among the new breed of tyrants was Agathocles who, in emulation of Dionysius I, imposed his tyranny over Syracuse and then gradually extended his control to include most of Sicily. Agathocles was the son of a potter but preferred to handle weapons rather than clay. He was twice exiled from Syracuse and on the first occasion became a captain of mercenaries in the service of Tarentum. On the second occasion he also acted as a captain of mercenaries but for his own purposes. He travelled to Morgantia where he recruited other Syracusan exiles and a force of Sicel mercenaries sufficiently large and menacing enough to persuade Syracuse to accept his return and his subsequent demand that he be appointed general. Agathocles had begun to raid Carthaginian possessions in Sicily in order to acquire sufficient means with which to pay his army, in much the same way as Timoleon had done a quarter of a century earlier. The Carthaginian reaction was predictable enough. In 311 BC, a 45,000-strong Carthaginian army under Hamilcar attacked and defeated Agathocles' army (which included up to 10,000 mercenary infantry) and laid siege to Syracuse itself.[14] Agathocles countered the Carthaginian success with a bold manoeuvre. Leaving a mercenary garrison in Syracuse, he collected 3,500 Syracusans, 2,500 Sicilian allied troops, 3,000 Greek mercenaries and 3,000 Sammite, Etruscan and Gallic mercenaries and attacked Carthage.[15] So unexpected was Agathocles' strategy that Carthage was forced to recall some of her troops in Sicily to meet the threat posed by his invasion force. Hamilcar sent 5,000 Greek mercenaries upon whom Agathocles inflicted a heavy defeat shortly after their arrival. He took 1,000 prisoners of whom more than half were Syracusan exiles. Agathocles' mercenary troops, having trounced those of the enemy, ravaged the countryside around Carthage but were unable to capture the city itself. Then Agathocles began to have difficulty in providing regular pay and some of his mercenaries deserted to the Carthaginians. His situation further deteriorated when he was forced to return precipitately to Sicily in order to suppress rebellions in a number of cities he had incorporated into his domain. Upon returning to Carthage he found that nearly half of his army had been destroyed owing to the poor leadership of the officers he had left behind to continue the siege. Agathocles fled ignominiously, leaving his army to come to terms with the Carthaginians. Many of his mercenaries, less than impressed by Agathocles' behaviour, changed sides. Carthage had survived but, exhausted by the struggle, she sued for peace. Back in Sicily, Agathocles was involved in a new war against Hamilcar's Greek mercenary commander,

Deinocrates. Having abandoned his army at Carthage, Agathocles was only able to recruit some 6,000 men while Deinocrates had closer to 28,000, of whom 8,000 were Syracusan exiles.[16] Nevertheless, despite this numerical disadvantage, Agathocles emerged triumphant. He treated Deinocrates with notable leniency and made him a general in his own army. Agathocles' victory did much to restore his credibility as an employer of mercenaries. His subsequent campaigns were centred on the Italian mainland where he was employed as a mercenary commander-in-chief by the Tarentines who were being plagued by the Bruttii and other hill tribes of southern Italy. During his Italian adventure, Agathocles found himself once again unable to pay 2,000 Etruscan and Ligurian mercenaries but solved his pecuniary difficulties by massacring the entire contingent.[17] When his financial situation improved he merely hired a new group of mercenaries. Agathocles seems to have had considerable success against the enemies of Tarentum but died in 289 BC before completing his operations.

Few details exist regarding the tyrants who ruled Sicilian cities in the interval between the death of Agathocles and the rise of Hiero II, whose attack on the Campanian mercenaries of Messana ultimately led to the First Punic War and the Roman conquest of Sicily. It is almost certain, however, that the power of those little-known tyrants must have been based on the use of mercenaries. Few tyrants, if any, could rely solely on citizen militia levies, particularly in cities where the population was predisposed towards democratic government.

The circumstances leading to the advent of Hiero II are not known with any precision. Like his predecessors, he was elected to the post of general and then became tyrant and finally King of Syracuse. Shortly after he became ruler, Hiero led his army, composed of citizen levies and veteran mercenaries, in an attack upon the city of Messana, which was under the control of a band of Campanian mercenaries called the Mamertines (Mamers was the Oscan word for Mars). The city had been seized in 289 BC by the Sons of Mars, who had hitherto been in the service of Agathocles. They used Messana as a base from which they conducted piracy and brigandage on an impressive scale and extracted tribute from other Greek cities in return for dubious promises, which ostensibly bound them not to attack centres blackmailed into paying protection money. The Mamertines were somewhat akin to the free companies of medieval Europe and, needless to say, were a law unto themselves.

Hiero would undoubtedly contribute to the stability of Sicily by ridding the island of an unruly element which had been a chronic nuisance to Syracuse and, for that matter, to the Carthaginians. But Hiero also had an ulterior motive for he wished to rid himself of his veteran mercenaries, many of whom he had inherited from Agathocles. They had undoubtedly supported his elevation to the generalship of the Syracusan armies and consequently they expected to be paid regularly and to exert influence over the young Hiero. Whatever the precise nature of their grievances, the veteran mercenaries were, according to the Greek historian Polybius, unreliable, unruly, seditious and potentially mutinous.[18] Thus, Hiero sent the mercenaries to attack the Mamertines while he held his Syracusans in reserve as if he intended to attack the enemy at another point. Much to his satisfaction, the Mamertines destroyed Hiero's mercenaries while he withdrew to Syracuse, having achieved his immediate goal in much the same way as Dionysius I had deliberately betrayed his mercenaries during the Carthaginian siege of Syracuse in 397 BC.

Hiero then personally selected a large number of new mercenaries who owed their loyalty directly to him rather than the Syracusan state, thus securing his continued domination over the city. The relative ease with which Hiero replaced the defunct mercenaries provides further evidence, if indeed any is needed, that there was a plentiful supply of adventurous or impoverished souls from all over the Hellenistic world ready and willing to perform mercenary service. Hiero also raised his native Syracusan levies, put them through intense training and, together with his mercenary troops, marched the entire army out on a second campaign against the Mamertines who had grown even more daring and arrogant after their destruction of Hiero's original mercenary force. On the plain of Mylae he defeated the Campanians and captured their leaders. As a result of his victory, Hiero became King of Syracuse and was recognised as such by all his Sicilian allies.

While Hiero made preparations to besiege Messana, the defeated Mamertines split into two factions, one of which appealed to Carthage for help while the other sent a delegation to Rome. Carthaginian control over northern Sicily was perceived as a threat to the Italian mainland and the fear – real or imaginary – of another foreign invasion was enough to persuade the Romans to undertake their first overseas military expedition.

The First Punic War (264–241 BC), as the conflict came to be known, began and ended with Roman successes. A Roman army under the consul Appius Claudius entered Messana without difficulty when the Carthaginian commander, Hanno, panicked and withdrew his forces from the city. Hiero, alarmed by this easy Roman victory, temporarily forgot traditional enmities and allied himself with the Carthaginians. The unlikely allies launched another attack on Messana but Appius was able to defeat Hiero, who fled to Syracuse, and to rout the Carthaginians on the following day. He lifted the siege of Messana and began that of Syracuse. When the Roman senate heard of Appius' double victory, it despatched another four legions to Sicily. Hiero clearly saw that Roman power was at least a match for that of Carthage and decided to surrender but he was allowed to remain King of Syracuse and was henceforth a loyal friend and ally of Rome.

Having lost their Syracusan ally, not to mention considerable battle casualties, the Carthaginians reinforced their army with fresh troops by recruiting large numbers of Ligurian, Celtic and Iberian mercenaries and concentrating them at Agrigentum, a major commercial centre in southern Sicily. Fifty thousand mercenary troops stood ready to march northwards against the Romans. The Romans, however, struck the first blow by marching rapidly across the island and besieging Agrigentum. For five months the Romans besieged the Carthaginian stronghold. The Carthaginian commander, Hannibal Gisco, appealed to Carthage for aid. Reinforcements duly arrived and the Romans found that they had become besieged as well as besiegers. But the relief force under General Hanno (not the Hanno at Messana, who was crucified for abandoning the city) could make no impact on the Roman siege lines. A preliminary cavalry action between Numidian mercenaries and Roman horsemen ended largely in favour of the Carthaginians but two more months passed with nothing more than daily skirmishes. As the famine grew steadily worse within Agrigentum, Hanno at last decided to give battle. The ensuing fight lasted most of the day but the Romans finally overcame the Carthaginian mercenaries and the entire relief force was routed with great loss. The triumphant but exhausted Romans failed to maintain a sufficiently vigilant watch and Hannibal broke out of the city at night with his entire mercenary army and escaped. The Romans broke into Agrigentum, enslaved some 25,000 inhabitants and took a large quantity of loot.[19]

The capture of Agrigentum gave Rome virtual control of all Sicily and encouraged wider ambitions than the strictly limited aims that had originally led to Roman intervention.

The sheer momentum of their success inspired the Romans to imitate Agathocles and strike directly at Carthage itself. The Roman expeditionary force encountered the Carthaginian fleet off Cape Ecnomus and crashed through, sinking some thirty enemy ships and capturing sixty-four, and sailed

on to Africa, landing unopposed near Carthage. Under the command of the
consul Marcus Atilius Regulus, the Roman army marched rapidly towards
the Carthaginian capital, capturing the town of Apsis along the way. At Adys,
the Carthaginians made a resolute stand. Their mercenaries pushed back an
entire Roman legion but advanced too far, so that they were surrounded and
routed by the rest of the Roman forces.[20] Carthage was now in a perilous
position and was prepared to negotiate with Regulus. The Roman general's
conditions, however, were so harsh that the Carthaginians decided on further
resistance, despite their catastrophic defeats.

It was during Carthage's hour of maximum danger that one of her
recruiting officers returned from Greece with a substantial number of
mercenaries and a first-class mercenary commander, Xanthippus of Lacedaimon. Xanthippus immediately realised that the Carthaginian generals were
inexperienced, that they were using their cavalry and elephants ineffectively
and that the Carthaginian troops were still powerful and merely needed to
regain inspiration and confidence. The Carthaginians accepted the mercenary
commander's criticisms and appointed him general-in-chief. Xanthippus
reorganised and revitalised the Carthaginian forces and in 255 BC inflicted a
crushing defeat on Regulus' army at the battle of Tunes. Both armies were
equally matched in size – just under 20,000 men – and the Romans fought
extremely well against the Greek mercenaries, of whom they killed about
eight hundred. But against the 100 elephants (imported from India together
with their trainers) and the Carthaginian cavalry the Romans had no answer.
The Roman cavalry was severely handled by the Carthaginian horsemen
while large numbers of infantry were flattened by the elephant corps.[21] Less
than 5,000 survivors escaped and were rescued by a Roman fleet. On the way
back to Sicily the fleet ran into a violent storm and more than three quarters
of the ships were lost, complete with soldiers and crewmen. Xanthippus,
meanwhile, suddenly left Carthage at the height of his success and returned
to Greece for reasons unknown.

The heavy losses suffered by the retreating Roman fleet encouraged the
Carthaginians to send reinforcements to the few surviving outposts in Sicily.
The Carthaginian general Hasdrubal landed in Lilybaeum with some 25,000
men and 140 elephants but this force was skilfully defeated by Lucius
Caecilius Metellus and, emboldened by their success, the Romans besieged
Lilybaeum, which was defended by 10,000 Greek and Celtic mercenaries.[22]
An early end to the siege seemed imminent when several senior commanders
of the Carthaginian mercenary troops secretly made their way to the Roman

camp and offered to hand the city over to the besiegers. The conspiracy was reported to the Carthaginian commander, Himilco, by an Achaean mercenary named Alexon. Promising substantial rewards, Himilco appealed to the remaining commanders who in turn appealed to their men to remain loyal. When the conspirators returned and demanded entry into the city in order to explain Roman offers to the rank and file mercenaries, they were met with missiles thrown from the walls.[23] Carthage had barely escaped another disaster. Her troops at Lilybaeum made an attempt to destroy the Roman siege engines but the legionaries managed to contain the Carthaginian sortie and the siege continued with every prospect of success until the Romans were suddenly struck by two naval disasters which ended any immediate chance of victory.

Publius Claudius Pulcher, commander of the 120 Roman ships blockading Lilybaeum, sailed to the port of Drepana where a Carthaginian relief fleet had arrived. He expected an easy victory but the Romans suffered a major defeat at the hands of the Carthaginian admiral Adherbal. Several days later, a savage tempest annihilated a second Roman fleet. Rome was, for the moment, incapable of naval operations. For five years neither side could achieve a decisive victory but ultimately Roman resilience proved stronger than that of Carthage. After defeats at Lilybaeum and Drepana and at sea, Carthage had no choice but to make peace. She withdrew her surviving troops from Sicily, agreed to pay Rome 3,200 talents and consoled herself by crucifying Hanno, just as she had executed his namesake at Messana. Twenty-four years of war ended in Rome's favour. She was now inextricably involved in the wider Mediterranean, with Sicily as her first overseas province.

The First Punic War was fought by two armies whose character and composition could not have been more different. The armies of Rome, made up of Roman citizen militiamen led by native Roman officers and supported by allied militiamen, were practically the antithesis of the Carthaginian armies, which were almost entirely composed of multinational bands of mercenaries under the overall command of Carthaginian officers. The earliest Carthaginian armies were, needless to say, citizen militias but towards the beginning of the sixth century BC, Carthage began to use mercenaries and auxiliaries, the latter being conscripts from among the Libyan tribes under Carthaginian control and from other north African tribes whose rulers were independent chieftains. It was not that militia forces were no longer mobilised but henceforth they would be called upon to serve only in times of dire emergency, when Carthage was directly attacked by Agathocles, Regulus or the irate mercenaries she had tried to disband without full payment at the end of the First Punic War.

Whenever necessary, Carthage was able to mobilise about 10,000 militia-men and these troops performed effectively enough and were particularly stubborn and courageous when hard-pressed but Carthage was essentially a naval and commercial empire and few native Carthaginians were imbued with a love of the military life for its own sake, unlike the Iberians, Gauls or Numidians whom they employed. Thus, from a relatively early time, Carthage progressively entrusted its defence to foreign mercenaries and auxiliaries while Carthaginians could pursue their business interests without the incon-venient interruption of military service. Furthermore, as Plutarch observed, Carthage preferred to use mercenaries simply because, in the Carthaginian estimation, at least, they were expendable and if a battle ended in defeat the losses were largely borne by foreigners.[24] The 10,000 Carthaginians slaugh-tered at Crimisus by Timoleon's mercenaries represented an unusual and exceptionally large presence of native Carthaginian troops, particularly in an army sent overseas. Most armies fielded by Carthage contained few of her own nationals, other than those of the high command.

Carthage's first foreign troops came, naturally enough, from Africa. They were not mercenaries but conscripted auxiliaries drawn from the Libyan tribes living under Carthaginian domination. The Libyans had been reduced to a state of slavery in the earliest period of their subservience to Carthage but by the mid-third century BC their status had somewhat improved so that they became free cultivators, albeit they were required to pay tribute and perform military service.[25] They provided both infantry and cavalry and their attitude varied between sullen resentment and active cooperation, the former being more usual. Initially, Carthage seems to have conscripted large numbers of Libyans but, as other foreigners became available, she placed less reliance on disaffected tribesmen. By the time of the First Punic War, the Libyans in her employ may have been more akin to mercenary hirelings rather than conscripts.

Polybius in his account of the Punic Wars refers to the Libyans as mercenaries but whether this is indicative of a real change in their status or more a misunderstanding on the part of the Greek historian remains a matter for speculation. G.T. Griffith suggests that Carthage may have suspended the levying of less than reliable subject troops who might be tempted to desert to the Romans, in favour of hiring more mercenary soldiers from beyond the borders of their empire. According to his explanation, the Libyans would henceforth be required to pay contributions in lieu of military service (presumably over and above the tribute already extracted by the Carthaginian government). Thus, the Libyan mercenaries repeatedly mentioned by Polybius may indeed have been true mercenary volunteers hired in much the same way as other foreign troops. The volunteers would have been more reliable than potentially hostile conscripts, provided, of course, that they were paid a regular wage (the one unvarying proviso underlying successful use of the mercenary system). Griffith's interpretation is both logical and plausible but, as he himself recognises, cannot be substantiated with irrefutable proof.[26]

More reliable than the Libyan conscripts were the so-called Liby-Phoenicians. These were Libyans who had imbibed Carthaginian culture or were of mixed Libyan and Carthaginian blood. The Liby-Phoenicians were the most important component of the Greek-style phalanxes used by the Carthaginian heavy infantry and were armed and dressed in the manner of Macedonian hoplites. They were not strictly speaking mercenaries, in that they were Carthaginian subjects, but they were not anywhere near as reticent about soldiering as the pure Libyans.

Other African troops employed by Carthage came from outside Carthaginian territory. The Numidians were, perhaps, the archetypal light horsemen of the Ancient World. Trained from childhood, they were armed with javelins and rode small, fast and agile mounts bareback and without stirrups (which had not yet been invented). They lived in a land that was largely rugged and mountainous save for a small fertile coastal strip, their society made up of small nomadic clans of herdsmen, each with its individual ruler. The Numidians were exclusively horsemen and were particularly suited to ambushes, raids, skirmishing and the pursuit of broken enemies rather than to full-scale cavalry encounters. In the face of an enemy cavalry charge they simply scattered independently and returned by a circuitous route to attack the flanks and rear of the oncoming force, using hit-and-run tactics. When they were routed they often disappeared from the field, not always rejoining the rest of the army in which they were employed. During the fourth century BC they seemed to have worked for Carthage on an individual basis as mercenaries but in the third century they were hired in large groups by arrangement between Carthage and their tribal chiefs. They were not conscripts but volunteers who willingly provided their own horses and equipment (such as it was) and were thus both mercenaries and auxiliaries – auxiliary by status and certainly mercenary in motivation and behaviour. The Moors of Mauritania, like their Numidian neighbours, were nomadic tribesmen independent of Carthaginian rule and also worked for Carthage as mercenary-auxiliaries by agreement between the Carthaginian government and their own rulers. They provided Carthage with light troops, both cavalry and infantry.

As Carthaginian domination and influence spread to the western shores of the Mediterranean, Carthage began to employ non-African mercenaries, of whom the most prominent were Iberians and Celt-Iberians from Spain, Balearic islanders and Celts and Ligurians from the Alpine region covering southern France and northern Italy. The Iberians were the original inhabitants of Spain but their exclusive occupation of the peninsula gradually came to an end as Celtic tribesmen came southwards over the Pyrenees in migratory waves in the period between the eighth and sixth centuries BC while along the south-eastern coast commercial colonies were established by the Ionian Greeks and the Carthaginians, with the latter progressively ousting the former. The southern Iberians came under the influence of Hellenic and Phoenician culture and also that of Egypt, whose trading ships visited the Spanish coastline. By the third century BC, the population of Spain consisted of three main groups, each of which was divided into several tribes. In the north there were the Celts while the centre was occupied by the Celt-Iberians who, as the name suggests, were the product of a gradual merging of original inhabitants and Celtic migrants. In the south were the Iberians, who were influenced not just by their contact with Greek and Carthaginian colonies but also by returning Hispanic mercenaries. The Iberians and Celt-Iberians – in particular, the latter – had already established a substantial tradition of mercenary service long before their regular employment by Carthage. Celt-Iberians often served other Hispanic tribes as mercenaries of auxiliaries during inter-tribal wars. Thus, for example, the Iberian Turdetani tribe hired some 10,000 Celt-Iberians during one neighbourly conflict.[27] By the beginning of the fifth century BC, Hispanic warriors had also served overseas in Sicily, Greece and Egypt and, indeed, in most locations in the Mediterranean world. Those who survived came home influenced by the more advanced culture of their foreign employers. In Carthaginian service Hispanic mercenaries played a vital role, particularly during the Second Punic War. They provided their employers with horsemen who were every bit as expert as the Numidians with the added advantage of being a heavier type of cavalry, more useful at the centre of a battle than the mounted skirmishers. Hispanic footsoldiers came in various types and, although they were armed with throwing spears, they were essentially sword-and-shield men. The Iberians were usually armed

[225]

with a characteristic curved sword called a *falcata* while the Celt-Iberians normally carried the straight Celtic sword. While Spain provided the Carthaginians with some of their best heavy infantry, by far the most effective light troops came from the Balearic Islands, whose Hispanic inhabitants had established an awesome reputation throughout the Mediterranean area for their expertise with the simple but deadly sling. Trained, like the Numidians, from early childhood, the Balearic islanders were legendary for their accuracy and their ability to project a missile right through the helmet or breastplate of an opponent.

In terms of character, the Hispanic troops were fierce and courageous in the attack, stubborn in defeat and were highly valued by their employers. On the negative side, they were proud and independent and given to ill-discipline. Their relations with the Carthaginians did not always run smoothly for they were somewhat unreliable and did not approach engagements made between themselves and their employers with unimpeachable fidelity and seriousness. When Rome recovered after the disasters of Trebbia, Lake Trasimene and Cannae and it became obvious that the conflict between Carthage and Rome would be decided in favour of the latter, Hispanic troops did not hesitate to change sides. They were, after all, mercenaries and had no particular affection for the Carthaginians. In the defence of their own territory, however, the Iberians and Celt-Iberians only accepted Roman domination after a furious and protracted struggle, which sometimes involved the mass suicide of entire Spanish garrisons in preference to surrender.

Among Carthage's other western European mercenaries were the Ligurians, hill tribesmen living in north-western Italy. They were hunters, herdsmen and foresters and their dire poverty led them to engage in looting raids, piracy and mercenary service. Armed with sword, dagger, shield and a bundle of javelins they worked for Carthage, Syracuse and then for Rome.

The Carthaginian army also contained Gauls and other Celtic peoples who, as inveterate enemies of Rome, served Carthage with savage enthusiasm. After their disastrous performance against Timoleon's mercenary hoplites at Crimisus, the Carthaginians immediately appreciated the superiority of the Greeks and began to hire them on a regular basis within a year of their defeat. Greek mercenary phalanxes fought for Carthage during the First Punic War and, as described, it was a Greek mercenary general who saved the city from capture by the Romans.

Such were the various nationalities to be found in Carthaginian service, each one usually commanded by kings, nobles, chieftains or officers of the same ethnic origin. The Carthaginians made no attempt to impose uniformity on this polyglot mass of soldiers. Indeed, it would have been impossible to impose any standardised weaponry or battle tactics for each component nationality had its own way of fighting and its own preferred armament. Surprising though it may sound, fighting is a cultural activity, not, of course, in the sense that it enhances civilisation and cultural identity – no sensible argument could be made in support of that proposition – but in the sense that different cultures have fought and to some extent continue to fight in different and distinctive ways determined by their psychological makeup, their geographical origins and their predilection for particular types of weapons. Religions, laws, traditions, customs, festivals, music, art, literature, architecture and gastronomy are all reflections of culture or that more advanced state of culture, civilisation. Fighting styles are also indicative of the nature of a particular culture even though they represent an uncivilised activity. Not for nothing have the strengths and weaknesses of soldiers of different nationality been constantly compared throughout the ages by historians and military men.

The multinational mercenary army of Carthage was commanded, as previously observed, by native Carthaginian generals. Being a Carthaginian general was a frustrating not to mention risky business. The Carthaginian government was niggardly both in the provision of money and men. It was not just the mean commercial mind at work, for the government also feared that some of its generals with too many mercenaries at their disposal might contemplate the establishment of their own kingdoms or the overthrow of the Carthaginian government. Thus, relations between the government and the military were often difficult and characterised by mutual distrust. The danger in being a general lay in the fact that Carthage was unforgiving to those who failed in their tasks. Crucifixion was the penalty and it was no idle threat, as more than one general found out during the First Punic War.

While Rome rejoiced at the outcome of her first war with Carthage, the fortunes of the latter went from bad to worse, for the Carthaginian government, in demobilising its mercenaries, tried to underpay them. Carthage now sought to reduce the size of her army. This was accepted practice in peacetime and perfectly understandable now that she had lost her Sicilian possessions and no longer needed to maintain garrison troops and field armies to defend them. The mercenaries accepted demobilisation as a matter of course but the Carthaginian government's attempt to cheat them of their wages was a particularly foolish policy given Carthage's long-standing and

[227]

self-imposed reliance on mercenaries for her defence. Then again, the Carthaginians had tried to fight their entire war with Rome on a tight budget, for their commercial instinct was so much stronger than their grasp of military necessity. One of the underlying causes of her defeat had been Carthage's failure to provide her field commanders with sufficient resources. While Rome could mobilise more men than she actually needed and replace losses of material with remarkable speed, the Carthaginian generals were hampered by a government whose cost-cutting and half-measures seriously weakened their ability to respond effectively to Roman armies that were very often superior in numbers. Despite government parsimony, the war had still been costly and now there was a substantial indemnity to be paid to the victors. Thus, the Carthaginian government's desire to save money by defrauding its mercenaries was in keeping with its mercantile mind and even understandable in the circumstances in which Carthage now found itself but it was a move fraught with dangerous consequences.

In observance of Carthage's treaty with Rome, the mercenaries were to be removed from Sicily and transported back to Carthage. General Gisgo, who was in charge of the evacuation, was sensible enough to send the mercenaries back in separate contingents at staggered intervals so that the government might pay off one group before the next one arrived. But the Carthaginian government, much less sensible, allowed each contingent into the city without making any attempt to provide pay. During the war, Carthage had accumulated a huge debt and had not paid her mercenaries by the month or, indeed, at any regular interval. She now hoped that the mercenaries would accept a reduced wage. Irritated by the government's tardiness in handing over their hard-earned money, the mercenaries behaved with increasing surliness and ill-discipline. The Carthaginians requested that the mercenaries should move to another city and reside there until their pay was ready. Surprisingly perhaps, the mercenaries agreed to go and agreed to a further request to take their families with them. This was a major tactical blunder by the Carthaginians for it deprived them of hostages who could be used to ensure moderation and good behaviour on the part of the mercenaries. The Carthaginian general Hanno was sent to parley with the disgruntled foreigners and tried to persuade them to accept a lesser sum. The mercenaries, however, were fully aware of the correct amount they were owed and reacted by marching on Carthage. There were Iberians, Gauls, Ligurians, Balearic islanders and Greeks among their ranks but the most numerous were Libyan mercenaries.

In keeping with their international composition, the insurgents were led by men of different nationalities. There was Mathos, a Libyan who aggravated an already tense situation by inciting rebellion among the Libyan tribes dominated by Carthage. His fellow ringleaders were Autarichus, the leader of a 2,000-strong Gallic contingent, and the Campanian, Spendius, a runaway slave who, understandably enough, found life as a mercenary infinitely more congenial than rowing in a Roman galley.

The mercenaries were supplied with generous monetary donations by the Libyan tribes, who saw in the revolt a chance to gain their freedom. Such was their liberality that the mercenaries soon had more money than the total sum owed by Carthage. But there was no stopping now and the Carthaginians found themselves at war with the mercenaries and the Libyan tribesmen. It was a particularly merciless war even by the standards of the time, complete with sanguinary battles that ultimately destroyed most of the mercenaries, the slaughtering of prisoners rather than their enslavement and atrocities that impressed eyewitnesses long inured to the habitual cruelty of their times. The mercenaries' revolt soon escalated from an armed brawl over money into a full-scale social crisis as the soldiers found willing supporters among the subject peoples of the Carthaginian empire. The insurgents declared themselves to be a separate state and even issued a range of coins to emphasise their independence. To meet the crisis, the Carthaginians mobilised their 10,000-strong militia and, despite the object-lesson they were receiving on the perils of the mercenary system, hired new mercenaries, presumably on the promise of future payment, from traditional recruiting grounds in western Europe. Old habits die hard. Carthage recruited in Spain, France and northern Italy with the forbearance of Rome. Although the Carthaginians had been yesterday's enemy, the Romans were alarmed at the possible emergence of a rogue mercenary state which would undoubtedly engage in piracy and plundering and constitute an international threat. Thus, when Carthage's mercenaries in Sardinia went into open revolt in sympathy with their fellow soldiers in Africa, the Romans at first refused – hard though refusal may have been – an offer from the mercenary garrison to place the island under Roman control.

By 238 BC, the Carthaginian general Hamilcar had managed to restore order and had destroyed the great mass of the insurgent mercenaries. He had received considerable help from the Numidians who had remained friendly to Carthage. One Numidian prince supplied 2,000 cavalrymen.[28] The resurgence of Carthage caused Rome to change her policy in a rather perfidious manner. When the mercenary garrisons on Sardinia renewed their offer, the Romans accepted and occupied the island. Shortly thereafter, they annexed Corsica and utterly compromised Rome's reputation for good faith and honourable dealing. Carthage, exhausted from her ordeal, could do nothing. But Roman treachery deepened Carthaginian resentment and the desire for revenge. Shut out from the northern Mediterranean, Carthage now sought to extend her dominions in the Spanish peninsula to compensate for her recent losses to the Romans and despatched three great generals, Hamilcar, Hasdrubal and Hannibal, to achieve her ambitions. Spain was an attractive prize, both as a source of mineral wealth and of mercenary soldiers. The Carthaginians annexed most of Spain up to the River Ebro without undue difficulty, as much by diplomacy as by military action, for the Hispanic tribes were disunited and there were plenty of Hispanics quite willing to help the Carthaginians effect their conquest.

Lying within the area taken by Carthage was the city of Saguntum, which had commercial links with the pro-Roman city of Massilia (Marseilles) and was itself decidedly pro-Roman. In 226 BC the Romans signed a treaty with the Carthaginians stipulating that Saguntum would remain independent of Carthaginian control and that Hasdrubal was not to advance northwards beyond the Ebro. For the Carthaginians, the existence of what amounted to a Roman outpost in its sphere of influence was ultimately unacceptable and war between the two rivals was inevitable. From 225 BC, Rome was temporarily preoccupied with yet another invasion by Gallic tribes supported by mercenaries from Trans-Alpine Gaul. The Romans mobilised 130,000 men, including allied contingents, and defeated the invaders at the battle of Telamon (224 BC). This marked the last Gallic attack on Italy. The Romans advanced northwards and conquered practically all of the sub-Alpine region.

In Spain, Hamilcar had died by drowning (229 BC) and Hasdrubal was assassinated in 221 BC, leaving Hannibal in sole command. Hannibal decided that he would no longer tolerate the existence of an independent Saguntum and besieged the city in 219 BC. The Romans did nothing at first but, when the city fell after an eight-month siege and its inhabitants were sold into slavery, they demanded that the Carthaginian government surrender Hannibal into their hands. When the Carthaginians refused, the Romans declared war.

Polybius, in describing this second war between Carthage and Rome, argues that wars in general have a cause, a pretext and a beginning, three factors not to be confused with each other.[29] Thus, Hannibal's assault on Saguntum precipitated renewed conflict but was neither its pretext nor its cause. The specific pretext was the existence of a pro-Roman enclave in

Carthaginian-controlled territory while the real cause was the continuing struggle between Rome and Carthage for military control of the western Mediterranean, which would provide the victor with exclusive access to its resources. Given the importance of the prize and the mutual hatred of the antagonists, the outcome of the struggle could only be determined by war rather than negotiation and compromise.

The Romans intended to strike at Hannibal on Spanish soil and to attack Carthage itself but in March 218 BC, Hannibal crossed the Ebro, subdued the pro-Roman Pyrenean hill tribes and marched overland through eastern Gaul. Hannibal's army was not large, less than 38,000 men, by the time he reached the Alps. His crossing of the Alps was also made in the face of attacks by hostile hill tribes and across mountains covered by premature autumn snows. The Romans believed that no invading army could successfully cross the mountains in such wintry conditions, menaced by ambushes and avalanches, but Hannibal achieved the seemingly impossible and descended into the Po valley, his army reduced to 26,000 men.[30] Against this force Rome could potentially raise up to 700,000 infantry and 70,000 cavalry from among her own citizens and her allies.

The army which Hannibal led from Spain to Italy contained all the nationalities which Carthage had traditionally employed. Notwithstanding desertions in Spain, the percentage of Hispanic mercenaries was much larger than in previous Carthaginian armies for the simple reason that Hannibal had nearly the entire country as a recruiting ground. While there were substantial numbers of disaffected Spanish tribesmen unwilling to perform military service for Carthage, there were plenty of mercenary volunteers. Cisalpine Gaul also provided enthusiastic recruits, as did Liguria, for those regions had not gladly accepted Roman rule.

At the Ticinus river, the Roman consul Publius Cornelius Scipio attacked the exhausted Carthaginian army but the veteran African and Spanish troops repulsed the Roman force and as a result the local Gauls, who had initially hesitated to support such a depleted and unprepossessing invasion force, now committed themselves to Hannibal's cause. Some 4,000–5,000 Gauls immediately joined the Carthaginian army. When the Roman general Sempronius attacked Hannibal at the River Trebbia, the Gallic mercenaries helped to defeat the 40,000-strong Roman army, which lost three quarters of its men. The Romans were forced on to the defensive and withdrew from northern Italy. But worse was to come. In April 217 BC, Hannibal surprised and slaughtered a 30,000-strong Roman army which he had lured into a defile close to Lake Trasimene. For the loss of 1,500 men (largely Celtic mercenaries) Hannibal destroyed 15,000 Romans and captured 10,000.

The Carthaginians had broken a Roman army but the catastrophe did not break Rome itself. Nor did Hannibal attempt to march on the city. He lacked an adequate siege train and a secure supply base. Furthermore, to his disappointment, not a single Italian allied city had yet defected from Rome, despite his resounding victory. There were few Romans who appreciated that Hannibal's failure to win over any allied city was a major blow to Carthaginian strategy. The harassing tactics used by Quintis Fabius Maximus against Hannibal aroused impatience in the Roman senate which was bent on a renewal of offensive strategy. Upon expiry of his six-month term as temporary dictator, Fabius was replaced by two consuls, Aemilius Paulus and Terentius Varro, each of whom exercised command of the army on alternate days, and each of whom believed he could defeat Hannibal in open battle.[31]

The battle of Cannae was Hannibal's greatest triumph and the greatest disaster in the military history of Rome. It was perhaps, the most notable victory won by a mercenary army, inspired by the personality of a charismatic leader rather than ideology, over a patriotic citizen army. Hannibal deliberately allowed the Roman legions to push back his centre giving the impression of a Carthaginian retreat while on his left his Celtic and Spanish heavy cavalry crushed the Roman horse and then wheeled right to attack the rear of the Roman army. On Hannibal's right the Numidian cavalry under Maharbal pinned down the cavalry of the Roman allies until the Celtic and Spanish cavalry linked up with them and completed the encirclement of the Roman army. Such, in a terse and over-simplified form were the main events at Cannae. The encirclement was a remarkable feat in itself for Hannibal had little more than 40,000 men while the Romans, if they did not have the 80,000 men quoted by Polybius, certainly had upwards of 50,000. About half of the Roman force was killed outright. Another 10,000 fought their way out of the trap while the rest were taken prisoner. Hannibal had lost 4,000 Celts, 1,500 Spanish and African troops and about 200 (Numidian?) cavalry.[32]

At last Hannibal's strategy began to take effect as the cities of the south, and in particular Capua, the second most important city in Italy, seceded from the Roman Confederation. New allies came from further afield, for Hannibal was able to make an alliance, albeit of limited use, with Philip V of Macedon. In other theatres of war events also favoured the Carthaginians. A Roman army under the Scipio brothers (the father and uncle of Publius Cornelius) was defeated in Spain by Hasdrubal, while in Sicily the Carthaginians were able to re-establish control over Syracuse after the timely death of Hiero and were in a good position retake the whole of Sicily.

Hannibal did not march on Rome despite the exhortations of his general, Maharbal, who complained, not without some justification, that the Carthaginian leader knew how to win brilliant victories but not how to exploit them to full advantage. Hannibal had neither the desire nor the means for a direct and necessarily costly assault on Rome. Roman fortifications were formidable and extensive and the city's garrison alone contained some 40,000 men and was only marginally smaller than Hannibal's entire army.

Although he had finally won over most of the south, his strategy had failed, for the cities of central Italy, which the Romans had treated generously, remained steadfastly loyal to the Confederation. Hannibal had thus far won all the battles but had lost the war. For the next thirteen years after Cannae, Hannibal remained in southern Italy – no mean feat in itself – but despite a number of victories against Roman armies at Capua, Herdonia and Numistro (212–210 BC), he had made little progress towards weakening Roman power. In 212 BC, the Romans recaptured Syracuse, finally overcoming the ingenious defensive engines devised by the seventy-four-year-old mathematician, Archimedes, who was killed by a Roman soldier ignorant of his identity. There was a further decline in Carthaginian fortunes when a Roman army under Publius Cornelius Scipio invaded Spain and captured New Carthage, the chief city of the Carthaginian domain. In 208 BC Scipio inflicted a defeat on Hasdrubal, Hannibal's brother. Hasdrubal, however, escaped from Spain with his troops and marched towards Italy, intent on reinforcing the Carthaginian army. His disappearance enabled Scipio to conquer most of Spain but his reappearance in Cisalpine Gaul with an army of 20,000 men, soon swelled to 30,000 by enthusiastic Gallic recruits, alarmed the Roman Confederation.

By a supreme effort Rome mobilised enough men to maintain an army in the north as well as the south. Hannibal waited in Apulia, for he needed to know his brother's line of march before moving northwards but at the River Metaurus the Romans forced Hasdrubal to fight. Outnumbered by at least 10,000 men, the Hispanic, Ligurian and Gallic troops were cornered and cut to pieces, losing 10,000 men, while the Romans suffered 2,000 casualties. Hasdrubal died gallantly in a suicidal charge and when his head was later delivered to Hannibal's camp by catapult, Hannibal retreated into Bruttium in the extreme south of Italy – where he remained unmolested but ineffective until his recall by Carthage.

[233]

It was the invasion of Africa by Cornelius Scipio (Africanus) with 30,000 men that caused Carthage to recall its most eminent warrior. The Carthaginians were heavily defeated in battle at Utica and Bagradas (203 BC), where the Numidian cavalry of Massinissa, a Roman ally, routed the Carthaginian horse while Scipio's Italian cavalry drove back Numidian mercenary cavalry in Carthaginian employ. Encircled by Roman troops, a 4,000-strong contingent of Celt-Iberians newly recruited by Carthage died to the last man.

Hannibal returned just after the disasters at Utica and Bagradas and Carthage levied new troops around the nucleus of the 18,000 troops he had brought with him from Italy. With 45,000 infantry but only 3,000 cavalry, Hannibal marched out for a final confrontation with Scipio.[33] In terms of size there was little difference between the two armies – Scipio had 34,000 infantry and 9,000 cavalry – but in terms of quality and composition the Roman army had a decided advantage. Hannibal's Gauls, Ligurians and Bruttians were veteran troops but at least half of his army consisted of hastily-mobilised and poorly trained levies. At Zama (202 BC) Hannibal's levied troops in the centre of his line were quickly defeated by Scipio's infantry but the mercenary veterans stood their ground and the fight swayed back and forth indecisively until Massinissa returned from pursuing the enemy Numidians and attacked the rear of the Carthaginian army. This manoeuvre did much to decide the battle in favour of the Romans. In the carnage that followed, the Carthaginians lost 20,000 men and 15,000 prisoners but Hannibal was fortunate enough to escape from the field. In Scipio he had finally met a general who possessed comparable skill if, perhaps, not quite the same level of genius. Scipio's battles were often fought using the techniques Hannibal had so brilliantly employed at Cannae.

The battle of Zama effectively ended the Second Punic War. Rome gained control of the entire western Mediterranean while Carthage was required to pay double the previous indemnity imposed by Rome. Her navy was reduced to ten ships and she was henceforth required to obtain Roman permission before engaging in war. This effectively meant that she could no longer hire mercenaries without Roman knowledge and approval. The western European recruiting grounds were now firmly in Roman hands while Massinissa, who had become King of Numidia, was an enemy and very unlikely to provide Carthage with Numidian recruits. On the contrary, he had designs on Carthage itself. Denounced by enemies for plotting against Rome, Hannibal ultimately fled into Bithynia where he committed suicide to avoid capture by the Romans (183 BC).

Military historians have argued over the relative merits of the great commanders – Alexander, Hannibal, Caesar, Genghis Khan, Gustavus Adolphus and Napoleon, among others – and have reached far from unanimous verdicts. Hannibal may or may not have been ahead of his colleagues in the pantheon of great generals but he was certainly one of the most remarkable military geniuses in history and not least remarkable as a leader of mercenary armies. All the others commanded armies that were predominantly composed of troops having the same nationality as their commander. Alexander and Caesar used mercenaries in an auxiliary function but they relied mainly upon the Macedonian phalanx and the Roman legion respectively for their principal forces. During the Thirty Years' War, King Gustavus Adolphus recruited large numbers of German, Scottish and English mercenaries among other nationalities but the nucleus of his army consisted of the highly trained and disciplined Swedish regiments. One might quibble at Napoleon's Corsican origin but, during the first half of his reign at least, the French army was almost entirely made up of French nationals and Napoleon was, after all, emperor of the French and was regarded as a Frenchman by his adopted country.

Hannibal, by contrast, led an army that was overwhelmingly mercenary, an army that consisted of half a dozen nationalities at least, each with its own distinctive way of fighting, its own language, customs and character. Hannibal knew the strengths and weaknesses of each national group intimately and was able to turn undisciplined and individualistic tribesmen like the Gauls into effective units capable of fighting in coordination with troops of other
· nationalities. His command of the Greek language gave him access to all the extant Greek texts on Hellenistic warfare, a subject on which his knowledge was vast. With his mercenary army he achieved some of the most dramatic victories in military history. It was not that Hannibal's soldiers were necessarily better fighters than the Romans. In fact, a good case could be made for the opposite viewpoint. But the numerically superior Roman armies were, on the whole, indifferently led, until the advent of Scipio Africanus, whose own talent could match that of Hannibal.

Hannibal possessed extraordinary ability both as a tactician and a leader. He commanded an army whose main motive had initially been the acquisition of plunder, an army without emotional or ideological commitment to the Carthaginian cause. He won the personal loyalty of his men and kept them for fifteen years in hostile territory exposed to constant danger without ever having to face a mutiny. Unlike Alexander's men, they did not refuse to

[235]

march any further nor did they demand higher pay as the price of their continued service, as Cyrus' Greeks had done. That Hannibal was able to hold together a mercenary army of diverse nationalities for such a length of time, even in moments of adversity, by sheer force of personality was, perhaps, even more remarkable than his battlefield victories and testifies to the intense charisma that he undoubtedly possessed.

Rome's victory over Carthage enabled her to turn her attention to the east and, in the interval between the Second and Third Punic Wars (202–149 BC), she defeated Macedonia and Syria and established a Roman protectorate over Macedon, Greece and Anatolia. In the west there were recurrent but unsuccessful revolts against Roman rule in Spain.

Marcus Portius Cato, who feared the shadow of Hannibal, finally persuaded the Roman senate into declaring war on Carthage on a mere technicality after Carthage declared war on Rome's ally, Massinissa (149 BC). With national survival at stake, the Carthaginians fought desperately for three years. Their army was now almost entirely made up of citizens, for the Carthaginians had no access to former mercenary recruiting areas. To Cato's intense delight, Carthage finally fell in 146 BC. Nine-tenths of the population was destroyed in six days of bitter street fighting and the survivors – some 50,000 inhabitants – were sold into slavery to work in private households, galleys, mines or large farming estates that had come into being after the Second Punic War. In the same year Rome crushed the Achaean league led by Corinth. The city was captured and burnt and its inhabitants, needless to say, joined the growing population of slaves on which the Romans increasingly relied for manual labour.

CHAPTER THIRTEEN

Rome: From Militia to Mercenary

THE SECOND PUNIC WAR wrought a fundamental change in the structure of Roman agriculture, which in turn altered the traditional organisation of the Roman army. Farming had hitherto been the province of small land-holders, the same small proprietors who became militiamen in time of war. Those who had survived Lake Trasimene and Cannae returned to find their farms ravaged and were forced into debt in attempting to revitalise their properties. Other militiamen simply regarded their holdings as unworkable and sold them cheaply to wealthy entrepreneurs who created vast *latifundia* (estates) worked by large numbers of slaves recruited from all the territories conquered by Rome. The militiamen did what impoverished rural inhabitants did from time immemorial and continue to do. They drifted to the cities where work might be found as manual labourers and entertainment was either free or cheap, and swelled the ranks of the urban poor, living in the most abject and squalid conditions while those who had dispossessed them lived in spacious and elegant residences.

The dispossession of the small farmers represented a deep social crisis. Those who had migrated to Rome in search of work were often unable to support their families and were embittered at open displays of wealth by the senatorial aristocracy. The degraded status of the former militiamen led to a recruitment crisis in the Roman army. Military service had traditionally been regarded as an honour and had consequently been restricted to those possessing sufficient means to purchase and maintain their own equipment. The rank of individual recruits was determined by the amount of property they owned. During Hannibal's invasion, the property qualifications had been lowered (although not abolished), for recruits were badly needed to replace

Rome's heavy losses. After the Punic Wars, the requirements were lowered again. Even so, there were many farmer-soldiers who could not meet the minimum qualifications. The militia system was breaking down at both ends of the social scale. Many of the farmers were too poor to be recruited while the aristocracy, desirous of enjoying its wealth, no longer wanted to be recruited now that the threat from Carthage was no more. There was a serious decline in the number of militiamen available for conscription but Rome needed troops for her wars in the east and her armies there were made up of volunteers attracted by the chance of acquiring booty along with such militia troops as could still be recruited. Many of the latter re-enlisted after their mandatory period of service for similar mercenary reasons.

Gaius Marius, elected consul and supreme commander an unprecedented six times between 107–101 BC, is credited with the transformation of the Roman army from a citizen militia to a paid volunteer professional force. The Marian reforms, as they are known, which created a new model army had far-reaching consequences but they were essentially the confirmation of a trend towards professionalisation and proleterianisation that had begun during the Second Punic War – with the lowering of the property qualifications and the appeals for volunteers to replace those citizens who either shirked military duty or demanded their immediate discharge after the mandatory period or were simply too poor to qualify.[1]

Marius' remodelling of the army occurred in two stages, both of which were the result of events beyond the confines of Italy. The first of these involved a struggle among the descendants of Massinissa for the control of Numidia. In an attempt to resolve the dispute, Rome partitioned Numidia between two rival princes, Adherbal and Jugurtha, giving the latter the less developed half of the country. Jugurtha responded by besieging and capturing the city of Cirta, massacring the Italians resident there and torturing Adherbal to death, thus launching the so-called Jugurthine War (112–106 BC). Jugurtha inflicted a few minor but humiliating defeats on the Roman army sent by the Senate which, according to Gaius Sallustius Crispus (Sallust, 86–35 BC), chronicler of the Jugurthine War, was

> an indolent and unwarlike army, in no fit state to face danger or toil, readier to brag than to fight, and so undisciplined and ill behaved that it plundered its allies and allowed itself to be plundered by the enemy. Its demoralised condition caused its new commander so much anxiety that he could entertain little hope of being helped much by its numerical strength.[2]

[238]

The new commander was Quintus Caecilius Metellus, a competent general who reorganised the demoralised army, restored its morale and discipline and led it to victory over Jugurtha at the battle of the River Muthul (108 BC). Jugurtha, however, escaped into the Sahara Desert where he raised a force of mercenaries from among the Gaetulians, a barbarian tribe living a partly nomadic, partly sedentary existence, and trained them to fight as a coordinated group.[3] Jugurtha himself had previously commanded a Numidian contingent in Roman service in the Spanish penisula and was conversant with the fighting techniques of both the Romans and the Hispanics. He made a military alliance with the Moorish king Bocchus and undertook a guerrilla war against the Romans, making good use of his mercenary troops. Metellus countered Jugurtha's attacks successfully enough but was unable to defeat Jugurtha. It was at this juncture that Gaius Marius was elected consul and replaced Metellus. In order to raise fresh troops he broke with established practice. He recruited soldiers,

> not in accordance with traditional custom, from the propertied classes, but accepting any man who volunteered – members of the proletariat for the most part. Some said he did this because he could not get enough of a better kind; others, that he wanted to curry favour with men of low condition, since he owed to them his fame and advancement. And, indeed, if a man is ambitious for power, he can have no better supporters than the poor: they are not concerned about their own possessions, since they have none, and whatever will put something into their pockets is right and proper in their eyes.[4]

In this revealing passage, Sallust not only describes Marius' method and source of recruitment but touches on the relationship between the soldiers and their commander, a relationship very much at variance with that which existed between militiamen and the amateur generals of previous eras. Marius was the prototype, perhaps even the archetype, of a new breed of generals. Most of his predecessors had been consummate politicians and indifferent generals. Those that followed Marius and became embroiled in the civil wars of the first century BC were competent if not outstanding commanders but indifferent politicians.

It was to some extent true that Marius could not recruit sufficient troops 'of a better kind', which presumably meant propertied militiamen. Those who could still meet the necessary qualifications had become reluctant to go on lengthy overseas campaigns which kept them away from more lucrative civilian pursuits, and demanded to be released immediately after their mandatory period of service. Clearly, such half-hearted recruits had to be replaced by men of greater commitment, men who were soldiers by choice and who preferred army life to civilian poverty. Thus, it was among the dispossessed that Marius found men who were soldiers first and citizens second; men whose primary allegiance was to their commander not to the Republic, much less the Senate. Constitutional government was largely irrelevant to them. These were soldiers who were willing to support the personal ambitions of their generals even if these ambitions amounted to treason and led to dictatorship. They were indifferent to the causes of a war and merely hoped that a particular conflict would drag on for as long as possible. The loyalty of the soldiers was not just a function of gratitude, devotion or the receipt of a regular wage. As military men they were removed from civilian life and felt a sense of comradeship and of belonging to a special organisation. Not least important, they saw their general as a sort of paternal figure who would act in their interest, give out rewards for meritorious service and provide for their security in old age. In return, they afforded him the means to pursue private goals, impose his will on the Senate if need be and undertake lengthy overseas campaigns. There was a personal bond between soldier and general that was rarely seen in the old militia armies. The relationship between the new professional soldiers and the new type of general was an example of the system of patronage and clientage underlying the entire fabric of Roman society.

Marius sailed to Numidia with his volunteer army, including some Ligurian auxiliaries, and there he trained his men, using a mixture of strict discipline and rough humour beloved of professional soldiers, until they had reached a high standard of efficiency. The Romans performed well against Jugurtha's Gaetulian mercenaries and Bocchus' Moorish troops, capturing large areas of Numidia, although they were unable to crush Jugurtha who fought with a savage determination. Twice Jugurtha caught and attacked the Roman army on the march and inflicted severe casualties before being driven off with heavy losses. In the event, Jugurtha was not defeated in battle but was betrayed into the hands of Marius' deputy, Lucius Cornelius Sulla, and was subsequently conveyed to Rome where he died in prison in 104 BC.

While Rome restored its hegemony over Numidia, its northern borders were menaced by wandering Germanic tribes, the Cimbri and Teutoni, who had migrated from Jutland. At Arausio (Orange) in 105 BC, the Cimbri annihilated a Roman army which, together with its civilian followers, numbered some 80,000 souls. For Rome, the loss of her army represented the greatest catastrophe since Cannae and seemed to portend an imminent invasion of Italy. But the Cimbri and the Teutoni turned south and entered Spain, where they were met and repulsed by tough Celt-Iberian tribes who were still independent of Roman rule. The Germanic tribes' decision to turn south had given Marius two precious years in which to prepare for their return. For the Numidian campaign he had merely ignored rather than abolished the property qualification. Now he completed the task of reform by abandoning it altogether. Henceforth the army was permanently open to all volunteers irrespective of their wealth, or rather, lack of it. Recruits signed on for long service and their loyalty was directed to the personalities who led them. Marius happened to be the agent of change but perhaps the creation of a professional army would have been inevitable, in any case. The Roman empire was growing larger and would continue to grow until it took in the entire Mediterranean. Such a large area required permanent long-service soldiers to garrison and defend its borders and strategic points, a function not suited to part-time militiamen who had grown increasingly loath to perform extended military service.

Marius reorganised his legions, replacing the maniples with a larger unit, the cohort (ten to a legion), standardised all equipment and put the soldiers through gruelling exercises with plenty of forced marches in full kit. In 102 BC the Cimbri and Teutoni reappeared in Gaul. Marius crushed the Teutoni at Aquae Sextiae (Aix-en-Provence), using Hannibal's favourite tactic of yielding ground to a frontal attack by the enemy and launching an enveloping counter attack on the enemy's rear. The following year Marius and Quintus Lutatius Catulus defeated the Cimbri at Vercellae in the Po valley, ending the Germanic threat.

Marius' army and those that came after, in the late Republican period and the early Empire, were professional armies but they were not mercenary armies. Although the military forces were open to volunteers of any class, Roman citizenship was still an essential requirement for acceptance into the ranks. Rome had begun to use mercenaries on a limited scale during the Punic Wars, always in an auxiliary capacity and only for the duration of a particular campaign. Often, whatever mercenaries were present on the Roman side were not directly recruited by Rome but were supplied by allies like Hiero of Syracuse, who contributed 500 Cretan archers and 1,000 light troops to the Roman army that Hannibal went on to destroy at Lake Trasimene.[5]

Such mercenaries as the Romans did employ during the late second and throughout the first century BC were recruited to make up for Roman deficiency in missile weapons but Rome relied primarily on her own citizen volunteers in the legions for her victories. There were also foreigners in the cavalry arm, both mercenary and auxiliary, but they also were recruited purely on a temporary basis and were sent home after the conclusion of hostilities. Julius Caesar employed Gallic and Germanic cavalry, most of whom were auxiliaries rather than true mercenaries, both in the sense that they were support troops and in the sense that they had largely been recruited from friendly or subdued tribes. Nor were the Greeks and Macedonians serving in the Roman army led by Sulla against Mithridates VI true mercenaries. Macedonia and Greece were part of the Roman empire and the troops they supplied were subjects of Rome. Rome's use of mercenaries was circumspect. Not for a moment did she consider a Carthaginian-style reliance on foreigners. There were too many inherent dangers, as was clearly demonstrated by the mercenaries' revolt of 238 BC. Rome did not emulate the Greek city-states of the fourth century BC, who hired out whole contingents of mercenary hoplites to foreign employers in Asia, more or less indifferent to the cause of the paymaster. Roman armies sent overseas to support foreign monarchs went as allies not as mercenaries provided as a money-making venture and they were sent in accordance with the perceived interests of the Roman government in pursuit of specific foreign policy goals.

The late Republican period – the eight decades between the consulships of Marius and the accession to power of Octavian (Augustus) in 30 BC – was a time of recurrent social, economic and political upheaval complete with foreign and civil wars, dictatorships and assassinations, although it was not without its cultural achievements, for the period produced two of the greatest poets of Latin literature, Lucretius (c.94–55 BC) and Catullus (c.86–54 BC).

The first of several civil wars – the Social War of 91–89 BC – was caused by Rome's refusal to extend citizenship to her allies. The Allies resorted to war, raising an army made up of their own legionaries (many of whom were veterans of Marius' campaigns), supported by mercenary contingents of Cretan archers and Hispanic cavalry. The Roman army also had foreign auxiliary forces – Gauls, Spaniards and Numidians. The war, like all civil wars, was particularly savage and Rome fought for its continued existence as the paramount city in Italy. Despite some initial defeats, the Romans gradually managed to gain the upper hand but the war was terminated not by decisive Roman victories but by a belated recognition of the validity of Allied demands.

The revolt progressively died out when Rome extended full citizenship. The Social War and its aftermath, the civil war between the supporters of Marius and those of Sulla (88–82 BC), clearly showed the changing status of the Roman army *vis-à-vis* the Roman government. Roman military forces, directly recruited by their commanding generals, had become *de facto* private armies over which the government had completely lost control. Admittedly, Sulla used his 40,000-strong army and his one-year dictatorship to restore the authority of the Senate at the expense of the tribunes who represented plebeian interests. But this temporary restoration of senatorial power was effected by an army under the control of an unscrupulous and vicious general who was not much different from a *mafia* gang boss and who happened to believe in oligarchic rather than democratic government. Sulla proscribed and murdered thousands of his opponents. He freed their slaves, bestowed Roman citizenship and thereby created a force of virtual thugs who owed their allegiance to a species of gangster chief. Sulla voluntarily gave up the dictatorship, well satisfied with his work on behalf of the Senate and died shortly thereafter, in 78 BC. He had shown that an ambitious general with a sufficiently large army could make or break the government of Rome. What he had done, others could do.

Sulla's constitution did not outlast its author. After his death, three generals rose to prominence, each with his own private army: Pompey, Crassus and Caesar. All three coveted the position of *princeps*, that is, the leading citizen of Rome, and sought to outdo each other in the acquisition of military glory. Pompey, who had been one of Sulla's deputies, gained renown fighting for his former mentor in Sicily and Africa. He enhanced his reputation, rather undeservedly, when he defeated the forces of the pro-Marian general Quintus Sertorius, who had established an independent regime in Lusitania (Portugal and western Spain) with the aid of his own army. Sertorius' legionaries were fully prepared to support their leader, even if this entailed treason to Rome. Initially, Pompey performed badly against Sertorius, who was one of Rome's best generals. But when the latter was murdered by his own second-in-command, Pompey quickly overcame the demoralised rebel army and returned to Italy in 71 BC. He was just in time to assist Marcus Licinius Crassus in crushing the slaves' revolt led by Spartacus, a Thracian who had been an auxiliary soldier in the armies of Rome and whose insurgent forces included Gauls, Germans and Thracian ex-mercenaries.

While Crassus remained in Italy, absorbed in monetary speculation,

Pompey acquired further military glory by sweeping the Mediterranean free of pirates. He then campaigned in Asia Minor against Mithridates VI, whose hatred of Rome rivalled that of Hannibal. Mithridates' army had already been heavily defeated by Pompey's predecessor, Lucullus, and Pompey merely struck the final blow. At the River Lycus, the Romans and their foreign auxiliaries utterly destroyed Mithridates' forces, which were made up of diverse nationalities. Among other elements, Mithridates had been able to levy auxiliary troops from Asia Minor, Scythia and Sarmatia. He most likely recruited Anatolian Greeks, although there are few conclusive indications other than references to phalanxes that may have been provided by Sinope and other Greek cities on the Black Sea. He also recruited substantial numbers of Thracians who were pure mercenaries hired from lands beyond Mithridates' control. There were also Roman officers supplied by Sertorius with whom Mithridates had an alliance and a not inconsiderable number of Roman deserters who were among his best troops. Mithridates, however, was overwhelmed by vastly superior forces and escaped into the Crimea where he committed suicide.

Pompey followed up his success by annexing Syria and Palestine and terminating the Seleucid dynasty. He returned to Rome late in 62 BC, replete with riches that made him even more wealthy than Crassus and abundant military glory. Pompey asked the Senate to ratify his actions in the east, all of which had been taken without consultation. Notwithstanding his success and the enormous loot and glory he had brought home, the Senate was unimpressed and failed to approve of the arrangements Pompey had made for the government of the eastern provinces. Nor did the Senate accede to his second demand that his soldiers be rewarded with land grants in addition to the share of booty they had received. Crassus rejoiced, hoping to further increase his influence by siding with the Senate against Pompey, but he was also snubbed, owing to his involvement in a dispute between the Senate and tax-gatherers. The Senate compounded its blunders by attempting to obstruct Caesar's candidacy for the consulship of 59 BC. Caesar responded by making an alliance with Pompey and Crassus, known as the First Triumvirate. He became consul, obtained the land grants for Pompey's veterans, increased Crassus' control over tax collection in the Asian provinces and procured the governorship of Cisalpine and Transalpine Gaul and Illyricum (Dalmatia).

In 58 BC, Caesar began his nine-year campaign to conquer Gaul. The most detailed account of the conquest is, of course, Caesar's own *Commentaries*, which, however, has to be read with Caesar's ulterior motives in mind. The

Commentaries is a grand *apologia* for an unprovoked war of aggression, which included several Roman atrocities, undertaken by Caesar on the pretext of helping the Aedui, a friendly Gallic tribe, against their enemies.

Caesar's legions were supported by Gallic and Numidian cavalry, Balearic slingers and Cretan archers. Many of these auxiliaries were not permanent troops and were disbanded at the end of the campaigning season. Their battle record was a mixed one. The Gauls and Numidians performed well during Caesar's war with a coalition of Belgic tribes but were routed in a subsequent action against the Belgic Nervii tribe and were saved by the timely assistance of the 10th legion.[6] Caesar's confidence in the trustworthiness of his Gallic levies was not always unreserved. When he agreed to a parley with the German chieftain Ariovistus, he dismounted his Gallic cavalry and created a temporary bodyguard by using the infantrymen of his favourite 10th legion as a mounted escort.[7] On the whole, Caesar's Gallic auxiliaries proved loyal enough but their loyalty might be attributed as much to their fear of Caesar as to any genuine attachment to his cause. For his second expedition to Britain in 54 BC, Caesar raised up to 4,000 cavalry from the Gallic tribes and took care to include all the tribal chieftains, save for a few of proven loyalty. The chiefs were ostensibly the leaders of their respective contingents but in reality Caesar was taking them as hostages so that there should be no rebellion in Gaul during his absence. Later, during his struggle with Vercingetorix, Caesar recruited 400 German cavalry. At Noviodunum, they played a vital role in rescuing his Gallic horsemen, who were being mauled by Vercingetorix's cavalry.[8] Caesar used his auxiliaries for the classical functions of scouting, pursuit, protecting the flanks of the infantry and countering the attacks of enemy cavalry. He was sometimes ruthless in using non-Roman troops. In 53 BC, during his campaign against the Germanic Eburones tribe, he deliberately sent his Gauls into forest areas where the Germans were waiting in ambush so as to preserve his legionaries.[9] He fully appreciated that Roman troops were far less suited to warfare in the woods.

The successful outcome of the siege of Alesia and the surrender of Vercingetorix marked the collapse of Gallic resistance to Caesar's conquest. To a large extent he owed his final victory to the versatility and toughness of his legions and he himself was a fighting general who was always present at the crucial moments of a battle, often in the most dangerous and threatening situations. But he might not have succeeded in his Gallic enterprise had the native tribes been united. His conquest was undoubtedly facilitated by the dissension he found among the Gauls. He obtained active cooperation from friendly tribes when he took the field against their enemies. Conquests were often achieved with the full support of a particular segment of the local population. Thus did Cortez, for example, gain willing help from Mexican indians hostile to the Aztecs. Thus did Britain conquer India with the support of local princes. Vercingetorix's rebellion had been the closest that the Gauls had come to a unified show of force but even then their tribal loyalties prevented an effective and coordinated defence against Caesar's aggression.

Caesar had to fight one last action – the siege of Uxellodunum – before he could turn his full attention to events in Italy, where the Senate, jealous of his success and fearful of his intentions, had grown increasingly hostile and had thrown its support behind Pompey. A showdown was inevitable now that Pompey had sided – not without some hesitation and self-reproach – against his fellow triumvir. Caesar could either return to Italy as a private citizen to face certain oblivion or he could fight for survival backed by his legions. Needless to say, he chose the latter option but he could not remove his legions from Gaul without ensuring that the Gallic tribes would remain subdued. He decided on lenient treatment of the Gauls, thus enabling him to recruit auxiliary troops more easily. He needed to recruit a large body of these because Pompey would undoubtedly have substantial numbers of his own auxiliaries, drawn from Greece, Anatolia and Syria.

That Caesar and Pompey had come into open conflict was partly due to the unexpected demise of Crassus in 53 BC. While Caesar was still in Gaul acquiring an immortal reputation as a great commander, Crassus, anxious to enhance his own reputation as a successful general, embarked on an ill-fated expedition to attack the Parthians. Refusing help from Artavasdes, King of Armenia and an enemy of Parthia, Crassus marched to Carrhae (Haran), where a Parthian army under Surenas caught the Romans in territory eminently suited to cavalry operations. The Parthian army was smaller that Crassus' expeditionary force, containing no more than 1,000 cataphracts (heavy cavalry lancers) and 10,000 horse archers, but it surrounded and defeated three times its number.

The Romans were forced into square and neither the light troops or the legionaries were at any stage able to close with the enemy. The light troops made a charge which petered out under a veritable shower of arrows. When the legionaries attempted to break out of the encirclement, the Parthians merely retreated a short distance, firing as they withdrew. The Romans endured the nearly incessant bombardment, reasoning that the Parthians must sooner or later run out of missiles, but the enemy had brought up a camel train loaded with huge quantities of arrows with barbed heads that inflicted excruciating wounds on the hapless legionaries. The Romans locked shields in their customary fashion but the slightly undulating ground prevented the creation of an effective wall of shields and the Romans continued to fall in their thousands. The Romans were pounded by volley after volley, fired in high trajectories, until the fall of night brought blessed relief. Under cover of darkness they retreated from Carrhae, leaving behind 4,000 wounded men to be slaughtered by the Parthians on the following morning. The Parthians did not press the Romans too closely and merely wiped out small contingents that had lost contact with the main army. Surenas invited Crassus to a conference during which the latter was struck down by a Parthian soldier. Crassus had sacrificed his army, his son and his own life in the vain quest for glory. Rome and Parthia had hitherto enjoyed neutral if not friendly relations. Now, thanks to Crassus, Parthia was a bitter and irreconcilable enemy. Five thousand Romans managed to escape from Carrhae. Twenty thousand had perished and 10,000 were taken prisoner.[10]

The destruction of Crassus' legions at Carrhae had a curious sequel. Some of the surviving Roman prisoners were turned into mercenaries, not so much by their own volition but by the force of circumstances, and ended their days in north-western China in a garrison city whose Chinese name, Li-jien, meant 'Rome'. That Roman legionaries wound up so far eastwards may seem at first glance to be no more than a good theme for a pseudo-historical adventure novel but the evidence for a Roman settlement is considerable. The theory that some of Crassus' men got as far as China and worked as mercenaries for the Han Dynasty was first proposed in 1955 by Homer Hasenpflug Dubs, Professor of Chinese at Oxford University, and has since been confirmed by the more recent research carried out by the Australian writer and historian David Harris. The details of Professor Dubs' thesis may be found in *A Roman City in Ancient China*, and David Harris has described how he identified the approximate site of Li-jien in his *Black Horse Odyssey*.[11] The process by which the legionaries reached China is to some extent known from the writings of Pliny who recorded that the prisoners were marched eastwards to Margiana where they were used as border guards to protect Parthia's eastern frontiers against the Huns.[12] The next solid reference to soldiers who could only have been Romans is to be found in Chinese chronicles and paintings related to a campaign against the Huns in 36 BC, and these Romans could only have come from among the survivors of Crassus' legions.[13] There is no extant information as to the eventual fate of the Roman garrison troops while they were in Parthian service but the fact that some of them were found in the army of Jzh-jzh, King of the Huns, clearly suggests that a small number deserted from the Parthian border posts and made their way further east. How many exactly remains unknown but the Chinese chronicles state precisely that the Chinese general Chen Tang captured 145 foreigners who had been arranged 'in fish-scale formation' near a double wooden palisade built outside the walls of the Hun capital.[14] The Chinese did not use the word 'Roman' in describing these exotic foreigners but the visual and written evidence in their records places their nationality beyond reasonable doubt. Chen Tang could find no better description than 'fish-scale' for a battle formation he had never seen before, one that could only have been the *testudo* of linked shields characteristic of the Romans. The Chinese, the Huns, the Bactrians and indeed any other Asiatic peoples did not use this formation. Nor could the Greek or Macedonian phalanxes with their round shields fit Chen Tang's description. Both Greeks and Macedonians fought in a somewhat more open order than the Romans. Furthermore, the double wooden palisade mentioned by Chen Tang was also characteristic of Roman fortification and was not known among the Chinese or the Huns, let alone the Greeks. A final clue to the identity of the foreigners is provided by Chen Tang's paintings of what he saw during his campaign against Jzh-jzh – paintings that unambiguously show the influence of Roman military art.[15]

The Romans who deserted the Parthian outposts really had no choice but to head east. There was little chance that they could safely cross nearly 2,000 kilometres of hostile territory and reach the nearest Roman province. If they were captured by the Parthians they would be executed as deserters and even if they managed to return to Rome they would be stripped of their citizenship for having been mercenaries for the Parthians, no matter how unwillingly. Rome was unforgiving to those who failed her, irrespective of the circumstances. Thus, the more intrepid Romans, bored by a lonely and degraded existence as border guards, opted for mercenary service in the Hun army. Jzh-jzh was ruler of a considerable empire that stretched from Manchuria across Mongolia and northern China to Sogdiana and was consequently well able to pay mercenary troops. He was a renowned warlord, an enemy of the Parthians and hence an attractive employer for the Romans. At the same time, Jzh-jzh would have fully appreciated both the fighting skill and the advanced military engineering techniques of the legionaries.

The Chinese also seem to have been impressed by the legionaries, who were obviously superlative fighters and would be useful in defending China's north-western border against any further incursion by the Huns. Thus was founded the city of 'Rome' in China – somewhere between the Qilian mountains and the Yongchang plains not far from the Silk Road. The precise centre of Li-jien remains controversial for ruins have been discovered in various locations, although the approximate area is no longer in doubt. Satellite photographs have revealed traces of ancient fields – each one 720 metres by 720 metres – precisely the same size as the fields around Ancient Rome.[16] The Roman settlers undoubtedly married Chinese women and their descendants were gradually absorbed into the wider Chinese population until no visible trace of their half-Roman ancestry remained. The city of Li-jien continued to exist for nearly eight centuries before being destroyed by Tibetan invaders in AD 746. The Huns, repulsed by the Chinese, never returned. They moved westwards and their descendants were destined to conquer Rome.

While the survivors of Crassus' legions were living out the rest of their lives as mercenaries far from home, the Roman empire was torn by a civil war that began in 49 BC, when Caesar crossed the Rubicon stream to settle his differences with Pompey and the Senate, and ended in 30 BC with the suicide of Antony and Cleopatra and the triumph of Caesar's grand-nephew, Octavian. For several years before Caesar returned to Italy, Rome had been in a state of anarchy as gangs of armed thugs fought each other in the streets. One group, led by Clodius, supported Caesar's interests in his absence while another under Milo worked for Pompey. Clodius was murdered while Pompey was given the task of eradicating the gangs. He was made sole consul and induced to sever his alliance with Caesar.

In a rapid and daring move typical of the man, Caesar crossed the river of no return with only the 5,000 veterans of one legion and 300 Gallic cavalry and marched southwards along the Adriatic coast. He left behind in Gaul some 40,000 legionaries and 20,000 auxiliaries whom he would employ at a chosen moment.[17] Potentially, his great rival could mobilise a large army but Caesar's rapid advance caught Pompey by surprise and he had but two legions immediately at hand while the rest of his forces were still being recruited. Most of Pompey's men stationed in Italy had not fought in twelve years, while his most effective legions were at that moment operating in Spain. Caesar's men, on the other hand, were fresh from their victories in Gaul. Pompey realised that Italy was untenable and fled Rome along with the Senators, whose panic did not prevent them from taking along as much of their property as they could carry. He made his way to Greece with five legions (about 25,000 men) and began to recruit a larger army, anticipating that his rival would soon follow. Caesar gives a fairly precise catalogue of the forces Pompey gathered together: nine Roman legions, of which five were from Italy, two from Asia, one from Crete and one from Macedonia. He expected two more from Syria. There were 3,000 archers – both mercenary and auxiliary – from Crete, Lacedaimon, Pontus, Syria; 1,200 slingers (of unspecified provenance but likely to include Balearic islanders); 7,000 cavalry, including 600 Galatians, 500 Cappadocians, 500 Thracians, 200 Macedonians; 200 Syrian mounted archers; and a number of Dardanians and Thessalians, for whom Caesar gives few details beyond the observation that some were mercenaries and others conscripted troops.[18]

Caesar did not pursue Pompey. He lacked a sufficiently large fleet because Pompey had commandeered most of the available vessels in Brindisium during his escape. Instead Caesar secured his position in the west by campaigning in Spain with some 37,000 men. He was heavily outnumbered by two armies whose combined strength amounted to seven legions and about 40,000 auxiliaries, the latter largely made up of Celt-Iberians, Cantabrians and Lusitanians who had the advantage of local knowledge. Caesar raised some 6,000 Gallic cavalry and recruited auxiliaries from among the Aquitani of south-western Gaul and Pyrenean hill-tribesmen. There were skirmishes between the Pompeians and Caesar's forces but both sides were keen to avoid a major confrontation. In the Spanish campaign Caesar's Gallic cavalry played a much more important role than he normally assigned to his foreign troops. He used his Gauls to cut off his opponent's supply lines so that one of the Pompeian armies under Afranius and Petreius found itself practically without food and water. Large numbers of the Pompeian auxiliaries, driven by raging thirst and a healthy respect for Caesar's reputation, deserted to his army. There was a considerable amount of fraternisation between the legionaries of the opposing sides. Many of the Pompeians sought out kinsmen, friends and fellow-villagers serving in Caesar's army. Fraternal meetings notwithstanding, Caesar continued to deny the Pompeians access to water for he preferred to inflict discomfort rather than death on the enemy and to avoid heavy casualties among his own troops. Thus, his cavalry and German light troops guarded the banks of the Sicoris river which flowed through Ilerda, where both armies were camped in sight of each other. The Pompeians surrendered and Caesar enrolled some of their legionaries and disbanded the rest, requiring the demobilised men to leave Spain. Caesar compensated those who had owned property with a cash payment and was forced to resolve wage disputes when

Afranius and Petreius were unable to meet the strident demands of the Pompeian legionaries for arrears in pay.[19] These legionaries were far removed from the militiamen of pre-Marian times and their preoccupation with money provides some indication of the extent to which Roman armies had become mercenarised in motive if not in status. The surrender of Afranius and Petreius induced the other Pompeian army to submit to Caesar and he now controlled Spain, Gaul and Italy itself. His only setback had occurred in Africa, where his legate, Scribonius Curio, had been defeated by Pompeian forces operating in alliance with the Numidian king, Juba. Curio's 500-strong Gallic cavalry had initially scored a notable success against a much more numerous Numidian force but Juba reinforced the Pompeian army with the 2,000 Spanish and Gallic cavalry of his mercenary bodyguard. Curio was lured into an ambush in the Bagradas valley, where he died fighting, along with his two legions and most of his Gallic horsemen.[20]

Caesar would regulate his affairs in Africa at a later date. Reinforced by Mark Antony, he now attacked Pompey's main base at Dyrrhachium with some 30,000 men, boldly besieging the Pompeians, who were twice as numerous. But, for once, Pompey's numerical advantage forced Caesar to break off the siege. He retreated to Thessaly, followed by Pompey, who mounted another lacklustre pursuit. The final confrontation came at Pharsalus (9 August 48 BC) and was the largest battle fought between two Roman armies. Caesar had about 22,000 men while Pompey disposed of 35,000–40,000 men. Pompey's mercenary and auxiliary cavalry outnumbered Caesar's Gauls by seven to one and quickly overcame them but the legionaries of Caesar's army were veterans of the Gallic Wars and they shattered Pompey's infantry. Like all great commanders, Caesar was not renowned for modesty, false or otherwise. He claimed that 15,000 Pompeians had fallen and 24,000 were captured while he had lost 230 killed.[21] Whatever the real total was, the result was beyond doubt. Pompey fled to Egypt where he was murdered by the ministers of the young Pharaoh, Ptolemy XII. Caesar, anxious to take Pompey alive, followed with a mere 3,000 men. In Alexandria he arbitrated in a dynastic dispute between Ptolemy XII and his half-sister Cleopatra. When he seemed to favour Cleopatra he was attacked by the 20,000-strong Ptolemaic army made up of foreign mercenaries, Syrian and Cilician pirates and Romans who were more or less a law unto themselves and were living in Alexandria independent of direct control by Rome. Caesar was rescued from a perilous position by the timely arrival of a Roman ally, Mithridates of Pergamon. Together, Caesar and Mithridates managed to defeat Ptolemy XII, who was killed. Cleopatra became Queen of Egypt, protected by a substantial bodyguard of Galatian mercenaries.

When Caesar returned to Italy in August 49 BC, his first task was to support a mutiny, not among disaffected auxilaries or former Pompeian soldiers but among the 10th legion, which had served him so well in Gaul. Caesar's particular affection for the men of this legion had made them feel indispensable. He had repatriated them ahead of his own return and they had marched straight to Rome, demanding larger bounties. They terrorised the city until Caesar confronted them and ended their mutiny solely by the sheer force of personality. Commenting on this episode, the Roman historian Suetonius (AD 60–*c*.140), observed that: 'Caesar's men did not mutiny once during the Gallic War, which lasted ten years. In the Civil Wars they were less dependable, but whenever they made insubordinate demands he faced them boldly, and always brought them to heel again – not by appeasement but by sheer exercise of personal authority.'[22] In calming the legionaries, Caesar had addressed them as 'citizens', to which they responded, 'We are your soldiers, Caesar, not civilians!'[23] This response clearly illustrates the attitude of post-Marian soldiers towards their leaders and towards society in general. They owed their loyalty not to the state but directly to the generals and they felt a remoteness from, and by implication, a superiority to, sloppy civilians. The whole incident was a further indication of just how much the Roman soldier had become motivated by pecuniary rather than patriotic motives.

Before he could establish undisputed mastery of the Roman empire, Caesar had to fight two more campaigns. After some hard fighting he decisively defeated the Pompeian-Numidian forces in north Africa at Thapsus and then sailed to Spain where he crushed the legions and Spanish auxiliaries of Gnaeus Pompey at the battle of Munda (March 45 BC). Returning to Rome, Caesar was made dictator for life in January 44 BC. He planned a second expedition against Parthia partly motivated by a desire to avenge Crassus and partly inspired by the prospect of surpassing Alexander the Great. Caesar had drawn the obvious conclusions from the disaster at Carrhae and intended to invade Parthia by way of Armenia. He also ordered the recruitment of auxiliary horsemen and a large number of archers who would counter the Parthian horse archers. Just as he was about to join his army, Caesar was murdered (March 44 BC). His demise led to a renewed outbreak of civil war. Mark Antony (Marcus Antonius), Octavian and Lepidus formed the Second Triumvirate and in 42 BC defeated Brutus and Cassius in two separate battles at Philippi in Greece. In 36 BC, around the time when the more determined survivors of Crassus' ill-fated expedition were meeting their strange destiny in China, Mark Antony embarked on an ill-fated expedition of his own against Parthia. He suffered the loss of half his army of 70,000 men (which included 10,000 Gallic and Spanish cavalry) but managed to retreat. Lepidus attempted to seize the island of Sicily but his army mutinied and surrendered him to Octavian, who kept him prisoner in opulent surroundings for some twenty-three years. In 33 BC came the rupture between Octavian and Antony and two years later they fought their final battle at Actium off the western coast of Greece. Octavian invaded Egypt in 30 BC and Antony and Cleopatra committed one of the famous suicides of history. Cleopatra's Galatian mercenaries were not unduly affected by the loss of their employer for Octavian merely gave them to the Judean king, Herod, who had been a protégé of Mark Antony but was not slow to perceive where his interests now lay. The Galatians joined other Celts, Thracians, Greeks and Germans already in Herod's employ. Whether or not the mercenaries took part in the Massacre of the Innocents attributed to Herod can only be a matter for conjecture, but they would have been admirably suited to such a task given that they were foreigners without any racial ties with the local population. They would have carried out Herod's orders unhindered by feelings of sympathy and compassion towards Herod's victims.

After leaving Egypt, Octavian came home to a tumultuous welcome, hailed by the Roman people as the enforcer of peace after three long and bitter civil wars. He was, for the moment, fabulously wealthy, for he had thoroughly plundered Egyptian treasures, above all those of Cleopatra, which she herself had expropriated from temples and estates confiscated from her opponents. He was able to discharge large numbers of his troops with a cash bonus of 3,000 *denarii*, that is about thirteen years' pay. Octavian resettled his demobilised forces at his own expense in existing colonies or in newly-created establishments all over the empire. Such were Octavian's financial resources that he distributed part of his surplus to the common citizens of Rome, an act which, needless to say, added to his prestige and popularity. Of course, such largesse at the beginning of his reign could not become a regular event. It was partly as a cost-cutting measure that Octavian radically reduced the size of the military forces he had inherited from both sides in the civil wars. There had been no lack of volunteers and Octavian found himself with over sixty legions to maintain. Clearly, such a large number of soldiers would impose a heavy burden on his financial resources and had perforce to be reduced once the treasures taken overseas were used up in payments and resettlement.

Mindful of Caesar's fate, Octavian did not impose a dictatorship on Rome nor did he abdicate power as Sulla had done. He outwardly respected the forms of republican government and ostensibly shared power with the Senate, which he had, of course, purged of any member who had supported Antony or Lepidus. He left the actual details of day-to-day civilian government to the Senate and the Equestrian order and, as *princeps*, he was ostensibly *primus inter pares* in relation to the Senate. However, he was in fact a monarch in all but name and confirmed his pre-eminent position by adopting the cognomen of 'Augustus', which conferred an almost mystical semi-divine status and at the same time was a symbolic severance with his past as Octavian the triumvir.

The power of the *princeps* rested primarily on his control of financial administration, foreign policy and the army. Augustus retained absolute control of the military forces partly because he owed his own position to his prestige among the soldiers and partly because he wanted to prevent ambitious officers from using the legions as private armies with which to threaten the government, as had happened during the civil wars. On the one hand he reimposed stern discipline on the army but, on the other, he encouraged an *ésprit de corps* and a competitive spirit among the legions and ensured regular remuneration. Augustus undertook a fundamental reorganisation of the army, changing its status, its composition and its very *raison d'être*. He reduced the number of legions from sixty to twenty-eight but the remainder became a regular army. Before Marius, soldiers had been part-time talented amateurs. After Marius, the armies were filled with volunteers who had decided to make soldiering a profession and who signed up for an unspecified and indefinite period, hoping that the war would be lengthy. But their professionalism notwithstanding, post-Marian armies were not intended to be permanent formations. Thus did Sulla and Crassus, for example, give up their commands at the end of a campaign. It was the extended duration of the civil wars that made the contending armies semi-permanent, not the conscious desire on the part of their generals to create regular forces for their own sake. Augustus, then, was the true creator of the Imperial Roman army. His second innovation was to incorporate the auxilia into the army on a permanent basis, each legion having its corresponding auxiliary unit. Prior to Augustus' military reorganisation, the auxiliary units had been irregular forces which were raised independently of the legions and were quickly dismissed when they were no longer required. Caesar had prepared the way for their absorption into the Roman army by his regular use of Gallic cavalry, Cretan archers and Balearic slingers but, again, it was Augustus who took the decisive step of recruiting auxilia on a permanent basis. Whereas the legions were still largely recruited in Italy at this time, the auxilia came exclusively from the provinces. As subjects of Rome they were not mercenaries by status, whatever the nature of their motives may have been, but neither were they citizens. Citizenship still remained as a qualification for recruitment into the legions, although Caesar had broken the rules by recruiting legions from Cisalpine Gaul, which in his day had not received the full citizenship rights that had been won by the Italian allies.

Augustus' third innovation was to fix the periods of service for both legionaries and auxiliaries. For the legionaries the period was sixteen years, later raised to twenty, while the auxiliaries were expected to serve for twenty years and later twenty-five years. Upon termination of service, the legionaries and auxiliaries were discharged, not without considerable delay. The legionaries were initially rewarded with land grants but monetary bonuses became the more common form of payment towards the end of the Augustan period and in subsequent reigns. The auxiliaries received the Roman citizenship they had been promised at the time of enlistment. Augustus was very conservative in extending the franchise. Citizenship was granted only in return for meritorious service but he honoured the promises made to the foreign recruits. Later emperors were more liberal in dispensing citizenship so that when the Emperor Caracalla (r. AD 211–217) extended Roman citizenship to all free-born inhabitants of the empire in AD 212, he was merely bringing to a logical conclusion a process that had begun at least a century earlier. Caracalla's extension of the franchise removed any remaining social distinctions between the Romans and those whom they had conquered. It gave the provincials rights they had hitherto been denied and a sense of truly belonging to the Roman empire, but there were disadvantages. Caracalla's main motive had been to increase the number of people on whom he could impose several indirect taxes which were paid only by Roman citizens. His extension of the franchise also removed the primary incentive for enlistment in the auxiliary forces. There was no longer any need to enter a profession that offered the supreme boredom of garrison duty on the one hand and the risk of death in battle on the other.

The regular army that Augustus created from the remnants of the civil wars contained some 300,000 men (150,000 legionaries, 150,000 auxiliaries), a force barely sufficient to defend Roman territory and one which allowed only one major military campaign at a time beyond the borders of the empire. Cutting expenditure was not Augustus' only reason for reducing the size of his forces to the bare minimum he considered necessary for the effective defence of Roman acquisitions. In the hands of an ambitious general, a large army stationed near Rome was a threat to the established government. Alternatively, the presence of such an army close to the capital within easy call of the *imperator* might make Augustus seem autocratic. Thus, he did not establish a central reserve which might be used to reinforce border garrisons or to threaten Rome itself. His army was almost entirely positioned on the most sensitive parts of the imperial frontiers, primarily on the Rhine, the Danube and to a lesser extent in Egypt and Spain where revolts were a recurrent possibility. The primary task of this army was border defence rather than the long-range offensive campaigns characteristic of the Republican period.

The destruction of three legions in the Teutoberg forest caused him to abandon any further attempt to establish Roman rule beyond the Rhine. The loss of those legions and their auxiliary units was a severe blow for, although Augustus was able to recruit two new legions made up of provincial recruits, his army was barely adequate in numerical terms for the defence of Roman borders. He was unable to reinforce a threatened sector of the frontier without leaving another sector dangerously exposed. He resorted to conscription only on a very limited basis in times of emergency and confined such recruitment to the provinces. Conscripts were not suitable for frontier defence, which required long periods of garrison duty. Furthermore, conscript militias tended to be more loyal to their recruiting general than to the *imperator* and Augustus required the personal loyalty of his soldiers. The professional troops swore an oath of allegiance to the emperor and it was to him that they looked for rewards, for security in their declining years and for the resolution of any grievances.

Up until the Augustan period Rome had used mercenaries on a relatively modest scale as compared with the previous empires of the Ancient World and nearly always on a temporary basis. A certain distinction can be made between true mercenaries – those hired from territories which in the Republican period were not under Roman control – and auxiliaries hired as a result of arrangements with tribal chieftains. Thus, the armies of Pompey, Crassus and Caesar contained both mercenaries and auxiliaries, with the latter category already preponderant over the former. In establishing a regular army and in making the auxilia part of the permanent establishment, Augustus set the development of the Roman army on a rather different course to that taken by the armies of Rome's predecessors. The preceding empires had in general followed a recurrent pattern entailing a substantial if not complete mercenarisation of their armies. Roman armies certainly underwent a radical transformation so that there was no resemblance between the citizen militias of the early Republic and the armies of the late empire. But, although the Romans wound up being defended by foreigners, this did not entail a straight progression from militia to mercenary. Rome's citizen armies were first professionalised, then provincialised and finally barbarised. Marius had confirmed a pre-existing trend towards professionalism which Augustus brought to completion. Augustus intended that the legions should be solely made up of Italian volunteers but he was forced to recruit provincials in a partial replacement of the legions destroyed by Arminius. His legions, however, remained predominantly Italian.

After the reign of Augustus, there was a progressive provincialisation of the legions as the enrolment of non-Italians became more and more common. The process was well-advanced during the reigns of Claudius (AD 41–54) and Nero (AD 54–68), and in Trajan's time (AD 98–117) provincial recruits outnumbered Italians by nearly five to one. Along with the growing tendency to rely on non-citizens came an increasingly luke-warm attitude among Italians towards the performance of military service. From the early years of the third century, Rome was faced with a deepening crisis as Germanic tribes began to intensify the pressure on the northern borders. In the east, meanwhile, the resurgence of Persia under the Sassanid Dynasty (founded AD 226) posed a new threat to Roman domination. With fewer legions stationed in the west, Rome was unable to resist Germanic pressure. The crisis was worsened by Rome's inability to raise sufficient manpower. But there was also the fact that only a limited number of men could be recruited from the countryside without imperilling agricultural production. Furthermore, from the reign of Marcus Aurelius (AD 161–180), there was a palpable decline in the Italian birthrate.

The third century AD was an age of internal turmoil as well as external danger. The Praetorian Guard, deeply involved in domestic politics and a law unto itself, regularly made or destroyed emperors often by recourse to assassination. The Praetorians were a major source of instability until they were finally disbanded by Constantine (AD 306–337) after the battle of the Milvian Bridge (AD 312), where they had supported his rival, Maxentius. Constantine replaced the Praetorians with his own bodyguard, largely consisting of German recruits. Encouraged by Roman domestic chaos, the barbarian tribes – Franks, Alemanni, Goths, Quadi, Sarmatians and Heruli, among others – continued their attacks on the imperial frontiers, penetrating the Roman garrisons without undue difficulty.

During the second half of the century, the barbarians were contained by the Illyrian emperors – Claudius II, Aurelian, Probus and Carus – but this was only a reprieve from the relentless Germanic invasion. The reign of Diocletian (AD 284–305) saw a complete restructuring of the Roman army that effectively terminated the Augustan system, which had been based solely on frontier defence. Diocletian's new army was made up of garrison troops – the descendants of the legions – whose status was henceforth downgraded in favour of mobile reserves.

Volunteer enlistment of recruits from within and without the Roman empire was still the primary source of effective soldiers. Conscription failed to produce good-quality troops, no matter how vigorously it was applied and the Roman government began to accept money in lieu of unwilling recruits – money that could be used to pay more enthusiastic Germans. Long gone were the days of the early Republic when military service was considered an honour and one that ought to be restricted to the propertied classes.

Rome's solution to the problem of inadequate manpower was to import barbarians – to barbarise its army, which essentially meant a Germanisation of the military forces. Germans would be recruited to fight other Germans. The idea was feasible because the Germanic tribes were not a single entity. There was a considerable degree of inter-tribal warfare, which had worked for a long time in Rome's favour by preventing a coordinated attack on her territory. Now that some of the tribes were showing signs of a combined effort, it was essential for the Romans to enlarge the size of their armies.

What was the attraction of German troops for Roman emperors? Firstly, they were noted for a deep sense of personal loyalty to and reverence for their chiefs. Secondly, they were big, strong and tough and were formidable fighters whom the Romans had never really conquered. Thirdly, they were uninvolved in Roman domestic politics. They spoke little or no Latin and were less susceptible to the persuasion of any potential rebels against imperial authority.

Germans had been living within imperial borders ever since the foundation of the Roman empire by Augustus, albeit as a tiny minority among the provincial population. Some were volunteers attracted by the prospect of a land grant and a share in the prosperity of the empire. Others, whose

[258]

incursions into Roman territory had made them a chronic nuisance, were forcibly resettled and required to join the army. There were also prisoners of war whose release from slavery was conditional on the performance of military service. The Germans recruited during the first, second and third centuries became in varying degrees Romanised, not always unwillingly, because there was a sense of prestige in belonging to a glorious empire with a superior culture. Once inducted into the army, they were armed with Roman weaponry and trained to fight using Roman tactics. Most of these recruits were not true mercenaries. The volunteers were subjects living within the empire while the resettled tribesmen and the prisoners were serving more or less under compulsion, and compulsory military service is not associated with mercenaries.

The third century saw a substantial increase in the recruitment of barbarians by voluntary or forced enlistment, on an individual basis or in whole tribes, from within or beyond imperial frontiers. Those recruited individually or as part of small free companies were clearly mercenaries. But the status of entire tribal groups taken into service and resettled on Roman territory is less clear cut. In the sense that they were serving a foreign power in return for land grants (at the expense of provincial Roman landowners who were required to vacate their holdings) and whatever other rewards Roman civilisation could provide, they were mercenaries. However, with the exception of those groups who had been forcibly resettled, the Germanic tribes served Rome as a result of negotiations between tribal leaders and the Roman government and the arrangement was ostensibly a mutual-assistance pact. Thus, the Germans were akin to allies rather than genuine mercenaries, but the distinction between mercenaries and auxiliaries was somewhat blurred.

The German tribes, known to the Romans as *federati*, operated under their own chiefs, who received from the Roman emperor a yearly payment in cash and goods with which to pay their men. Although their attitude ranged from absolute loyalty to undisciplined behaviour, if not rebellion, the Germans did not actively contemplate a takeover of the Roman empire, despite their growing and ultimately dominant presence in the army. Faced with the unrelenting hatred and racial prejudice which Roman citizens reserved for outsiders, the Germans gradually began to lose any sense of loyalty towards Rome and came to despise the Italians in their turn. They were not liked, let alone assimilated, but they were required to defend the Romans against invasion by other Germans, for the Romans had abdicated all responsibility for their own defence. After the reign of Diocletian, all the major battles against barbarian invaders were fought with barbarian troops – Germans and Huns. Constantine (AD 306–307) continued to recruit Germanic troops in large numbers. His armies were the last to employ traditional Roman fighting tactics based on close coordination and manoeuvre. After his reign, 'Roman' armies used traditional Germanic brute force and went into battle with German war cries. In the fifth century, the German tribes who had settled in Spain, Gaul and in Italy itself were completely autonomous although in the eastern Roman empire, based on Constantinople, German troops remained under imperial control for they were not nearly as numerous as in the West and the Byzantine emperors had alternative sources of recruitment.[24]

Although Rome was sacked by the Goths under Alaric and the Vandals under Gaiseric, the city was not obliterated in one cataclysmic moment like the destruction of Nineveh. The decline of Rome was a gradual affair. Destabilised by internal political disorder, entrusting its defence to barbarians, unable to stem repeated invasions from the north, afflicted by a declining birthrate and an increasingly inefficient agricultural sector, the Roman empire collapsed, sapped of energy and vitality, devoid of any creative urge and lacking any further *raison d'être*. The year AD 476 traditionally marks the end of the western empire but most of its provinces were effectively under German control earlier in the fifth century. The last Roman emperor, Romulus Augustulus, was ousted by *federati* led by the mercenary captain Odoacer, and the Germanic kingdoms which replaced the Roman empire were the logical consummation of a process begun two centuries before when the Romans began to barbarise the army. The mercenaries and auxiliaries of the Roman republic had been its servants but those of the Roman empire ultimately became its masters.

Epilogue

The history of mercenaries is a story over 5,000 years long. It has neither a precise beginning nor is it likely to have a tidy ending, given that humanity has signally failed to go beyond war as a means of resolving disputes, notwithstanding the existence of modern peace-keeping organisations. War, by its very nature, tends to produce mercenaries ready to serve foreign employers purely for pay or for a particular ideology, secular or religious.

In the Ancient World there is little evidence that mercenaries served their employers for anything other than financial gain and, in some cases, the social advancement conferred by membership of a sovereign's bodyguard or promotion to some sort of officer status. The ancient mercenaries sought to escape poverty and hunger and the rigours of life in mountainous or desert homelands. Nubian tribesmen, Arabian desert nomads, Libyan 'sand-dwellers' and the hardy inhabitants of unproductive mountainous regions from Iberia to Anatolia and beyond were attracted by the opulence of superior civilisations and the lure of financial rewards, as were the Teutonic tribes living among the then extensive forests of Germany. The ancient mercenaries were primarily economic determinists – mercenaries in the purest sense, untramelled by moral considerations or pious justifications, genuine or hypocritical, as to the nature of their service. In a pre-ideological age, they offered no pretensions related to patriotism or the defence of some cause such as democracy, as it is understood in the Western world. The patriotic mercenary – ostensibly a contradiction in terms – as routinely featured in publications such as the American *Soldier of Fortune*, is a relatively recent character born of the ideological conflicts of the twentieth century.

At best, the ancient mercenaries might have chosen to serve one employer over another, drawn by the sheer charisma of an outstanding leader, one perceived to be a winner of victories. Hannibal was, of course, the archetypal example of such a personality and his maintenance of a multinational mercenary army in hostile territory for fifteen years was one of the truly amazing events of world history. Cyrus the Younger was also a charismatic figure, although to a lesser degree than the incomparable Hannibal. But the support by mercenaries of a specific cause was an accident of being employed by a particular leader and not attributable to a deeply held principle. Any identification with Cyrus' cause among the Greeks – if it existed at all – was heavily subordinated to pecuniary interests, as Xenophon's account clearly shows. Perhaps the Philistine mercenaries of King David's bodyguard came closest to representing foreign soldiers with a genuine attachment to the cause of their employer, but for the great mass of the ancient mercenaries described in these pages, money was the paramount motive.

That mercenaries should appear so early in the history of human civilisation is not particularly surprising. The effective maintenance of empires was to a greater or lesser degree intimately connected with the employment of mercenary troops, who could be used to ensure law and order and to garrison frontier outposts. There were substantial reasons for which employers resorted to the mercenary system. For Sargon and Hammurabi it was the perceived need of a reliable bodyguard. For the Egyptians it was the need to compensate for less-than-enthusiastic militia troops. The Assyrians, for their part, needed to garrison an over-extended empire, while the Persians sought to hire a superior type of soldier and found no lack of volunteers among the very people that they had twice attempted to subjugate. For Greek tyrants, the employment of mercenaries was founded on the very understandable desire for personal protection in the face of insurrection by their own native subjects. Alexander the Great, who relegated mercenaries to a secondary role in battle, nevertheless used substantial numbers to garrison the newly created cities and fortresses of his far-flung empire. For the Romans it was the need of an effective cavalry and of soldiers specialising in missile weapons that led to the employment of foreigners, albeit as auxiliaries in every sense of the term rather than as pure mercenaries. In the late Roman empire, a declining birth rate and a growing unwillingness to perform military service on the part of native Italians resulted in an outright mercenarisation of the army. Although their paths to ultimate mercenarisation might have varied from empire to empire, the final result was the same.

There were a number of advantages in hiring mercenary troops, in that they were usually experienced professionals or members of warrior societies who could be expected to give many years of faithful service, given the right conditions. Their loyalty was to their employer and they could be relied upon to defend the ruler's interests in the face of a revolt by native citizens and to provide external security against foreign invaders ... as long as they were paid – that was also the chief problem associated with the mercenary system. A sudden lack of funds or a deliberate attempt at cheating mercenaries out of their pay could well result in a full-scale revolt, as happened with the mercenary insurrection against Carthage. Furthermore, mercenaries liked to be on the side perceived to be winning and were prone either to desert or to actually change sides when the fortunes of their employer turned sour. There were, occasionally, mercenaries who stood by an employer at the cost of their own lives, but it was not the business of mercenaries then or now to die a martyr's death.

Notes

Chapter One: *The Earliest Mercenaries*

1. For a detailed discussion of the origins of human violence see John Keegan, *A History of Warfare*, London, 1993, Chapter 2, pp. 79–136.
2. C. Leonard Woolley, *The Sumerians*, Oxford, 1929, p. 57.
3. Georges Roux, *Ancient Iraq*, London, 1964, pp. 120–125.
   I. M. Diakonoff, *Structure of Society and State in Early Dynastic Sumev*, Moscow, 1959, Los Angeles, 1974, p. 10.
   C. Leonard Woolley, op. cit., p. 57.
4. Ibid. p. 59.
5. Ibid., p. 60.
6. Jean-Jacques Glassner, *La chute d'Akkadé*, Berlin, 1976, p. 21.
7. Ibid., p. 21
8. For a detailed list of sources relative to the motives of Sargon's wars see ibid., pp. 22–25.
9. On Hammurabi's code of laws see George Roux, op. cit., pp. 183–188.
10. D. J. Wiseman, *Nebuchadnezzar and Babylon*, Oxford, 1985, p. 16.
    Yvon Garlan, *War in the Ancient World*, London, 1975, p. 94.
11. For a detailed treatment of the *habiru–Sa-Gaz* problems see Jean Bottero, *Le problème des Habiru*, Paris, 1954.
12. Ibid., pp. 87–96.
13. Ibid., pp. 97–99.
14. Ibid., p. 104.
15. Ibid., p. 72.
16. Ibid., p. 124.

Chapter Two: *Egypt from the Old Kingdom to the New*

1. Etienne Drioton and Jacques Vandier, *Les Peuples de l'Orient Méditerranéen*, Paris, 1952, p. 208.
2. G. Maspero, *Life in Ancient Egypt and Assyria*, London, 1891, p. 78.
3. Ibid., pp. 78–80.
4. Etienne Drioton and Jacques Vandier, op. cit., p. 169.
5. Bruce G. Trigger, *Nubia Under the Pharaohs*, London, 1976, pp. 57–59.
6. Ibid., pp. 60–63.
7. Ibid., p. 63.
8. Leonard Cottrell, *Life Under the Pharaohs*, London, 1955, pp. 118–125.
9. John A. Wilson, *The Culture of Ancient Egypt*, Chicago, 1952, p. 163.
10. J. F. C. Fuller, *The Decisive Battles of the Western World Vol. 1*, London, 1970, p. 26.
    For the battle of Megiddo see also John A. Wilson, op. cit., pp. 177–180.
    James Henry Breasted, *A History of Egypt*, London, 1924, pp. 285–292.
    Yigael Yadin, *The Art of Warfare in Biblical Lands*, London, 1963, pp. 100–103.
11. Etienne Drioton and Jacques Vandier, op. cit., p. 408.
12. James Henry Breasted, op. cit., p. 330.

Chapter Three: *Imperial Egypt: The Sea Peoples and the Hittites*

1. For a detailed analysis of problems related to the Sea Peoples see R. D. Barnett, *The Sea Peoples* in *Cambridge Ancient History, Vol. 2*, Chapter 28, Cambridge, 1969.
   Alessandra Nibbi, *The Sea Peoples and Egypt*, New Jersey, 1975.
   N. K. Sanders, *The Sea Peoples*, London, 1978.
2. A. R. Burn, *The Pelican History of Greece* (revised edition), Harmondsworth, 1978, p. 51.
   N. K. Sandars, op. cit., p. 107.
3. Claire Lalouette, *L'empire des Ramses*, Paris, 1985, p. 114.
4. Sir Alan Gardiner, *The Kadesh Inscriptions of Ramesses II*, Oxford, 1960, p. 56.
   James Henry Breasted, op. cit., London, 1924, p. 424.
5. For a detailed analysis of the events at Kadesh see Mark Healy, *Qadesh 1300 BC*, London, 1993.
6. Sir Alan Gardiner, op. cit., pp. 9–14.

7. G. Maspero, op. cit., London, 1891, p. 185.
8. Etienne Drioton and Jacques Vandier, op. cit., p. 425.
9. Claire Lalouette, op. cit., pp. 273–274.
10. Alessandra Nibbi, op. cit., p. 75.
11. N. K. Sandars, op. cit., p. 165.
12. James Henry Breasted, op. cit., p. 482.
13. Herodotus, *The Histories*, (translated by Aubrey de Sélincourt), Harmondsworth, 1954, Bk2, p. 154.
14. H. W. Parke, *Greek Mercenary Soldiers*, Oxford, 1933, p. 5.
15. Herodotus, op. cit., Bk1, pp.103–108.
16. Ibid., Bk2, pp. 170–172.
17. Ibid., Bk3, pp. 11–13.

Chapter Four: *Israel*

1. Roland de Vaux, *Ancient Israel: Its Life and Institutions*, London, 1961, p. 219.
2. Chaim Herzog and Mordechai Gichon, *Battles of the Bible*, London, 1978, p. 86.
3. Roland de Vaux, op. cit., p. 219.
   J. Alberto Soggin, *A History of Israel*, London, 1984, p. 50.
4. Roland de Vaux, op. cit., p. 95.
   J. Alberto Soggin, op. cit., p. 50.
5. Chaim Herzog and Mordechai Gichon, op. cit., p. 86 *et seq.*
6. Roland de Vaux, op. cit., p. 219.
7. J. Alberto Soggin, op. cit., pp. 64–65.
8. Roland de Vaux, op. cit., p. 222.
9. Ibid., p. 222.

Chapter *Five: Assyria*

1. Bustenay Oded, *Mass Deportation and Deportees in the Neo-Assyrian Empire*, Wiesbaden, 1979, p. 20.
2. Ibid., p. 20.
3. See Bustenay Oded, op. cit., for detailed information on the aims and objectives of Assyrian deportations and the nature and status of deportees.
4. See Florence Malbran-Labat, *L'armée et l'organisation militaire de l'Assyria*,

Paris, 1982, for detailed information on the Assyrian system of couriers, fortresses and intelligence gathering.

5. Ibid., pp. 96–99.
6. Ibid., p. 90.
7. For more information on famine as a means of mercenary recruitment see ibid., Chapter 7.
8. See C. J. Gadd, *The Fall of Nineveh*, London, 1923, for information on the role of the Scythians in the destruction of Assyria.

Chapter Six: *Greece and Persia*

1. Nick Secunda, *The Ancient Greeks*, London, 1986, p. 17.
2. Peter Connolly, *Greece and Rome at War*, London, 1981, p. 41.
3. Herodotus, op. cit., Bk3, p. 39.
4. H. W. Parke, op. cit., pp. 7–8.
5. A. R. Burn, *The Pelican History of Greece*, Harmondsworth, 1966, p. 123.
6. For an analysis of Xenophon's account of Thymbra see J. K. Anderson, *Military Theory and Practice in the Age of Xenophon*, Berkeley, 1970.
7. Jack Cassin-Scott, *The Greek and Persian Wars 500–323 BC*, London, 1977, p. 5.
8. A. R. Burn, op. cit., p. 160.
9. N. G. L. Hammond, *A History of Greece to 322 BC*, Oxford, 1959, p. 216.
10. Peter Connolly, op. cit., p. 15.
11. N. G. L. Hammond, op. cit., pp. 236–237.
12. Peter Connolly, op. cit., p. 25.
    A. R. Burn, op. cit., p. 184.
13. Herodotus, op. cit., Bk8, pp. 74–78.
14. J. B. Bury, S. A. Cook and F. E. Adcock, *The Cambridge Ancient History Vol. 5: Athens 478–401 BC*, Cambridge, 1969, p. 324.
15. Herodotus, op. cit., Bk9, p. 73.

Chapter Seven: *Sparta and Athens: The Peloponnesian War*

Note: The content of this chapter is primarily based on Thucydides' account of the Peloponnesian War, still the best and most readable source of information.

1. Thucydides, *The Peloponnesian War*, (translated by Rex Warner), Harmondsworth, 1954, Bk 1, p. 23.

2. Ibid., Bk1, p. 60.
3. A. R. Burn, op. cit., p. 105.
4. Thucydides, op. cit., Bk5, p. 2.
5. Ibid., Bk5, p. 6.
6. Ibid., Bk5. p. 10.
7. Ibid., Bk6, p. 6.
8. Ibid., Bk6, p. 45.
9. Ibid., Bk7, p. 57.
10. Ibid., Bk6, p. 90.
11. Ibid., Bk7, p. 19.
12. Ibid., Bk7, p. 11.
13. Ibid., Bk7, p. 13.
14. Ibid., Bk7, p. 48.
15. Ibid., Bk7, p. 87.
16. Ibid., Bk7, p. 29.
17. M. I. Finlay, *The Ancient Greeks*, London, 1963, p. 89.
18. Yvon Garlan, op. cit., London, 1975, p. 94.
19. M. I. Finlay, op. cit., p. 89.

Chapter Eight: *Greece and Persia: The Ten Thousand*

1. Xenophon, *The Persian Expedition*, (translated by Rex Warner), Harmondsworth, 1949, Introduction: G. L. Cawkwell, pp. 18–19.
2. Ibid., Bk6, Chapter 2.
3. H. W. Parke, op. cit., pp. 23, 28.
   J. G. P. Best, *Thracian Peltasts and their Influence on Greek Warfare*, Groningen, 1969, p. 45.
4. G. T. Griffith, *The Mercenaries of the Hellenistic World*, Cambridge, 1935, p. 259 .
5. Xenophon, op. cit., Bk2, Chapter 6.
6. Ibid.
   H. W. Parke, op. cit., p. 28.
7. Xenophon, op. cit., Bk6, Chapter 4.
8. Ibid., Bk2, Chapter 6.
9. Ibid., Bk6, Chapter 4.
10. Ibid., (introduction: G. L. Cawkwell, p. 18).
11. Ibid., Bk1, Chapter 9.
12. Ibid., Bk1, Chapter 2.

13. Ibid.
14. Ibid.
15. Ibid., Bk1, Chapter 3.
16. Ibid., Bk1, Chapter 4.
17. Ibid.
18. H. W. Parke, op. cit., p. 27.
    G. B. Nussbaum, *The Ten Thousand*, Leiden, 1967, pp. 121–122.
19. Xenophon, op. cit., Bk1, Chapter 7.
20. J. B. Bury, *History of Greece*, London, 1900, p. 521.
    G. B. Nussbaum, op. cit., p. 100.
21. Xenophon, op. cit., Bk1, Chapter 8.
22. Ibid., Bk2, Chapter 2.
23. Ibid., Bk2, Chapter 6.
24. Ibid., Bk3, Chapter 2.
25. Ibid., Bk3, Chapter 3.
26. Ibid., Bk3, Chapter 4.
27. Ibid., Bk4, Chapter 1.
28. Ibid.
29. Ibid.
30. Ibid., Bk6, Chapter 3.
31. Ibid., Bk6, Chapter 5.
32. Ibid., Bk7, Chapter 2.
33. Ibid., Bk7, Chapter 3.
34. Ibid., Bk7, Chapter 6.
35. Arrian, *The Campaigns of Alexander* (translated by Aubrey de Sélincourt), Harmondsworth, 1971 (introduction: J. R. Hamilton, p. 17).
    Xenophon, op. cit., Bk2, Chapter 5.

Chapter Nine: *Greece: Civil War*

1. J. B. Bury, op. cit., p. 543.
2. H. W. Parke, op. cit., pp. 46–47.
3. J. B. Bury, op. cit., pp. 544–545.
4. H. W. Parke, op. cit., pp. 50–51.
5. J. K. Anderson, op. cit., pp. 122–123.
   H. W. Parke, op. cit., p. 53.
6. J. K. Anderson, op. cit., p. 121.
7. Ibid.

8. J. G. P. Best, op. cit., p. 90.
   J. K. Anderson, op. cit., p. 128.
9. J. G. P. Best, op. cit., p. 90.
   J. K. Anderson, op. cit., p. 128.
10. J. G. P. Best, op. cit., p. 91.
    J. K. Anderson, op. cit., p. 129.
11. H. W. Parke, op. cit., p. 58.
    J. G. P. Best, op. cit., p. 94.
12. H. W. Parke, op. cit., p. 58.
    J. G. P. Best, op. cit., p. 94.
13. Ibid.
14. Ibid., p. 60.
15. H. W. Parke, op. cit., p. 105.
    Nick Secunda, *The Persian Army 560–330 BC*, London, 1992, p. 27.
16. J. B. Bury, op. cit., p. 558.
17. A. R. Burn, op. cit., p. 319.
    J. G. P. Best, op. cit., p. 112.
18. Ibid.
19. Ibid., p. 98.
20. Ibid., p. 100.
21. Ibid., p. 99.
22. H. W. Parke, op. cit., p. 85.
23. R. Ernest Dupuy and Trevor N. Dupuy, *The Encyclopedia of Military History*,
    London, 1970, p. 43.
    J. B. Bury, op. cit., p. 595.
24. H. W. Parke, op. cit., pp. 88–89.
25. J. B. Bury, op. cit., p. 591.
    H. W. Parke, op. cit., p. 102.
26. Ibid.
27. Ibid., pp. 136–137.
28. Ibid., p. 137.
29. J. B. Bury, op. cit., p. 699.
30. Ibid., p. 712–713.

Chapter Ten: *Macedonia, Persia and India*

1. Duncan Head, *Armies of the Macedonian and Punic Wars 359 BC to 146 BC*,
   Sussex, 1982, p. 106.

2. H. W. Parke, op. cit., pp. 155–164.
3. Duncan Head, op. cit., p. 12.
4. Ibid., p. 158.
   G. T. Griffith, op. cit., pp. 12–13.
5. Ibid., p. 14.
6. H. W. Parke, op. cit., p. 198.
7. Arrian, op. cit., Bk1, p. 17.
   Peter Green, *Alexander of Macedon*, London, 1970, Harmondsworth, 1974, p. 180.
8. Arrian, op. cit., Bk1, p. 24.
9. Peter Green, op. cit., p. 201.
10. Arrian, op. cit., Bk1, p. 29.
11. J. B. Bury, op. cit., p. 758.
12. J. B. Bury, S. A. Cook, F. E. Adcock, *The Cambridge Ancient History Vol 6: Macedon 401–301 BC.* (rev. edn.), Cambridge, 1975, Chapter 10, p. 368.
13. Arrian. op. cit., Bk2, p. 11.
14. Ibid., Bk2, p. 11.
15. Peter Green, op. cit., p. 305.
16. Ibid., pp. 322–323.
17. Ibid.
18. Ibid., p. 323.
19. Ibid., p. 338.
20. Ibid., pp. 421, 450.
21. Ibid., p. 353.
22. Peter Green op. cit., p. 381.
23. Romila Thapar, *A History of India: Vol. 1.*, Harmondsworth, 1966, pp. 50–53.
24. Arrian, op. cit., Bk4, p. 27.
25. Arrian, op. cit., Bk7, p. 9.

Chapter Eleven: *The Hellenistic World*

1. J. B. Bury, S. A. Cook, F. E. Adcock, *The Cambridge Ancient History Vol.6: Macedon 401–301 BC*, Cambridge, 1975, Chapter 14, p. 457.
2. Ibid., Chapter 15, pp. 461–504.
   See also Arthur Cotterell (ed.), *The Penguin Encyclopedia of Classical Civilisations*, London, 1993, pp. 46–56.
3. J. B. Bury, S. A. Cook, F. E. Adcock, op. cit., Chapter 15, p. 502.
4. G. T. Griffith, op. cit., p. 63.

5. Ibid., p. 64.

6. Ibid., p. 70.

7. J. B. Bury, S. A. Cook, F. E. Adcock, op. cit., Chapter 16, p. 509.

8. Duncan Head, op. cit., p. 22.

9. G. T. Griffith, op. cit., p. 118.

10. Duncan Head, op. cit., p. 24.

11. Stylianos Spyridakis, *Cretica: Studies on Ancient Crete*, New York, 1992, p. 56.

12. Duncan Head, op. cit., p. 18.

13. Titus Livy, *Rome and the Mediterranean* (translated by Henry Bettenson), Harmondsworth, 1976, Bk55, p. 30.

Chapter Twelve: *Carthage, Syracuse and Rome*

1. Michael Grant, *History of Rome*, London, 1978, p. 11.
   M. Cary, *History of Rome*, London, 1938, p. 36 *et seq.*

2. Duncan Head, op. cit., p. 73.

3. Peter Connolly, op. cit.

4. J. B. Bury, op. cit., pp. 635–638.

5. H. W. Parke, op. cit., p. 67.

6. J. B. Bury, op. cit., p. 651.

7. Ibid., p. 654.

8. H. W. Parke, op. cit., p. 115.

9. Ibid., p. 118.

10. Ibid., p. 119.

11. Ibid., p. 172.

12. J. B. Bury, op. cit., pp. 675–676.

13. H. W. Parke, op. cit., p. 173.

14. G. T. Griffith, op. cit., p. 198.

15. Ibid., p. 199.

16. Ibid., pp. 200–201.

17. Ibid., p. 200.

18. Polybius, *The Rise of the Roman Empire* (translated by Ian Scott-Kilvert), London, 1979, Bk1, p. 9.

19. Ibid., Bk1, pp. 17–19.

20. Ibid., Bk1, p. 30.

21. Ibid., Bk1, p. 34.

22. Ibid., Bk1, p. 42.

23. Ibid., Bk1, p. 43.

24. Plutarch, *Timoleon*: p. 28 in *The Age of Alexander* (translated by Ian Scott-Kilvert), London, 1973.
25. Terence Wise, *Armies of the Carthaginian Wars 265–146 BC*, London, 1982, p. 7.
26. G. T. Griffith, op. cit. pp. 219–220.
27. Duncan Head, op. cit., p. 36.
28. G. T. Griffith, op. cit., p. 221.
29. Polybius, op. cit., Bk3, p. 6.
30. Ibid.
31. See Mark Healy, *Cannae 216 BC*, London, 1994, pp. 60–64 for a reassessment of Varro's role and character.
32. Polybius, op. cit., Bk3, p. 117.
33. R. Ernest Dupuy and Trevor N. Dupuy, op. cit., p. 70.

Chapter Thirteen: *Rome: From Militia to Mercenary*

1. Yvon Garlan, op. cit., p. 106.
2. Sallust, *The Jugurthine War The Conspiracy of Catiline* (translated by S. A. Handford), Harmondsworth, 1963, Chapter 6, p. 45.
3. Ibid., Chapter 8, p. 81.
4. Ibid., Chapter 9, p. 86.
5. Polybius, op. cit., Bk 3, p. 75.
6. Caesar, *The Conquest of Gaul* (translated by S. A. Handford), Harmondsworth, 1951, rev. edn. 1982, Bk 2, pp. 9–10, 26–28.
7. Ibid., Bk1, p. 42.
8. Ibid., Bk7, p. 13.
9. Ibid., Bk6, p. 34.
10. Ibid., p. 31.
11. Homer H. Dubs, *A Roman City in Ancient China*, London, 1957.
    David Harris, *Black Horse Odyssey*, Adelaide, 199.
12. Homer H. Dubs, op. cit., pp. 4–5.
13. Ibid., pp. 10–15.
14. Ibid., p. 15.
15. David Harris, op. cit., p. 7.
16. Ibid., p. 276.
17. R. Ernest Dupuy and Trevor N. Dupuy, op. cit., p. 107.
18. Caesar, *The Civil War* (translated by Jane F. Gardner), London, 1967, Part 3, p. 4.

19. Ibid., Part 1, p. 87.

20. Ibid., Part 2, p. 42.

21. Ibid., Part 3, p. 99.

22. Suetonius, *Caesar*: Chapter 1, p. 69 in *The Twelve Caesars* (translated by Robert Graves), London, 1957.

23. Ibid., Chapter 1, p. 70.

24. Michael Grant, *The Fall of the Roman Empire*, London, 1990, pp. 203–204.

Bibliography

AESCHYLUS, *The Persians* in *Prometheus Bound and other Plays* (translated by Philip Vellacott), Harmondsworth, 1961.

ANDERSON, J. K., *Military Theory and Practice in the Age of Xenophon*, Berkeley, 1970.

ANDREWES, ANTONY, *Greek Society*, London, 1967.

ARNOTT, PETER, *Introduction to the Roman World*, London, 1970.

ARRIAN, *The Campaigns of Alexander* (translated by Aubrey de Sélincourt), Harmondsworth, 1971.

ASTON, TREVOR (ED.), *Crisis in Europe 1560–1660*, London 1964.

BARKER, PHIL, *The Armies and Enemies of Imperial Rome*, Sussex, 1981.

BAR KOCHVA, BEZALEL, *The Seleucid Army*, Cambridge, 1976.

BARNETT, R.D., *The Sea Peoples* in *Cambridge Ancient History: Vol. 2*, Chapter 28, Cambridge, 1969.

BEST, J.G.P., *Thracian Peltasts and their influence on Greek Warfare*, Groningen, 1969.

BIKERMAN, E., *Institutions de Seleucids*, Paris, 1938.

BOARDMAN, JOHN, *The Greeks Overseas*, Harmondsworth, 1964.

BOTTERO, JEAN, *Le problème des Habiru*, Paris, 1954.

BREASTED, JAMES HENRY, *A History of Egypt*, London, 1924.

BREASTED, JAMES HENRY, *Ancient Times: A History of the Early World*, London, 1935.

BRISSON, JEAN-PAUL, *Problèmes de la guerre à la Rome*, Paris, 1969.

BURN, A. R., *The Pelican History of Greece*, Harmondsworth, 1978.

BURNE, A. H., *The Art of War on Land*, London, 1944.

BURY, J. B., *History of Greece*, London, 1900, 1951.

BURY, J. B., COOK, S. A., AND ADCOCK, F.E., *The Cambridge Ancient History: Vol. IV*, Cambridge, 1975.

BURY, J. B., COOK, S. A., AND ADCOCK, F. E., *The Cambridge Ancient History: Vol. 6: 401–301 BC.*, Cambridge, 1933, rev. edn., 1975.

CAESAR, JULIUS, *The Conquest of Gaul*, (translated by S. A. Handford), Harmondsworth, 1951.

CAESAR, JULIUS, *The Civil Wars* (translated by Jane F. Gardner), London, 1967.

CARY, M., *History of Rome*, London, 1935.

CASSIN-SCOTT, JACK, *The Greek and Persian Wars 500–323 BC*, London, 1977.

CASTELLAN, GEORGES, *Histoire de l'armée*, Paris, 1948.

CERNENKO, E. V., *The Scythians 700–300 BC*, London, 1983.

CHARLES-PICKARD, GILBERT AND COLETTE, *Daily Life in Carthage*, London, 1961,

CHEESEMAN, G., *The Auxilia of the Roman Imperial Army*, Oxford, 1914.

CHILDE, V. GORDON, *New Light on the Most Ancient East*, London, 1935.

COHEN, ROBERT, *La Grèce et l'Hellénisation du monde antique*, Paris, 1948.

COOK, S. A., ADCOCK, F. E., CHARLESWORTH, M.P., *The Cambridge Ancient History: Vol. 18: Rome and the Mediterranean: 218–133 BC*, Cambridge, 1970.

COOK, S. A., ADCOCK, F. E., CHARLESWORTH, M.P., *The Cambridge Ancient History: Vol. 9: The Roman Republic*, Cambridge, 1966.

CONNOLLY, PETER, *Greece and Rome at War*, London, 1981.

CONTAMINE, PHILIPPE, *War in the Middle Ages* (translated by Michael Jones), Paris, 1980; London, 1984.

CONTENAU, G., *La Civilisation d'Assur et de Babylone*, Paris, 1951.

CORVISIER, ANDRÉ, *L'armée Française*, Paris, 1964.

COTTERELL, ARTHUR, *The Penguin Encyclopedia of Classical Civilisations*, London, 1993.

COTTRELL, LEONARD, *Life Under the Pharaohs*, London, 1955.

COWELL, F. R., *Cicero and the Roman Republic*, London, 1948.

DANIEL, GLYN, *The First Civilisations*, London, 1968.

DIAKONOFF, I. M., *Structure of Society and State in Early Dynastic Sumer*, Moscow, 1959; Los Angeles, 1974.

DRIOTON, ETIENNE, AND VANDIER, JACQUES, *Les Peuples de l'Orient Méditerranéen*, PARIS, 1952.

DUBS, HOMER H., *A Roman City in Ancient China*, London, 1957.

DUDLEY, DONALD R., *The Civilisation of Rome*, New York, 1960.

DUPUY, R. ERNEST, AND DUPUY, TREVOR N., *The Encyclopedia of Military History*, London, 1970.

DUNAN, MARCEL (ED.), *Larousse Encyclopedia of Ancient and Medieval History*, Paris, 1963; London, 1966.

EFFENTERRE, HENRI VAN, *La Crète et le Monde Grec*, Paris, 1948.

ERMAN, ADOLF, *The Ancient Egyptians*, New York, 1966.

FINLEY, M. I., *The Ancient Greeks*, New York, 1963.

FINLEY, M. I., *Aspects of Antiquity*, London, 1968.

FULLER, J. F. C., *The Decisive Battles of the Western World: Vol. 1*, London, 1954, 1970.

FULLER, J. F. C., *The Generalship of Alexander the Great*, New York, 1960.

GADD, C. J., *The Fall of Nineveh*, London, 1923.

GARDINER, SIR ALAN, *The Kadesh Inscriptions of Ramesses II*, Oxford, 1960.

GARELLI, PAUL, AND NIKIPROWETZKY, V., *Le Proche-Orient asiatique*, Paris, 1974.

GARLAN, YVON, *War in the Ancient World*, London, 1975.

GAVAGHAN, PAUL F., *The Cutting Edge: Military History of Antiquity and Early Feudal Times*, New York, 1990.

GLASSNER, JEAN-JACQUES, *La chute d'Akkadé*, Berlin, 1986.

GLOVER, T. R., *The Ancient World*, Cambridge, 1935.

GRANT, MICHAEL, *History of Rome*, London, 1978.

GRANT, MICHAEL, *The Army of the Caesars*, London, 1978.

GRANT, MICHAEL *The Fall of the Roman Empire*, London, 1990.

GREEN, PETER, *Alexander of Macedon*, Harmondsworth, 1974.

GRIFFITH, G. T., *The Mercenaries of the Hellenistic World*, Cambridge, 1935.

GURNEY, O. R., *The Hittites*, Harmondsworth, 1952.

HAMMOND, N.G L. *A History of Greece to 322 BC*, Oxford, 1967.

HARMAND, G., *La guerre antique de Sumer à Rome*, Paris, 1973.

HARRIS, DAVID, *Black Horse Odyssey*, Adelaide, 1991.

HARRISON, G. W. M., *The Romans and Crete*, Amsterdam, 1993.

HEAD, DUNCAN, *Armies of the Macedonian and Punic Wars 359 BC to 146 BC*, Sussex, 1982.

HEALY, MARK, *Cannae 216 BC*, London, 1994.

HEALY, MARK, *New Kingdom Egypt*, London, 1992.

HEALY, MARK, *Qadesh 1300 BC*, London, 1993.

HEALY, MARK, *The Ancient Assyrians*, London, 1991.

HERODOTUS, *The Histories* (translated by Aubrey de Sélincourt), Harmondsworth, 1954, 1972.

HERZOG, CHAIM, AND GICHON, MORDECHAI, *Battles of the Bible*, London, 1978.

HINZ, W., *The Lost World of Elam* (translated by J. Barnes), London, 1972.

HUOT, JEAN-LOUIS, *Les Sumérians*, Paris, 1989.

INGPEN, ROBERT, AND WILKINSON, PHILIP, *Encyclopedia of Mysterious Places*, London, 1990.

JONES, A. H. M., *The Later Roman Empire 284–602: Vol. 1*, Oxford, 1964.

KEEGAN, JOHN, *A History of Warfare*, London, 1993.

KENDRICK-PRITCHETT, W., *The Greek State at War: Vol. 1*, Berkeley, 1971.

KINDER, HERMANN, AND HILGEMANN, WERNER, *The Penguin Atlas of World History: Vol. 1*, Munich, 1964; London, 1974.

KITTO, H. D. F., *The Greeks*, Harmondsworth, 1951.

KRAMER, SAMUEL NOAH, *History Begins at Sumer*, Pennsylvania, 1956.

LALOUETTE, CLAIRE, *L'Empire des Ramses*, Paris, 1985.

LAUNEY, MARCEL, *Recherches sur les armées hellenistiques*, Paris, 1949.

LE BOHEC, Y., *L'armée romaine*, Paris, 1989.

LEVY, PETER, *Atlas of the Greek World*, Oxford, 1984.

LEWIS, NAPHTALI, *Greeks in Ptolemaic Egypt*, Oxford, 1986.

LIVY, TITUS, *The War with Hannibal* (translated by Aubrey de Sélincourt), Harmondsworth, 1965.

LLOYD, E. M., *A Review of the History of Infantry*, London, 1908.

LOT, FERDINAND, *L'art militaire et les armées: Vol. 1*, Paris, 1946.

MACDOWALL, SIMON, *Late Roman Infantryman 236–565 AD*, London, 1994.

MACKSEY, KENNETH, *The History of Land Warfare*, New York, 1974.

MCMAHAN, JEFF, *Reagan and the World*, London, 1984.

MACQUITTY, WILLIAM, *Abu Simbel*, London, 1965.

MALBRAN-LABAT, FLORENCE, *L'armée et l'organisation militaire de l'Assyrie*, Paris, 1982.

MANCHIP WHITE, J. E., *Ancient Egypt*, London, 1952.

MASPERO, G., *Life in Ancient Egypt and Assyria*, London, 1891.

MICHELL, H., *Sparta*, Cambridge, 1964.

MOCKLER, ANTHONY, *Mercenaries*, Paris, 1964.

MOCKLER, ANTHONY, *The New Mercenaries*, London, 1985.

MYERS, HUGH BOLTON, 'The Best Aspect of Assyrian Culture was that it was destroyed', unpublished essay, Sydney, 1994.

NEWARK, TIM, *The Barbarians*, Dorset, 1985.

NIBBI, ALESSANDRA, *The Sea Peoples and Egypt*, New Jersey, 1975.

NUSSBAUM, G. B., *The Ten Thousand*, Leiden, 1967.

ODED, BUSTENAY, *Mass Deportations and Deportees in the Neo-Assyrian Empire*, Wiesbaden, 1979.

PARKE, H. W., *Greek Mercenary Soldiers*, Oxford, 1933.

PARKER, H. M. D., *A History of the Roman World from AD 138 to 337*, London, 1935, 1958.

PARKER, H. M. D., *The Roman Legions*, Cambridge, 1958.

PLUTARCH, *The Age of Alexander: Nine Greek Lives* (translated by Ian Scott-Kilvert), London, 1973.

PLUTARCH, *Fall of the Roman Republic* (translated by Rex Warner), London, 1972.

POLYBIUS, *The Rise of the Roman Empire* (translated by Ian Scott-Kilvert), London, 1979.

RACHEWITZ, BORIS DE, *Egyptian Art*, London, 1960.

RADICE, BETTY, *Who's Who in the Ancient World*, London, 1971.

RANKOV, BORIS, *The Praetorian Guard*, London, 1994.

RAWLINGSON, GEORGE, *The Five Great Monarchies of the Ancient World: Vol. 2*, London, 1864.

RICE, MICHAEL, *Search for the Paradise Land*, London, 1985.

ROUX, GEORGES, *Ancient Iraq*, London, 1964.

SALLUST, *The Jugurthine War/The Conspiracy of Catiline* (translated by S. A. Handford), Harmondsworth, 1963.

SALMON, E. J., *A History of the Roman World from 30 BC to AD 138*, London, 1944.

SANDARS, N. K. *The Sea Peoples*, London, 1978.

SAGGS, H. W. F., *The Greatness that was Babylon*, London, 1962.

SAGGS, H. W. F., *The Might that was Assyria*, London, 1984.

SCHMOKEL, H., *Sumer et la civilisation sumérienne*, Paris, 1964.

SECUNDA, NICK, *The Army of Alexander the Great*, London, 1984.

SECUNDA, NICK, *The Ancient Greeks*, London, 1986.

SECUNDA, NICK, *The Persian Army 560–330 BC*, London, 1992.

SECUNDA, NICK, *Early Roman Armies*, London, 1995.

SIMKINS, MICHAEL, *The Roman Army from Caesar to Trajan*, London, 1984.

SIMKINS, MICHAEL, *Warriors of Rome*, London, 1988.

SNELL, HEBER C., *Ancient Israel: Its Story and Meaning*, Utah, 1948.

SPYRIDAKIS, STYLIANOS V., *Cretica: Studies on Ancient Crete*, New York, 1992.

STILLMAN, NIGEL, AND TALLIS, NIGEL, *Armies of the Ancient Near East: 3000 BC to 539 BC*, Sussex, 1984.

STROUHAL, EUGEN, *Life in Ancient Egypt*, Cambridge, 1992.

SUETONIUS, *The Twelve Caesars* (translated by Robert Graves), London, 1957.

THAPAR, ROMILA, *A History of India: Vol. 1*, Harmondsworth, 1966.

THUCYDIDES, *The Peloponnesian War* (translated by Rex Warner), Harmondsworth, 1954; rev. edn., 1972.

TREVINO, RAPHAEL, *Rome's Enemies: Spanish Armies 218 BC 1–19 BC*, London, 1986.

TRIGGER, BRUCE G., *Nubia under the Pharaohs*, London, 1976.

VAUX, ROLAND DE, *Ancient Israel: Its Life and Institutions*, London, 1961.

VERNANT, JEAN PIERRE (ED.), *Problèmes de la guerre en Grèce ancienne*, Paris, 1968.

WEBSTER, GRAHAM, *The Roman Army*, Chester, 1956.

WILCOX, PETER, *Rome's Enemies: Parthians and Sassanid Persians*, London, 1986.

WILHELM, GERNOT, *The Hurrians*, Warminster, 1989.

WILSON, JOHN A., *The Culture of Ancient Egypt*, Chicago, 1952.

WISE, TERENCE, *Ancient Armies of the Middle East*, London, 1981.

WISE, TERENCE, *Armies of the Carthaginian Wars 265–146 BC*, London, 1982.

WISEMAN, D. J., *Nebuchadnezzar and Babylon*, Oxford, 1985.

WOOLLEY, C. LEONARD, *The Sumerians*, Oxford, 1929.

XENOPHON, *The Persian Expedition* (translated by Rex Warner), Harmondsworth, 1949.

YADIN, YIGAEL, *The Art of Warfare in Biblical Lands*, London, 1963.

Personalities

ABIMALEK (and JEPHTHAH)

First Hebrews known to have recruited mercenaries.

ADAEUS THE COCK

Commander of mercenaries in army of Philip of Macedon. His sobriquet was a reference to his vainglorious personality rather than an acknowledgement of sexual prowess.

AGATHOCLES

Syracusan tyrant. Used multinational mercenary armies to fight Carthaginians.

AGESILAUS

Spartan king. Aged eighty-four, twice performed mercenary service for Persians and Egyptians so that impecunious Sparta could hire mercenaries.

ANTIMENES OF MYTILENE

Exiled mercenary in the service of Babylonian monarch, Nebuchadnezzar. Friend of poet, Sappho.

ARCHILOCUS OF PAROS

Poet, gold miner, and mercenary leader flourished c.650 BC. Lost his shield in Thrace.

ARCHON (and PELEKOS)

Greek mercenaries in service of Psammeticus II. In an early example of vandalism, left graffiti at Abu Simbel.

ARRIAN

Author of *Anabasis Alexandri* and a remarkable man in his own right. Greek governor of Cappadocia and commander of two legions – an almost unique position for a non-Roman.

AUTARICHUS

Commander of 2,000 Gallic troops in mercenaries' revolt against Carthage (240–238 BC).

BASIAS

Arcadian mercenary in the Ten Thousand killed by Kurdish archer during the retreat.

BENAIAH BEN JEHOIDA

Commander of King David of Israel's mercenary bodyguard.

BRASIDAS

Spartan general and mercenary leader. Captured Amphipolis. Defeated Athenian general, Cleon (423 BC).

CHABRIAS

Athenian general. Led mercenary peltasts to assist Evagoras of Cyprus against Persians. Later in employ of Egyptian Pharaoh, Achoris, but recalled to Athens. Killed at Chios (357 BC).

CHARES

Athenian mercenary commander. Assisted Persian satrap Artabazus against Artaxerxes Ochus.

CHARIDEMUS

Euboean mercenary general. Mercenary service in Thrace. Married Thracian princess.

CHIRISOPHUS

Elected general of the Ten Thousand after death of Clearchus. Probably *de facto* commander-in-chief. Died of illness during retreat.

CLEARCHUS

Initially commander of Greek troops in the Ten Thousand. Betrayed by Persian satrap Tissaphernes. Executed in Babylon.

COES OF MYTILENE

Lesbian auxiliary in army of Persian monarch, Darius.

CTESIAS

Greek doctor in service of Persian king, Artaxerxes. Wrote account of Cyrus' campaign – fragments survive.

CYRUS THE YOUNGER

Recruited the Ten Thousand – 13,000 Greek mercenaries – including Xenophon to overthrow his brother. Killed at Cunaxa near Babylon 40 BC.

DAVID

King of Israel (1010–973 BC). Prior to becoming king was mercenary commander in the service of Philistine ruler, Achisk of Gath. As monarch, created Philistine and Canaanite mercenary bodyguard.

DEXIPPUS

Mercenary leader in service of Syracuse (406 BC). Later member of the Ten Thousand. Deserted before Cunaxa.

[283]

DION

Syracusan exile. Recruited mercenary force to overthrow Syracusan tyrant, Dionysius II (357 BC). Succeeded but killed by mercenaries sent by a trusted friend.

HANNIBAL OF CARTHAGE

Needs no introduction. Commander of a mercenary army *par excellence*.

HARKHUF

Egyptian diplomat and recruiter of Nubian mercenaries and dancing dwarfs for Pharaoh Merenre (*c.*2300 BC).

HIERO II

Syracusan tyrant and employer of mercenaries against the Mamertines of Messana.

IPHICRATES

Athenian commander of mercenary light troops. Fought with great success against Spartans. After King's Peace (387 BC) married Thracian King Coty's daughter.

ISOCRATES

Athenian orator and bitter critic of Greek mercenary service.

JASON OF PHERAE

Thessalian tyrant. Private army of 6,000 mercenaries. Might have imposed his rule on Greece but murdered, 370 BC.

LEONYMUS

Spartan mercenary in the Ten Thousand. Killed by Kurdish archer during the retreat.

LYCIDAS

Aetolian commander of Alexander the Great's Greek mercenary garrison in Egypt.

MATHOS

Libyan co-leader of the mercenaries' revolt against Carthage (240–238 BC).

(NUBANDA) MARDUNE

Captain of Amorite mercenaries in bodyguard of Sargon of Akkad. 'Nubanda' seems to have been a rank rather than a name.

MEMNON OF RHODES

Greek mercenary commander married into Persian nobility. Opposed Alexander the Great.

MENON THE THESSALIAN

Mercenary officer in the Ten Thousand and bitter rival of Clearchus.

MILTIADES OF CHERSONESUS

Greek auxiliary officer in service of Darius. Changed sides when Persians invaded Greece 490 BC. Present at Marathon.

MNASIPPUS

Spartan general and commander of mercenaries. Tried to cheat mercenaries of their pay. Killed at Corcyra (*c.*374 BC).

NEON OF ASINE

General in the Ten Thousand. Replaced Chirisophus.

NICHARCHUS THE ARCADIAN

Mercenary officer in the Ten Thousand. Deserted after Cunaxa.

PARMENIO

Macedonian commander of mercenary troops in armies of Philip and Alexander the Great.

PASION OF MEGARA

Mercenary officer in the Ten Thousand. Deserted at Myriandrus.

PHANES OF HALICARNASSUS

Disgruntled Greek mercenary in service of Psammeticus III. Deserted to Persians.

PROXENUS

Theban mercenary general in the Ten Thousand.

PSAMMETICUS I

Founder of Saite Dynasty in Egypt. First known Egyptian employer of Greek mercenaries known as 'the men of bronze' (Ionia and Caria).

PYRRHUS

King of Epirus and mercenary commander. Famous for his pyrrhic victories. Defeated at Beneventum by Romans aided by pigs. Killed at Argos.

RITTI MARDUK

Renegade Elamite lord in Nebuchadnezzar's army.

SEUTHES

Minor Thracian king. Hired the remnants of the Ten Thousand to settle domestic political disputes. First Thracian employer of Greek mercenaries.

SHESHONK

Libyan mercenary commander. Established Libyan dynasty in Egypt.

SHULGI

Monarch of the Third Dynasty of Ur. Recruited Elamite legion for Sumerian border defence.

SOCRATES THE ACHAEAN

Mercenary officer and recruiter in the Ten Thousand.

SOPHAENETUS OF STYMPHALUS

Arcadian general in the Ten Thousand. Wrote an account of Cyrus' campaign, now lost save fragments.

SOSIS THE SYRACUSAN

Mercenary officer and recruiter in the Ten Thousand.

SPENDIUS

Campanian runaway slave and co-leader of mercenaries' revolt against Carthage.

TIMASION

Elected general of the Ten Thousand after death of Clearchus. Commanded rear
guard together with Xenophon during retreat.

TIMOLEON

Corinthian leader of mercenaries. Liberated Syracuse from local tyrants and
Carthaginians.

TJHEMAU

Nubian mercenary officer in Egyptian service during Middle Kingdom.

XANTHIPPUS

Lacedaimonian mercenary commander in Carthaginian service. Saved Carthage
from total defeat by Romans during First Punic War at battle of Tunes
(255 BC) then left suddenly.

XENIAS THE ARCADIAN

Greek mercenary officer in the Ten Thousand. Deserted at Myriandrus.

XENOPHON

Elected general of the Ten Thousand after death of Clearchus. Wrote *Anabasis*,
most famous of all works on mercenary soldiers.

Index

INDEX